PROVENCE

Ma douce Provence!

Provence and the Côte d'Azur are among the classic tourist destinations of Europe. By the 19th century better-off Britons had discovered the favourable climate that makes the coast between the Camargue, the broad mouth of the Rhône, and the Italian border near Menton such an agreeable winter residence. And the abundance of light in the Provence can be intoxicating for northern Europeans – as was demonstrated by the Dutch painter Vincent van Gogh, whose painting style, under the influence of the Mediterranean, developed a palette of vibrant colours.

In fact, Provence is very much a sensual landscape. There is the wide variety of scents in the lavender fields and cultivated flowers, which threaten to overpower the visitor in the world-famous perfume town of Grasse. There is the breathtaking violence of the mistral winds that sweep down from the Alpine regions through the Rhône valley towards the sea. There are the grand gorges that have been hewn out of the rock by untamed rivers, and the sedimentary plains of the Camargue, deposited by the Rhône over the last few thousand years – even now white horses and black bulls roam through the wide sand and marsh areas. The senses are assaulted by the variety of experiences.

Greek, and later the Roman, colonisers were quick to appreciate the wealth of this land. They founded remarkable settlements, the remains of which are much visited today – Nîmes (Nemausus), Orange (Arausio) and Marseiles (Massalia/Massilia) are among the classical towns. The Trophée des Alpes, still visible from afar, was erected at la Turbie to celebrate the subjugation of the Alpine peoples by Emperor Augustus. A living

Boules is the most popular sport in France

Colourful essential oils
advertise the perfumes of Grasse

Pastoral landscape
in Haute-Provence

survivor of the Roman colony is the Occitan language that developed out of the vulgar Latin spoken by the troops. It became a tuneful means of expression for the troubadours, and today is consciously preserved by Provençals to mark their own heritage.

Provence remained a scene of historic events. During the great migrations, Visigoths, Ostrogoths and Frankish tribes penetrated as far as the Riviera; and in the 14th century, Avignon was the residence of seven popes during their exile from Rome. In 1481 Provence was incorporated into the French kingdom, but the maritime Alps and Nice, which until then belonged to the duchy of Piedmont, were not integrated until 1860. The Route Napoléon, a much-frequented tour through grandiose countryside, also has historic origins: it follows the route that Napoléon took on his return from Elba to Paris, where he briefly seized power again.

Altogether, Provence is a destination that impresses with its great geographical and cultural diversity. In addition, the legendary pleasures of the French cellar and cuisine continue to invite the traveller, as do the renowned spas. And last but not least, winter-sports enthusiasts are amply catered for in the upper reaches of the maritime Alps.

CONTENTS

Principal Sights

★★

Aigues-Mortes	
Aix-en-Provence	
Ardèche	
Arles	
Avignon	
Les Baux-de-Provence	
Calanques	
Camargue	
Corniches de la Riviera	
Ganagobie	
Gordes	
Gorges d'Ollioules	
Gorges du Cians	
Gorges du Verdon	
Marseille	
Menton	
Monaco	
Mont Ventoux	
Nîmes	
Pont du Gard	
Route Napoléon	
St-Gilles	
St-Maximin-la-Ste-Baume	
St-Paul-de-Vence	
Le Thoronet	
Toulon	
Villeneuve-lès-Avignon	

★

Antibes

Biot

Bonnieux

Cannes

Draguignan

Entrecastaux

Entrevaux

Esterel

Eze-Village

Fontaine-de-Vaucluse

Fontvieille

Fréjus

★

Gap

La Garde-Adhémar

Gorges de la Nesque

Gorges des Alpes-Maritimes

Gorges du Loup

Gourdon

Grasse

Grignan

Grimaud

Haut-de-Cagnes

Hyères

Lubéron

Massif des Maures

Montmajour

Montpellier

Nice

Orange

Peillon

Roquebrune

Roussillon

St-Rémy-de-Provence

Stes-Maries-de-la-Mer

St-Tropez

Salon-de-Provence

Sénanque

Silvacane

Sisteron

Tarascon

La Turbie

Uzès

Vaison-la-Romaine

Vallauris

Vence

Following the tradition established by Karl Baedeker in 1846, buildings, places of natural beauty and sights of particular interest are distinguished by one ★ or two ★★ stars. The places listed above are merely a selection of the principal sights – there are of course many other sights in Provence, to which attention is drawn in the guide by the Baedeker stars.

Orange: the Roman Triumphal Arch ➤

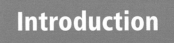

Introduction

Facts and Figures

General

Topography

The expressions Provence and Côte d'Azur, however familiar they may be, are geographically, historically and politically not easy to define.

Provence

The regional name Provence comes from the Roman Provincia Gallia Narbonensis which was founded from 125 BC onwards, after the conquest of what is present-day France. Subsequently the political borders and affiliations of the Provence area altered frequently and today it comprises the political region Provence-Alpes-Côte-d'Azur, one of the 22 *régions* of France, the *départements* of Alpes-de-Haute-Provence, Hautes-Alpes, Alpes-Maritimes, Bouches-du-Rhône, Var and Vaucluse. Surrounded by this territory on the Mediterranean is the independent Principality of Monaco.

Côte d'Azur

Even the expression Côte d'Azur is difficult to define. It indicates the azure blue coast between St-Raphaël and the French-Italian frontier but it is generally applied to the whole French Riviera as far west as Marseille.

The area described in this guidebook does not completely coincide with Provence-Alpes-Côte-d'Azur as a political region. It takes in the chief places of interest (Gorges de l'Ardèche, Nîmes, Montpellier) on the edge of the area, but only briefly refers to the winter resorts far to the north-east.

Regional structure

Provence, which comprises the south-east of the French mainland, is rich in beauty and culture. It is divided into three regional areas each with its own character and wealth of scenic forms – the lower Rhône valley, the coast and the mountainous hinterland.

Rhône valley

The Rhône is France's second longest and most abundant river. It rises in Switzerland near the Furka Pass, flows through the Valais and Lake Geneva and divides in the Défilé de l'Ecluse in the Jura Mountains. Its lower valley begins near Lyon, where the more abundant Saône joins it. Below Lyon the Rhône flows southwards through the Rhône rift valley (part of the Mediterranean-Mjosen Zone), between the foothills of the French Alps and the Massif Central (Cévennes) to its mouth. In this area the wide valley is terraced and used for intensive cultivation of grapes, fruit and vegetables. South of Avignon the river has many tributaries. It finally reaches Arles, where heavy sediment has extended its mouth towards the sea by between 10 m and 55 m a year. The Rhône forms a delta here, bordered by the Grand Rhône (with its mouth in the east at Port St-Louis in the Gulf of Fos) and the Petit Rhône (with its mouth in the west at Stes-Maries). The Rhône delta encloses the Camargue, an unspoilt area of particular charm.

Long before Greek and Roman times – and certainly no later than the Bronze Age – the Rhône valley was a much-used transport route and an important cultural link between the Mediterranean on the one hand and Britain and Gaul on the other.

Coastal region

Provence's coastal region extends between Cap Couronne in the west and the Italian border in the east and is divided into four sections; the Côte à Calanques (Blue Coast), the Côte des Maures (Crimson Coast), the Côte de l'Esterel and the Côte d'Azur in its narrowest sense.

Côte à Calanques

The Côte à Calanques (Côte Bleue, Blue Coast) forms the first section. With the Rade de Marseille (Roadsteads of Marseille) and some offshore islands it is characterised by the Calanques, torturous coastal indentations which are

difficult to reach – the name comes from the Provençal *calanco* (falling steeply) – and forms part of the ancient karstic limestone massifs of the Provençal coast. The imposing coastal formation arose as a consequence of the combination of a drop in sea level during the Pleistocene age and a simultaneous rise in the limestone heights, in which karstic development played an important role.

Côte des Maures

The Côte des Maures or Côte Vermeille (Crimson Coast) begins at Sanary-sur-Mer and is bounded in the east by the estuary of the Argens river. With the offshore Hyères Islands this coastal area has to be included with the mountains of the Département of Var, as is illustrated by the nature of the Massif des Maures, consisting of granite, gneiss, mica-schist and phyllite, some 60 km long, 30 km broad and rising to a height of 779 m. Extensive bays with, in places, excellent beaches form the line of the coast and sometimes, for example near Toulon and St-Tropez, penetrate deeply inland.

Massif de l'Esterel

The Massif de l'Esterel, extending between St-Raphaël and Cannes, is geologically of the same nature as the Massif des Maures. This mountainous gneiss area is 20 km long, about 12 km broad and up to 618 m in height which in many places, particularly on the coasts, is broken by volcanic outcrops. The reddish porphyry of the coast with its numerous bays and offshore islets contrasts charmingly with the blue of the sea.

To the east of the Siagne estuary this coastline is characterised by the dipping of the sub-Alpine chain and the western Alps to the south into the Ligurian Sea. To the east beyond Cannes the coast rises in terraces; the Cap d'Antibes stands out impressively, and then there follows the estuarial area of the Var, the course of the river reveals clear tectonically limited boundaries. Bays and promontories, with the backdrop of mountain slopes like an amphitheatre, give the landscape its particular attraction which, however, is becoming increasingly spoiled by development as big business has transformed the whole area into a unique centre of tourism.

Côte d'Azur: view from the Massif de l'Esterel over Nice and the Alps

France

— Boundaries of régions
Boundaries of départements

Provence and the Côte d'Azur
are among the most visited
holiday areas of France.

Alpes-Maritimes
Between Nice and Menton (where the Italian border begins) the chalk foothills of the maritime Alps fall away steeply into the sea. This leaves little room for human habitation, only the Principality of Monaco (covering an area of about 2 sq km and able to increase its size through deposits building up in the sea) and Èze, lying at an altitude of 427 m above sea level.

Crau
The coastal hinterland, comprising Haute-Provence and Basse-Provence, is bordered in the extreme west by the Crau Plain, once the delta of the Durance, whose smooth pebbles had been washed down from the Alps during the ice age. Originally dry, about 60 per cent of the area is now irrigated and used as pasture and for market

gardening. The territory around the Étang de Berre, a lake of about 160 sq km but only up to 10 m deep, serves as an industrial relief zone for Marseille.

To the east lies a stratified region, consisting primarily of chalk, clay and conglomerates, the highest terrace of which forms part of the basin of Aix-en-Provence. To the east and south-east of Aix the mountain chains of Provence become more prominent. Examples are the steep slopes of the Montagne Ste-Victoire, the Montagne du Cengle, the Chaîne de l'Etoile and the Massif de la Ste-Baume. But even ranges such as the Chaîne de l'Estaque between the Étang de Berre and the Golfe du Lion or the Lubéron range to the east of Avignon, consisting predominantly of Jurassic and cretaceous limestone, belong to the mountain system of the Pyrénées and Provence. The depression zone around

Toulon–Cuers–le Muy, with its extensive vineyards, separates these chains from the uplands of the coast.

The deposits of bauxite in the vicinity of Brignoles bear witness to the emergence of an upland zone from the inlet of the sea which once covered an extensive area of Provence. The products of a considerable weathering of laterite became accumulated in karstic hollows forming storage places for this aluminium ore.

The river systems of the Durance and the Verdon characterise the north of the hinterland. The Lower valley of the Durance, between Avignon and Mirabeau, is broad and follows the Pyrénées-Provence axis. It has only a few tributaries and a relatively small gradient. North of Mirabeau there is an increase in gradient and in the number of tributaries, and the Durance turns towards the north-east.

Verdon

The central reaches of the Verdon, which is controlled by important flood barriers, is an exception. It has cut its bed into great Jurassic limestone banks, in part like the Dolomites.

This stretch, called the Grand Canyon du Verdon, with the deepest gorges in Europe, is an example of an ancient breach valley. Even the tributaries of the Verdon reveal an astonishing independence from the present structure of the land. North of the lower Verdon stretches the Plateau de Valensole, a hollow filled with huge mounds of gravel. South of the Grand Canyon du Verdon extend the undulating karstic reliefs of the Grand Plan de Canjuers and the plain of Comps.

The east of the hinterland is mainly formed by heavily fissured fold mountains of the Alpine foothills of Grasse, to which the Montagne de Thorenc, the Montagne de Cheiron and the Montagne de l'Audiberque also belong. The rivers, however, sometimes follow the north-south direction of the maritime Alps to the east of the Var, as is shown by the example of the Loup. The highest point of the maritime Alps, the Cime dell'Argentera (3297 m) is actually in Italy.

◀ Autumn in Haute-Provence (near Séderon)

Mediterranean

The waters around the Mediterranean coast (Golfe du Lion, Ligurian Sea) are relatively warm; because of the latitude, evaporation and salt content are relatively high. Even at quite great depths the temperature is rarely below 13°C. The surface temperature in winter ranges between 10 and 13°C and in summer can reach 25°C.

High and low tides have a difference of only 25 cm, but the waves are frequently subject to fluctuation; strong air currents sometimes cause short-lived but violent waves which can be dangerous to swimmers.

Unfortunately the quality of the sea water in several places leaves much to be desired. Sewage from coastal settlements, pollution of the rivers and rubbish from ships have recently necessitated regular monitoring of rivers, bacteriological control and the setting up of a warning system when excessive pollution is threatened.

This warning system proved of little use against the oil pollution that occurred when the tanker Haven exploded and sank off Genoa in April 1991. In just two weeks the escaped oil reached the beaches of the Côte d'Azur and threatened the Hyères beaches and the National Park Port-Cros. Special ships which were meant to vacuum up the oil could not be used as the waves were too high and the carpet of oil had broken up. Fortunately the tanker did not break up and so the spillage was only relatively light; even in the bay of St-Tropez, which faces east, only a few patches of oil were washed ashore.

Beaches

The beaches vary in nature, depending on the sea currents on the one hand, and on the other hand on the morphology of the coasts. Established tourist centres such as Monaco and Nice have partly rocky coasts and very coarse sand, while more modern resorts, such as St-Tropez and Hyères, can offer spacious beaches with fine sand. Artificial beaches have been and continue to be laid down.

The submarine terrain has naturally the same geological conditions as the coast. Steep shelving, shallows and precipitous rock formations require constant vigilance from those in boats. There are excellent opportunities for experienced sub-aqua sportsmen and sportswomen.

Climate

Coastal area

Most of the built-up areas near the coast – and above all the Côte d'Azur – are extraordinarily well favoured from the point of view of climate. Although the annual precipitation is between 550 mm and 820 mm and is, therefore, not very different from that in northern regions, the annual sunshine amounts to about 3000 hours. In the east especially, where the mountains rise like an amphitheatre and the slopes are exposed to the sun for the whole of the day, cool north winds are kept at bay. In the west the mistral occasionally makes its unpleasant presence felt.

For the coastal area favourable pressure distribution provides clear sunny days with fresh winds and predominantly dry air in winter. In this season average day temperatures of between 6°C and 12°C are reached; maximum temperatures are between 2°C and 4°C higher, corresponding approximately to conditions to the south of Rome. Frost and snow are rare on the coast. The windiest month is March which is also rainy; April and May are the most suitable months for visitors seeking a healthy break. Summer is not too hot (July average 24°C). Sultry weather and storms are rare in the vicinity of the coast, but there is a considerable drop in temperature at night and at times heavy dew. Moderate rainfall occurs mainly in autumn when it is almost possible to talk of a rainy season in October (maximum 97 mm) and November. Precipitation and the frequency of frost increase in relation to altitude and topography.

Upland region

Climatic conditions in the more northerly upland mountain areas are quite different, as a continental type of climate competes more strongly with the moderating influence of the sea. In this region precipitation occurs throughout the year, without noticeable peaks in spring or autumn. In the higher parts the snow lies for quite a long time; in the high Alpine regions generally excellent conditions for winter sports prevail. Even in the summer months it remains cool here.

Mistral

The mistral, a notorious wind, which hurls itself down the Rhône valley and roars over Provence, occurs when there is low pressure over the Golfe du Lion and simultaneously high pressure over the Massif Central. The constriction of the air currents between the latter and the Alps causes, by means of a kind of jet effect, high wind speeds. At the same time low-pressure areas which are caused by solar heat rising from the North African shotts – saline depressions – and the flat expanses of sandy desert, contribute in causing localised mistrals.

The mistral generally blows in periods of from three to ten days, normally beginning about 10am and lasting until sunset. When such a period comes to an end, several pleasant days without any wind follow.

Sirocco

Sometimes in summer the sirocco reaches Provence. This is a hot dry wind from North Africa (the Sahara).

Flora and Fauna

Flora

As a consequence of the favourable Mediterranean climate the flora is exceptionally varied. Silver-grey olive trees, which are found everywhere on the slopes up to 500 m and more above sea level, orange and lemon plantations, vines, pines, palms, cypresses, aloes, agaves, cacti and many more are now taken for granted as typical plants of the Côte d'Azur, but were in some cases brought here from other countries in Roman times.

Of the original vegetation that has suffered from human intrusion as well as catastrophic fires in forest and plain, pines take a leading place (Aleppo, maritime, stone and northern pines). In addition there are holm, kermes and cork oaks, hornbeam and sweet chestnut. The principal plant of the *garrigue* (in Provençal *garoulia*), a special form of the maquis (undergrowth of hard-leafed evergreens, bushes, shrubs), is the holm oak. The outer surface of its leaves are thickened and covered with a wax layer, and the underside is protected with a felty coating. This prevents evaporation occurring too quickly.

The large number of sweetly scented bushes and herbs (lavender, rosemary, thyme, cistus) is striking. Edible fungi often occur in the forests, particularly

Holm oaks in bloom in the Lubéron

Thyme in the Tricastin

truffles in Vaucluse which are tracked down with the help of trained dogs. The flowers of the Riviera have become legendary, the intensive cultivation of cut flowers such as mimosa for export (in winter) or of sweet-smelling blossoms (violets, roses, lavender, oranges) for perfume production plays an important role in the economy.

Fauna

There is a wide variety of fauna, particularly reptiles (tortoises, lizards, geckos, snakes, vipers) and insects, which find perfect living conditions in areas which are difficult of access. Only a few animals suitable for hunting survive in the hinterland as the sport is traditionally very popular. Thrushes and other songbirds, quails, pheasants, partridges, hares, roe deer and deer as well as trout, whitefish and river crabs are all sought after outside the few protected areas. The sea is also intensively exploited so that (just as with hunting) stocks are being increasingly exhausted. Sea creatures under particular protection include mussels, prawns and octopuses as well as sea eels, perch,

bream, tuna and sardines together with fur seals and ray.

Economy

The natural potential of Provence has led to land development which is characterised on the one hand by agriculture, forestry and fishery (the last named partly in decline), and on the other hand, by reason of a rapid development of industry, mining, energy production and tourism, a heavy concentration of population and the urbanisation of entire stretches of the coast.

Population

The Provence-Alpes-Côte-d'Azur region is one of the most densely populated areas of France, with the coastal region being one of the most densely populated anywhere. The intensity of settlement here continues as shown by the increase in population (doubled since the second world war) and the density of settlement; from about 100 inhabitants per sq km at the end of the 1970s to 136 per sq km today. The numbers are even more striking when the sharp contrast in population density between the coast and inland areas can be seen by comparing the figures (1989) for the different *départements*: Alpes-de-Haute-Provence 19, Hautes-Alpes 20, Var and Vaucluse 128, Alpes-Maritime 226, Bouches-du-Rhône 346 inhabitants per square kilometre. In total the region has about 4.25 million inhabitants of which 1.45 million form the working population employed in the following fields – 4.2 per cent in primary industry, 22.4 per cent in the secondary sector and 73.4 per cent in the service industry (with about 250,000 unemployed).

Industry

Marseille
The favourable geographical situation of the coastal area is of extreme economic importance. Marseille, at the 'Gateway to Africa and the East' has become a leading industrial and commercial centre, and the zone of the Étang de Berre is a major petrochemical Europort. An annual turnover of about 100 million tonnes (about 90 per cent of the imports consists of oil) makes the port of Marseille one of the largest in Europe. With an annual refining capacity of 30 million metric tonnes, this industrial zone is the second largest in France (a pipeline from Fos to Karlsruhe in Germany is 782 km long).

As well as large complexes of the chemical and petrochemical industries, there are also aluminium works which produce about 85 per cent of the total French output. In addition there are large iron and steel plants, aircraft and engineering works and shipyards. Another important branch of the economy is the food industry (sugar, bread, cakes and pastries, jams, milling and abattoirs).

In addition to Marseille, **Toulon** is also notable as a regional economic centre, owing to its natural advantages as a military and commercial port (1138 ha; the largest naval port in France).

Côte d'Azur
The Côte d'Azur has also developed over the last 20 years into an important industrial centre, concentrating mainly on new 'smoke-free' technology. The turnover of the tourist trade is being surpassed in the meanwhile by the development of service, electronic and computer companies (e.g. Texas Instruments, IBM, Digital Equipment, Thomson) and of chemical and biotechnological research and business centres. Nice airport is France's second largest and deals with five million passengers a year; about 20 flights a week arrive here from Paris. Direct flights connect Nice with the rest of the world. The long-term goal is to establish Nice as a second centre of industry after Paris and the location of the technology park (Sophia Antipolis at Antibes with 2300 ha, Toulon) is intended to be a step in this direction. Jacques Médecin, mayor of Nice from 1966 to 1990 and initiator of the Côte d'Azur Développement company founded in 1983 to provide support for the economy, believed that the region could become the centre of an economically successful southern Europe. Médecin considered it to be an exaggeration to suppose that the limit of the ecological maximum capacity of the area could be reached.

Other industries
An important role is played by bauxite-mining in the vicinity of Brignoles (about 70 per cent of the total French supply); this supply is important for the industrial area of Marseille.

Of regional importance is the limestone and cement industry between Marseille and Cassis. Productive salt pans are located in the area of the Étang de Berre as well as near Hyères and Giens.

The fresh and preserved food industry, which processes agricultural produces, plays an important role.

Perfume industry
The centre of the highly developed and traditional perfume industry is the small town of Grasse and the countryside around it. Here more than 30 large concerns annually process several million kilograms of flower blossoms (orange, rose, jasmine, thyme, rosemary, mignonette, violet). There are also factories producing synthetic perfume and these are gaining in importance. The distillation of lavender is primarily confined to the catchment area of the Verdon, where almost 80 per cent of the world's lavender oil is produced.

Energy

Water exploitation

A decisive factor in the provision of water is the landform with its deeply incised valleys, especially in the catchment area of the Durance. The numerous dams and canals leading to the south are not only used to generate electricity, but also to control the water supply by holding back floodwater, thus creating a reserve for periods of drought, irrigation (for example in the Crau) and providing a supply of drinking water. The waters of the larger rivers, especially the Rhône, are used for cooling the reactors in **nuclear fuel plants** (Cruas, Marcoule, Tricastin). Cruas and Tricastin combined have more than eight reactor blocks which produce almost 50 billion kilowatt-hours a year, supplying about 14 per cent of France's electricity requirements. Tricastin and Marcoule are also important for their enriched areas of fissile uranium. Cadarache, the centre for atomic development, is located south of Manosque at Verdon.

Agriculture

Irrigation

Agriculture and forestry have great importance as suppliers of basic materials. Once poorly supplied with water, Provence developed into the fertile region it is today through the building of a network of tightly knit canals. The initiator of this project was Adam de Craponne (1527–76). Born in Salon-de-Provence, he built the canal between the Durance and the Crau (opened in 1554) which carries his name.

Cultivation

Extensive areas devoted to vegetable and fruit growing as well as numerous vineyards are to be found principally in the fertile valleys of the hinterland but also on the artificially irrigated fields of the Crau. The produce is not only valuable for the local food and canning industry but is also exported.

The less fertile land (the gravelly areas of the Durance karst and the high terrain of the Alpine foothills) serves either as pasture or for growing fodder for cattle or for sheep. Increasing demands for beef and veal in the

Lavender harvest near Valensole

Nice around 1900, promenade des Anglais

tourist centres has led to a considerable increase in the rearing of cattle.

In the mountainous regions near the coast supplies of timber (olive, oak, beech and tree heather – briar roots, especially for pipes) are much in demand. The production of olive oil and cork plays an important agricultural role.

Between Toulon and Menton some 8000 specialist firms are engaged in the growing of flowers (principally under glass). The blossoms are used for the production of perfume and essential oils. The Alpes-Maritimes *département* alone produces about 50 per cent of France's cut flower exports.

The main source of income for the farmers on the plateau between the Durance and the coast is the harvesting of lavender, together with a small amount of cereals and hay.

Transhumance

Flocks of sheep graze everywhere between Crau and the maritime Alps. The ancient custom of transhumance – the seasonal moving of livestock to new pastures – is adhered to strongly here. For centuries in early summer, when the grass on the plains had already withered, flocks of sheep were driven along paths (known as *drailles* or *carraires*) up into the heights of the Cevennes, the Massif Central and the Alps. They often covered distances of 100 km or more. Nowadays the flocks total some 500,000 animals, a fraction of former numbers, and are mostly transported by freight train or lorry. The sight of the brightly marked and decorated animals, bleating noisily and with their bells jingling as they are moved across the fields and through the villages, presents a unique picture (☞Practical Information, Walking).

Fishing

Fishing both in the sea and in inland waters only plays a subordinate commercial role today. It is strictly regulated within the protective zone created in 1992 for sea mammals. While commercial fishing has lost its importance, coastal and deep-sea fishing have become increasingly popular with tourists.

Tourism

Already by the first half of the 18th c.

the great beauty and mild climate of this coastal region was talked about in circles where people could indulge in journeys for pleasure and recuperation. At first it was the wealthy English who spent winters here, first in Nice and later in Cannes. Nice, the climate of which was found to be very healthy, became fashionable as a health resort.

War and revolution caused a considerable reduction in the burgeoning tourism, but the Côte d'Azur experienced a rise in prosperity in the 19th c., not least through the building of railway lines and roads. The pattern of settlement was altered when promenades along the shore, splendid gardens, luxury villas and well-appointed inns were built, and there arose an attractive winter health resort area of international renown. Cannes, Nice, Monaco and Menton were the resorts preferred by the European aristocracy.

Côte d'Azur
In 1887 the socialite and author Stephen Liégeard published a book about the life of the upper crust on this as yet nameless coast, entitled *Côte d'Azur*. The book's success caused its title to be included in *Larousse*, France's famous dictionary, in 1888. The world's playground had acquired its name.

Mass tourism
The first world war brought another crisis. However, through skilful advertising wealthy people from all over the world were attracted to Provence for holidays for their health. After 1930 new coastal and beach settlements emerged, dependencies of villages situated further inland, and this relieved pressure on the older seaside resorts, while their beaches attracted more summer visitors. From the original health resorts, which were visited only in winter, there arose a holiday area with visitors all year round, and with summer as the high season.

Economic and ecological importance
The favourable climatic conditions, the beauty of the coasts with their bays and sandy shores and the relative proximity of the winter sports area resulted after the second world war in the development of a tourist region which has few equals. The *département* of Alpes-Maritimes alone receives about eight million tourists every year and employs some 100,000 people in tourism. In the wake of modern mass tourism followed a frantic building of hotels, holiday villages, second homes, marinas, campsites and leisure complexes. Further development is planned. Warnings by biologists and town planners about the destruction of flora and fauna and about the enormous intrusion into the delicate ecology of the coastal region have, until now, been ignored. With the increase in local holiday traffic, overcrowding of the beaches, water pollution and shortage of accommodation have become the norm. There has also been a considerable increase in criminal activity (theft, stealing from vehicles, muggings).

Recently, in addition to local and holiday tourism, business meetings and conferences have contributed to the growth of tourism. Cannes, Nice and Monte Carlo in particular have made great efforts to stage various events – fairs, festivals and congresses – and the international airport Nice-Côte d'Azur has been of great service in this respect.

Famous People

The following are famous historical personalities, all linked to Provence either through birth, residence, work or death and famous throughout the world. The list is arranged alphabetically.

André-Marie Ampère
(1775–1836)

The mathematician and physicist André-Marie Ampére, born in Lyon on January 22nd 1775, did fundamental work in the field of natural science. He developed a theory of electromagnetism, built an electrotelegraph and discovered the direction of circulation of a magnetic field surrounded by a conductor through which the current was flowing. Even today the measure of the strength of a current is named after him. Ampère died on June 10th 1836 at the age of 61 in Marseille.

Louis Bréa
(ca 1450–1522/3)

Louis Bréa, born in Nice, was the most important artist living between the end of the 15th c. and the beginning of the 16th c. in the Nice-Liguria region, a region remote from contemporary trends. Little is known about the models he chose or his influences. He worked mainly in Genoa, Taggia, Ventimiglia, Monaco and Nice. For a long time he remained closely attached to the antiquated taste of his patrons, mainly orders of penitent monks; his altarpieces consist of several fields mounted in wooden frames, each depicting only a few figures portraying deep contemplation and peace. The simplicity and naivity of his figures cause him to be known as the 'provincial Fra Angelico'. After 1500 he painted in the Renaissance style and from 1510 the influence of the Lombardy School became noticeably stronger. Bréa died between March 1522 and March 1523 in Nice. His paintings can be found in churches in Monaco, Nice, Biot, Antibes, Gréolières, Lucéram and Fréjus.

Paul Cézanne
(1839–1906)

Born the son of a prosperous banker on January 19th 1839 in Aix-en-Provence, Paul Cézanne came to painting after studying law for a short time. At first he modelled himself on classical masters; he admired and copied Michelangelo, Delacroix and Tintoretto. His school friend Zola introduced him to the Impressionists, of whom Camille Pissarro influenced him most strongly. In 1873 Cézanne accompanied Pissarro to Auvers-sur-Oise and worked with him there in the open air outside the studio – a novelty of Impressionist art. He began to use strong colours to reproduce distinctive moods of light, air and nature. After taking part in the first group exhibition mounted by the Impressionists in 1874 and reaping only scorn, he moved back to Aix and spent the next 27 years there in strict seclusion.

Only after 1899 did he gradually become known to a wider public. He is regarded as the master of post-Impressionism; and from his words 'la réflection modifie la vision' (contemplation alters what one sees) he is counted as one of the forerunners of modern art. By returning to classical aesthetics and to form he gave considerable impulse to modern representational art (fauvism, cubism). Cézanne died on November 22nd 1906 in Aix.

Marc Chagall
(1887–1985)

Marc Chagall, born in Vitebsk (White Russia) on July 7th 1887, studied at the Petersburg Academy of Art and then lived from 1910 to 1914 in Paris, where he became friends with Cendrars and Apollinaire; at that time his tendency to fantasy was already becoming apparent. He made the acquaintance of the cubists, whose influence can only be sensed, however, in his composition. His first solo exhibition was arranged by Herwarth Walden in 1914 in his Berlin gallery The Storm. Chagall returned to the Soviet Union until 1923, when he finally turned his back on his homeland. After another period in France he went to live in America from 1941–7 (in 1945 he designed the staging and costumes for Stravinsky's ballet *The Firebird*) and then returned to France to live in St-Paul-de-Vence from 1949.

Chagall's work has its roots in the Jewish tradition of the East and in Russian popular art. From Jewish-mystic and rural elements he created mysterious, melancholy or effusive compositions in a uniquely fantastic style; his works contain mainly lyrical characters. Chagall is also important as an illustrator of books (Gogol, La Fontaine, the Bible) and he also worked with ceramics and stained glass, including the windows of the Frauenmünster in Zürich in 1970 and Rheims Cathedral in 1974. The most important museum in Provence featuring Chagall is the Musée National Message Biblique in Nice. Chagall died on March 28th 1985 in St-Paul-de-Vence.

Alphonse Daudet
(1840–97)

Alphonse Daudet was born in Nîmes but spent his youth in Lyon. In 1860 he obtained the post of private secretary to the duke of morny, through whose patronage he gained entry to interesting literary circles and thus acquired the basis of a commercially successful career in writing. Daudet's cheerfully ironic stories make him the most important humorist of his time. Under the influence of the naturalists he also turned his hand to themes critical of society, although he did not adopt their general ideological claims. Through Frédéric Mistral, Provence plays a large part in his works. He used the windmill near Arles as the fictitious place of origin of his *Lettres de Mon Moulin* (the stories were written in Paris). The windmill now houses a Daudet museum and has become a leading French tourist attraction. Georges Bizet wrote the music to accompany a dramatisation of one of the letters, *l'Arlesienne*. Daudet also created the well-known figure of Tartarin of Tarascon, an ironically drawn Frenchman of the south on whom the ever present discrepancy between fantasy and reality plays many tricks. Daudet died on December 16th 1897 in Paris.

Auguste Escoffier
(1846–1935)

Escoffier, the creator of the modern culinary art, was born on November 28th 1846 in Villeneuve-Loubet and died on February 12th 1935 in Monte-Carlo. He served his apprenticeship with his uncle in Nice and then went on to work in Paris, Lucerne and Monte-Carlo before making a great career for himself in London, becoming 'the king of chefs and the chef of kings'. In 1898 he became chef de cuisine at the London Carlton and remained in this position until he retired in 1921 at the age of 75. He was decorated with the Order of the Legion of Honour.

Escoffier's extensive works still form the basis of professional cookery, especially *Le Guide Culinaire* (1903), *Livres des Menus* (1912) and *Ma Cuisine* (1934). He not only created many classic recipes (peach melba is merely his best known) but also reorganised and rationalised the working kitchen and its employees and introduced a code of behaviour (cooks were to practise cleanliness and precision in the kitchen and they were not to smoke, drink or shout there). Escoffier modernised some methods of preparation such as making heavy Spanish and German sauces more subtle. A cookery museum was set up in 1966 in the house in which he was born at Villeneuve-Loubet.

Jean-Henri Fabre
(1823–1915)

Fabre was a brilliant scientist and is regarded as the father of modern behavioural research – a fact little known outside France. Born the son of a poor farmer in 1823 in St-Léons (Aveyron), the intelligent boy discovered his love of nature at an early age but satisfied his thirst for knowledge with a variety of interests. At the age of 16 he gained a scholarship to a teacher training college in Avignon, eventually teaching in Carpentras, Ajaccio and Avignon. He gained his doctorate although, in order to support his large family, he had to supplement his meagre income by giving private lessons. Fabre's first and greatest discovery, the behaviour of digger wasps, brought him to the attention of Darwin, with whom he exchanged letters over many decades.

Fabre was already over 60 years old when, with the help of a loan from the famous English philosopher John Stuart Mill, he was able to buy an estate at Sérignan-du-Comtat called Harmas (Provençal for fallow land). Here he could continue with his experiments. The publication of his 10-volume major work *Souvenirs Entomologiques* between 1879 and 1907 introduced him to a wider audience. Fabre died on November 11th 1915 in Sérignan; Harmas has been turned into a museum.

André-Marie Ampère

Jean-Henri Fabre

Vincent van Gogh

Vincent van Gogh
(1853–90)

Vincent van Gogh was born on March 30th 1853, the son of a pastor in Zunden near Breda in the Netherlands. To begin with he was an assistant to an art dealer in Den Haag, then a lay preacher in the southern Belgian workers' settlements of the Borinage. After failing at theological studies, he began to paint in 1880 without any artistic training, portraying the farmers and workers of his native land in heavy, dark colours. In 1886 he went to Paris to live with his brother Theo, a successful art dealer, and came into contact with many other artists, including Paul Gauguin. Van Gogh began to paint in the Impressionist style, brightening the colours of his still life subjects and his portraits, and even verged on pointillism.

On moving to Arles in 1888 van Gogh was completely overcome by the intensity of light and colour, and developed a new and unique style. He painted landscapes and town scenes, still life (such as *Sunflowers*), and portraits in loud, expressive colours with his characteristically rough strokes. After several attacks of mental derangement (after a fight with Gauguin in December 1888 he cut off one of his ears) van Gogh first entered a psychiatric home at St-Rémy-de-Provence in 1889, then one at Auvers-sur-Oise, all the time working with vehement energy until his suicide on July 29th 1890 at the age of 37.

During his lifetime van Gogh remained almost unknown and he depended on the financial help of his brother. It was some decades after his death that he was discovered as the successor to Impressionism; his work inspired the expressionists. Today such pictures as *Sunflowers* and *The Bridge at Arles* fetch astronomical prices.

Henri Matisse
(1869–1954)

Henri Matisse, born on December 31st 1869 at le Cateau-Cambresis, belonged in his early days as an artist to the school of Impressionism. Under the influence of Gauguin, Cézanne and Monet he became around 1900 one of the most important artists to overcome the direction into which this style was leading; his paintings became more two-dimensional and more intensive in colour. Matisse and the painters of his circle were first disparagingly called *Les Fauves* (The Wild Ones). Fauvism preferred to compose pictures with large expanses of colour, abstaining from the delicate shades of Impressionism, and the effect was only obtained by colour and contrast. Matisse's book illustrations and drawings are also important; his last great fresco is the painting of the rosary chapel in Vence (1947–51). Matisse died on November 3rd 1954 in Nice-Cimiez.

Darius Milhaud
(1892–1974)

The composer Darius Milhaud who was born in Aix-en-Provence and was a pupil of the famous Conservatoire de Paris, belongs to the Groupe des Six, which included Arthur Honegger; the group had been formed in 1918 and its aim was to give new life to contemporary music. Milhaud was an extraordinarily prolific composer; his works include operas (*Christophe Colombe*, *Medée*), ballet music, symphonies and chamber music.

From 1947 until 1962 he gave lessons in composition at the Paris Conservatoire.

Hippolyte Mège-Mouriès
(1817–80)

In 1869 this food chemist, born in Draguinan, developed a butter substitute based on beef suet as an entry for a competition run by Napoléon III, who was looking for a cheap and long-lasting fat for sailors. It was called margarine on account of its mother-of-pearl appearance (from the Greek *margaron* meaning pearl). Only after 1900, with the discovery of fat hardening, was plant oil substituted.

Prosper Mérimée
(1803–70)

After studying art and architecture, this son of an affluent merchant family (born on September 29th 1803 in Paris) became an inspector of historical statues and in this capacity travelled around France and the Mediterranean countries, in particular Spain. Many important historical monuments, which make up an essential part of Provence's cultural landscape, owe their preservation to him. His literary works are characterised by a preference for romantic, spine-chilling, exotic and unusual themes; nevertheless, he wrote in a deliberately factual, anti-romantic style. He achieved true mastery of the novella and through the operatic production of his novella *Carmen* in 1845 by Georges Bizet he remains famous until this day. In 1848 he became a member of the Académie Française and in 1853 a senator; nevertheless he maintained friendship with Stendhal and other opponents of the Restoration. He died on September 23rd 1870 in Cannes.

Frédéric Mistral
(1830–1914)

Frédéric Mistral was born in Maillane, not far north of St-Rémy, the son of a farmer. The impetus for his literary work and his enthusiasm for the sonorous Provençal dialect came from his earlier acquaintance with Joseph Roumanille who was 12 years his senior. In 1859 appeared the first of the major works of Mistral, the novel *Mirèio* (in French *Mireille*).

Mistral (his real name) is the most important innovator of the Provençal language and its poetry. With Théodore Aubanel and Joseph Roumanille he founded in 1854 the Felibrige, a group of poets dedicated to this revival. Their work and aims are still highly regarded in Provence. In 1904 Mistral received the Nobel Prize for Literature.

Nostradamus
(1503–66)

Michel de Nostre-Dame was born in St-Rémy-de-Provence, the son of a family converted to Judaism. After studying liberal arts in Avignon and medicine at Montpellier University (founded in 1289 and the most famous medical faculty in the western world) he became the personal physician of Catherine de' Medici and Charles IX of France. Like many humanists he Latinised his name and henceforth called himself Nostradamus.

Considerable success in treating patients in several epidemics, mainly by the use of disinfected implements and by insisting on rules of hygiene, earned him the mistrust of his colleagues and forced him into hiding. During this time his intensive preoccupation with astrological and cosmic subjects began. From his observations of the constellations he drew conclusions which he set down in his sombre esoteric prophecies. His work, composed in gloomy four-line verse, was published in 1555 in Lyon under the title *The Centuries*. It caused a great furore (the Vatican blacklisted it as it foresaw the decline of the papacy) and has continued to exert influence in later centuries.

Less well known is his book which appeared in the same year in which he foresaw the production of make-up and perfumes and of jams. Nostradamus died on July 2nd 1566 at Salon-de-Provence where he had lived since 1547.

Francesco Petrarca
(1304–74)

The Italian poet, philosopher and humanist, born in Arezzo, moved with his family to Avignon in 1311 and studied law from 1317 in Montpellier and then from 1323 in Bologna. Having moved back to France he met in 1327 the lady whom he immortalised in his poetry as 'Laura'. It was a meeting that held importance for the whole of the rest of his life and for his artistic development. Between 1330 and 1347 he was the servant of Cardinal Giacomo Colonna. After extensive journeys through France, the Netherlands and Germany, where he searched for old manuscripts in libraries, he moved back to Fontaine-de-Vaucluse near Avignon in 1337 to fulfil his poetic inclinations there. In 1353 he left Provence and

Nostradamus

Francesco Petrarca

Pablo Picasso

worked for eight years for the Milanese Visconti as an envoy (including some time in Prague), from 1362 he lived entirely in Venice. Petrarca was a pioneer of humanism and of the Italian Renaissance. His writings in Latin gave new life to what was old and the content of his Italian poems, which are characterised by the formation of the suffering and reflective soul and by an inner-worldly ideal of the beautiful woman, became formal models for European love poetry (Petrarchism). He has become known as the 'First Modern Man', proof of which is his famed ascent of Mount Ventoux on April 26th 1336, a climb made not for gain but with the sole purpose of experiencing the landscape.

Gérard Philipe
(1922–59)
The actor Gérard Philipe, born in Cannes, lived only for 37 years. Better known than his stage appearances were the international films in which he appeared (*Fanfan la Tulipe, Le Diable au Corps*). He is buried in the upland village of Ramatuelle near St-Tropez.

Pablo Picasso
(1881–1973)
Pablo Ruiz Picasso, the Spanish painter, sculptor, illustrator and potter, was born on November 25th 1881 in Malaga. He is held to be the greatest artist of modern times, having influenced 20th c. art for eight decades.

After having been apprenticed to his father, Picasso studied at the academies of Barcelona and Madrid (from 1896) and, following several extended stays in Paris, moved to his chosen homeland of France

in 1904. He finally settled on the Côte d'Azur in 1936 – 'Then I realised that this landscape was my landscape' – after repeated trips to Provence and the coast. He worked chiefly in Mougins, Golfe-Juan, Antibes, Vallauris, Cannes and Vauvenargues. His early works, which are divided into the Blue and the Pink periods according to the most-used colour, are characterised by melancholy, yet graceful figures. With his epoch-making key work, the *Demoiselles d'Avignon* of 1907, Picasso (together with Georges Braques, and later also Juan Gris and Fernand Léger) created the requirements necessary for the development of cubism. After the first world war Picasso returned to figurative representation and came close to surrealism; his use of forms became blurred, his pictures were filled with motifs of movement and extremely vivid people. At the end of the 1920s he devoted himself increasingly to sculpture. Book illustrations, works portraying the Spanish civil war and the greyness of war in general (*Guernica*, created after the bombardment of the Basque town by the German Condor Legion, was a further highpoint), depictions of bullfights, portraits and variations on the theme of 'artist and model' were now his main subjects.

After the second world war Picasso became very involved with ceramics and also produced many graphics (drawings, etchings and lithographs). This resulted in a life's work that shows a unique mastery of using the history of art, of his own history and of the most varied artistic methods and techniques. Picasso died on April 8th 1973 in Mougins; his grave is at Vauvenargues where he worked for three months in 1958.

History

900,000 BC First signs of human life (cave finds at Vallonet near Roquebrune-Cap-Martin); objects made of bone and pebbles.

700,000 BC Oldest burnt spots in the cave at l'Escale, near St-Estéve-Janson (Bouches-du-Rhône).

380,000 BC Terra Amata finds at Nice: coastal settlement of large huts, burnt spots.

300,000 BC Cave finds at Baoussé-Roussé near Menton.

4000–3000 BC Stone Age culture, decorated and painted pottery; cave dwellings, burial grounds (finds at Roquepertuse, near Velaux).

Ca 800 BC Ligurians take the coastal area and set up strongholds; development of modest trade along the Riviera.

Ca 600 BC Greeks from Phocaea in Asia Minor found the port of Massalia, later Marseille. They introduce the vine and the olive tree as well as their important ceramic industry. Greek culture spreads through Gaul from here.

600–100 BC Further Greek settlements on the coast, increasing clashes with the Celto-Ligurian population.

181/154 BC The Greeks from Massalia summon their Roman allies to help against the Celto-Ligurians.

150–50 BC Roman incursions into the present-day area of Provence: Provincia Gallia Narbonensis.

125–121 BC The amalgamation of the Celts leads the Romans to occupy the land (destruction of the Oppidum d'Entremont, an important stronghold of the Saluvier).

124 BC Founding of Aix to protect the land route to Spain; construction of the Via Domitia. Founding of the first Roman province on the other side of the Alps: Gallia Transalpina or Gallia Narbonensis (founding of Narbonne 118 BC).

58–52 BC Caesar's conquest of Gaul.

50/49 BC Julius Caesar conquers Massalia (Latin Massilia), which had taken the side of Pompeii against him. Roman veterans are settled in Arles and Fréjus. Further colonies in Avignon and Orange.

Up to AD 14 Augustus conquers the Alpine tribes. Construction of the Trophée des Alpes, the victory monument near la Turbie. Various magnificent buildings of the Imperial Age such as the triumphal arch in Cavaillon.

2nd c. AD Heyday of the Pax Romana, which lasted until the 3rd c. AD. Extension of the Gallo-Roman towns and the first beginnings of Christianity.

3rd c. AD Arrival of nomadic peoples.

4th/5th c. AD Christianity gains in importance; coffins are produced in Marseille and the Church of St-Victor is built.
 Legend of the landing of the three Maries (Stes-Maries-de-la-Mer).

419–78 The Visigoths conquer Arles and occupy the area south of the Durance; Burgundians settle north of the Durance.

507 After their victory at Vouillé the Ostrogoths take control of the Riviera.

536 The Franks gain the ascendancy.

591 Plague in Marseille.

736–9 Saracens invade southern France; emergence of many refuge settlements (*villages perchés*). Construction of baptisteries (baptismal churches).

714–41 Charles Martel defeats the Saracens and invades Provence.

768–814 Charlemagne brings 'peace' to the region.

843 As a result of the Treaty of Verdun, in which the Carolingian empire was divided, Lothar gains Provence.

855–63 Provence first becomes a kingdom.

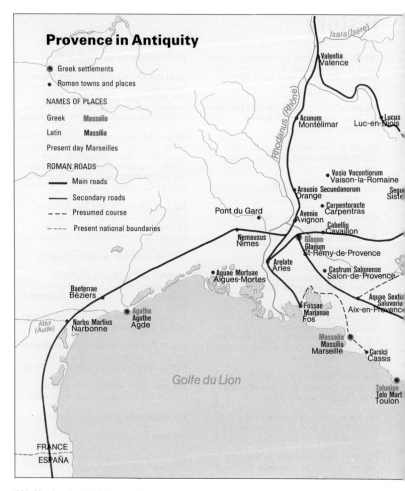

Provence in Antiquity

- ● Greek settlements
- · Roman towns and places

NAMES OF PLACES

Greek	**Massalia**
Latin	**Massilia**

Present day Marseilles

ROMAN ROADS

—— Main roads

—— Secondary roads

--- Presumed course

---- Present national boundaries

Isara (Isère)

Valentia
Valence

Rhodanus (Rhône)

Acunum
Montélimar   Luc-en-Diois   Lucus

Vasio Vocontiorum
Vaison-la-Romaine

Arausio Secundanorum
Orange   Segu
Siste

Carpentoracte
Carpentras

Pont du Gard   Avenio
Avignon   Cabellio
Cavaillon

Nemausus
Nîmes   Glanon
Glanum
St-Rémy-de-Provence

Arelate
Arles   Castrum Salonense
Salon-de-Provence

Aquae Mortuae
Aigues-Mortes

Aquae Sextia
Saluvoriu
Aix-en-Provence

Baeterrae
Béziers

Fossae
Marianae
Fos

Atax
(Aude)   Agathe
Agathe
Agde

Narbo Martius
Narbonne

Massilia
Massilia
Marseille   Carsici
Cassis

Golfe du Lion

Telunion
Telo Mart
Toulon

FRANCE
ESPAÑA

869 Charles the Bald, king of France, annexes Provence.

879 Under Boso, brother-in-law of Charles the Bald, Provence becomes part of the kingdom of Lower Burgundy.

9th c. Spasmodic incursions by the Saracens who settle in the Massif des Maures.

933 Lower and Upper Burgundy combine into one kingdom with Arles as the main city.

947 Kingdom of Provence-Burgundy under Conrad, founding of the new earldoms of Arles, Apt, Avignon.

973 Saracens are expelled from Fraxinetum (la Garde-Freinet?).

1033 Affiliation of the kingdom of Burgundy with the Salic empire (Emperor Conrad II).

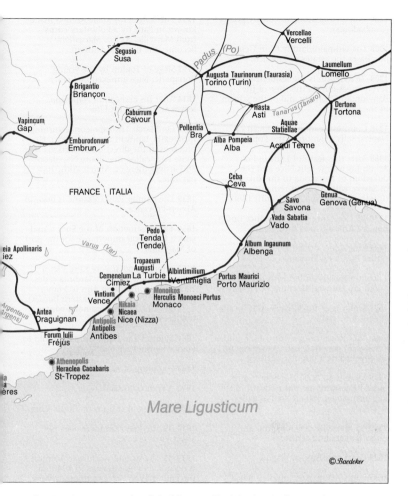

11th c. First Romanesque church building. The family of the counts of Provence break into three factions, the counts of Barcelona, Toulouse and Forcalquier, who feud against one another.

1125 Raimond Bérenger III, count of Barcelona, receives the land between the Rhône, the Durance, the Alps and the sea, the count of Toulouse, Alphonse Jourdaine, the land north of the Durance.

Battles between the Catalan counts and the dukes of les Baux (1142–62).

Participation in the crusades.

12th c. Flourishing of the ports following the crusades (trade with the Levant).

1175 Founding of Silvacane Abbey.

1246 Charles I of Anjou, brother of Ludwig the Holy, becomes duke of Provence by marriage and, through the conquest of the kingdom of Naples in 1266, king of Provence.

12th–14th c. Flourishing of courtly poetry (troubadours).

1308 The Grimaldi family from Genoa purchases the estates of Monaco.

1309–76 Avignon is the residence of seven Popes during the time of the Babylonian Captivity and of the schism in the Church.

1348 Countess Jeanne (also queen of Naples) sells Avignon to the Pope.

1388 After the death of Ludwig I of Anjou his widow sells Nice and the dukedom of Barcelona to the dukedom of Savoy, with whom it remains (interrupted by Napoléon) until 1860.

1434–80 Flowering of the province under René of Anjou (Good King René).

1442 King René, driven from Naples, settles in Aix-en-Provence.

1481 Provence is united with the French kingdom; Ludwig XI, count of Provence.

1524 Building of the Château d'If on the island of Marseille.

From 1524 Royal troops (from 1536 under Charles V) penetrate into Provence and are repelled by a popular uprising.

1545 More than 2000 Huguenots and other Protestants are put to death in the Lubéron range; 800 are sold as galley slaves.

1580–95 Marseille develops into an important trading centre.

1629 Great epidemic of plague.

1635 Louis XIV makes Toulon a naval port.

1641–60 After uprisings Marseille is subjected to the central power of Louis XIV.

1691 The French take over Nice.

1710 Prince Eugene advances to the Riviera.

1720–2 Years of severe plague.

1715–50 Flowering of the art of faience in Moustiers-Ste-Marie and Marseille.

1792 The *Song of the Rhine Army* is made known in Paris by a voluntary corps from Marseille. As *The Marseillaise* it becomes the national anthem.

1793 Siege of Toulon by the young Bonaparte; Nice annexed by French.

1814 After his abdication Napoléon leaves St-Raphaël for Elba.

1815 On March 1st Napoléon, returning from exile, lands in the Golfe-Juan. He proceeds in the direction of Paris via the route later called the 'Route Napoléon' and arrives there on March 20th. 100-day rule.

1839 The painter Paul Cézanne is born in Aix-en-Provence.

1859–69 Construction of the Suez Canal, which is of great importance for the port of Marseille.

1860 After a popular vote King Victor Emanuel II of Piedmont-Sardinia cedes Nice and the maritime Alps to France (alteration of the French eastern border).
   The Côte d'Azur becomes a winter holiday resort.

1861 Menton and Roquebrune are sold to France by the Prince of Monaco.

1866 Founding of Monte-Carlo.

1870–1 Franco-Prussian war.

1878 Opening of casinos in Monte-Carlo.

1914–19 The first world war does not affect Provence.

1939–45 The second world war. Menton is occupied by the Italians in 1940. At the end of 1942 German troops occupy the Riviera in retaliation for the Allied landing on November 8th in North Africa. The French war fleet is scuttled on November 27th at Toulon.
   Within the framework of the invasion strategy, which has been proceeding since the beginning of June in Normandy, on August 15th enormously strong Allied forces land on the Côte des Maures. With the support of the Resistance they take Toulon (August 26th), Marseille (August 28th) and Nice (August 30th). German units remain in the mountainous hinterland until April 1945.

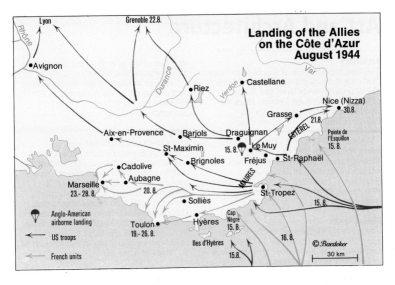

Landing of the Allies on the Côte d'Azur August 1944

Lyon
Grenoble 22.8.
Rhône
Avignon
Durance
Riez
Verdon
Castellane
Var
Nice (Nizza) 30.8.
Grasse • 21.8.
ESTEREL
Pointe de l'Esquillon 15. 8.
Aix-en-Provence • Barjols • Draguignan
St-Maximin   Le Muy 15. 8.
• Brignoles   Fréjus • St-Raphaël
Cadolive
Aubagne
Marseille • 23.- 28. 8.
20.8.
MAURES
• Solliès
St-Tropez
15. 8.

Anglo-American airborne landing

US troops

French units

Toulon • 19.- 26. 8.
Hyères
Cap Nègre 15. 8.
Iles d'Hyères 15.8.
16. 8.
© Baedeker
30 km

1947 Italy cedes the territory of Col de Tende to France.

1956 Inauguration of the first French ceramic works, Marcoule on the Rhône.

1959 On December 2nd the town of Fréjus is stricken by a catastrophic flood caused by a breach in the Malpasset Dam. 421 people are killed.

1962 The airport Nice-Côte d'Azur is opened and quickly achieves more than regional importance.

From 1965 Construction of the industrial harbour of Fos at the Étang de Berre after Marseille harbour becomes too small.

1972 During the course of regionalisation the *départements* of Bouches-du-Rhône, Vaucluse, Hautes-Alpes, Alpes-Maritimes and Alpes-de-Haute-Provence are combined into the Provence-Alpes-Côte-d'Azur *région*.

1973 The painter Pablo Picasso is buried in Vauvenargues.

1980 Motorway A8 'La Provençal' links Provence to the French and the Italian motorway networks.

1981 A new policy of decentralisation begins under the newly elected president François Mitterrand; the aim is to bring more political independence to the regions.

1992 September 22nd. A severe storm with flooding devastates large areas of Vaucluse and the Ardèche; the valley of the Ouvèze was particularly badly affected around Vaison-la-Romaine.

Art and Architecture

Prehistory
The first monuments of significance date from the time of pre- and early history. These include finds from the Sanctuary of Roquepertuse near Velaux, from the Oppidum Entremont near Aix-en-Provence and from Cavaillon near Avignon.

About 600 BC Greeks from Phocaea bring the first breath of classical Mediterranean culture to the Riviera with the founding of Massalia (Marseille). There are also traces of settlement in Nice, Antibes and Greek Antipolis.

Roman times
There are many remains of the Roman epoch including the arena and baths of Cimiez (part of Nice), fine granite pillars in Riez, the Greco-Roman town of Glanum near St-Rémy, the arena and theatre in Arles, the arena and theatre in Fréjus, the fine victory statue in la Turbie, the triumphal arches in Orange and Cavaillon as well as the temple site at Vernègues near Salon.

A large amount of stonework is kept and displayed in the museums in the relevant towns.
Ancient

Early Christianity
From the Early Christian and Carolingian periods date remarkable round buildings (baptisteries), which can still be admired today in Fréjus, Aix-en-Provence and Riez. The crypt of St-Maximin contains the sarcophagi of, amongst others, SS Maria-Magdalena, Sidonius and Maximin; there are more sarcophagi in the Musée d'Art Chrétien in Arles. One of the most important monuments of this age is the Church of St-Victor in Marseille.

Romanesque
The 12th c. architecture in this region experiences a considerable uplift, which manifests itself particularly in secular

Arles: the Roman arena

Cloister of le Thoronet

building of the Romanesque-Provençal style. Under the influence of the Cistercians there arise churches of uncomplicated design, with simple façades and plain interiors; the square bell towers reveal the influence of Lombardy. The best-known buildings of this period are the cathedrals at Aix-en-Provence and Avignon and the abbeys of Sénanque, le Thoronet and Silvacane.

Gothic
French Gothic reaches its zenith in Avignon with the Church of St-Pierre and the famous Papal Palace. Other leading buildings of this time are the Basilica of St-Maximin and the Cathedral of Fréjus.

Renaissance
Few architectural monuments remain from the Renaissance but, on the other hand, it left a legacy of very many paintings. Of note is the Avignon school that developed further the work of Simone Martine who came from Tuscany, and which united artists from different countries at the court of the popes. The most important examples are *Coronation of the Virgin Mary* by Enguerrand Quarton (1453) in the museum at Villeneuve-lès-Avignon (see entry) and Nicolas Froment's triptych *Maria in the Burning Bush* (1485) in the Cathedral of Aix-en-Provence (see entry).

Inspired by the Italian Renaissance, a remarkable school of painting flourished in Nice, the head of which, Louis Bréa (ca 1440–1523) is considered the 'Fra Angelico of Provence'. Works of the school of Bréa, which are characterised by a naive purity and simplicity, are to be found in numerous rural churches of south-eastern Provence.

Baroque
During the time when baroque art was gaining momentum, above all in Italy and Germany, **classicism** was developing in France. This movement consciously dissociated itself from the baroque, and in essence also preserves a greater formal discipline. Yet in south-eastern France the influence of the Italian view of art cannot be ignored and here one can confidently speak of baroque art.

Avignon: the Papal Palace

Aix-en-Provence: Pavillon de Vendôme

The new theatre in Nice (by Yves Bayard and Henri Vidal)

The most prominent examples of this form of art are found in Aix-en-Provence; as a single work the Pavillon de Vendôme, a little outside the town, is outstanding. Also belonging to this period is the good ceramic work of Moustiers-Ste-Marie. Definitely influenced by baroque was the Marseille painter and architect Pierre Puget (1620–94), probably the most important French sculptor of the 17th c.; as well as many other striking sculptures he created the caryatids on the portal of the Old Town Hall in Toulon.

Classicism
18th c. classicism is reflected in the works of Parrocel, van Loo and Fragonard. Jean-Honoré Fragonard, born in 1742 in Grasse, was effectively the court painter of the Parisian aristocracy and is famous today for his stately boudoir and pastoral scenes.

Neo-Romanesque
In the 19th c. an architectural style based on Romanesque-Byzantine historical models was widespread. Shining examples are the Church of Notre-Dame-de-la-Victoire in St-Raphaël,

the Church of Notre-Dame-de-la-Garde and the Cathedral of la Major in Marseille.

19th and 20th centuries
Increasing numbers of artists of more modern and contemporary painting have been attracted to the Riviera since the end of the 19th c. Impressionists, the master of whom is Cézanne, born in Aix-en-Provence, include Berthe Morisot who painted in Nice, Monet in Antibes and Renoir in Cagnes. In 1892 Signac, an exponent of pointillism, chose St-Tropez as his home and brought others, including Bonnard and Matisse, with him. The reaction in the form of fauvism was principally represented by Dufy and Matisse who were later resident in Nice. Picasso, one of the initiators of cubism, spent his time principally in Vallauris, Cannes and Mougins. The cubist Léger was active in Biot, the surrealist Chagall found in Vence themes for his colourful dream pictures. Other famous artists who lived and worked on the Riviera include Braque in St-Paul-de-Vence, Kandinsky in la Napoule, Cocteau in Menton and van Dongen in Cannes. Their works can be seen in many local museums.

The Unité d'Habitation, built in Marseille by Le Corbusier between 1947 and 1952, together with modern marinas and leisure and residential layouts, such as Port-Grimaud, Port Camargue or Marina Baie des Anges, are impressive (if not of great merit in all respects) examples of contemporary architecture. The important art centre, Fondation Maeght in St-Paul-de-Vence, is a work of art in itself. In earlier times Nîmes and Nice distinguished themselves as centres of modern architecture.

Villages perchés

Amid the long line of scarcely indistinguishable picturesque coastal villages and small and large towns the many *villages perchés* are of particular interest. These hill settlements, also known as *nids d'aigle* (eagle's nests), situated on the hilltops, slopes, outcrops, ridges or terraces, were once used as refuges against foreign invaders or would-be conquerors, especially those threatening attack from the sea.

Lack of space compelled the inhabitants to build their houses on the smallest possible piece of ground (*maisons en hauteur, maisons tour*), as close together as possible and frequently intermingled. Typical examples close to the coast are Castellar, Èze, Gorbio, Gourdon, Peillon, Roquebrune, Tourettes-sur-Loup and Vence. There are many other examples inland, such as those to be found on the hilltops east of Avignon, including Gordes, Roussillon, Bonnieux, Ansouis, Lacoste and Ménerbes.

Some years ago these hill villages were being abandoned by their inhabitants as a result of an unfavourable economic situation and the problems of access and supply (for example, drinking water). Today, when money and technology make a more comfortable life possible, they are inhabited once more and restored as second or holiday homes, protected from total decay but often robbed of their originality.

Language of Provence

Provençal, which is widely spoken in south-eastern France, varies significantly from classical French. It is known as *la langue d'oc* in southern France (*oc* being the word originally used to mean 'yes'), whereas in the rest of the country the word was *oil* and French spoken elsewhere was called *la langue d'oil*.

History

Like all living Romance languages, Provençal is derived from vulgar Latin, which had penetrated into the country with Roman colonisation. In Provence about the year 1000 this dialect was the basis of the language of the troubadours and of courtly poetry, a trend that would be paralleled in German-speaking countries. This old Provençal was basically an artificial language. From the 13th c. the concept of 'Proensal' gained currency at the expense of the former idiom known as *lenga Romana*. In subsequent centuries although Provençal was still being used as a spoken language, it was surpassed by written French, and more particularly in the field of literature by 'classical' French which had developed from the northern French tongue, the so-called *langue d'oil*.

Provençal renaissance

It is certainly no accident that at the time when nation-states were beginning to emerge in the first half of the 18th c., there arose in Provence a new awareness of its own history and a new assessment of its own language. In 1854 the Félibrige (Association of Félibres) was founded, a group of poets of whom Fréderic Mistral was the most important. One of the principal contributions of the Provençal renaissance of that year was the comprehensive stocktaking of the linguistic heritage of the south of France. The conscious nurture of the *langue d'oc* and the pride of the people of southern France in belonging to the area where it

Fréderic Mistral

Bilingual road signs

is spoken are now increasingly apparent. In spite of this the *langue d'oc* is rarely their first language; indeed, a survey of 1987 revealed under 1 per cent of speakers who named both French and the *langue d'oc* as their mother tongue.

Linguistic characteristics

Provençal differs from standard French through the richness of its vowels. Whereas in classical French unstressed vowels tend to become reduced to a voiceless *e* or in some cases to disappear altogether, Provençal still makes use of the whole range of vowels. The chief characteristics are the maintaining of *a* in an open syllable (Provençal *pra* = French *pré*, the mutation of the *a* to *ié* (Provençal *marchié* – from the Latin *mercatus*), the distinction of four final vowels (*a, e, i, o*; Provençal *a, e*; French *e*), the *-o* ending of the first person of the verb, the regional distinction between nominative and accusative, and the shaping of certain sounds. There are, of course, unusual features in the vocabulary, both in the stock of words and in the meaning.

Quotations

Tobias Smollett
(1721–71)
[Nice] When I stand upon the rampart and look round me, I can scarce help thinking myself enchanted. The small extent of country which I see, is all cultivated like a garden. Indeed the plain presents nothing but gardens full of green trees, loaded with oranges, lemons, citrons, and bergamots, which make a delightful appearance. If you examine them more nearly, you will find plantations of green pease ready to gather; all sorts of sallading, and pot herbs, in perfections; and plats of roses, carnations, ranunculas, anemonies, and daffodils, blowing in full glory, with such beauty, vigour, and perfume, as no flower in England ever exhibited.
Travels through France and Italy, 1766

Henry Swinburne
(1743–1803)
The Provençal is all alive, and feels his nerves agitated in a supreme degree by accidents and objects that would scarce move a muscle or a feature in the phlegmatic natives of more northern climes; his spirits are flurried by the slightest sensations of pleasure or of pain, and seem always on the watch to sieze the transient impressions of either; but to balance this destructive propensity, nature has wisely rendered it difficult for those impressions to sink into their souls; thus daily offering a surface smoothered afresh for new pains and pleasures to trace their light affections upon. But this by no means excludes warm attachments and solid friendships; when time and habit afford leisure for the impression to penetrate deep enough, it will, no doubt, acquire and retain as firm a hold in their breast as in any other, and perhaps be stamped with still greater warmth and energy.
A Journey from Bayonne to Marseilles, 1775 and 1776

Philip Thicknesse
(1719–92)
Avignon is remarkable for the number seven; having seven ports, seven parishes, seven colleges, seven hospitals, and seven monasteries; and I may add, I think, seven hundred bells, which are always making a horrid jingle; for they have no idea of ringing bells harmoniously in any part of France ...

[Nîmes] It is said, and I have felt the truth of it, in part, that there does not exist, at this day, any building, ancient or modern, which conveys so secret a pleasure, not only to the connoisseur, but to the clown also, whenever, or how often soever they approach [the Maison Carrée]. The proportions and beauties of the whole building are so intimately united, that they may be compared to good breeding in men – it is what every body perceived, and is captivated with, but what few can define.
A Year's Journey through France and Spain, 1789

Henry Crabb Robinson
(1775–1867)
[Nîmes] I took Wordsworth to see the exterior of both the Maison Carrée and the Arena. He acknowledged their beauty, but expressed no great pleasure. He says: 'I am unable from ignorance to enjoy these sights. I receive an impression, but that is all. I have no science, and can refer nothing to principle.' He was on the other hand delighted by two beautiful little girls near the Arena, and said: 'I wish I could take them to Rydal Mount.'
Diary, April 3rd 1837

Charles Dickens
(1812–70)
The town [Aix-en-Provence] was very clean; but so hot, and so intensely light, that when I walked out at noon it was like coming suddenly from the darkened room into crisp blue fire. The air was so very clean, that distant hills and rocky points appeared within an hour's walk; while the town immediately at hand – with a kind of blue wind between me and it – seemed to be white hot, and to be throwing off a firey air from the surface.
Pictures from Italy, 1846

Charles Lewis Meryon
(1821–68)
The Provençal language ... is a most disagreeable jargon, as unintelligible even to those who understand French, as

to those who do not, and delighting in intonations of the voice, which always reminded me of a crying child.
Travels with Lady Hester Stanhope, 1846

JC Hare
(1795–1855)
At Avignon I saw some large baths in the garden by the temple of Diana, built on the foundations of the old Roman ones. 'Does anybody bathe here now?' we askt; for we could see no materials for the purpose.

'No'; the guide answered. 'Before the Revolution, the rich used to bathe here; but they wanted to keep the baths to themselves; and the poor wanted to come too; and now nobody comes'. What an epitome of a revolution!
Guesses at Truth (with A Hare), 1847

Algernon Charles Swinburne
(1837–1909)
Of all the beasts of countries I ever see, I reckon this [Menton] about caps them. I also strongly notion that there ain't a hole in St. Giles's which isn't a paradise to this. How any professing Christian as has been in France and England can look at it, passes me. It is more like the landscape in Browning's 'Childe Roland' than anything I ever heard tell on. A calcined, scalped, rasped, scraped, flayed, broiled, powdered, leprous, blotched, mangy, grimy, parboiled, country, without trees, water, grass, fields – with blank, beastly, senseless olives and orange-trees like a mad cabbage gone indigestible; it is infinitely liker hell than earth, and one looks for tails among the people. And such females, with hunched bodies and crooked necks carrying tons on their heads, and looking like Death taken seasick. Ar-r-r-r-r! Gr-r-r-rn!
Letter to Pauline Trevelyan, January 19th 1861

Edward Lear
(1812–88)
This place [Nice] is so wonderfully dry that nothing can be kept moist. I never was in so dry a place in all my life. When the little children cry, they cry dust and not tears. There is some water in the sea, but not much: – all the wet-nurses cease to be so immediately on arriving: – Dryden is the only book read: – the neighbourhood abounds with Dryads and Hammerdryads; and veterinary surgeons are quite unknown. It is a queer place, – Brighton and Belgravia and Baden by the

Mediterranean: odious to me in all respects but its magnificent winter climate …
Letter to Chichester Fortescue, February 24th 1865

Henry James
(1843–1916)
Aigues Mortes presents quite the appearance of the walled town that a school-boy draws upon his slate, or that we see in the background of early Flemish pictures – a simple parallelogram, of a contour almost absurdly bare, broken at intervals by angular towers and square holes … It is extraordinarily pictorial, and if it is a very small sister of Carcassonne, it has at least the essential features of the family. Indeed, it is even more like an image and less like a reality than Carcassonne …

There are places that please, without your being able to say wherefore, and Montpellier is one of the number . . . The place has neither the gaiety of a modern nor the solemnity of an ancient town, and it is agreeable as certain women are agreeable who are neither beautiful nor clever.
A Little Tour in France, 1882

Sights from A to Z

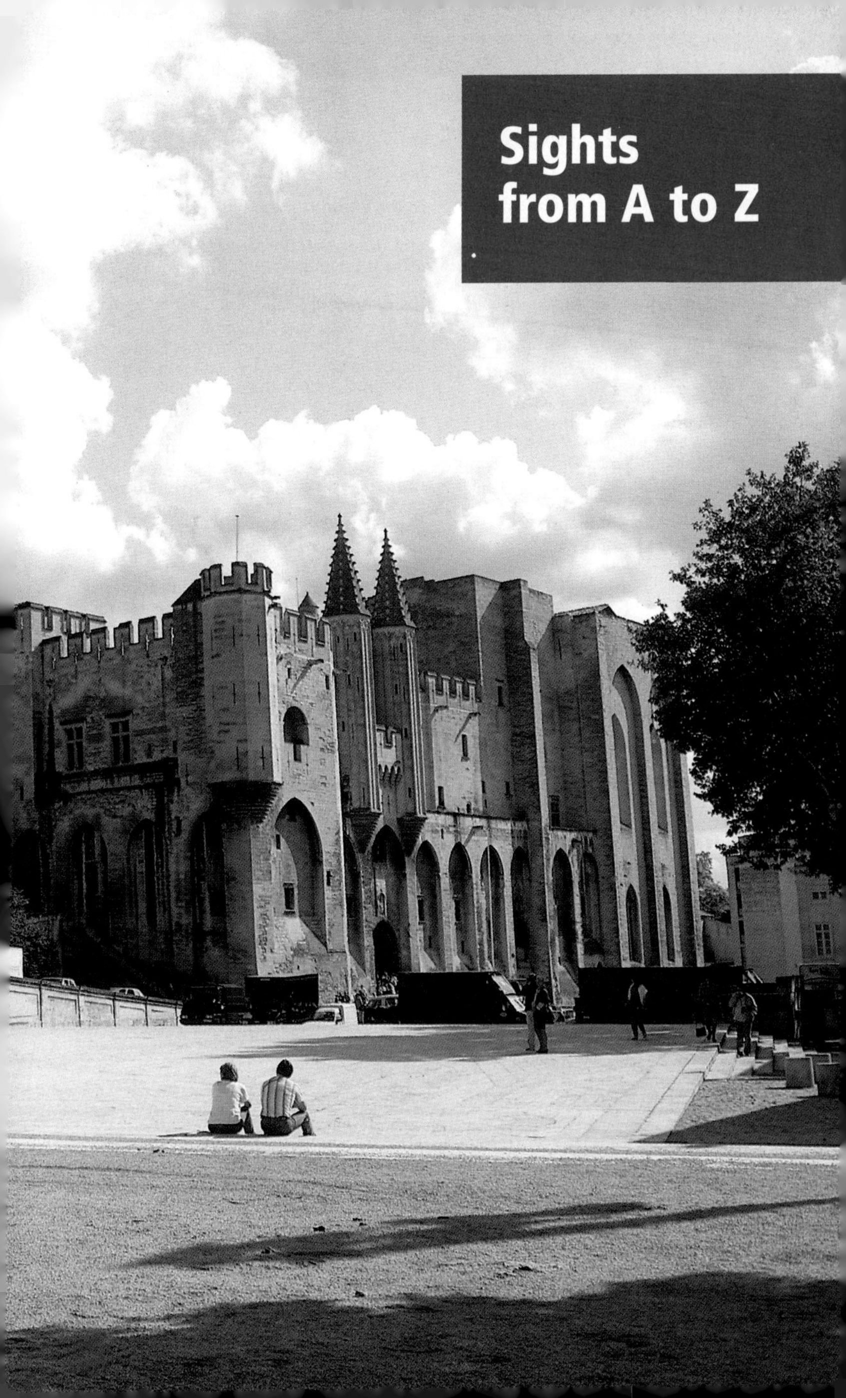

Suggested Routes

These suggested routes are intended to offer plenty of ideas to those travelling by car or by motorcycle without denying them the freedom of individual planning and choice. The triangular area enclosed by Avignon, Aix/Marseille and Aigues-Mortes, in particular, contains so much of interest that it is almost an impossible task to select one outstanding itinerary in this region.

The routes have been devised to include the main places of interest in the area. Nevertheless, many of the places described in this guide can only be reached by making detours. The suggested routes can be followed by using the map that accompanies this travel guide, which should help to simplify the detailed plans.

Places included in the Sights from A to Z section under a main heading appear in the suggested routes in **bold type**. Descriptions of other places included can be found by referring to the index.

Timetable
Those who follow the complete routes (including all detours, they cover a total of approximately 4500 km) and who want to have sufficient time to visit the principal points of interest, must allow about four weeks for the itinerary. Even when the detours are omitted, the whole tour will still take three weeks.

Provence
In its most general sense the Provence of scenic beauty and of important cultural monuments encompasses the area of land between the lower Rhône (approximately between Montélimar and Aigues-Mortes) and the Var at Nice as well as the French Alps rising in the hinterland. In contrast, the historical province of Provence stretches across the area of the present-day *départements* of Bouches-du-Rhône and Vaucluse as well as the Languedoc-Roussillon region in the Gard *département* (Nîmes).

The first section of suggested routes deals with this triangular area usually considered by tourists to be Provence.

Côte d'Azur
The second section covers the French

◀ The Palais des Papes at Avignon

holiday resorts *par excellence*, the Mediterranean coast between Marseille and the Italian border at Menton as well as its immediate hinterland.

Haute-Provence/Alps
By following these suggested routes it is possible to return to northern France via Gap, Grenoble, Geneva or Lyon. One possibility is to follow the Route Napoléon (described in the third section of routes); however, not from the south to north but from the north to the south as an interesting alternative to the normal way of getting to Provence by car.

Splendid views of the French Alps can be enjoyed by following the Route des Grandes Alpes (also known as the Route d'Eté des Alpes) which is another alternative for the return journey. From Nice it passes through Briançon and Chamonix and on to Geneva. The third section of routes details the stretch as far as Barcelonette, from where Serre-Ponçon Lake and Gap can be reached.

1a: Loriol–Orange (150 km)

Provence begins – so it is generally said – at Loriol: landscape, vegetation and light soon take on a Mediterranean flavour. Leave the motorway here and cross to the right bank of the Rhône. Enter Cruas with its noteworthy Romanesque church, its medieval ruins and its nuclear power station. From Rochemaure château enjoy a wonderful view across the Rhône valley to **Montélimar**. This historic Provençal town, famous for its white nougat, is dominated by a 12th–14th c. château.

Heading towards Orange it is worth making a detour through the Tricastin, a hilly triangular area enclosed by Montélimar, Nyons and Orange. The hillsides are mainly planted with olive trees, holm oaks and pines, while fruit and vegetables are grown wherever possible in the valleys. Discerning gourmets associate truffles in particular with this area. Leaving Montélimar on the D4 drive through **Grignan** with its splendid 16th c. château where Madame de Sévigné, famed for her letters, lived.

Continue to Suze either in an easterly direction through Valréas, centre of the Enclave des Papes (Enclave of the Popes), and Nyons or proceed westwards past the ruins of the chapel of Val des Nymphes to the small medieval town of **la Garde-Adhémar**, located on a mountain spur across the Rhône and offering, as well as an impressive Romanesque church, a good general view of the whole Tricastin region. The principal town, St-Paul-Trois-Châteaux (a mistaken translation of the Celtic word Tricastin), contains remains of a former fortress and a 11th–12th c. cathedral built in the Provençal Romanesque style. The imposing château in Suze-la-Rousse bears witness to the town's great importance during the Middle Ages. Looking up from the Var valley, Bollène becomes visible, with the remains of its 14th c. fortress built on a hill blessed with fine views across the Rhône valley.

It is possible here to make a round trip to view the Gorge of the **Ardèche** and the famous stalactite caves; to do this cross the Rhône at Pont-St-Esprit.

An excursion to the north can be undertaken from Bollène. Where the Rhône is diverted by the Rhône dam at Donzère pass the enormous Blondel power station and ascend to Barry, a small hamlet built on a rocky outcrop. Here experience a fantastic panoramic view across the complex of the **Donzère-Mondragon** dam and the nuclear power station of Tricastin.

Leaving Mondragon, Orange can soon be reached via the N7 (A7) from Montélimar. It is more interesting, however, to follow the route along the D12 through Rochegude (detour along the D206), Uchaux and across to Sérignan where the scientist Fabre lived and worked. At last we come to **Orange**, located in a fertile plain exposed to the Mistral. Its Roman theatre is one of the largest and best preserved.

1b: Orange–Mont Ventoux–Apt–Aix–Marseille (310 km)

This varied journey demonstrates Provence's differing landscapes: first Orange's fertile plain with its olive and mulberry trees, then Mont Ventoux with its wooded slopes but bare limestone crest offering a view right across Provence as far as the Alps, then the Vaucluse plateau with its picturesque gorges and Fontaine-de-Vaucluse made famous by Petrarch (where the Sorgue has its source). After crossing the Lubéron range in the densely forested Combe de Lourmarin the visitor finally reaches the plain of Aix-en-Provence, surrounded by bare mountain chains and intensively farmed. The route from here to Marseille passes through Vauvenargues, St-Maximin, Nans-les-Pins and the Col d'Espigoulier and reveals the many unique characteristics of Provence.

Begin the journey from **Orange** to **Mont Ventoux** by driving east along the D950 and D55 to Beaumes-de-Venise, a village famous mostly for its Muscat wine. Then proceed northwards along the foot of the Dentelles-de-Montmirail, a mountain chain resembling the edge of lace. On the way pass the Romanesque Chapel of Notre-Dame-d'Aubune, with its elegant bell tower visible from some distance, the famed wine villages of Vacqueyras, Gigondas and Séguret, finally reaching **Vaison-la-Romaine**. Countless excavations verify the importance of the town as a trading centre in Roman times. Continue to Malaucène at the western foot of Mont Ventoux (Provencal *ventour*, windy mountain, after the many heavy storms). The impressive towering chalk ridge is an isolated continuation of the Pyrénées.

From the summit it is worth continuing via Sault through large fields of lavender (destined for the perfume industry) along Lavender Road (this tourist route, not described here, leads from Avignon via Carpentras and Malaucène to Sault and on through the small town of Forcalquier and Gréoux-les-Bains, a spa town located in the lower Verdon valley, to the Gallo-Roman township of Riez, from there via Moustiers-Ste-Marie, Castellane and Grasse to Nice).

From Sault, drive through the Gorges de la Nesque, a wooded rocky valley cut into the Vaucluse plateau, a high chalk plain adjoining the south face of Mont Ventoux. Pass through Villes-sur-Auzon, noted for its ochre production, to **Carpentras**, an industrial town rich in tradition, located on the Auzon with France's oldest maintained synagogue. Not far away to the south east, the village of Venasque contains a noteworthy church and a baptistry (6th and 12th c.). From Carpentras the journey continues through Pernes-les-Fontaines, with its several pretty fountains, remains of a fortress and 12th c. church, to **Fontaine-de-Vaucluse**, picturesquely situated in a rocky amphitheatre (*vallis clausa*) and dominated by the ruins of a château once belonging to the bishops of Cavaillon. Allow time here for a stroll to the source of the Sorgue which begins as a spring at the end of a hollow surrounded by high chalk rocks and which was mentioned by Petrarch who lived in Avignon and Fontaine-de-Vaucluse for many years.

A detour through the pretty little town of **Gordes**, located on a rocky slope of the Vaucluse plateau (its château accommodates a Vasarely museum) and past medieval cottages called *bories* and constructed from stone slabs without mortar, leads to **Senanque**, a Romanesque Cistercian monastery. Continue to Roussillon, France's main ochre-producing centre built on a plateau of ochre. Apt, with its fruit and preserves industries, lies in the Coulon valley; of note is the Cathedral of St-Anne in the town centre.

Further south, drive through fine fertile countryside reminiscent of Tuscany to the **Montagne du Lubéron**, a mountain chain between the valleys of the Coulon and the Durance. Continue to Bonnieux, a pretty hillside town, either directly along the D943 or by travelling further east through Buoux. Bonnieux affords a fine view northwards to Mont Ventoux. The road winds its way southwards among forests of holm oaks and chalk rockfaces through the Combe de Lourmarin; the village of Lourmarin possesses a Renaissance château as well a cemetery where the author Albert Camus is buried. He spent the later years of his life in this town. From here, either follow a direct route to Cadenet in the Durance valley or arrive there via the former Waldenses (☞Sights from A to Z, Lubéron) villages of Cucuron and Ansouis, with its impressive château. Cadenet's church contains an ancient font.

After visiting the former Cistercian abbey at **Silvacane** (cross the Durance and then turn right towards la Roque-d'Anthéron), continue to Aix-en-Provence; drive along the D543 past Bassin-de-St-Christophe, a reservoir supplying water to Marseille, and the small town of Rognes to the D10. Head west again to Ventabren and the Roquefavour aqueduct and then on via les Milles (D65) to **Aix-en-Provence**, Provence's historic centre. Allow plenty of time to visit its many places of interest.

Beyond Marseille, use the motorway A51, which cuts through a hilly landscape, offering a very impressive panoramic view of surrounding bare mountain chains. Drive east and follow the eroded and twisty road around the Montagne-Ste-Victoire to the massif of Ste-Baume and on down into Marseille. The D10 passes Bimont reservoir and on to Vauvenargues, famous for the château where Picasso lived for some years. Walkers would find the climb to the Croix de Provence a unique experience. Passing through le Puits-de-Rians and Pourrières, the tour then reaches **St-Maximin-la-Ste-Baume**. This attractive little town nestles in the basin of a former lake and possesses Provence's only important Gothic church.

Leaving Tourves and Nans-les-Pins, Plan d'Aups is reached at the foot of the Massif de la Ste-Baume, which like St-Maximin and Stes-Maries-de-la-Mer is bound up with the legend surrounding St Mary Magdalene. Another real feast for walkers is the ascent of St-Pilon; also of interest here are the woods, whose plant life is not typical of the area. The double bends of the Col d'Espigoulier lead down to Gemenos, a holiday resort, and to Aubagne, birthplace of Marcel Pagnol (his stories are mainly based in this area) and headquarters of the Foreign Legion. The Etoile mountain chain rises in the north west with the characteristic rocky peak of the Garlaban. Follow the D2 to **Marseille**, France's second largest and oldest town, on the Golfe du Lion; the entrance to Marseille is dominated by the view of high densely built apartment blocks in front of the towering rocks.

1c: Marseilles–Arles–Nîmes–Avignon (310 km)

Leave Marseille in a north-westerly

direction and arrive first at L'Estaque, a seaside resort frequented by local people; it has a small fishing harbour and some industry. The N568 leads via the picturesque bare Chaîne de l'Estaque which separates the Étang de Berre from the Mediterranean and through the Vallon de l'Aigle up to the coast at Carry-le-Rouet, a small seaside town. Then follow the coastline to Sausset (and to Cap Couronne), finally head inland to **Martigues**, once the centre of a principality on the **Étang de Berre** which is linked to the Mediterranean by the Canal de Caronte. Traversed by several channels, the Old Town is known as the Venice of Provence.

The harbour areas of Lavéra, Port-de-Bouc and the enormous Port de Fos (industrial zone) form Marseille's giant harbour. Cross the Rhône canal and also a side canal by a small *pontet* (bridge) and drive along the west bank of the Étang de Berre whose white chalk rocks and green landscape offer a charming alternative to the industrialised east bank around Marignane (airport, salt works, natural gas refineries, chemical industries). The route continues via St-Mitre-les-Remparts, with its medieval fortifications, eventually by means of a detour via the Chapel of St-Blaise across the Etang de Lavalduc, near to which the remains of a Greek fortress (4th c. BC) and a basilica have been excavated, to Istres (Latin for oyster pond) on the bank of the small Etang d'Olivier where remains of an ancient Greek town have been found. Allow time to visit the hill town of Miramas-le-Vieux, which still has its walls, before travelling along rural roads lined with plane trees via St-Chamas and the well-known small wine village of Cornillon-Confoux finally reaching **Salon**, centre of olive processing and the home town of Nostradamus.

The straight N113 leads immediately from here through the Crau, called Campus Lapideus or Cravus by the Romans, a bare plain formed by Pleistocene gravels of the Durance where sheep graze and where market gardening is carried on to **Arles**, Provence's unofficial capital, with its unique atmosphere and impressive historic monuments from Roman and medieval times.

From here, choose either the direct route to Stes-Maries-de-la-Mer or a diversion via les Baux; to the north-east outside Arles the ruins of the former 10th c. Benedictine abbey of **Montmajour** and the unusual Chapel of Ste-Croix-en-Jérusalem (12th–13th c.) lie on a mountain ridge. Then comes the small town of Fontvieille with its impressive limestone quarries and the windmill made famous by Alfonse Daudet in his *Lettres de Mon Moulin*. Continue into the white mountain chain of the Alpilles to the ruined town of **les Baux-de-Provence**, picturesquely located on a rocky plateau and once the chief town of a medieval barony and centre of troubadors. In 1632 les Baux was destroyed and today is only a small place, living exclusively by tourism; it has restored 14th and 15th c. houses, a former Waldenses (Protestant) church, the grandiose fortress ruins and a fantastic view.

Continuing in the direction of St-Rémy-de-Provence, cross the **Alpilles** chain whose richly fossilised white Miocene rocks proved an excellent building material (partly quarried underground). To the south of **St-Rémy-de-Provence** with its classical domed church, worthy of a visit, lies the Greco-Roman settlement of Glanum, destroyed by the Visigoths in AD 480, of which extensive excavations bear witness; still preserved are a triumphal arch and the 18 m high mausoleum. To the north-west of St-Rémy is the village of Maillane, birthplace and resting place of the Provençal poet Frédéric Mistral, a champion of Provençal traditions.

Next head for the town of **Tarascon** on the left bank of the Rhône, known through Alphonse Daudet's Roman character *Tartarin de Tarascon*. Next to the bridge leading to neighbouring Beaucaire stands the imposing 12–15th c. château of King René. Beaucaire, on the right bank of the Rhône, once famous throughout the western world for its market dating from 1217 but today of lesser importance, is crowned by the ruins of a fortress (fine panoramic view); also recommended is an excursion to the Abbaye de St-Roman across the Grand Rhône.

From Beaucaire either follow the D999 directly to **Nîmes** or travel along the Canal du Rhône à Sète which forms a connection to the Mediterranean at

Aigues-Mortes to **St-Gilles**. This small town, which grew up around one of the abbeys founded by St Egidius, possesses a Romanesque church famous for its extraordinarily richly decorated facade. From St-Gilles, on the northern edge of the **Camargue**, a trip can be undertaken through the Rhône delta with its flat lagoons and reed marshes, extensive salt works and sand dunes; either follow the D37 southwards and along the east bank of the Etang de Vaccares to Salin-de-Giraud and to Plage du Piémanson or follow the D570 (from Albaron) to **Stes-Maries-de-la-Mer**, the Camargue's largest town. The route continues along the Petit Rhône to **Aigues-Mortes** about 6 km from the sea, located between marshes and ponds which give the town its name 'dead waters' (*acquae mortuae*). The medieval harbour and crusader town still possesses mighty fortified walls. To the south-west of Aigues-Mortes lie the modern seaside resorts of le Grau-du-Roi and **la Grande-Motte**, loved by French holidaymakers.

After driving through St-Laurent and Aimargues (east of Codognan is the bottling plant for Perrier mineral water), reach **Nîmes** (the French town most blessed with historic buildings) and continue via **Uzès** with its château and the elegant round Tour Fenestrelle to **Pont du Gard** (in summer only via Remoulins, one way road system). The 49 m high and 275 m long aqueduct, probably built around 19 BC, spans with its three tiers of arches the deep valley of the Gard and is one of the most spectacular and best-preserved Roman constructions in existence. From here continue along the N100 through hilly country (to the north the vineyards from which comes Tavel, the best known rosé wine of Provence) to the one-time papal residence of **Avignon**, the centre of tourism in Provence.

2a: Marseille–Toulon–Cannes–Nice (250 km)

Leaving **Marseille**, the route leads first to the little port of Cassis, located on a small semicircular bay and famous for its excellent white wine. A detour exists to the west of Cassis to the Calanques, narrow deep inlets between steep white chalk cliffs. Well worth experiencing is the drive from Cassis to la Ciotat on the Corniche des Crêtes, which encircles Cap Canaille, at 363 m France's highest cliffs. The red cliffs of the Bec de l'Aigle tower boldly above the port of la Ciotat. The journey continues via the seaside towns of la Ciotat-Plage, les Lecques and **Bandol** to Sanary-sur-Mer from where there is a fine view of the coast and also from where an excursion to Ollioules and to le Gros Cerveau can be made. At this point the D559 divides the Cap Sicié peninsula and passes Fort de Six-Fours, with its many excellent views, before reaching **Toulon**, France's largest military port.

The N98 provides a direct link to Hyères. However, it proves more interesting to follow the coast road to the Glens peninsula, an island first linked to the mainland during Roman times. Trips to the Hyères islands, with their impressive cliffs and rich plant life, depart from la Tour-Fondeau. The most important island in this group is the Île de Porquerolles with its port of the same name. About 10 km to the east lies the island of Port-Cros, a nature reserve with wonderful walks. **Hyères**, built not far from the sea on a steep hillside, is the oldest health resort in the Mediterranean. The Old Town is bordered to the south by Hyères-les-Palmiers, a new town named after its many date palms. The hill to the north, where a château once stood, offers an extensive panoramic view although this is surpassed by the view from the Fenouillet, the highest peak of the Maurettes.

Now follow the N98 as it returns inland, past extensive salt fields, through Massif des Maures covered with woods (cork extraction), moorland and maquis. Behind Mauvanne the D559 turns off to the small town of Bormes-les-Mimosas, arriving at the coast again at **le Lavandou**. The splendid Corniche des Maures runs along this part of the coast, rich in bays and cliffs and with a number of seaside resorts, continuing via the charming hillside health resort of le Rayol to the sheltered bay of Cavalaire. Cross magnificent forests (partly planted with cork trees) to the Cap Camarat peninsula and continue via Moulins de Paillas and a detour to Cap Camarat (a far-reaching view of the Plage de Pampelonne, the Côte d'Azur's largest and finest beach) to **St-Tropez**, the famous little port lying on the south side of the gulf of the same name. This small town still thrives as a meeting place for artists and international society, even though its prominent inhabitants have long since retired into quieter areas and well-protected villas.

The N98 continues through the Giscle estuary and along the Gulf of St-Tropez to **Port-Grimaud**, a harbour and holiday town built in the mid-1960s in a Venetian style by the architect François Spoerry, and to the resort of Ste-Maxime. The coast road continues around the Cap des Sardinaux, les Issambres and encircles further foothills, all with fine views. Behind St-Aygulf (good sandy beach) cross the estuary of the Argens to reach **Fréjus**, a small town located between the Massif des Maures and the Esterel mountains, which in Roman times as Forum Iulii was an important port. The historic buildings, especially the cathedral with its font and cloisters, are well worth visiting.

Beyond Cannes the N7 from Fréjus leads in a north-easterly direction through the **Esterel** mountains. It is worth climbing Mont Vinaigre, the highest peak of the Massif. The coast road, meanwhile, follows the Gulf of Fréjus via the seaside resort of **St-Raphaël** (whose Old Town contains an impressive Templar church) to the red porphyry rocks Lion de Mer and Lion de Terre. The Corniche de L'Esterel (Corniche d'Or) continues on to Agay. From Agay the coast road passes through the seaside resort of Anthéor on the Calanque of the same name, with its many cliffs, and then follows a picturesque route via the Pointe du Petit-Caneiret, with its view of the fire-red porphyry cliffs of Cap Roux and the less impressive Rocher de St-Barthélemy. An excursion should be planned here to the Pic du Cap Roux, the Esterel's best vantage point with a fine view of the coast of St-Tropez as far as Bordighera, the maritime Alps and sometimes Corsica.

Drive through St-Barthélemy, nestling in a valley, across the Cap Roux peninsula and around the Baie de la Figueirette until Miramar appears. Behind the Point de l'Esquillon ascend many twisty mountain roads admiring the view of Napoule Bay, Cannes, the Lérins islands and the maritime Alps. Above the popular seaside resort of la Napoule, a

14th–18th c. château stands in solitary splendour on a ridge.

Crossing the wide estuary of the Siagne, we reach fashionable **Cannes**, regarded as the most distinguished health resort on the Côte d'Azur thanks to its mild climate, varied subtropical vegetation, splendid beaches and international film festival. Boats sail several times a day to the Lérins islands of Ste-Marguerite and St-Honorat. The trip crosses the fine Juan Bay to the port of Golfe-Juan where Napoléon landed in 1815 on his return from Elba. The somewhat inland little town of Vallauris is known for its pottery, Picasso having worked here. On the western side of Cap-d'Antibes lies the famous resort of Juan-les-Pins. Its yearly summer jazz festival enjoys international acclaim.

From here to Antibes the route passes around Cap-d'Antibes with its villas and gardens of which the Jardin Thuret, laid out in the 19th c., invites a stroll. **Antibes**, in an impressive location on the north-east side of the like-named cape between the small bays of Anse St-Roch in the north and Anse de la Salis in the south, is a centre of flower cultivation and export. Visit Fort Carré, a survivor of the fortifications, and the medieval town wall with the Front de Mer promenade, which borders the heart of the Old Town on the seaward side, as well as the former Grimaldi château, which houses a Picasso museum.

For the journey from Antibes to Nice, choose either the N7, a little away from the sea, or drive directly (N98) along the wide Baie des Anges (Bay of Angels) – with a detour to Biot – past the enormous pyramid-shaped apartment buildings, Marina Baie des Anges and, on the other side of the Var past the Nice-Côte d'Azur airport, to the main town of the Riviera – **Nice**. Stroll through the narrow alleys of the lovely, lively Old Town and along the palm-lined promenade des Anglais.

An alternative recommended route from Cannes to Nice is via Mougins to **Grasse**, the centre of the perfume industry, then on to Gourdon and to the Gorges du Loup and across to Tourrettes-sur-Loup. The appealing little towns of **Vence** and St-Paul-de-Vence hold particular interest for art-lovers (Fondation Maeght). Rejoin the coast through Villeneuve-Loubet or at Cros-de-Cagnes.

2b: Nice–Monaco–Menton (30 km)

From Nice, three different corniches (road along edge of cliff, coastal road with extensive views), of which the Moyenne Corniche and the Grande Corniche count among Europe's finest roads, follow the slopes or the feet of the maritime Alps to Menton.

The distance between Nice and Menton on all three routes measures about 35 km. Those wishing to make the journey twice, perhaps as a round trip from Nice, should choose for the outward journey the Moyenne Corniche, as it reveals the full beauty of the landscape, while the return journey on the Grande Corniche offers a grandiose panoramic view.

★Corniche du Littoral

The Corniche due Littoral (N98), also called the Corniche Inférieure or Petite Corniche, follows the edge of the sea and offers fine views but takes second place to the two higher routes. Traffic is heavy here and this leads above all to congestion through the many towns.

After leaving **Nice**, the Corniche du Littoral leads first around the foothills (many fine views) of Mont Boron, past the excellent roadstead of Villefranche-sur-Mer harbour and the like-named holiday resort with its romantic Old Town. Behind here a road branches to the south to the elegant villa town of St-Jean-Cap-Ferrat on the eastern side of the peninsula. Here a round trip to a vantage point (belvédère) and up on to the headland can be made.

The road continues to the pleasant little town and holiday resort of **Beaulieu-sur-Mer**, located very close to Villefranche on a broad waterway, dominated by steep rocky cliffs. After Menton, Beaulieu counts as France's warmest town, this having earned the town the name of Little Africa. Now drive through the magnificent chalk cliffs of Cap Roux to reach the elegant seaside town of Èze-Bord-de-Mer. The journey continues via Cap d'Ail, whose wonderful cliff-hidden bays are excellent for swimming, and St-Antoine, with its impressive Château de l'Ermitage, to the Principality of Monaco, whose people are so closely linked to their French neighbours. Crossing Pont St-Roman leave the principality again and follow the N7 to **Menton**, at the foot of the maritime Alps right on the Italian border. In contrast to many other seaside resorts, Menton, despite some new building, has managed to preserve the character of a developed Mediterranean town.

★★Moyenne Corniche

Completed in 1939 and ending in Monaco, the Moyenne Corniche passes halfway up the cliffs across several bridges, from where there are fine views, and through galleries. It is certainly the finest of the three routes, as it lies closer to the sea than the Grande Corniche, and offers the chance to sample the beauty of the coast in a more detailed way.

Continue along the N7 via the Col de Villefranche (view of Nice, the coast and the maritime Alps, south of the pass across the Vallon de la Murta) to the Col de Caire, to drive beyond here via a picturesque route over cliffs and through a long tunnel to the St-Michel valley, with its olive groves and across a 57 m high viaduct to the mountain settlement of Èze-Village. The village was built in a bold, scenic position high above the sea on a cliff crowned with an ancient Ligurian refuge. After leaving Èze-Village the road soon curves through the Vallon de St-Laurent and around the Tête de Chien, where a fork leads past the Jardin Exotique (worth visiting) to **Monaco** and from there to **Menton**.

★★Grande Corniche

The highest route is the Grande Corniche, climbing to 530 m. Built during the time of Napoléon I, it offers a splendid extensive view.

The Grande Corniche (D2564) follows a wide curve from Nice past the observatory around Mont Gros, with its magnificent view across the Paillon valley and the maritime Alps to Nice and the western coastline. Following the Col des Quatre-Chemins are the Belvédère (view across the coast) and the Col d'Eze, from where the peaks of the maritime Alps are visible. Drive along the southern slope of Mont Camps de l'Allé to la Turbie, a small Provençal coastal town on the saddle between the Tête de Chien (fantastic view down across Monaco) and Mont de la Bataille, dominated by the Trophée d'Auguste or Trophée des Alpes. The road continues along the slopes of Mont Agel, past the village of **Roquebrune**, picturesquely built on a group of cliffs with narrow, vaulted, stepped alleys and the fine ruins of a château, to climb finally to the start of the Corniche du Littoral, leading to the health resort of **Menton**.

3a: Gap–Digne–Nice/Cannes (220 km)

The Route Napoléon, a tourist route inaugurated in 1932 and generally open to traffic throughout the year, stretches from Grenoble via Gap and Grasse to Cannes. It encompasses the extremely charming and varied landscape of the Alpine peaks around Gap, the mountainous scenery of Haute-Provence to the Mediterranean coastal region. The route follows in reverse that which Napoléon took after he landed in Golfe-Jun on March 1st 1815 on his return from Elba and is marked by small eagles. Using a legacy from Napoléon, six shelters (named Réfuges Napoléon after him) were built on the particularly exposed mountain passes, of which only three still remain. From Barrême the most southerly section of the Route d'Hiver des Alpes forms the connection to Nice.

The descriptions in this guide do not cover the whole approximately 350 km Route Napoléon but only the stretch between Gap and Cannes/Nice. As a result some information about the route between Grenoble and Gap is included in the following suggestion.

Behind Grenoble pass first Vizille with its imposing 17th c. château built by Connétable Lesdiguières. The Monument du Centenaire stands outside it, dedicated to the group of representatives who, on July 21st–22nd 1788, decided to refuse to pay their taxes thus sparking the French Revolution. After la Mure it is worth making a detour along the Corniche du Drac, past the monastery of Notre-Dame-de-Commiers and the Château de la Motte, while the N85 (which the Route Napoléon follows) ascends to the lakeland district of

Laffrey, a small area much visited for its delightful situation, where Napoléon encountered the regular troops opposing him on his return from Elba. Continue either via the Col de la Morte or past Laffrey's pretty lakes to la Mure, a small mining town, then onward and upward through Beaumont, in the foothills of the Alps, to Obiou at the summit. Next head for Corps, departure point for visits to the Sautet reservoir and la Salette, the famous place of pilgrimage with its imposing church on the slopes of Mont Gargas.

Beyond Gap there is a worthwhile alternative route to the Route Napoléon exists. Drive around Lac de Sautet on the D537, then through the narrow pass Défilé de la Souloise and les Etroits and continue via St-Etienne-en-Dévoluy to Col du Noyer, with its fine views. The Route Napoléon can be rejoined at St-Bonnet as it climbs from Corps to Col Bayard, where a fine view of the Dauphiné Alps exists.

With a look back at the Massif des Ecrins, enter the ever-widening Gap valley. **Gap**, the Roman Vapincum, is the principal town of the Hautes-Alpes *département*, with a 19th c. cathedral and a noteworthy district museum. Continuing on the N85, the Route Napoléon reaches the Durance valley and follows its left flank through the little town of Tallard up to Lac de Serre-Ponçon while, just before **Sisteron**, the Route d'Hiver des Alpes descends the valley and joins it.

The Route d'Hiver des Alpes, identical to the Route Napoléon from Sisteron to Barrême, now follows the course of the mainly dried-up Durance downstream to the elongated town of Château-Arnoux, crosses the Durance and continues alongside a canal to Malijai and then into the Bléone valley to **Digne-les-Bains**, the Roman Dinia. Its Old Town is a maze of streets and has a noteworthy church. Finally the traveller reaches Barrême where the Route Napoléon turns off to Castellane (Grand Canyon du Verdon), while the Route d'Hiver des Alpes leads into the Asse de Moriez valley and via the Col des Robines into the Verdon valley, wide at this point, to St-André-les-Alpes. From there it passes Verdon's fine reservoir the Lac de Castillon, via Annot and **Entrevaux** to **Nice**.

From the little town of Castellane in the Verdon valley, dominated by an impressive chalk cliff with the Chapel of Notre-Dame-du-Roc, an excursion around the **Grand Canyon du Verdon** can be undertaken. At this point, take the road through the Verdon valley with the two narrow passes Porte de St-Jean and Clue de Chasteuil, then continue via Trigance to the Balcons de la Mescla with a breathtaking view down into the deep Verdon gorge and beyond on to the Corniche Sublime high above the Falaise des Cavaliers. Drive around Vaumale, encircled by rocks, across the Col d'Illoire and via the Verdon, dammed here, to reach the small town Moustiers-Ste-Marie, famous for its faïence (pottery), with a notable Romanesque Gothic church as well as the Chapel of Notre-Dame-de-Beauvoir. Return to Castellane via la Palud and Point-Sublime.

Leave the Verdon valley behind Castellane and drive through a partly wooded mountain landscape via the Col de Luens, Escragnolles, the Pas de la Faye and St-Vallier-de-Thiey, from where an excursion via the Col de la Leque and past the tumulus to the medieval village St-Cézaire-sur-Siagne and the dripstone cave Grotto Dozol can be made, down to **Grasse**, in a sheltered location on the slopes of Roquevignon. Now only a further 17 km remain to the luxurious seaside resort of **Cannes** on the Golfe de Napoule.

Alternative route

A very interesting alternative to one side of these well-trodden paths is the Sprint Final route, the final stage of the 1960 Monte-Carlo rally. In contrast to those drivers, two or three days should be allowed to enjoy the landscape and Provençal hospitality. From Gap follow the D942 or the A/D900B to Lac de Serre-Ponçon; at Ort l'Hotel change on to the D900C across the Durance to Selonnet. The D900 leads via the Col de Maure Pass and the Col de Labouret Pass as well as la Javie Pass to Digne. Follow the Route Napoléon (N85) as far as Séranon, then the D81/D79 to Gréolières and Coursegoules and finally the D8 to Bouyon and the D1 to le Broc and Carros in the Var valley. Head north on the N202 and after 2 km turn off to the right after Castagniers at les Moulins on the D614. From here follow the D719 to Tourrette-Levens and the D19 to St-André, pass twice under the motorway, and reach la Turbie and Monaco on the D2204A.

3b: Nice–Barcelonnette (160 km)

The following route is part of the Route des Grandes Alpes (Route d'Eté des Alpes), the most splendid journey through the French Alps. The very varied route leads from the subtropical Mediterranean coastal landscape through narrow valleys and gorges and the Maritime Alps, partly forming part of Provence, to the southern French Alps belonging to the Dauphiné.

From **Nice** ascend the at first wide Var valley upstream between the rocky slopes of the maritime Alps via Plan-du-Var, behind which the D2565 turns off into the Gorges de la Vésubie to the health and winter sports resort of St-Martin-Vésubie and through the narrow Défilé du Chaudan to the Tinée river.

Here the driver can take the uphill Route de la Bonette through Tinée valley via Isola and St-Etienne-de-Tinée to Col de la Bonette, the highest Alpine pass, eventually climbing to the Cime de la Bonette with its breathtaking panoramic view. Crossing the smaller Col de Restefond the Route des Grandes Alpes is rejoined in the Ubaye valley at Jausiers.

The Route des Grandes Alpes meanwhile leads from the Tinée river via the picturesque little hillside town of Touët-sur-Var in the direction of Puget-Théniers and **Entrevaux** with its impressive citadel. Immediately beyond Pont de Cians at Touët make time for a worthwhile detour through the wild and romantic Gorges du Cians, first through the 450 m high chalk sides of the Gorges Inférieures and then into the even wilder and deeper Gorges Supérieures which are carved into the dark red porphyry rock. Via Beuil and Col de Valberg in the centre of a small winter sports region, climb to Guillaumes where those drivers who have continued on the N202 from Entrevaux and later turned off right on the D902/D2202 through the Gorges de Daluis rejoin the route.

From Guillaumes the D2202 continues mostly along the slopes of the upper Var

Panorama on the Col de Turini

valley via the prettily located village St-Martin-d'Entraunes and past the source of the Var to the bare Col de la Cayolle where a fantastic view can be enjoyed. **Barcelonnette**, in the Ubaye valley, soon appears. From here, by following the Route des Alpes across passes or through the Ubaye and Durance valleys, Briançon can be reached – alternatively, change to the Route Napoléon after Gap.

Col de Turini
To conclude these suggested routes, the final stage of the Monte Carlo rally can be referred to again – in particular the journey along the Col de Turini ('Night of the Long Knives'). From Monaco take the D2204A to St-André and then ascend to l'Escarène on the D2204. Follow the D2566 up through Lucéram (whose church contains the most important collection of work by the Nice school of painting) and Peïra-Cava to the top of the pass (1607 m) from where the outstanding view is ample reward for the strenuous journey.

Sights from A to Z

In the following description of places (including their surroundings) the individual headings are so arranged that they follow a circular walk or circular drive.

The name of the *région* is given if the town or place concerned does not lie within the Provence-Alpes-Côte-d'Azur *région*.

To make it easier to locate the places listed in the Sights from A to Z section of the guide, their coordinates on the fold-out map are shown at the head of each entry.

★★Aigues-Mortes off map

Région: Languedoc-Roussillon
Département: Gard
Altitude: sea level
Population: 4500

Famous for its medieval fortifications, the little town of Aigues-Mortes lies some 30 km east of Montpellier on the western edge of the Camargue, the delta of the Rhône, which is here dotted with numerous lagoons. Two navigable canals, the Chenal Maritime and the Canal du Rhône à Sète, link the town with the sea, 6 km distant.

History

The town owes its name 'town of the dead waters' (*aquae mortuae*) to the bogs and shallow lagoons of the surroundings. St Louis (King Louis IX) possessed no lands bordering on the Mediterranean, so in 1240 he purchased the region from the monks of Psalmody (the remains of their abbey some 4 km to the north have been excavated). He then bestowed a number of privileges on the town, which rapidly developed and prospered in commerce and trade as well as in the traditional economies of fishing and salt mining. The Seventh Crusade in 1248 and the Eighth in 1270 sailed from here. The building of the town walls, financed by means of taxes, was expensive and continued – with some interruptions – from 1266 to the end of the 13th c. At that time Aigues-Mortes had 15,000 inhabitants. It started to decline in the middle of the

14th c. as the waterways gradually silted, but nevertheless remained an important trading port until the end of the 15th c., when Marseille was elevated to the status of royal town.

In the Hundred Years War, the great controversy about the succession to the French throne, the Burgundians, supported by England, conquered the town in 1418 and settled here. Afterwards the Gascons laid siege to Aigues-Mortes, penetrated the town one night and defeated the Burgundians. Their corpses were thrown into the south-west tower (now known as the Burgundian Tower) of the town walls and covered with salt in order to prevent decay.

In the Wars of Religion Aigues-Mortes became a refuge for the Huguenots, but following the Edict of Nantes in 1685 its towers served as their prison.

Sights

★★Town walls

The massive walls took over 30 years to build; they form a rectangle which is still complete and which surrounds the town. The ring of walls has 15 towers and 10 gates, some protected by towers; it comprises an area measuring 567 × 497 × 301 × 269 m.

Because of the narrow streets in the Old Town a visit on foot is recommended. There are car parks on the northern edge of the Old Town, near the Tour de Constance (charge) and outside the south-west town wall.

The tour of the ring of walls starts at the Porte de la Gardette, a few steps east of the Tour de Constance. A broad path inside the wall enabled the defenders of the town to get quickly from one place to another to repulse attackers.

It is also worthwhile following the ring of walls on the outside. There is a fine view of the Tour de Constance from the bridge that spans the canal, the Chenal Maritime. The south-west front – nearly 500 m long – is particularly impressive. At one time the quays were situated here, which is why it has more defensive towers.

Tour de Constance

The mightiest tower in the town walls is known as the Tour de Constance; its name is said to come from that of a daughter of King Louis VI. It is also sometimes called the Tower of Steadfastness. Forming the northern corner of the ring of walls, it is separated from them by a moat filled with water and spanned by a bridge. 54 m in height and with walls 6 m thick and measuring 22 m in diameter, it is the epitome of a medieval defensive construction. From the earliest times it served as a state prison, for it was considered impregnable. Among those imprisoned here were, at the beginning of the 14th c., members of the Order of Templars, who had been taken prisoner by Philip IV on the pretext of heresy and immorality, from the 17th c. many Huguenots, and finally a group of Protestant women who were released in 1768 by clemency of the governor; among these prisoners was the well-known Marie Durand, who spent 38 years in this tower and was renowned in France for her steadfastness. It was last used in 1815 to imprison Napoléon's officers when the Royalists took Aigues-Mortes.

It is interesting to climb up to the turret which is crowned by an iron cage and served as a lighthouse for centuries when the town was still a port. From here there is a panoramic view of the town and the surrounding countryside, as far as the Cévennes in the north and the concrete pyramids of la Grand-Motte in the west, salt mines and the Camargue in the east.

Tour Carbonnière

The 14th c. Tour Carbonnière, about 3 km to the north-east along the D58 road, guards the only entrance to the town from the land side. The road passes through the tower, the gates of which were once secured by a portcullis and mantraps inside. The little round tower, which protrudes from the top of the square edifice, probably dates from the 16th c., when the tower was in Protestant hands.

★★Aix-en-Provence   H 8

Département: Bouches-du-Rhône
Altitude: 177 m
Population: 155,000

Aigues-Mortes: town walls and the Tour de Constance

Flamingoes in the Camargue

Aix (Provençal Ais), the former capital of Provence, lies barely 30 km north of Marseille in a fertile plain surrounded by mountains. Four palaces, dating mainly from the 17th and 18th c., and many fine churches and museums bear witness to the town's glittering past. As the home of a famous university and the seat of an archbishop it remains the spiritual centre of Provence to this day.

As well as being a spa town and deriving considerable income from tourism, an important part of its economy lies in the preparation of almonds for the confectionery trade; its *Calissons d'Aix*, a tangy almond sweet, are famous.

The lightly radioactive hot springs, rich in minerals, were already known in Roman times. Their chief constituents are bicarbonates, calcium, sulphates, silicates, chlorine and magnesium.

Music Festival

The International Music Festival which is held annually in July/August attracts large audiences. Information and tickets (by post or by telephone) from:
SERVICE LOCATION FESTIVAL D'AIX
13100 Aix-en-Provence
☎ *0442173435, fax. 0442961261.*

History

Soon after the destruction of the Celtic settlement (121 BC) to the north near Entremont, Aix-en-Provence was founded by Caius Sextius as the first Roman settlement in Gaul and called Aquae Sextiae Saluviorum. Twenty years later the Roman commander Marius defeated the Teutons near here as they advanced into Italy. Its medicinal springs, which had been known for a long time, and its strategic position on the Via Aurelia, led to a rapid development of the new settlement.

After serious setbacks, caused by migrations and attacks by Saracens, Aix became the capital of the county of Provence and also, especially in the time of the art patron René of Anjou (1409–80), a cultural centre of Provençal poetry. In 1409 the university was founded, and in 1481 the town passed to France. It was badly affected in the Wars of Religion. From 1630 there were violent clashes with Richelieu and Mazarin which could be settled only by the good offices of Michel, the brother of Mazarin and archbishop of Aix.

An extensive building programme in the 17th and 18th c. determined the town's architectural image. The painter Paul Cézanne (1839–1906) was born and died in Aix. From 1958 Picasso lived in the palace at Vauvenargues (☛Surroundings), where he is also buried.

Sights

★Cours Mirabeau

The broad cours Mirabeau, laid out in 1651, borders the Old Town in the south, separating it from the Mazarin Quarter. This idyllic shady promenade is planted with aged plane trees (which are regularly and heavily pruned). Along the road are set four beautiful fountains, including the great Fontaine de la Rotonde (19th c.) at the western end in place du Général-de-Gaulle; in the centre of cours Mirabeau stand the Fontaine des Neuf-Canons (17th c.) and the Fontaine d'Eau-Chaude (18th c.), which is fed with warm spring water.

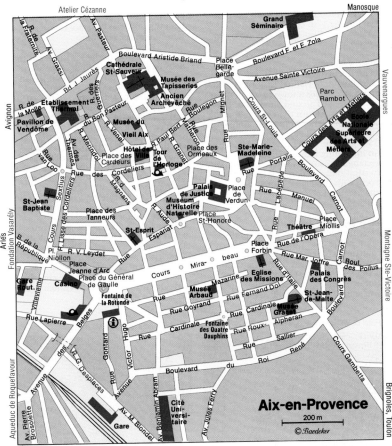

Aix-en-Provence
200 m
© Baedeker

There are several impressive **buildings** in the street, among them the Hôtel des Villars (No. 4; 1710), the Hôtel d'Isouard de Vauvenargues (No. 10; 1710), the Hôtel d'Arbaud Jouques (No. 19; early 18th c.), the Hôtel de Forbin (No. 20; 1656) and the Hôtel de Maurel de Pontevès (No. 38; 1647–50; now the offices of the principal of the university). At the east end of cours Mirabeau stands the Fontaine du Roi-René, the work of David d'Angers (19th c.) and the Chapel of the Oblats, part of the Carmelite monastery designed by a pupil of Puget and restored about 1700. The Deux Garçons café dates from the 18th c.

North of cours Mirabeau the Old Town extends as far as the Hôtel de Ville (Town Hall) and is largely a pedestrian precinct.

Musée d'Histoire Naturelle
Near the Fontaine d'Eau-Chaude on cours Mirabeau, rue Clemenceau leads into the heart of the Old Town. At the end of the little place St.-Honoré rue Espariat branches off to the left, and near it stands the Museum of Natural History. Its collections, particularly the dinosaur eggs which were found in Provence, are well known in specialist circles. The museum is housed in the

Hôtel Boyer d'Eguilles, a town mansion built in the 17th c.
Mon.–Sat. 10am–noon, 2pm–6pm, Sun. 2pm–6pm.

Place d'Albertas

Place d'Albertas lies a short way west of the Museum of Natural History. On its south side stands a town house of three wings grouped around a fountain. Here visitors should turn right and follow rue Aude in a northerly direction, noting on the left the Hôtel Peyronetti, built in 1562 and one of the oldest in Aix, with an interesting facade of double rectangular columns and a frieze of bulls' heads. Continue along rue du Maréchal-Foch, with the 17th c. Hôtel d'Arbaud on the left, until place de l'Hôtel-de-Ville is reached.

Place de l'Hôtel-de-Ville

Place de l'Hôtel-de-Ville, the central point of the Old Town, features a fountain (1755) around which the busy flower market is held every day. On the south side of the square stands the former Halle aux Grains (Corn Exchange), with a magnificent gable,

built in 1759–61 and embellished with sculptures by Jean Pancrace Chastel. It now houses the post office.

On the west side of the square stands the **Hôtel de Ville** (Town Hall), built between 1652 and 1668 and modelled on Italian baroque; it encloses the courtyard and was badly damaged during the French Revolution. Its wrought-iron balcony rail and the beautiful gateway are also 17th c.

On the right side of the facade of the Hôtel de Ville rises the **Tour de l'Horloge** (clock tower of 1510), which was erected on the Roman foundations of a former town gate. In 1661 the astronomical clock below the balustrade was installed.

Palais de Justice

On place de Verdun to the south-east stand the Palais de Justice, completed in 1831, and the Church of Ste-Marie-Madeleine, which contains an Annunciation scene ca 1440. The Renaissance-style facade of the church dates from 1860, while the church itself was rebuilt in 1905.

Hôtel de Ville and Tour de l'Horloge

Hôtel de Forbin on cours Mirabeau

Musée du Vieil Aix

Passing through the clock tower and continuing north along rue Gaston-de-Saporta, with its fine town houses, we come to the Musée du Vieil Aix (Museum of Civic History), which is located in the 17th c. Hôtel Estienne de St-Jean (No. 17).

Ⓘ *Tue.–Sun. 10am–noon, 2.30pm–6pm, winter 2pm–5pm.*

Also in rue Gaston-de-Saporta are the Hôtel de Châteaurenard, with its richly decorated staircase, and the Hôtel de Maynier d'Oppède, once the seat of the Faculty of Letters.

★Cathédrale St-Sauveur

In rue J de la Roque, in the north of the Old Town, stands the Cathedral of St-Sauveur. It was built in various stages from the 12th to 17th c., and dedicated in 1534.

In the 15th–16th c. Gothic **doorway**, where the stone figures were severely damaged during the French Revolution, hang beautiful walnut doors carved mainly between 1508 and 1510 by Jean Guiramand; these are normally concealed behind protective shutters, which the sacristan will open on request. The lower part of the doors already reveals elements of the early Renaissance.

The **interior** of the cathedral is entered through a Romanesque doorway, to the right of the Gothic part of the facade. On the right is an Early Christian baptistry, dating from the 6th c. and renovated in 1577, with a 4th c. font. On the right of the main nave can be seen the triptych *The Burning Bush*, by Nicolas Froment (1435–84); in the left panel will be found a portrayal of *Good King René* (1434–80). In the central nave and south aisle hang Flemish tapestries from 1511 representing the Passion and the story of the Virgin, with representations of English ladies at court. Behind the high altar lies the Chapel of St-Mitre, dedicated to the patron of the town, whose tomb can be found in the first chapel on the right. There is a small, but beautiful, Romanesque cloister adjoining the church on the south wall.

★Musée des Tapisseries

The Musée des Tapisseries is housed in the Ancien Archevêché (former archbishop's palace; 1648), adjoining the cathedral on the west in place des Martyrs-de-la-Résistance. On show are tapestries from Beauvais in Picardy which date from the 17th and 18th c. and include a series of scenes from the life of Don Quixote. Musical events are held in the inner courtyard during the summer.

Ⓘ *Wed.–Mon. 10am–6pm.*

Établissement Thermal (Thermes Sextius)

The Établissement Thermal (thermal baths), which is reached from the cathedral by following the rue du Bon-Pasteur in a south-westerly direction, was built in the 18th c. on the site of the roman baths of Sextius (2nd c. BC). The water issues at a temperature of 34°C and is used both for drinking and bathing, especially for metabolic disturbances, circulatory disorders, nervous diseases and post-operative complaints.

Pavillon de Vendôme

In rue Célony, not far west of the Établissement Thermal and outside the town walls as they were at that time, stands the pavilion built in 1664–7 for the duc de Vendôme and reconstructed in the 18th c. It is surrounded by a small park. The sculptural decoration is noteworthy, and inside are 17th and 18th c. furniture and paintings.

Ⓘ *Daily 10am–noon, 2pm–6pm, winter 2pm–5pm.*

Atelier Paul Cézanne

The studio of the famous Impressionist painter Paul Cézanne, born in Aix, is situated to the north outside the Old Town at 9 avenue Paul-Cézanne, and is reached along avenue Pasteur. In addition to mementos of the master painter there is an audio-visual exhibition.

Ⓘ *Wed.–Mon. 10am–noon, 2.30pm–6pm, winter 2pm–5pm.*

Quartier Mazarin

In the years 1646–53, at the suggestion of Michel Mazarin, archbishop of Aix and brother of the famous cardinal and politician, the quarter named after him and the broad street known as cours Mirabeau were laid out, necessitating the demolition of part of the town walls. The rectangular area is characteristic of 17th c. town planning; it is bounded on the south by boulevard du Roi-René and boulevard Carnot, part of which follows the line of the former town walls. The

VI·ME·INVENERIT·INVENIET·VITAM·ET·HAVRIET·SALVTEM·A·DOMINO

centre of the area is formed by place des Quatre-Dauphins, with the 1667 fountain of the same name which is adorned with sculptures of four dolphins.

Musée Paul Arbaud

Standing to the north of the Fontaine des Quatre Dauphins on rue du Quatre-Septembre, the Hôtel d'Arbaud is one of the finest town mansions in the quarter. Built in the 18th c. it now houses the Académie d'Aix and the Musée Paul Arbaud. This collection contains important examples of faience and pictures and also has a large library.
🔘 *Mon.–Sat. 2pm–5pm.*

Musée Granet

The Musée Granet (Museum of Fine Arts and Archaeology) in place St-Jean-de-Malte, east of the Fontaine des Quatre-Dauphins, is one of the most comprehensive museums in Provence. It is housed in the former Priory of The Knights of St John of Malta (Palais de Malte), dating from 1671. Most of the exhibits were formerly the property of the collector and painter François Marius Granet (1775–1849); they include Celto-Ligurian sculptures from the Oppidum d'Entremont (see below), Greek reliefs, Roman fragments, an Early Christian sarcophagus, medieval sculpture and works by European painters (including Rubens, Rembrandt, Ingres and Cézanne).
🔘 *Wed.–Mon. 10am–noon, 2pm–6pm.*

St-Jean-de-Malte

The Church of St-Jean-de-Malte, which adjoins the palace on the east, was once part of the priory. Erected late in the 13th c., it is the earliest Gothic building in the town. In 1682–93 it was extended with additional chapels. The 14th c. bell tower is 67 m high. Inside, the graves and paintings are note-worthy.

Cité Universitaire

The Cité Universitaire is located in the Quartier des Fernouillères, south of boulevard du Roi-René. The foundation of the university with its Faculty of Philosophy (1409) dates from the reign of Louis II. University institutions are still housed in the old buildings in place de l'Université, but in 1950 it became necessary to remove a considerable part

of the university out of the Old Town. There are now about 20,000 students in Aix.

Bibliothèque Méjanes

The valuable collection of the Méjanes Library – 350,000 18th c. volumes, manuscripts, incunabula – was once housed in the Hôtel de Ville (Town Hall), but now forms part of the Espace Culturel Méjanes, a former match factory converted into the municipal library at 8–10 rue des Allumettes in the west of the town. The nucleus of the collection was provided by the Marquis de Méjanes (1726–86), a teacher born in Arles, who donated 80,000 volumes to the native town.

The St John Perse Foundation, a research centre for poets, diplomats and 1960 Nobel prizewinners, has also been transferred here. Temporary exhibitions are held twice a year.

★Fondation Vasarely

The Vasarely Foundation lies in avenue Marcel-Pagnol, in the Jas de Bouffan district in the west of the town. In this modern and unconventional building, some 87 m in length, visitors can see 42 huge wall paintings – *integrations murales* – as well as some 800 others by the Hungarian-French artist Victor Vasarely (1908–97), the main advocate of the abstract constructivist school of painting and of op art (☛Gordes).
🔘 *Wed.–Mon. 9.30am–12.30pm, 2pm–5.30pm.*

★Oppidum d'Entremont

The archaeological site of the Celto-Ligurian settlement of Oppidum d'Entremont lies some 3 km north of Aix, off the D14 road. This settlement, which comprised an Upper and a Lower Town, was strategically placed on high ground. About 4 ha have been uncovered, and pieces of broken pillars enable one to discern the outlines of some individual buildings and parts of the settlement. A mosaic floor and remains of what were apparently charnel houses are all that is left of a sanctuary on the hill, destroyed in 123 BC.
🔘 *Wed.–Mon. 9am–noon, 2pm–6pm.*

◄ *The Burning Bush* (1475–6) by Nicolas Froment

Place d'Albertas in Aix

Surroundings

Vauvenargues
The D10 road leaves Aix and leads
northward through the charming
countryside on the north bank of the
Bimont reservoir. The latter is not visible
from the road, and it is worth making a
detour to the wall of the reservoir in
order to enjoy the impressive view of the
bold triangular mountain peak, the
Montagne Ste-Victoire.

About 12 km east of Aix, above the
river which supplies the reservoir, lies
the village of Vauvenargues, known for
the abundance of game and wildlife in
the surrounding countryside. The pretty
village church dates from the 12th and
16th c., and the Renaissance palace,
where Luc de Clapiers, marquis de
Vauvenargues, wrote his famous 18th c.
philosophical maxims, was purchased by
Picasso in 1958. Picasso and Jacqueline
Roque, his second wife, are buried in the
park.

Today the palace is owned by the
daughter of Jacqueline Roque and is not
open to visitors. Jacqueline wanted to
install a Picasso museum here, but the
local authorities would not allow it, for
fear that the little village and quiet
valley would be spoiled by hordes of
artists and other visitors.

★★Croix de la Provence
To the south of Vauvenargues towers the
Montagne Ste-Victoire ridge, made
famous by Paul Cézanne. From the little
hamlet of les Cabassols to the west a
road – part of the GR9 walking trail –
leads to Croix de la Provence (945 m).
The climb – about 5 km and taking
about 1½ hours – is mainly over gravel
and rocky ground; stout shoes and a
good standard of fitness are essential.
The superb panoramic view – on a clear
day – from the Camargue in the west
across the Maures massif as far as the
Alps in the south make the effort
worthwhile. The masses of flowers
among the rocks are also impressive.

★Ventabren
Ventabren is a picturesque *village perché*,
or hillside village, dominated by a ruined
château high above the valley of the Arc,
some 15 km west of Aix. Few other places
can so clearly portray what is meant by
the term *perché:* 'like a bird perched high
up in a tree' is one description of it. The
11th–12th c. Church of St-Denis is worth
visiting. There is a magnificent 180° view
from the château ruins over the idyllic
landscape to the north of the Étang de
Berre and Martigues on the southern
bank of the river.

★Roquefavour Aqueduct
4 km south of Ventabren along, a
charming lateral valley of the Arc, we
come to Roquefavour Aqueduct, an
imposing construction conveying the
Durance Canal over the valley towards
Marseille. The aqueduct – three tiers,
internal height 83 m and length 375 m –
was constructed between 1842 and 1847;
although modelled on the Pont du Gard
and in fact considerably larger, its modern
construction is rather too perfect and thus
it fails to achieve the same powerful effect.

The upper level of the aqueduct is
accessible from the D64; coming from
Ventabren, turn left towards Petit-
Rigoués just before reaching the D65,
and then turn right to the watchman's
house.

Roquepertuse
4 km west of Ventabren in the valley of
the Arc lies the Celtic rock sanctuary of

Roquepertuse; an unsigned footpath leads southward from the junction of the D65 and D10. Most of the important finds made here can be seen in the Borély Museum in Marseille (see entry).

Les Milles
From the autumn of 1939, when France entered the second world war, until mid-1940, some 3000 Germans, some of whom had already emigrated several years before, were interned in the brick works of this little town south-west of Aix (about 8 km on the D9). Amongst their numbers were Max Ernst, Lion Feuchtwanger, Walter Hasenclever and Alfred Kantorowicz. They had sought safety here, but had then found themselves the enemy. It was only thanks to the commander of the camp that many of them were able to escape again. The remainder were sent to German concentration camps together with a further 2000 Jews betrayed by the French Vichy government for whom, from 1942, les Milles was a transit camp. There is a plaque commemorating these events at the railway station.

In a beautiful park south of les Milles, by the D59, stands the 18th c. **Lenfant Palace**.

Alpilles   G 4–5

Département: Bouches-du-Rhône
Highest point: la Caume 387 m

The chain of the Alpilles (Little Alps) extends east of the Rhône between St-Rémy-de-Provence (see entry) to the north and les Baux (see entry) to the south. In spite of its relatively modest height the steep limestone massif has a thoroughly Alpine appearance. Geologically the Alpilles are a continuation of the Lubéron (see entry), the mountain range adjoining on the east which runs parallel to the northern bank of the Durance. The western (Alpilles de Baux) and the eastern (Alpilles d'Eygalières) parts are different in character. The first discoveries of bauxite were made in the Alpilles.

A quarry and Montagne Ste-Victoire (1898) by Paul Cézanne

La Caume

The highest point of the Alpilles is the Caume (387 m). The summit, from which there are excellent views, can be reached on a road – sometimes closed – which branches off to the east on the D5 between St-Rémy and les Baux. The panorama extends as far as the mouth of the Rhône and the Camargue in the west and to Mont Ventoux and the valley of the Durance in the east.

★Antibes   H 18

Département: Alpes-Maritimes
Altitude: sea level
Population: 63,000

The town of Antibes – to which the resorts of Cap-d'Antibes and Juan-les-Pins belong – lies to the east of Cannes at the western end of the Baie des Anges (Bay of Angels), which reaches as far as Nice. Cap-d'Antibes, which extends south into the Mediterranean, separates the huge sweep of the Baie des Anges from the Golfe Juan. The actual area of the town occupies the peninsula of Garoupe.

Economy

Flower growing is of great importance to the economy; roses, carnations and other flowers are grown under about 3 sq km of glass.

8 km inland along the D35/103 the Sophia Antipolis Industrial and Technological Park has been developing since 1972 and has become known as Europe's 'Silicon Valley'. It now covers an area of 4,000 ha, on which about 1,100 firms with 17,000 employees are established. Of those some 100 are international firms, and 900 companies and organisations are working in advanced fields of technology such as electronics and telecommunications, energy and environmental research, chemistry and biotechnology. More than a half of the work force are white-collar workers, and of them 40 per cent are from 60 different countries. Sophia Antipolis has an international boarding school. Advantages are also expected from the proximity of the Nice-Sophia Antipolis University, which considers itself a European university and currently has 30,000 students.

Antibes: the Old Town, with the Bastion St-André

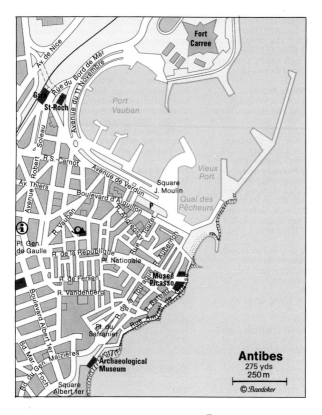

Antibes
275 yds
250 m
© Baedeker

History

Antibes was founded in the 5th c. BC by Greeks from Phocaea and named Antipolis, meaning the town lying opposite the settlement of Nikaia Polis (Nice). The settlement became a Roman municipium, later a stronghold against the barbarians. From the 14th c. onwards it was a frontier town between Savoy and France. In 1481 the town together with the whole of Provence fell to the French throne. Later the fortifications were remodelled by Vauban and Fort Carré, of which only a few remains exist, was built. The château in the Old Town was for many years the seat of a bishop and a holiday residence of the Grimaldi family.

Today Antibes, Cap-d'Antibes and Juan-les-Pins (see below) form a tripartite community.

Town

Antibes has a fine situation on the north-east side of the cape between the little bays of Anse St-Roche in the north and Anse de la Salis in the south. Above Anse St-Roche rises the picturesque 16th c. Fort Carré, a relic of the town defences. Nearby is a sports and youth centre.

South of the fort lies the harbour (Port Vauban), which was laid out by Vauban himself.

Église de l'Immaculée-Conception

South of the harbour – with a good general view from avenue de Verdun on its south side – on the coastal road (avenue Amiral-de-Grasse) stands the Church of the Immaculée-Conception which in the Middle Ages was a cathedral.

The nave dates from the 17th c. and there is little to see of the former 12th c. Romanesque building. The church houses a notable altarpiece from 1515 by Louis Bréa, *The Madonna with Rosary*, as well as a figure of Christ dating from 1447.

Château Grimaldi, Musée Picasso

The former château of the Grimaldis stands to the south of the church. When it was built in the 16th c. remains of the Roman fort were used in its construction. However, the defensive tower dates from the 13th/14th c.

Today the château contains the interesting ★Musée Picasso, a collection of modern and contemporary art, with works by Pablo Picasso, de Stael, Ernst, Mirò, Léger, Hartung, Atlan, Richier, Adami, Modigliani, Saura, Cesar, Arman and Alechinsky. There is also a wall tapestry, *Judith and Holofernes*, by Jean Cocteau.

The first floor is devoted to Picasso himself, with exhibits of pictures, ceramics and sculptures which he produced during a two-month stay in the château in 1946.

ⓘ *Jul.–Sep. Tue.–Sun. 10am–6pm.*

Musée Archéologique

The coastal promenade continues south to the Bastion St-André, also a relic of the Vauban fortifications. Here is situated the Musée Archéologique (Museum of Archaeology). Among its exhibits are some portraying the history of the Greek town, especially submarine archaeological finds.

ⓘ *Dec.–Oct. Wed.–Mon. 9am–noon, 2pm–7pm, winter 6pm; closed pub. hols.*

Cap-d'Antibes

The spit of land about 4 km long that leads to Cap-d'Antibes is dotted with villas and gardens. Its highest point is the Plateau de la Garoupe (78 m; lighthouse) on which stands an observation platform and an orientation table. The panorama takes in the town and the coast with the offshore islands of Lérins (☛Cannes, Surroundings) as well as the Esterel mountains and the maritime Alps rising behind them.

★Notre-Dame-de-la-Garoupe

Also on the plateau stands the pilgrimage chapel of Notre-Dame-de-la-Garoupe; among its internal features are many votive tablets, frescos, a 14th c. icon from Sebastopol and two gilded wooden statues.

Jardin Thuret

The Jardin Thuret is situated not far west of the Plateau de la Garoupe on boulevard du Cap. The garden commemorates the botanist Gustave Thuret, who laid it out about 1856. In the botanical garden, which boasts many exotic plants, the eucalyptus tree, originating in Australia, was first planted on European soil.

Musée Naval et Napoléonien

To the south-west not far from the end of the cape – where there is a rock pool and luxury restaurant – we come to the Batterie du Grillon. This former defensive work now houses the Musée Naval et Napoléonien (Naval and Napoleonic Museum).

Juan-les-Pins

Picturesque Juan-les-Pins lies on the Golfe Juan which extends between Antibes and Cannes (see entry). The name is derived from an old pine grove. Juan-les-Pins is a very popular resort with many hotels and a casino.

Surroundings

Biot

Biot (pronounced 'beeyot'), once a chief place of the Ligurians, is a village with steep narrow streets and bumpy paths climbing up a hill. It is noted for its arts and crafts, which include gold and silver work, ceramics, glass blowing, carving in olive wood, weaving and silk-screen printing. In the Church of Ste-Madeleine-St-Julien are two beautiful altarpieces from the Nice school and a *Madonna with Rosary* by Louis Bréa.

Biot has become especially known for its ★Musée National Fernand-Léger, which is reached by taking chemin du Val-de-Pome, a little way out of Biot in the direction of the sea, and then turning left. The museum, established by Léger's widow Nadja in the 1950s, displays all the periods of his works in a most comprehensive fashion. The enormous mosaic (1948) on its outside wall was originally intended for the sports stadium in Hanover, Germany,

The Musée National Fernand-Léger in Biot

but was found to be too expensive. The portrait of the artist in wire on the staircase is by Alexander Calder.
🔘 *Apr.–Sep. 10am–noon, 2pm–6pm; Oct.–Mar. to 5pm.*

Marina Baie des Anges
See Cagnes-sur-Mer

Vallauris
See Cannes

★★Ardèche (Gorges de l'Ardèche)   C–D 2–3

Régions: Languedoc-Roussillon, Rhône-Alpes
Départements: Gard, Ardèche

The Ardèche is a tributary on the right bank of the Rhône, which it joins near Pont-St-Esprit, about 100 km north of the Mediterranean coast.
　The river, which has a total length of 120 km, rises at a height of 1467 m in the area of Vivarais on the eastern edge of the Massif Central. It drops unusually steeply in its upper course.
　The most impressive reach of the river from the point of view of scenery is between Vallon-Pont-d'Arc and Pont-St-Esprit, a stretch which is also designated as the Gorges de l'Ardèche. The following description is confined to this part of the river, which is about 30 km long.

Boats can be hired at many places on the road which follows the river. Canoeing down the Ardèche is a popular sport, sometimes unfortunately leading to overcrowding. Occasionally there are rapids in the river; also when there is heavy rainfall the water level can rise rapidly by several metres. For these two reasons boating is advised only for experienced canoeists. During the high season in May and June there are very many boats on the river, which tend to spoil it as a place of natural beauty.

Warning The scrub and bushes – the *garrigue* – that cover a large part of the higher slopes are extremely dry in summer and, therefore, fire is always a danger. Because of the extensive nature of the area and its lack of paths these fires are practically impossible to fight. Visitors should be extremely careful with

The great bend of the Ardèche river

naked flames and avoid discarding lighted matches and cigarettes.

★★Circular tour through the Gorges de l'Ardèche

The circular tour described below is approximately 150 km long. In addition to the wild romantic scenery this trip is also impressive for the karst caves, especially those of the Aven d'Orgnac, which are among the most important caves in France open to visitors. The vistas which open up on this drive are extremely impressive, particularly the many ever-changing views downwards to the rushing turquoise river.

The visitor who wants ample time to appreciate the scenery is recommended to devote a whole day to this tour.

Setting out

Leaving Pont-St-Esprit the road crosses the Rhône – not far north of its confluence with the Ardèche – on an old stone bridge nearly 1000 m long. There is an exceptionally charming view of the river frontage of the Old Town.

From Pont-St-Esprit follow the N86

for a short distance and then bear left on to the D901, signposted for Gorges de l'Ardèche. This road, which is not within sight of the river, gradually climbs to the undulating higher slopes which are covered with scrub and bushes. Near Laval-St-Roman turn right off the D901 on to the D174 and follow the signs for Aven d'Orgnac. It is a further 9 km to the village of Orgnac-l'Aven, near which lies the cave.

★★Aven d'Orgnac

Aven d'Orgnac is one of the most splendid caves in the country that are open to the public. In this dripstone cave, which was discovered on August 19th 1935, there is an almost constant temperature of 13°C, so that in addition to stout footwear warm clothing is recommended. A visit, with a guide, lasts about an hour.

In the hall of the building at the entrance a plan of the cave can be seen on the wall, and above it are displayed a number of objects which have been found there, including bones and pottery. The cave is entered by an artificial tunnel which leads to the Great Hall with its almost 25 m high stalagmites. Visitors are photographed inside the cave and can take the photographs away with them when they leave.

Only those parts of the extensive system of caves which were opened up by 1939 are accessible to the public. Continuations have been discovered since 1965 and have been largely explored. Near the entrance stands a memorial to Robert de Joly (1887–1968), the discoverer and first explorer of the caves.

🔵 *Mar., Oct.–Nov. 14th daily 9am–noon, 2pm–5pm; Apr.–Sep. to 6pm.*

Aven de la Forestière

Not far north-west of the Aven d'Orgnac we find the Aven de la Forestière, a dripstone cave with some interesting sinter formations; it was discovered in 1966 and since 1968 has been accessible to the public. It is, however, not nearly so impressive as the Aven d'Orgnac.

🔵 *Apr.–Sep. daily 10am–7pm.*

Leaving Orgnac l'Aven, follow the D317 (which later becomes the D176) west. In a few kilometres there is a rewarding view on the right. In Barjac, turn north and cross the Ardèche this side of Vallon-Pont-d'Arc. On the far side of the bridge turn right and follow the sign Route Touristique des Gorges de l'Ardèche. The road (D290) now follows the course of the river for the most part. At first it winds through rock galleries; here there are some little grottos including the Grotto of the Tunnel.

★Pont d'Arc

About 4 km from Vallon-Pont-d'Arc a large rock arch can be seen on the right and through it flows the Ardèche river. The arch has headroom of 34 m above the normal water level and a breadth of 60 m. The sandy stretches on the banks are popular as stopping places for people in boats. The best view of the Pont d'Arc is from a short distance away after driving round a little bluff.

Nearby, the **Grotte de Chauvet** was discovered in 1995, and contains some spectacular cave paintings dating back 20,000 years. It is not open to the public.

The road continues at varying distances from the river, which in this reach has dug its bed many hundred metres deep into the chalk. At the **viewpoints** (*belvédères*) there are adequate parking

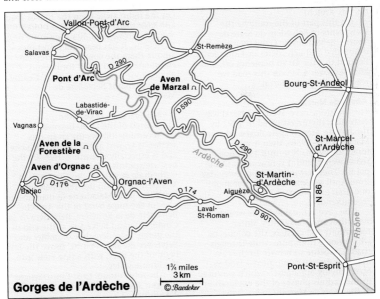

Gorges de l'Ardèche

1¾ miles
3 km
© Baedeker

Pont d'Arc

places; falling rocks are often a danger on this stretch.

On this part of the route lie the viewpoints of Belvédère du Serre de Tourre, Belvédères de Gaud, Belvédères d'Autridge and Belvédères de Gournier. Beyond this the D190 branches off, and after just over 5 km on this road we reach the Aven de Marzal.

★Aven de Marzal

The dripstone cave Aven de Marzal was systematically investigated in 1892 by the famous French speleologist Edouard Martel (1859–1938), then it was forgotten again. Not until 1949 was it rediscovered, and it is now open to the public. There are guided tours every day from April to October; these last about one hour and warm clothing is recommended.

The cave is notable for its wealth of stalactites and stalagmites, sinter formations and crystals, the colours of which range from pure white through shades of ochre to brown. In the cave museum there is equipment – ladders, boats, diving apparatus – which was used in the various phases of the exploration of the Aven de Marzal.

Grotte de la Madeleine

On the right, away from the tourist road and near the above-mentioned fork along a narrow road, lies the Grotte de la Madeleine. It has beautiful dripstones – among them the completely irregular *excentriques* – and sinter formations. A guided tour lasts about an hour. Nearby is the viewpoint Belvédère de la Madeleine.

★★Belvédères de la Corniche

The stretch of the D290 beyond the D190 turning follows the river; this section is known as the Haute Corniche and is especially charming. Here lie the best viewpoints – Belvédère de la Cathédrale (a view of the Cirque de la Madeleine), Balcon des Templiers and Belvédère de la Maladrerie (a magnificent view of the huge bend of the Ardèche), Belvédère de la Rouvière, Belvédère de la Coutelle, Grand Belvédère at the end of the gorge, Belvédère du Colombier and Belvédère du Ranc-Pointu, above the last bend of the river, with a fine view into the Rhône valley.

The return route to St-Esprit, where the tour started, is via St-Martin-d'Ardèche.

Alternative route

Visitors with less time can curtail the tour by taking the last part, the Haute Corniche, in the opposite direction from Pont-St-Esprit. In this case the views become more impressive as far as the Balcon des Templiers. The visit can end with the Aven de Marzal.

★★Arles   G 3

Département: Bouches-du-Rhône
Altitude: 9 m
Population: 51,000

The ancient town of Arles lies on the Rhône south of the point where the river divides into two arms – the Grand Rhône to the east and the Petit Rhône to the west – and flows through the Camargue, with its ponds and lakes, before entering the Mediterranean.

Impressive Roman and medieval monuments serve as a reminder of its great past. Some parts still remind the visitor of the painter Vincent van Gogh who lived in Arles from 1888 to 1889.

The famous Bridge of Arles, however, no longer exists, nor does Arles own any of van Gogh's paintings.

History

Arlath ('town in the marsh') was originally a Greek settlement, from 46 BC a Roman colony and competed with Massilia (Marseille) as a port. Quite early in its history it had a Christian community and was the venue in 314 for the first Council of the Roman Empire in the West. In 406 the town (Arelate) was the seat of the Roman Civil Government for the whole of Gaul. From the 10th c. it belonged to the kingdom of Burgundy and later to the Holy Roman Empire. In 1481 it and Provence fell to France.

Today Arles extends over 750 sq km and in area is the largest commune in France, Paris being only 105 sq km.

The beauty of the maidens of Arles was immortalised by Georges Bizet in his two-part concert suite *L'Arlésienne*, from the music written in 1872 for the drama of the same name by Alphonse Daudet (☛Montmajour, Fontvieille).

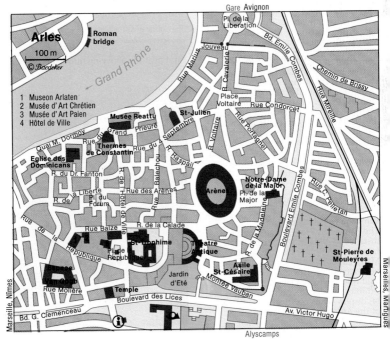

Arles

1 Museon Arlaten
2 Musée d'Art Chrétien
3 Musée d'Art Paien
4 Hôtel de Ville

100 m

© Baedeker

Note The streets in the centre of Arles are very narrow and there is a labyrinth of one-way streets, so motorists are recommended to leave their vehicle outside the Old Town which is partly surrounded by walls, and visit the town on foot.

Collective tickets at a reduced rate to all the sights in the town are obtainable from all ticket offices.

Sights

★Arènes

The Roman **amphitheatre** is the largest and most complete ancient monument in the town, dating probably from the early 1st c. AD. The great oval once had accommodation for 21,000 spectators. With a length of 136 m and a width of 107 m the arena was one of the largest in Gaul. The facade has a double row of arcades with 60 archways each 3.38 m wide; the four arches used as main entrances are 4.8 m wide.

Seating for the spectators was once on 34 tiers of steps; the arena itself was built into the bedrock of the site. Originally a wooden floor was provided over the rock; the holes in which the supporting joists were fixed can still be seen in the wall surrounding the arena.

In the Middle Ages the citizens converted the amphitheatre into a fortress by the addition of towers and the walling up of the arcades, of which there were originally three storeys; the third no longer exists. When Prosper Mérimée cleared and restored the arena 150 years ago three of the towers were left standing. The one over the entrance can be climbed and from it there is a charming view over the roofs of the Old Town and of the nearby ancient theatre. Nowadays bullfights take place in the arena in summer.

ⓘ *Apr.–Sep. daily 9am–7pm; Oct.–Mar. 10am–noon, 2pm–4.30pm.*

Van Gogh Foundation

The Fondation Vincent van Gogh was installed in 1984 in the nearby Palais de Luppé, at 26 Rond-Point des Arènes. Many famous artists, painters, photographers, writers and composers paid homage to van Gogh, and there are exhibits and documents covering his life on display. Thus his dream of a 'House of the Artist' has been realised.

ⓘ *Daily 10am–12.30pm, 2pm–7pm.*

Théâtre Antique

The **Roman theatre** is located in rue de la Calade/rue du Cloître; opening hours are the same as those for the Arènes.

It was built in the time of Augustus and, with seating for 8,000 on 33 tiers of steps, was as large as the theatre in Orange (see entry). In the early Middle Ages the theatre was used as a quarry, and with the material it provided the town wall was erected. Of the rear wall of the stage only a few stumps of pillars and two more or less complete columns remain. When the theatre is used to stage events during the July festival, it is protected on the outside by screens and the interior is somewhat spoiled by the necessary technical apparatus.

Most of the relics brought to light during excavation can be seen in the Musée Lapidaire d'Art Païen (Museum of Pagan Art, see below) – the most important of these is the *Venus of Arles*, a representation of the goddess Diana, which was discovered near a fountain in 1651 and is now in the Louvre in Paris.

Place de la République

Further west lies place de la République with an Egyptian obelisk 15 m high. It

The cloister of St-Trophime

was found in the amphitheatre and erected here in 1676.

On the north side of the square stands the Hôtel de Ville (Town Hall) built in 1673–5. Its bell tower dates from 1553 and came from the building which previously stood on the site.

★St-Trophime

The Church of St-Trophime in place de la République, once the cathedral, was founded it is believed in the year 606. Its patron was a Greek disciple who brought Christianity to Provence. In its present form it is a Romanesque basilica, built in the 11th and 12th c.

Here Frederick I, Barbarossa, married Beatrice of Burgundy in 1156 and in 1178 was crowned king of Arles, thus strengthening the affiliation between Provence and Burgundy.

The restored facade facing the square has a magnificent ★★doorway with some most impressive figures – a masterpiece of Provençal sculpture. It was placed in front of the existing Carolingian building in the 12th c. and shows a certain similarity to the doorway of the Church at St-Gilles (see entry). On the pillars are figures of saints and Apostles: on the extreme inside of the front on the left is St Trophime being crowned with a mitre by two angels and on the right the Stoning of St Stephen. Above the door in the tympanum can be seen the Last Judgment, surrounded by the symbols of the Evangelists and with the Twelve Apostles at its feet. This frieze is continued on the left and the right in the portrayal of the Last Judgment, with the 'chosen' on the left and the 'damned' on the right; below on the capitals on the left is the Annunciation and on the right the Birth of Jesus.

Both side doorways are considerably smaller than the main doorway and were added in the 17th c. They give access to the rather dim interior. All three aisles are very narrow and high and show the transition from Romanesque to Gothic, the transept being 11th c. and the centre aisle 12th c. In the first bays on the right and the left hang large Aubusson tapestries. The choir and its ambulatory are 15th c. Gothic.

The ★★cloister of St-Trophime adjoins the church on the south-east. It is accessible through the building to the right of the facade of the church and the

Musée d'Art Chrétien

courtyard behind it.

In the cloister pillars alternate with columns in pairs, the capitals of which are decorated with fine sculptures of Biblical scenes; on the pillars will be found figures of Apostles and saints, and between them reliefs of stories of Christ and the saints. The 12th c. north and east passages are the oldest parts, while the south and west date from the 14th c.; thus the cloister reveals both Romanesque and Gothic elements.

The **chapter house** adjoins the cloister; in it hang tapestries from Flanders and Aubusson (17th c.), and in the gallery is a small lapidary collection. The other rooms adjacent to the cloisters are used for temporary exhibitions. The stairs leading to the galleries and the rooms above also provide access to the terrace-like roof gallery which encircles the cloister and provides a charming view

🄖 *Jan. daily 10am–noon, 2pm–4.30pm; Feb. 10am–12.30pm, 2pm–7pm; Mar.–May 9.30am–12.30pm, 2pm–7pm; Jun.–Sep. 9am–7pm; Oct. 9.30am–12.30pm, 2pm–6pm; Nov.–Dec. 9.30am–noon, 2pm–4.30pm.*

Musée Lapidaire d'Art Païen

The Musée Lapidaire d'Art Païen (Lapidary Museum of Pagan Art) is located opposite St-Trophime in the former Church of Ste-Anne (1630). It exhibits works of the Roman period and especially of Hellenism. Most of the exhibits come from the Roman theatre, the former Forum and other ancient sites in Arles.

Musée d'Art Chrétien

The Musée d'Art Chrétien (Museum of Christian Art) lies a short distance north-west of the Musée Lapidaire on rue Balze. Housed in the chapel of the former Jesuit college which was built in 1652, it possesses one of the most important collections of Early Christian sarcophagi from the 4th c.; many of them come from the necropolis of the Alyscamps (see below) and from the Early Christian burial place of St Genest in the present-day suburb of Trinquetaille. The sarcophagi are decorated with reliefs showing scenes from the Old and New Testaments.

The Cryptoporticus, a partly

A 'Maid of Arles', Festival of the Gardian

subterranean arcade of the ancient Forum (see below), can be reached from the museum.

🄖 *May–Sep. daily 9am–12.30pm, 2pm–7pm; Oct.–Apr. 10am–noon, 2pm–4.30pm.*

Museon Arlaten

The Museon Arlaten (Museum of Arles) was founded in 1896 by the famous Provençal poet Frédéric Mistral. The Palais de Laval-Castellane, in which it is housed, is built on the remains of an ancient basilica, and was first a nobleman's palace and then a Jesuit college. Mistral, a Nobel prizewinner of 1904, donated his prize money in order to create in his native region a permanent museum. It is now the most important collection of Provençal folk art, displaying furniture, costumes, ceramics, tools and farming implements.

🄖 *Jul.–Aug. daily 9am–noon, 2pm–7pm; Sep.–Jun. Wed.–Mon. 9am–noon, 2pm–5pm.*

Forum

The Forum, the market and meeting place of the Roman town, was situated on the south side of the present-day place du Forum, north of the above-mentioned museums. The best-preserved part is known as the Cryptoporticus (crypt doorway ca 40 BC), a horseshoe-shaped loggia 89 by 59 m in extent, built probably to compensate for the slope of the site. Entrance is from the Musée d'Art Chrétien.

Thermes de Constantin

The Thermes de Constantin (Baths of Constantine), Roman bathing complex, dates from the 4th c. AD and is situated on rue D-Maîsto in the north of the town near the arm of the river called the Grand Rhône. Of the once-extensive series of buildings, which resembled a palace, only the caldarium (warm bath) and parts of the hypocaust (underfloor heating) and the tepidarium (warm-air room) remain.

Espace Van Gogh

The Dutch painter Vincent van Gogh (1853–90) spent 15 productive months in Arles in 1888–9. The artist – together with Cézanne and Gauguin, one of the main pioneers of modern painting – lived in this former hospital for a time, and portrayed it in several of his paintings. The 16th c. building is now a

Pont de Langlois (1888) by Vincent van Gogh

cultural centre and equipped as a School of Books.

Pont de Langlois
The Pont de Langlois, which once stood at the end of avenue du Plan-du-Bourg and was made famous by van Gogh, no longer exists. The drawbridge in rue G-Monge, which is often referred to as the Pont de Langlois, is some 2 km from the original and is a copy.

★Musée Réattu
The Musée Réattu, housed in a 15th c. building on rue du Grand-Prieuré once the Grand Priory of the Knights of Malta, stemmed from the collection of the painter Réattu (1760–1833) and exhibits drawings and paintings by Provençal artists of the 18th and 19th c., as well as a collection of contemporary art, largely owing to the generosity of Pablo Picasso. In addition to the gallery of photographs by Lucien Clergue and others, the drawings by Picasso himself make this friendly small museum particularly interesting; in the main they are portraits with the faces wearing loving or amused expressions, evidence of the humanity and sense of humour of the artist.

★Alyscamps
Along avenue des Alyscamps, on the south-eastern edge of the Old Town, stretch the Alyscamps (the Elysian Fields), an extensive Roman burial place, which, according to the legend of St Trophime, was dedicated as a Christian cemetery and, in the Middle Ages, was so famous that the dead were brought here for burial from considerable distances; Dante refers to it in his 'Inferno'. This led to the curious procedure of bringing the dead – in cleverly designed barrels together with a sum of money – along the Rhône to Arles, where they were fished out of the water by people employed for the purpose and duly interred. Their marble sarcophagi, which were later neglected, sold or destroyed, were not assembled again until the 18th c. Along the idyllic allée des Tombeaux (Street of Tombs), the only monuments to be seen are the plain

stone ones of the Middle Ages; the best ones are housed in the museums, especially in the Musée d'Art Chrétien, and in the Church of St-Trophime. See Arènes (amphitheatre) for opening hours.

At the end of the allée stands the Church of St-Honorat (12th c.), the only remains of which are the choir and the adjoining 15th–18th c. chapels. In the side chapel on the left is a beautiful sarcophagus dating from the 4th c. AD.

Surroundings

Camargue
See entry

Montmajour
See entry

Moulin de Daudet
See Montmajour

★★Avignon   F 4–5

Département: Vaucluse
Altitude: 23 m
Population: 93,000

The former papal residence of Avignon, today the capital of the *département* of Vaucluse, lies on the left bank of the Rhône where the river is divided into two by the island of Barthelasse, and at the foot of a limestone cliff on which stand the Papal Palace and the cathedral. South of Avignon its tributary the Durance flows into the Rhône. Avignon is much favoured by tourists for its art treasures and because it is an excellent base for excursions into Provence.

Festivals
More than 20 festivals are held annually in Avignon, the major and most attractive one being the great international Festival of Dramatic Art in July/August; including jazz and rock concerts which are held against the impressive backdrop of the Palais des Papes. Information from:
FESTIVAL D'AVIGNON
8 bis rue de Mons, 84000 Avignon
☎ 0490826708.

History
Avennio (or Avenio), the capital of the Gallic Cavares, later became a thriving

Roman colony. In turn the town fell into the hands of the Burgundians and the Franks, and in the 13th c. it was acquired, together with Provence, by Charles of Anjou. In the Albigensian Wars it supported the duke of Toulouse and the Albigens and was consequently conquered by Louis VIII in 1226.

Between 1309 and 1377 there resided here Popes Clement V (1305–14), John XXII (1316–34), Benedict XII (1334–42), Clement VI (1342–52), Innocent VI (1352–62), Urban V (1362–70) and Gregory XI (1370–8), a nephew of Clement VI. Only the return of Gregory XI to Rome ended the almost 70 years of Babylonian Captivity of the Church. After his death when schism set in, the popes Clement VII (1378–94) and Benedict XIII (1394–1424), resided in Avignon until 1403. The town with the surrounding county of Venaissin remained a possession of the curia until the Revolution united the papal city with France in 1791.

As a child Petrarch lived with his family for a time in Avignon. He returned in 1326 and a year later met the love of his life Laura de Noves.

After the popes had employed Italian masters, especially the Siennese Simone Martini who died here in 1344, an important school of painting flourished in Avignon until the 18th c.

★★Palais des Papes (Papal Palace)

The immediate reason for the erection of the papal residence was the removal of the curia from Rome to Avignon under Clement V. His successor, John XXII (Pope 1316–34), chose the palace of the bishop of Avignon, his nephew Arnaud de Via, as his official seat and initiated the first extensions. The present aspect of the fortress-like block of buildings is due mainly to the erection of the east and north-east wings (Palais Vieux – Old Palace) by Benedict XII (Pope 1334–42) and the west wing (Palais Nouveau – New Palace) by Clement VI (Pope 1342–52). Later Popes who resided in Avignon were responsible only for small extensions and completions.
🅖 *Guided tours Easter–Jun. daily 9–11.15am, 2–5.15pm; Jul.–Sep. 9am–6pm; Oct.–Easter 9–11.15am, 2–4.15pm.*

Exterior
The east of place du Palais is dominated

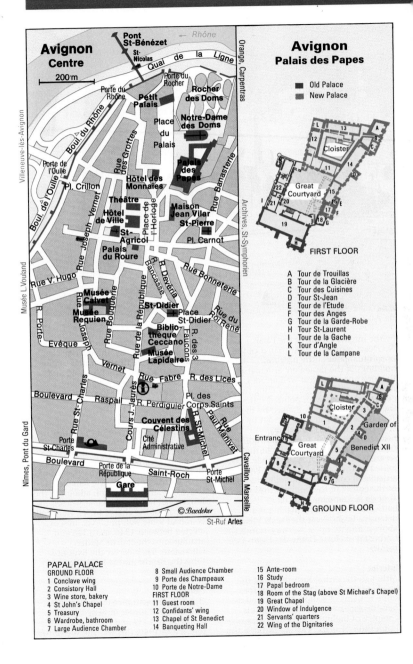

Avignon Centre

← Rhône

Pont St-Bénézet
St-Nicolas
Quai de la Ligne
Porte du Rocher
Porte du Rhône
Petit Palais
Rocher des Doms
Place du Palais
Notre-Dame des Doms
Boul. du Rhône
Rue des Grottes
Hôtel des Monnaies
Palais des Papes
Porte de l'Oulle
Pl. Crillon
Théâtre
Hôtel de Ville
Place de l'Horloge
Maison Jean Vilar
St-Pierre
St-Agricol
Pl. Carnot
Palais du Roure
Rue V. Hugo
Rue Joseph Vernet
Rue Bonneterie
Rue Bancasserie
Rue Banastarie
Musée Calvet
St-Didier
Place St-Didier
Musée Requien
R. Deveria
Rue du Roi René
Rue de la République
Biblio-thèque Ceccano
Musée Lapidaire
R. des 3 Faucons
Rue Bouquerie
Porte Evêque
Rue Fabre
R. des Lices
Vernet
Rue Fabre
Boulevard
Raspail
Cours J. Jaurès
R. Perdiguier
Pl. des Corps Saints
Couvent des Célestins
Rue Paul Manivet
Rue St-Michel
Porte St-Charles
Cité Administrative
Boulevard
Porte de la République
Saint-Roch
Porte St-Michel
Gare

200 m

Villeneuve-lès-Avignon
Orange, Carpentras
Archives, St-Symphorien
Cavaillon, Marseille
Nîmes, Pont du Gard
Musée L. Vouland

© Baedeker

St-Ruf **Arles**

Avignon Palais des Papes

■ Old Palace
■ New Palace

FIRST FLOOR

L 13 A
12 C
Cloister
11 14 D
22 15
Great Courtyard 16
21 20 17 F
19 G
H
I

GROUND FLOOR

L A
Cloister 3 C
10 1 Garden of
4 D
Entrance 2
Great Courtyard 5 Benedict XII
E
8 F
6 G
7
H

A Tour de Trouillas
B Tour de la Glacière
C Tour des Cuisines
D Tour St-Jean
E Tour de l'Etude
F Tour des Anges
G Tour de la Garde-Robe
H Tour St-Laurent
I Tour de la Gache
K Tour d'Angle
L Tour de la Campane

PAPAL PALACE
GROUND FLOOR
1 Conclave wing
2 Consistory Hall
3 Wine store, bakery
4 St John's Chapel
5 Treasury
6 Wardrobe, bathroom
7 Large Audience Chamber

8 Small Audience Chamber
9 Porte des Champeaux
10 Porte de Notre-Dame
FIRST FLOOR
11 Guest room
12 Confidants' wing
13 Chapel of St Benedict
14 Banqueting Hall

15 Ante-room
16 Study
17 Papal bedroom
18 Room of the Stag (above St Michael's Chapel)
19 Great Chapel
20 Window of Indulgence
21 Servants' quarters
22 Wing of the Dignitaries

The Palais des Papes (Papal Palace)

by the mighty facade of the Palais
Nouveau, more a fortress than a centre
of spiritual power. The irregular
buildings of the facade are articulated in
the lower part by great wall arcades.
Above the entrance gateway cling two
octagonal towers with pointed spires. On
the right the facade is flanked by the
Tour de la Gache and on the left by the
Tour d'Angle, two somewhat
insubstantial stump towers protruding
from the surface of the wall. On the left,
set back a little towards the facade, it is
joined by the Palace Vieux (Old Palace),
articulated completely by wall arcades.
At the corner of the building rises the
Tour de la Campane with its
battlemented pinnacle making it a
defensive tower. Near the Palais Vieux,
above a mighty open stairway, stands the
Cathedral of Notre-Dame-des-Doms (see
below).

Interior
Although the entire furnishings of the
inside of the Papal Palace, except for
some remains of sculptures and frescos,
have disappeared, the interior of this
complex of buildings offers a compulsive
impression of space. Passing through the

Porte des Champeaux, the entrance from
the open-air stairway, the Grande Cour
comes into view; this great inner
courtyard, around which the old and
new parts of the palace are grouped, is
from time to time the scene for open-air
dramatic performances.

Consistory
In the left-hand corner of the courtyard
will be found the entrance to the
Consistoire (Consistory), and, opposite,
the Cloister of Benedict XII (see below).
In the Hall of the Consistory measuring
11 × 48 m can be seen the remains of
frescos by Simone Martini; adjoining the
longer wall lies the Chapelle St-Jean, the
lower part of the chapel tower. Here will
be found some well-preserved frescos
created between 1346 and 1348 and
attributed to the Italian Matteo
Giovanetti. They depict the lives of St
John the Baptist and St John the
Evangelist.

Cloister
Opposite the entrance to the Consistory
Hall lies the Cloister of Benedict XII,
dating from 1339 and completely
restored in 1940; this was the site of the

earlier palace of John XXII. A staircase leads to the covered gallery above the cloister; note the alternation of double and considerably smaller simple windows up above.

Banqueting Hall
Adjoining this gallery is the former Banqueting Hall (Grand Tinel or Magnum Tinellum). It is situated immediately above the Consistory Hall; the wooden vaulted ceiling is modern. Hanging here can be seen four huge 18th c. Gobelin tapestries; from the short linking corridor in the left-hand corner of the hall that gives access to the Tour des Cuisines (Kitchen Tower) there is a charming view to the south-west over the Old Town.

St-Martial
The Chapelle St-Martial, which occupies the upper storey of the chapel tower, is – like its counterpart below – decorated with frescos by Matteo Giovanetti which date from 1344–5. They portray the miracles of St Martial, the 3rd c. patron saint of Limousin.

Bedchamber
The end of the Banqueting Hall leads into the Robing Chamber, the ante-room to the papal Bedchamber, in which two 18th c. Gobelins and a model of the Papal Palace are shown. The Bedchamber lies adjoining in the Tour des Anges. Of interest here are the (restored) polychromatic tiled floor, the painted beamed ceiling and the walls painted in tempera, predominantly arabesques on a blue ground; in the window niches are lodged painted birdcages. The Tour de la Garde-Robe, the tower adjacent to the Tour des Anges, houses the former study of Clement VI, known as the Chambre du Cerf (Room of the Stag), so called from the secular scenes, especially of hunting and fishing, painted on the walls. Also of interest is the painted coffered ceiling. The floor tiles are, like those in the Bedchamber, of more recent date but copied from traditional designs.

Grande Chapelle
A staircase now leads into the North Sacristy where there are plaster replicas of numerous tombs of cardinals and other spiritual dignitaries. Then comes the Grand Chapelle (Great Chapel), also called the Chapelle Clementine, a huge un-aisled church with a coffered roof.

On the walls hang a considerable number of baroque paintings; to the right of the altar stands the entrance to the South Sacristy in which will be found replicas of the tombs of Innocent VI, Clement V, Clement VI and Urban V. From the Great Chapel there is an entrance to the loggia where through the large traceried Fenêtre de l'Indulgence (Window of Indulgence) there is a view of the Great Courtyard. From this window the Pope used to give his blessing to the assembled faithful.

Grande Audience
Following the broad vaulted staircase down to the ground floor leads on the left to the door of the Grand Audience, the Great Audience Chamber, a twin-naved audience hall beneath the Chapelle Clementine. This, too, was embellished by Matteo Giovanetti in 1352 with wall paintings of prophets and sybils. In the Small Audience Chamber (also called the Audience des Contredites) ornamental grisaille paintings were introduced in the 17th c.

The way back to the entrance

Frescos in the Chapelle St-Martial

doorway is through the Corps du Garde (Guardroom).

Other sights

Cathédrale Notre-Dame-des-Doms
Near the Papal Palace on the north towers the Cathedral of Notre-Dame-des-Doms; it is mainly 12th c. but it was altered several times in the 14th–16th c. On the arch and gable of the main doorway are remains of frescos by Simone Martin. The gilded statue of the Virgin on the tower and the crucifixion group in front of the cathedral date from the 19th c.

In the interior, in the crossing to the left, can be seen a 12th c. bishop's chair of white marble; in the first side chapel on the north stands the former Romanesque main altar; in the fourth chapel on the south side the partly restored late Gothic monument to John XXII. At the entrance to the Baptistry Chapel – the ante-room on the right – can be seen early 15th c. frescos portraying the baptism of Christ and also showing the donor's family, the Spiefami from Luca. A beautiful silver sculpture of the *Scourging of Christ* is found in the north aisle. The Chapel of the Resurrection, the third chapel on the south side, was a gift from Archbishop Cibelli and also contains his tomb.

Rocher des Doms
The Rocher des Doms is a rocky spur that rises to the north of the Papal Palace and then falls steeply to the Rhône. There is a fine panoramic view from the beautiful park on its summit of the famous Pont St-Bénézet (see below) and the islands of Barthelasse and Piot in the river, as well as Villeneuve-lès-Avignon on the far bank.

★Pont St-Bénézet
Jutting out into the river at the foot of the Rocher des Doms lies what is probably the most famous bridge in the whole of France, immortalised in the children's song 'Sur le pont d'Avignon, on y danse tous en rond …'. Built in 1177–85, this fortified bridge over to Villeneuve-lès-Avignon originally had 22 arches and was 900 m long. A large part was destroyed in 1668 and only four arches remain; in the centre of these stands the two-storey Chapel of St-Nicholas, the lower part of which is Romanesque and

Pont St-Bénézet

the upper Gothic and with a bell gable. The chapel was restored in the 19th c.

Pont St-Bénézet (Provençal for Benedict) is also well-known because of the following legend attributed to it: it is said that in the year 1177 the shepherd Bénézet was instructed by the angels to build a bridge over the Rhône. The town fathers and citizens both mocked the idea, but he was given the strength to raise a giant lump of rock, which they then recognised as being a sign from God, further evidenced by the fact that the bridge was built in only eight years.
ⓘ *Apr.–Sep. daily 9am–6.30pm; Oct.–Mar. Tue.–Sun. 9am–1pm, 2–5pm; closed pub. hols.*

Musée du Petit Palais
On the north side of place du Palais stands the 14th c. Petit Palais, a Gothic palace which used to serve as episcopal offices and residence. It has a beautiful arcaded courtyard and the core of the building dates from the 13th c. At present it houses the Campana Collection of paintings by 13th–15th c. Italian masters, as well as a collection of works by the Avignon school of painters, established by Simone Martini (ca 1280–1344) and Matteo Giovanetti. At one time Napoléon II had purchased the collection for the Louvre.
ⓘ *Wed.–Mon. 9.30am–noon, 2pm–6pm; closed pub. hols.*

Porte du Rocher
A little way to the north the town wall is pierced by the **Porte du Rocher**, a gateway leading to the Pont St-Bénézet.

Hôtel des Monnaies
Opposite the Papal Palace stands the Hôtel des Monnaies, the former mint. Built in the early 17th c., this baroque building still displays a strong Italian influence; the facade is decorated with large figures of animals and bears the coat of arms of Pope Paul V, who came from the house of Borghese and whose vice-legate resided here. Today the palace houses the Conservatoire.

★Town walls
The Old Town is surrounded by a complete ring of walls, constructed 1355–68 by Pope Innocent VI. At irregular intervals eight gates and 39 towers were incorporated into the wall, the total length of which is 4˘8 km.

Some detailed restoration work was carried out in the 19th c.

St-Symphorien
Some distance east of the Papal Palace, on place des Carmes, stands the Church of St-Symphorien, dating mainly from the 15th c. It belonged to the former Monastery of the Unshod Carmelites, and was therefore also named the Église des Carmes. Inside will be found some 16th c. statues as well as paintings by Pierre Parrocel, a lesser-known member of the Parrocel family of artists, and others. A flea market is held on Sunday mornings on place des Carmes.

Place de l'Horloge
The idyllic place de l'Horloge south-east of the Papal Palace, dominated by street cafés beneath shady plane trees, is the centre of Avignon life. On its west side stand the theatre and the Hôtel de Ville (Town Hall; 1845) incorporating a 14th c. clock tower; life-size figures on the top, known as *jacquemarts*, strike the hours.

St-Pierre
A little to the east of the square stands the Church of St-Pierre; built in 1356 and extended in the late 15th c. and restored in the 19th c., it possesses a very beautiful Gothic facade and carved Renaissance wooden doors dating from 1550. Inside the church will be found some 16th c. statues of burial groups and a splendid baroque choral scene from the mid-17th c.

St-Agricol
A short distance south-west of the Town Hall is the Gothic Church of St-Agricol, a very sombre basilica with no transept, built by Pope John XXII in 1321–6.

St-Didier
To the east of rue de la République, the main street of the Old Town leading south from place de l'Horloge, stands the un-aisled Church of St-Didier, dating from the mid-14th c. It provides a further example of stern Provençal medieval architecture. It contains one of the earliest Renaissance works of art, the *Way of the Cross*, created between 1478 and 1481 by the Italian painter Francesco da Laurana, who had been working in France since 1476. Also worthy of note is the late Gothic pulpit with rich flamboyant-style decoration. More recently wall paintings dating from

Fort St-André at Villeneuve-lèz-Avignon

the 14th c. depicting the Crucifixion and Interment have been uncovered in the church.

★Musée Calvet

The Musée Calvet is the town's major museum. The museum has its origin in the private collection of the doctor, a native of Avignon, François Esprit Calvet (1729–1810) together with municipal collections. Since 1833 it has been housed in the Hôtel de Villeneuve-Martignan which dates from 1750 and is situated at 65 rue Joseph-Vernet, south-west of place de l'Horloge. The contents embrace antique sculptures, medieval paintings by Provençal masters, as well as a selection of French painters from the 16th to the 19th c., together with collections of coins and ceramics.

Musée Requien

The Musée Requien is located close to the Musée Calvet. A well as a large scientific library it possesses geological and botanical collections, including a large herbarium.

🕓 *Tue.–Sat. 9am–noon, 2pm–6pm; closed pub. hols.*

★Musée Lapidaire

The Musée Lapidaire (lapidary) can be found at 27 rue de la République, in the baroque former Jesuit church, joined by a bridge to the Jesuit college – now a secondary school – which was founded in 1564. The exhibits include Roman mosaics, fragments of the former triumphal arch, reliefs and ancient sculptures.

🕓 *Wed.–Mon. 9am–noon, 2pm–6pm; closed pub. hols.*

Couvent des Célestins

In the south of the Old Town, near the Porte St-Michel on the street of the same name, stands the former Célestine monastery, founded in the 14th century, once the largest monastery in the town. The interesting church has a superb apse by Perrin Morel; the cloister (ca 1400), which unfortunately is only partially preserved, has a 17th c. gateway.

Musée Louis Vouland

In the west of the Old Town, in rue Victor-Hugo near the Porte St-Dominique, can be found the Musée Louis Vouland, with French furniture, especially from the 18th c., pictures,

Gobelin tapestries and ceramics. Of interest too is the collection of Chinese porcelain and ivory sculptures.
🔘 *Jun.–Sep. Tue.–Sat. 10am–noon, 2pm–6pm; afternoons only Oct.–May.*

Bibliothèque Ceccano

The Bibliothèque Ceccano, the public lending library, is housed in a restored 15th c. building at 2 rue Laboureur.

Palais du Roure

The Palais du Roure at 3 rue Collège-du-Roure is the home of an institute specialising in archaeology and ethnology and the promotion of the Provençal language.
🔘 *Guided tours Tue. 10am, 3pm.*

Maison Jean Vilar

In Maison Jean-Vilar at 8 rue de Mons exhibitions are held depicting the history of the theatrical festival and providing information on the work of the producer Jean Vilar (1912–71), who was the festival director from 1947.

🔘 *Tue.–Fri. 9am–noon, 2pm–6pm, Sat. 10am–5pm.*

St-Ruf

Some distance to the south, outside the Old Town on the other side of the station on boulevard Gambetta, stands the Church of St-Ruf, the remains of a monastic foundation – Abbatiola Sancti Rufi – which goes back to Carolingian times; it was formerly a place of honour where the relics of St Justus were revered.

Villeneuve-lès-Avignon

A bridge over the southern part of the island of Barthelasse leads from Avignon to the little town of Villeneuve-lès-Avignon, which was laid out by Philip the Fair as a bastion against the papal residents.

On the bank of the Rhône opposite Pont St-Bénézet (see above) stands the Tour Philippe-le-Bel, built in 1307. In the collegiate Church of Notre-Dame,

Coronation of the Virgin Mary (1453) by Enguerrand Quarton (Museé Municipal, Villeneuve)

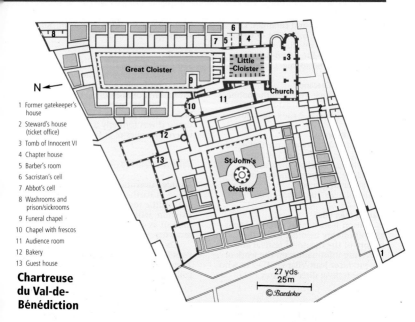

1 Former gatekeeper's house
2 Steward's house (ticket office)
3 Tomb of Innocent VI
4 Chapter house
5 Barber's room
6 Sacristan's cell
7 Abbot's cell
8 Washrooms and prison/sickrooms
9 Funeral chapel
10 Chapel with frescos
11 Audience room
12 Bakery
13 Guest house

Chartreuse du Val-de-Bénédiction

27 yds
25 m
© Baedeker

dedicated in 1333, are some good panels, a pietà and a noteworthy treasury.

★★Musée Municipal

The highlight of the Musée Municipal Pierre-de-Luxembourg on rue de la République is the *Coronation of the Virgin Mary*, painted by Enguerrand Quarton (or Charonton) in 1453, accompanied by works by Nicolas Mignard from the mid-17th c. and a 14th c. Madonna of painted elephant ivory. Some pieces removed from the Carthusian monastery (see below) are also found here, including a 17th c. door and cupboard and some pewter.

Fort St-André

From Fort St-André with its two mighty round towers, built in the late 14th c. by John the Good and Charles V, there is a magnificent view of Villeneuve, Avignon, Mont Ventoux and the Lubéron and Alpilles mountain ranges. The massive walls enclose the little town of St-André, a Benedictine monastery and the Romanesque Church of Notre-Dame-de-Belvézet.
ⓖ *Apr.–Jun., Sep. daily 9.30am–12.30pm, 2pm–6.30pm; Jul.–Aug. 9.30am–7pm; Oct.–Mar. 10am–noon, 2pm–5pm.*

★Chartreuse du Val-de-Bénédiction

In the northern part of rue de la République is the former Chartreuse du Val-de-Bénédiction (Carthusian monastery), which was founded in 1356 by Pope Innocent VI and soon became larger than its mother priory, the Grande Chartreuse at Isère. In the church – the choir of which is in ruins, thus giving a clear view of the fort – can be found the tomb of Innocent VI, in the first bay on the right; dating from 1362, it was preserved thanks to the efforts of Prosper Mérimée in 1834.

To the north of the monastic church lies the Petit Cloître (Little Cloister) and the elongated Cloître du Cimetière, measuring 20 × 80 m, adjoining which were the monks' cells.
ⓖ *Apr.–Sep. daily 9am–6.30pm; Oct.–Mar. 9.30am–5.30pm.*

Cavaillon

The little provincial town of Cavaillon – a centre of melon growing and of the canning industry – lies on the right bank of the Durance and on the western edge of the Montagne du Lubéron (see entry).

St-Véran

In the centre of the town stands the notable former cathedral of St-Véran, which was probably founded in the 12th c, as indicated by its Provençal Romanesque architecture. Its exterior is rather less attractive, but inside can be seen beautiful capitals in the apse and a fine cloister.

🄖 *Mon.–Sat. Apr.–Sep. 10am–noon, 3pm–6pm; Oct.–Mar. 10am–noon, 2pm–4pm; closed Mon. morning.*

Synagogue

The beautiful synagogue on rue Hébraïque is easily recognised by its arcades. Built in the rococo style in 1772 it was later altered; the former Kosher bakery on the ground floor houses the little Musée Judéo-Comtadin (Jewish Museum).

Musée Archéologique

In the chapel of the former hospital on cours Gambetta, with its rococo facade, can be found the Archaeological Museum with exhibits mainly from the Gallo-Roman period, including an interesting Merovingian altar. One room contains interesting items of equipment from the hospital dating from the 17th and 18th c.

Triumphal arch

South-west of St-Véran, in place F-Tourel on the edge of the town, can be found the only preserved building of the Roman era, the little triumphal arch of the former Roman Oppidum Cabellio. It was restored in 1880.

Bandol   L 10

Département: Var
Altitude: sea level
Population: 7000

The port and holiday resort of Bandol lies on the pretty bay between Marseille and Toulon. It possesses a casino and three beaches; Plage de Casino (500 m long, fine sand), Plage de Rènecros (500 m long, fine sand) and Plage Dorée (also 500 m, coarse sand and shingle). The promenades allées Alfred-Vivien and allées Jean-Moulin are charmingly planted with palms, pines and flowers. In the church the baroque woodwork is worth seeing. The surroundings of Bandol are among the best wine-producing areas of the French Mediterranean coast.

Surroundings

St-Cyr-sur-Mer

St-Cyr-sur-Mer, a community of several parts situated 9 km north-west of Bandol, has highly developed agriculture – flowers, capers, olives, grapes – and a ceramic industry.

The principal tourist area is the stretch of coast between the yacht harbours of les Lecques in the north-west and la Madrague in the south.

The Musée de Tauroentum – once the site of a Roman villa – has well-preserved mosaics from the 1st c. AD plus remains of pillars and amphorae.

Île de Bendor

The Île de Bendor is a rocky island 1 km south of Bandol, a trip of only 7 min. by boat (every 30 min.). Its attractions include a reconstructed Provençal harbour, the Musée de la Mer (Marine Museum), the Fondation Paul Picard, with art exhibitions and courses and a huge painting by Salvador Dali, the Exposition Universelle des Vins et des Spiritueux, a wine and spirits exhibition, the diving centre known as the Centre International de Plongée, a little zoo and a sea-water swimming pool.

Sanary-sur-Mer

Sanary-sur-Mer, 4 km south-east of Bandol, is a pretty former fishing village surrounded by wooded hills and with an extensive colony of villas. On a hill to the west of the village stands the Chapel of Notre-Dame-de-Pitié, built in 1560, which is well worth seeing and from which there is a splendid view.

Six-Fours-la-Plage

Six-Fours-la-Plage, 10 km south of Bandol, is a large community of several parts situated at the foot of a hill 210 m high, with magnificent views of the Roads of Toulon (☛Toulon) and the Fort de Six-Fours. At the foot of the hill stands the Church of Vieux-Six-Fours, part of which is a well-preserved Romanesque building, containing a fine 16th c. altarpiece.

Along the beach stretches an extensive complex of holiday homes.

Cap Sicié
Cap Sicié, south of Six-Fours-la-Plage, is the imposing steep slope of a wooded promontory. To the east in the sea can be seen the two rocks known as les Deux Frères (The Two Brothers). Not far west on the 358 m summit of the cape stands the pilgrimage church of Notre-Dame-du-Mai, from which there is an excellent panoramic view.

Îles des Embiez
About 5 km south of Six-Fours-la-Plage, on the southern edge of the Bay of Sanary, lie the Îles des Embiez. The Île de la Tour-Fondue (95 ha) is the chief island in this diverse group and has been developed into a centre for water sports. The south of the island, which is 64 m high and steeply sloping, is characterised by a salt works, vineyards and bathing beaches. The Observatoire de la Mer, a marine observation station and museum, is worth a visit.

Barcelonnette   C 15

Département: Alpes-de-Haute-Provence
Altitude: 1135 m
Population: 3300

Barcelonnette, the headquarters of the Sous-Préfecture des Départements Alpes-de-Haute-Provence, is situated some 70 km east of Gap in the Ubaye valley. This little town lies in magnificent mountain country, surrounded by fruit fields and meadows. The roads to the south lead over the well-known passes of Col d'Allos, Col de la Cayolle and Col de la Bonette; the latter, 2802 m above sea level, is the highest pass in the Alps.

History
Raimond Bérenger, count of Barcelona and Provence, built a fortress here in 1231; it was named Barcelone, from which developed the present name of Barcelonette. From 1388 Barcelonette, together with the whole of the Ubaye region, belonged to the house of Savoy until it was ceded to France under the Treaty of Utrecht in 1731.

Barcelonette was the birthplace of the politician Paul Reynaud (1878–1966), a staunch opponent of European unity after the second world war. In 1940 he was made president of the Council, resigned and was replaced by Marshal Pétain. He was interned by the Vichy government and deported to Germany between 1942 and 1945. After the liberation he was elected to and made president of the European Economic Commission.

Mexicains
In 1821 the Arnaud brothers from neighbouring Jausier emigrated to Mexico and opened a textile and clothing shop in Mexico City. From 1830 onwards they encouraged more emigrants from the valley, and by the end of the century more than 100 such shops in Mexico were owned by Barcelonnettes. Over a number of years more than a half of the men aged over 20 left the Ubaye valley to go to Mexico. Some became very successful; dealings in gold and silver began, and a group of them bought the Bank of London, Mexico and South America, which had the licence to issue banknotes for the whole of Mexico. In the 1880s the 'Mexicains' started to build luxurious villas in their home town, and these give the townscape its unusual character.

This golden age came to an end with the Mexican Revolution between 1910 and 1920, and a wave of the 'Mexicains' returned to Barcelonnette to settle.

The Musée de la Vallée (Ville de Barcelonnette) in la Sapinière villa on avenue de la Libération has a department devoted to the Mexican history of the Barcelonnettes.
ⓘ *Wed., Thu., Sat. 3pm–6pm, to 7pm in summer; open daily during school holidays in winter and summer.*

Townscape
Avenue de la Libération is lined with fine parks containing the villas built by the 'Mexicains'. One of the most lavish, la Sapinière, houses a museum and also the offices of the Mercantour National Park (Maison du Parc National du Mercantour); another villa is now a hotel.

Place Manuel lies outside the chessboard pattern of the historic centre. This broad square, with its colourful house fronts and cafés, is a favourite spot for tourists. The Tour Cardinalis, the bell tower of the Dominican priory, dates from the 15th c.

Surroundings

St-Pons
This little village, some 3 km to the north-west, has an interesting church, a relic of a Benedictine priory. The Romanesque parts – the west door and the choir and section immediately adjoining – date from the 12th c. The 15th c. south door has rich figure decoration, the theme being Death.

Le Sauze
The well-known winter-sports resort of le Sauze, 4 km south-east of Barcelonnette at a height of 1380 m, is one of the oldest in the Alps. Its sister resort of Super-Sauze lies at 1700 m.

Col de la Bonette
The direct road link with Nice, 149 km away, passes along the Route de la Bonette, built in 1832; the present road dates from 1963–4. Fortifications along the way are reminders of the strategic importance this route has always had, including the period of the second world war. A winding road – with a fine view of the Ubaye valley along the way – leads up to the top of the pass at 2802 m. From here it is a half-hour climb there and back to the Cime de la Bonette (2862 m), from where there is a superb panoramic view from Mont Pelvoux to Monte Viso in the north, and from the foothills of the Alps in Digne to the Maritime Alps in the south.

Col d'Allos
This road over the Col d'Allos (2240 m) together with the Col de la Cayolle (2327 m) provides the link with the valley of the Upper Var (☞Mercantour). While a wide road leads to the Pra-Loup winter-sports region, the road through the pass – closed in winter – is in a dreadful condition and requires strong nerves to negotiate it. Any barriers along the edge afford little more than token protection; large stretches should be taken at a snail's pace and a lookout kept for vehicles coming from the opposite direction!

Foux d'Allos
The Alpine view around this popular winter-sports resort (1425 m) is extremely impressive, but tends to be spoilt in summer by the effects of the skiing. Large areas of the grass turf on the gently rounded slopes have been badly damaged.

★★Les Baux-de-Provence   G 4

Département: Bouches-du-Rhône
Altitude: 280 m
Population: 450

The ruined town of les Baux is situated in the extreme west of Provence on the southern edge of the Alpilles (see entry), north-east of Arles. This unique ruined site occupies the plateau of a rock mass which rises above the Lower Town.

The entire place can be visited only on foot; parking is available outside the entrance to the Lower Town.

History
This elevated site was settled as long ago as the Palaeolithic. The first signs of overlords in les Baux are found around the year 950. In the 12th and 13th c. les Baux was the chief town of a county that embraced a great part of Provence and numbered more than 3000 inhabitants. The name probably comes from Provençal *li baus*, the rocks, or from the Ligurian words *balcius* or *baucius*, meaning hill or precipice. The Cour d'Amour, the rendezvous of the troubadours in the 13th c., was famous as the centre of courtly poetry which was later to find a parallel in German-speaking countries. Being a stronghold of Huguenots – there still exists a window from the former Protestant church of 1571 with the watchword *post tenebras lux*, or 'after the darkness, the light' – and a refuge for rebels from Aix, in 1631 Louis XIII ordered the duke of Guise to lay siege to the town and take it. The inhabitants longed for peace and asked the king to take over the whole town and to tear down the fortifications at their expense, which was done two years later. In 1642 les Baux was given as a gift to the Grimaldi family, who remained dukes of les Baux until 1791, when they were dispossessed during the French Revolution. Charles Maxime de Grimaldi, who died in 1880, was the last to hold the title of marquis des Baux.

At the beginning of the Industrial Revolution another aspect quickly became important. In the surrounding countryside in 1821 rich deposits of a mineral were discovered, which provides the main basic material for aluminium production, and which was named bauxite after the town.

Les Baux-de-Provence in the evening light

L'Oustau de Baumanière

This famous restaurant and hotel in the Vallon de la Fontaine – or rather its founder, Raymond Thuilier – has an astonishing history. Having grown up in a railway restaurant run by his mother at Privas in Ardèche, Thuilier entered the insurance profession in Paris. His hobby was cooking, but he was 50 before he devoted himself full-time to the culinary arts, and 80 when he became the doyen of French master chefs. In 1945 he came to Provence and built his own restaurant in a former oil mill. The official opening was performed by a young official from the ministry of tourism, the former teacher Georges Pompidou. Despite the remote location Thuilier's cuisine was a success, and the Michelin guide awarded him three stars as early as 1954. Since then the business has expanded, the Dèpendance Cabro d'Or built and a wine shop added. Thuilier was also mayor of les Baux.

★Lower Town

Passing the former 17th c. Town Hall and the Porte Eyguières, the ancient town gate, follow rue de l'Église to the attractive little place St-Vincent, the south side of which is formed from the rock (fine view westward).

St-Vincent

The sturdy Church of St-Vincent, dedicated to a 4th c. martyr, gives a surprising impression of space. Its present form is Romanesque and Gothic. The chapels leading off the right-hand aisle were hewn from the soft stone; in the centre one stands a font contrived from the actual rock. The right aisle is 10th c., from the Carolingian period. The 12th c. nave reflects the Cistercian Romanesque style. The left-hand aisle is 15th c. Gothic. Immediately behind here the marquis of les Baux lie buried; their tombs are not open to the public.

All the windows of the church were the gift in 1962 of Prince Rainier of Monaco, the successor to the dukes of les Baux.

At Christmas shepherds celebrate midnight vespers here. As only a few seats are available, anyone wishing to attend is advised to come early and dress warmly.

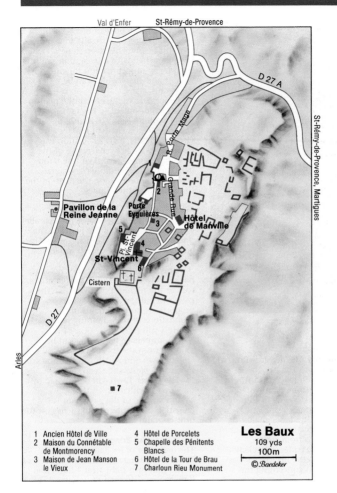

1 Ancien Hôtel de Ville
2 Maison du Connétable de Montmorency
3 Maison de Jean Manson le Vieux
4 Hôtel de Porcelets
5 Chapelle des Pénitents Blancs
6 Hôtel de la Tour de Brau
7 Charloun Rieu Monument

Les Baux
109 yds
100m
© Baedeker

Chapelle des Pénitents-Blancs
Opposite the church the square is closed off by the 17th c. Chapel of the White Penitents; inside can be seen some modern paintings by Yves Brayer.

Hôtel des Porcelets
On the left near the church stands the Hôtel des Porcelets, a 16th c. building which now houses Musée d'Art Moderne. On exhibition are works by modern artists, mainly from Provence.
Daily 8.30am–7pm, to sunset in winter; an entrance ticket for all museums and the Upper Town can be used here.

Hôtel de Manville
A lane going gently uphill on the left of the museum passes on the right the former Protestant church (Temple Protestant) and leads to the 16th c. Hôtel de Manville, with its beautiful inner courtyard. This now houses the office of the Mayor, the Office de Tourisme and the Musée d'Art Contemporain, which shows paintings, sculptures and photographs by Provençal artists.

Church of St-Vincent, Lower Town

Hôtel de la Tour-de-Brau

Coming from the Hôtel de Manville, rue des Fours and rue du Trencat, the latter a *chemin creux* (sunken road) cut into the rock, lead to the entrance to the Upper Town. The 14th c. Hôtel de la Tour-de-Brau on the right houses the Musée Archéologique et Lapidaire, exhibiting remains from the fortress and archaeological finds from the surrounding countryside – especially from graves of a Celtic necropolis – as well as information concerning the mining of bauxite.

★★Upper Town

The best time to visit the Upper Town is in the evening, in order to experience the special light when the sun goes down; the ticket office is open until 7pm.

Plateau

On the far side of the 12th c. Chapel of St-Blaise – which has been restored and contains an exhibition of olive production and processing – extends a large bare rocky plateau, the edge of which falls almost vertically to the foothills below. This steep slope should be approached with due caution, for it is completely unsecured and the often violent and gusty winds can be dangerous.

Quite near to the end of the plateau stands a monument to the Provençal poet Charloun Rieu (1846–1924), who belonged to the circle of *Félibres* around Frédéric Mistral. This association was responsible for the renaissance of the Provençal language and culture. From here there is a grandiose panorama across the Rhône valley, the plain of the Crau and over the Alpilles.

Ruins

The way to the ruined town runs parallel to the eastern edge of the plateau. The phenomenon of wind erosion which can be observed on the exposed surfaces is impressive.

Only scant remains of the château have survived. Right on the edge of the rock at the highest point is where the keep was built, with its spacious proportions; some remains of the foundations of the adjoining residential quarters still exist.

An impressive panorama can be enjoyed from the rocky crests round the Upper Town and which can be climbed by narrow paths and steep steps.

The Lower Town can be reached by a direct path which passes the Columbarium, or dove-cote, an Early Christian burial place with niches for the urns containing ashes.

★★Plâteau des Bringasses

The best view of les Baux is from the Plâteau des Bringasses; take the D27 road north, and turn right after 1 km. From here can be seen 'half of Provence', as well as Mont Ventoux and Lubéron, the Rhône valley and Camargue, Aix and Arles.

Cathédrale des Images

About halfway up to the Plâteau des Bringasses the road passes former quarries, some of which were underground. In one such quarry the artist Albert Plécy installed his *Cathedral of Images*, with slides on various subjects projected onto the giant stone walls some 400 m in length. Plécy's aim was to create a 'total picture', where the observer experienced the picture by actually standing within it rather than simply looking at it.

◎ *Mid–Mar. to mid–Nov. daily 10am–7pm.*

Surroundings

St-Rémy
See entry

Fontvieille
See Montmajour

Beaulieu-sur-Mer   G19–20

Département: Alpes-Maritimes
Altitude: sea level
Population: 4300

Beaulieu-sur-Mer, highly regarded as a marina, lies in the eastern part of the Côte d'Azur, about halfway between Nice and Monaco. Protected from the north winds by hills, Beaulieu-sur-Mer is a popular summer and winter resort. Abundant vegetation flourishes in the particularly mild climate.

Baie des Fourmis
The Baie des Fourmis (Bay of Ants), fringed by a palm-lined promenade, is picturesque.

On the spit of land that closes off the bay towards the north-east stands the **Villa Kerylos**, a reconstruction of an ancient Greek mansion. This building, which since 1928 has been owned by the Institut de France, has a remarkably fine interior with marble and bronze work, mosaics and furniture of the finest materials. However, only a very small number of these objects are in fact antique.

From the Baie des Fourmis avenue des Hellènes, boulevard Maréchal-Leclerc and the fine boulevard Alsace-Lorraine lead north-east to the yacht harbour which is one of the best on the French Mediterranean coast.

Petite Afrique
Not far east of Beaulieu the modern holiday seaside settlement of Petite Afrique (Little Africa) has been laid out. It is protected by steep cliffs up to 300 m high and has a good shingle beach.

Eze-Village and the Jardin Exotique

Èze

When travelling to Monaco on one of the Corniches de la Riviera (☞Suggested Routes, 2b), the two-part settlement of Èze is to be found 4 km north-east of Beaulieu.

★Èze-Village

Èze-Village, the old refuge settlement, has a picturesque situation 427 m up on a conical rock crowned by the ruins of a château from which there are marvellous views; it is still surrounded by 17th c. walls. In its narrow streets can be found many craft workshops and perfumeries. This is where Nietzsche drafted the third section of his *Thus spake Zarathustra* composition.

Of interest are the Musée d'Histoire Locale et d'Art Religieux (local history and religious art) and the Chapel of the Pénitents-Blancs with modern frescos by JM Poulin. The Jardin Exotique (exotic garden) offers flowering shrubs, cacti and a fine view.

Èze-Bord-de-Mer

On the coast, dominated by high cliffs, lies the fishing village of Èze-Bord-de-Mer. This place was already well known in antiquity and in more recent times has been developed into an important tourist centre.

St-Jean-Cap-Ferrat

This friendly villa colony is situated 4 km south-west of Beaulieu on the promontory of the same name, which extends far out into the sea. It has some excellent holiday residences and attractive gardens.

To the east of the picturesque village centre the Chapel of Ste-Hospice, with a bronze Madonna and a 16th c. tower, stands on the Pointe Ste-Hospice.

Musée Île-de-France

High above the sea in a magnificent park on the road towards Beaulieu is the Musée Île-de-France, founded by Ephrussi de Rothschild. It houses a ceiling fresco by Tiepolo, and paintings, furniture and other works of art from the 14th to the 19th c. from Europe and the Far East.

Cap-Ferrat

The most southerly tip of the peninsula is Cap-Ferrat with its lighthouse – well worth the climb – and a statue of the Virgin Mary.

Cagnes-sur-Mer   H18–19

Département: Alpes-Maritimes
Altitude: 77 m
Population: 35,500

Cagnes-sur-Mer, which consists of several parts, is situated about 12 km west of Nice on the far side of the Var river which flows into the Mediterranean at this point.

★Haut-de-Cagnes

Inland on a conical hill lies the picturesque village of Haut-de-Cagnes, with narrow little streets and houses built close together within the enclosing walls. It is overlooked by the 14th c. former Château Grimaldi. The château was taken over in 1536 and rebuilt at the beginning of the 17th c. Since 1939 it has been owned by the town and furnished as a museum, the Musée Ethnographique d'Olivier, Musée d'Art Méditerranéen Moderne and Musée Renoir du Souvenir, with an ethnographical collection, information about olive growing, works by Chagall, Matisse and Renoir. There is a fine view from the tower.

On the way towards the centre of the village stands the Chapel of Notre-Dame-de-la-Protection, with fine 16th c. frescos discovered 1936, and Maison les Colettes, the house in which Renoir (1841–1919) lived and died, a good example of Provençal architecture.

Cros-de-Cagnes

The historic fishing port of Cros-de-Cagnes, about 2 km south of the village at the mouth of the Cagne, is now a large seaside resort and yacht harbour.

Surroundings

La Colle-sur-Loup

This place, which is popular with artists, lies 6 km north-west of Cagnes, amid the fertile foothills of Vence, a scene of vineyards and flower growing. Of interest are the restored 12th c. church, and a chapel dating from the same period formerly owned by the monks of

Marina Baie des Anges ➤

Lérins. Nearby stands the Château le Gaudelet of King François I.

Villeneuve-Loubet

Situated 3 km south-west of Cagnes, Villeneuve-Loubet, originally a farming village and standing some 2 km from the coast high up on the left bank of the Loup, has a château, built originally in the 12th c., with a 30 m high defensive tower.

In the house where the famous chef Escoffier (1846–1935) was born there is a Museum of Culinary Art, displaying culinary objects of the 14th to 20th c. ⓒ *Tue.–Sun. 2–6pm; closed pub. hols.*

Marina Baie des Anges

A chain of low hills some 50 m high separates the old part of the village from the coastal settlement which was begun in 1930. Here apartment blocks built as pyramids and the new Marina Baie des Anges characterise the landscape.

Biot

See Antibes

★★Camargue   H–J 2–4

Département: Bouches-du-Rhône
Area: 92,000 ha

The marsh area of the Camargue – named after the Roman senator Camars who hailed from Arles – includes Grande Camargue, an area of some 720 sq km between the Grand Rhône and the Petit Rhône, the two arms of the river which divide just north of Arles, together with the Petite Camargue which covers an area of about 200 sq km west of the Petit Rhône. The river's western arm (Petit Rhône) forms the boundary between the regions of Provence-Alpes-Côte-d'Azur and Languedoc-Roussillon.

Agriculture

Camargue has been used for agriculture since the Middle Ages. It was probably at the end of the 13th c. that Arabs from Spain introduced rice to the marshes of the Camargue. Since 1942 rice growing has intensified, but subsequently declined as a result of competition and increased draining of the land. In recent years it has been revived, mainly in an attempt to help neutralise the salty nature of the soil. In 1985 50,000 tonnes of rice were grown here, equal to 18 per cent of France's requirements. The traditional rearing of beef cattle and horses, together with salt production and tourism, all play an important part in the economy of the region.

Landscape

In spite of tourism, parts of the Camargue are still completely isolated. The Camargue (Provençal Camargo) is a flat area with a thoroughly individual and often quite melancholy character. Over many centuries the Rhône has deposited detritus, sand and soil in its delta, pushing it ever further out into the sea. As a result, the historic port of Aigues-Mortes has receded some 5 km from the coastline in the course of some 600 years. While this has been happening in the western part of Camargue, the very opposite has occurred in the south-east; Stes-Maries-de-la-Mer, which was some distance inland during the Middle Ages, is now on the coast.

The part nearest the sea, around the lagoon of the Etang de Vaccarès, consists almost entirely of lagoons and reed marshes or dry salt expanses and dunes on which, in places, umbrella pines, juniper bushes and tamarisks thrive.

Waterfowl – in recent years there has been an increase of flamingos and herons – and even birds of prey are numerous; turtles and beavers can also be found. In winter especially, men on horseback (the traditional *gardians*) round up half-wild herds (*manades*) of small black bulls. The ancient breed of hardy Camargue horses (which are born black or brown and turn white at about four years) roam freely over the grassy marshland. They are ridden by the *gardians*, and in summer used at local festivities and hired out to tourists – in many places there are centres with Promenades à Cheval (horse-riding centres).

Drive through the Camargue

The best bases for a drive through the Camargue are Arles and St-Gilles (see entries). Road D570 coming from Arles – which is joined after 15 km near Albaron by the D37 from St-Gilles – leads south-west and ends in Stes-Maries-de-la-Mer (see entry). Initially the road runs through fields of sunflowers, rice fields and vineyards. As it nears the sea the landscape becomes more steppe-like and halophytes – plants well suited to the salty soil – take over.

Horses feeding in the marshes of the Camargue

Parc Régional de Camargue

This regional nature park was established in 1970; covering 820 sq km, it takes in roughly the whole of Grande Camargue. The aim is to preserve the traditional landscape, provide natural surroundings for the flora and fauna and foster tourism. The southern part, the Etang de Vaccarès (see below) and the adjoining coastal area have been a national reserve since 1975.

Musée Camarguais

Some 10 km south-west of Arles, on the marshy Plaine de Meyran, by the D570 just before Albaron, lies the Mas du Pont de Rousty. A one-time sheep farm now houses the Musée Camarguais, which provides information about the history of the region, its traditions and ways of life. A walk lasting some 1½ hours along a 3.5 km path will provide instruction on peasant life and rural conditions.

Apr.–Sep. daily 9.15am–5.45pm (Jul., Aug. to 6.45pm); Oct.–Mar. Wed–Mon 10.15am–4.45pm; Oct.–Mar.; closed pub. hols.

Centre d'Information

At the Etang de Ginès, a small coastal lake (about 4 km from Stes-Maries), the Centre d'Information de Ginès was established in 1976. It is dedicated to the first president of the Camargue Nature Park Foundation, François Huet (1905–72). An audio-visual display explains the geology and ecology of the Camargue. Between the information centre and the lake large windows afford a panoramic view of the bird sanctuary; telescopes are provided.

Apr.–Sep. daily 9am–12.30pm, 2–6pm; Oct.–Mar. Sat–Thu 9am–12.30pm, 2–6pm; closed pub. hols.

Parc Ornithologique
The Pont de Gau bird sanctuary covers more than 12 ha of marshland. Numerous species of birds, either native to the Camargue or resting during migration, can be observed. Many species which are difficult to observe in the wild can be seen here in aviaries constructed to be as near as possible to their native habitat.
◉ Mar.–Nov. daily 9am–sunset.

Etang de Vaccarès
Near Albaron (13th c. tower, remains of a fort) the D37 branches off from the D570, signposted Etang de Vaccarès. On the far side of Méjanes this road runs close to the Etang de Vaccarès surrounded by a girdle of reeds. This lake, which has an area of about 6000 ha – varying according to the water level – is by far the largest in the Camargue, but its average depth is only about 50 cm.
    Near Villeneuve the D36 B bears off to the right; this is a charming scenic stretch. It follows – often with fine views – the eastern shore of the lake which towards the south gives way to a number of lagoons dotted with sandbanks.

La Capelière
Here the Ministry of the Environment provides information regarding the Camargue National Reserve. There are also walkways with instruction boards and hides and observation huts.

Digue à la Mer
Near le Paradis, some 16 km south of Villeneuve, a little road branches off to the right. The path to the lighthouse, the Phare de la Gacholle, has to be negotiated on foot. There is a fine view from here, with a telescope for birdwatching. From there the road leads past the dyke known as Digue à la Mer as far as Stes-Maries-de-la-Mer (about 20 km). To the south lie more than 30 km of beaches of fine sand.

★Salin-de-Giraud
Near Salin-de-Giraud lie giant salt pans, where salt is obtained by the gradual evaporation of sea water. South of the village huge white heaps of salt are deposited. From an artificial hill, which is signposted, there is an extensive panorama of the mountains of sea salt and the huge evaporation basins, the water of which is coloured by microbes with shades of brown, red and violet.

Some of the salt undergoes further processing in chemical factories to produce bromide and magnesium salts.

La Palissade
The road now runs south between the embanked Rhône and the salt pans. Where the road leaves the river stands la Palissade Estate, which has exhibitions displaying flora and fauna from the Camargue, including slide-shows, a herbarium and an aquarium.
◉ Sep. 1st–Jun. 15th Mon.–Fri. 9am–5pm.

Plage de Piemanson
The road ends near the Plage de Piemanson, a broad beach of fine sand with no tourist facilities, lying at the eastern end of the Golfe du Lion.

The return journey can be made considerably more quickly on the D36, the course of which is parallel to the Rhône and which shortly before reaching Arles joins the D570. Alternatively, the Grand Rhône can be crossed by ferry near Salin-de-Giraud on to the D35, or the road via Martigues (see entry) and the Chaîne de l'Estaque to Marseille can be followed.

★Cannes   H 18

Département: Alpes-Maritimes
Altitude: sea level
Population: 73,000

The exclusive resort of Cannes marks the western end of the Côte d'Azur. It enjoys a sheltered situation on the wide Golfe de la Napoule, with the island group of the Îsles de Lérins offshore.

Because of its exceptionally mild climate, averaging 9.8°C in winter, its rich subtropical vegetation and its fine beach, Cannes is a tourist centre all year. After Paris, Cannes is the most important conference centre in France. The International Film Festival held in April–May is of particular importance.

History
Evidence of an early setlement on Mont Chevalier is shown by Celto-Ligurian finds. In the 2nd c. BC the Romans are said to have erected the Castrum Marsellinum here, and in the 11th c. a watchtower was built, around which a walled town later developed. In the

14th c. the town became part of Provence and in 1481 formed part of France. It only became a famous resort after having been discovered as a healthy place by the Englishman Lord Brougham (1778–1868), who had fled from Nice to Cannes to avoid a raging cholera epidemic. In 1838 the harbour was laid out, and 30 years later a beginning was made with a promenade along the shore.

Sights

Old Town

The le Suquet quarter, the Old Town, slopes up to Mont Chevalier (67 m), the summit of which is crowned by the 11th c. watchtower, from which there is a magnificent view. A few metres to the south stands the Musée de la Castre, which contains Egyptian, Phoenician, Etruscan, Greek and Roman antiques as well as art from the Far East and Central America.

North of the tower stands the Church of Notre-Dame-d'Espérance (1541–1648), with a notable 17th c. Madonna on the high altar and a wooden statue of St Anne, ca 1500.

Boulevard Jean-Hibert leads westward along the shore, passing the square of the same name, to the magnificent square Mistral. From here the 3 km boulevard du Midi connects with the Corniche de l'Esterel (Corniche d'Or).

Quartier Anglais

Above boulevard du Midi extends the Quartier Anglais (English Quarter) with its sumptuous villas. Boulevard Leader leads up to the Croix des Gardes. situated 164 m above sea-level in a copse of mimosa which blooms in February and March. This is a fine viewpoint with the best light towards evening. 1 km to the north-west the Rocher de Roquebillière lies 130 m above the little river of the same name.

★Vieux Port

To the east below the Old Town lies the Vieux Port, or Old Port, also known as Port Cannes I; at its north-eastern corner is the Gare Maritime (Marine Railway Station), built in 1957.

To the north the port is bordered by the pretty allées de la Liberté which are lined with plane trees. In the mornings

Hotel Carlton in Cannes, the epitome of the Côte d'Azur

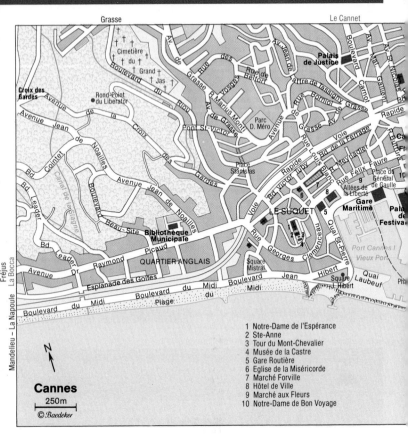

Grasse · Le Cannet

1 Notre-Dame de l'Espérance
2 Ste-Anne
3 Tour du Mont-Chevalier
4 Musée de la Castre
5 Gare Routière
6 Eglise de la Miséricorde
7 Marché Forville
8 Hôtel de Ville
9 Marché aux Fleurs
10 Notre-Dame de Bon Voyage

Cannes
250m
© Baedeker

the fine Marché aux Fleurs (Flower Market) is held here. At the western end of the allées stands the Hôtel de Ville (Town Hall) built in 1874–6.

Rue Félix-Faure, which runs parallel on the north, and its eastern extension, rue d'Antibes, are the town's main shopping streets.

Le Cannet
From the northern edge of the Inner Town the broad boulevard Carnot winds northwards to the beautifully situated villa settlement of le Cannet from which there are fine views.

★Palais des Festivals
On the east side of the Old Port, at

1 boulevard de la Croisette, stands the Palais des Festivals, opened in 1982. It is an impressive complex of buildings with three large auditoriums. There are eleven conference rooms, two exhibition halls, a casino, a nightclub and a restaurant. The annual film festival is held here.

★Boulevard de la Croisette
The centre of tourist activity is boulevard de la Croisette, which extends eastward from the Palais des Festivals along the Rade de Cannes, with its fine sandy beach; from it there is a magnificent view of the gulf and the offshore Îles de Lérins (Lérin Islands; see below). The boulevard is

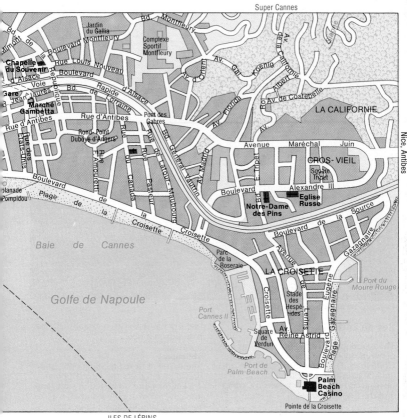

ILES DE LÉRINS

dominated by luxury hotels – some from the belle époque – and fashionable shops.

In the yacht harbour lies the pirate ship Neptune, built as the backdrop for an adventure film.

The eastern section of the boulevard bends south at the fine Parc de la Roseraie, skirts the new port layout of the Port Pierre Canto and ends at the southern tip of the Pointe de la Croisette by the Port du Palm-Beach and the Palm Beach Casino. On the east side of the peninsula the pleasant boulevard Eugène-Gazagnaire, with its fine beach, leads north to the Port du Moure-Rouge.

La Californie

From the eastern part of boulevard de la Croisette the road leads northwards through the district of Cros-Veil on the far side of the railway – where the Église Russe (Russian Church) on boulevard Alexandre-III is well worth seeing – to the especially charming part of the town known as la Californie, where Picasso lived in 1955. This area is overlooked by the Observatoire de Super-Cannes, which is 325 m high and has an observation tower, orientation table and the terminus of the funicular. Below, on boulevard des Pins, stands the notable Mémorial St-Georges, erected in memory of the duke of Albany.

The Vieux Port and le Suquet, the Old Town of Cannes

Îles de Lérins

The island group of the Îles de Lérins lies
between the Golfe de la Napoule and the
Golfe Juan. The two principal islands are
Ste-Marguerite and St-Honorat. The ferry
plies several times a day between Cannes
and the islands 4 km out.

History
As early as the 5th and 6th c. the islands
were an important centre of monastic
life. In the year 660 the monastery
assumed the Rule of St Benedict. Attacks
by the Saracens and later by pirates from
Genoa troubled the monks severely, and
in the 16th c. the convent began to
decline into obscurity.

Ste-Marguerite
Ste-Marguerite, 3 km long and up to 1
km wide, is the largest island of the
group and is covered with eucalyptus
and pine woods. On its northern side
stands a 17th c. fort, fortified by
Vauban, which served for a long time as
a prison. Towards the end of the 17th c.
the man known as the *Masque de Fer*
(Man in the Iron Mask), who was
surrounded in secrecy and whose

identity has never been established, was
held prisoner here.

St-Honorat
About 700 m from Ste-Marguerite, and
linked by ferry, lies the Île St-Honorat,
1.5 km long and up to 400 m wide, and
also covered with pine woods. On a
tongue of land in the south lie the
monastery buildings, which were once
fortified and, it is believed, were a
foundation of St Honoratus, bishop of
Arles, who died in 429. In the south by
the sea stands the impressive Château St-
Honorat, the tower built in the 11th c. as
a refuge against pirates and later altered;
there are beautiful cloisters on the
ground floor and on the first floor, and
extensive views.

There were formerly seven chapels
scattered about the island, but today the
only two remaining are the Chapel of St-
Sauveur, an Early Christian building,
with a diameter of almost 10 m, and the
Chapel of the Trinité, an early medieval
cemetery chapel.

Surroundings

Mandelieu-la-Napoule

The twin villages of Mandelieu-la-Napoule are situated 5 km west of Cannes between the mouths of the rivers Siagne and Argentière at the foot of the Massif du Tanneron, surrounded by mimosa plantations for the perfume industry.

Picturesquely situated by the sea and popular as a holiday resort, the village sector of la Napoule-Plage is overlooked by a restored 14th c. château (art exhibitions) standing on a porphyry rock.

From the nearby hill of San Peire, rising to 131 m above sea level and with a ruined chapel, there is a view of the coast, with apartment blocks and marinas.

Théoule-sur-Mer

In the western part of the Golfe de la Napoule lies the resort of Théoule-sur-Mer, which has an 18th c. soap works by the sea, remodelled into a mansion, and a harbour which dates from the 17th c. The slopes are lined with tiers of apartments in traditional Sardinian style;

in the vicinity of the yacht harbours Port de la Rague and Port de la Galère to the south lies Pointe de l'Aiguille, above which the settlement of Théoule-Supérieur is renowned as a holiday destination.

Vallauris-Golfe-Juan

The locality above the Golfe-Juan, 5 km north-east of Cannes, with the seaside estate of the same name, was originally called Vallis Aurea (golden valley). This little town with its potteries, vineyards and orange groves once belonged to the monks of Lérins.

The only relic of the Middle Ages is the Romanesque chapel; between 1952 and 1959 Picasso painted his famous picture *War and Peace* in the beautiful crypt. The monastery, which was fortified in the 12th c., was destroyed in 1569 and rebuilt during the Renaissance. Today it houses the Musée National d'Art Moderne (museum of modern art). In front of the church – where there is a market in the morning – stands Picasso's sculpture *Man with a Sheep*.

Pottery has been important in Vallauris since the time of the Romans. After the

Boulevard de la Croisette, the famous artery of Cannes

Man with a Sheep by Picasso

second world war the presence of Pablo Picasso gave the place a fresh impetus. Here in 1946 Picasso got to know the ceramic artists Suzanne and Georges Ramié and became enthusiastic about this medium. Today there are about a hundred potters working in Vallauris and their products are sold in the streets. The biennial pottery fair assures the future of this craft. The Madoura workshop near avenue Clémenceau, headed by Alain Ramié, still produces pottery based on Picasso's designs as well as some fine work of its own.

Carpentras   E 6

Département: Vaucluse
Altitude: 102 m
Population: 26,000

The little industrial town of Carpentras lies between Mont Ventoux to the north-east and the Plateau de Vaucluse to the south-east, in a plain which is open to the Rhône. The Auzon river flows north of the town centre.

History
The town is descended from the ancient Carpentoracte which, from 1320 until the French Revolution in 1789, was the capital of the papal county of Venaissin. From 1342 onwards it offered special protection to Jews and – as in Cavaillon and Avignon – they had their own quarter in the town.

Sights

St-Siffrein
In the town centre stands the former Gothic cathedral of St-Siffrein, started in 1405 and consecrated in 1519. The stump of a tower remain on either side of the west facade which was altered in the 17th c. but which nevertheless remains incomplete; in more recent times another tower was added on the south side. The south doorway of 1470–80, the Porte Juive (Jews' Gate), shows the late Gothic flamboyant style. Jews who wished to be baptised would enter by this doorway.

The nave has six bays, the last two combined into a vault, and is flanked by chapels. The differing texture of the walls bear witness to the long building period. The interior of the church is richly decorated and includes a number of remarkable panels as well as an altarpiece consisting of a radiant halo of gilded wood (1694) by Jacques Bernus. In a chapel to the left of the choir is a collection of religious art.

On the north side of the church are the remains of the Romanesque predecessor and a Roman triumphal arch dating from the 1st c. AD, which had been incorporated in the Romanesque church, and on the narrow side of which prisoners and trophies of war are represented. The prisoners, a German and possibly an Armenian, wear different attire.

Palais de Justice
Adjoining the north side of the church is the Palais de Justice, which was built in 1640 in imitation of Italian baroque. It was formerly the episcopal palace. The interior has some magnificently furnished rooms including the Bishop's Room (18th c. prayer-desk), the Council Room and the Criminal Court (cartouches with views of the towns of the Venaissin). A permit to visit can be obtained from the Office de Tourisme.

Museums

The most important museums of Carpentras are housed in a large mansion (on boulevard Albin-Durand) in the west of the Old Town.

The Musée Comtadin has collections of the ethnology of the region. The Musée Duplessis possesses several notable panels by local painters (Duplessis, Laurens) as well as some of Italian and Dutch origin; the Musée Sobirats houses artistic crafts.

🔘 *Wed.–Mon. 10am–noon, 2–6pm.*

The Musée Lapidaire, in the Chapel of the Pénitents-Gris (5 rue Stes-Maries) has finds from the Iron Age to the early Middle Ages as well as a collection of natural history. Visits by arrangement with the Musée Comtadin.

Bibliothèque Inguimbertine

The Bibliothèque Inguimbertine, the municipal library, is housed in the north wing of the museum complex. It is named after Bishop d'Inguimbert (in office 1735–57), a bibliophile who bought up numerous libraries. Later the collection was increased by donations, so that today there are about 220,000 volumes available as well as manuscripts and prints.

🔘 *Mon. 2–6.30pm, Tue.–Fri. 9.30am–4.30pm, Sat. 9.30am–noon.*

Synagogue

The Synagogue of Carpentras, the Maison de Prières (place Maurice-Charretier) is the oldest remaining in France. It was built in 1367, restored 1741–3 and again in 1929 and 1958. On the ground floor and in the basement are the ritual baths, some partly dating from the 14th c., as well as the kosher bakery; on the first floor is the place of worship which received its present furnishings in the 18th c.

🔘 *Mon.–Fri. 10am–noon, 3–5pm, closed pub. hols.*

Hôtel-Dieu

The Hôtel-Dieu (hospital; 1750) on place Aristide-Briand also goes back to the time of Bishop d'Inguimbert. This two-storey classical building at the southern end of the town centre comprises an inner courtyard with two fountains; a monumental staircase leads to the upper floor. On the ground floor the pharmacy

Cathédrale St-Siffrein: Porte Juive

with its original furnishings is of interest.

⊙ *Mon., Wed., Thu. 9–11.30 am.*

Surroundings

Venasque
South-east of Carpentras (11 km) the village of Venasque has a picturesque situation on the Vaucluse. Here the 13th c. church and the baptistery (6th and 12th c.) are worthy of note.

★Gorges de la Nesque
The Gorges of the Nesque is reached from Carpentras by driving east along D942 to Villes-sur-Auzon (17 km) or as a continuation of the drive over Mont Ventoux (see entry). The gorge with grey and light-brown rock walls begins a few kilometres beyond the picturesque village of Monieux (12th c. tower; medieval houses and gates). The road follows the right bank of the Nesque and in about 6 km reaches a viewpoint (*belvédère*; marked by pillars). Opposite is the deeply fissured Rocher de Cire (872 m). At the exit from the gorge there is a magnificent view of the cultivated plain around Carpentras to the south of Mont Ventoux.

Castellane   F 15

Département: Alpes-de-Haute-Provence
Altitude: 724 m
Population: 1400

The small town of Castellane lies in the south-east of Provence (54 km south-east of Digne) on the Route Napoléon (☛Suggested Routes, 3a) and on the Verdon river (see entry), which to the west flows through the well-known gorges. Castellane is, therefore, important as the starting point for a visit to the Grand Canyon du Verdon.

Town
On the northern edge of Castellane there are remains of the town walls, the most important relic of which is the Tour Pentagonale (five-angled tower).

At the western edge of the Old Town with its narrow streets rises the picturesque Tour de l'Horloge (14th c. clock tower). Of interest here are the Fountaine aux Lions (Lion Fountain; partly Romanesque) and the Church of St-Victor, originally 12th c. but altered later on several occasions.

The mighty rock of Castellane

Vineyards at Châteauneuf-du-Pape

Notre-Dame-du-Roc

Over the little town towers a mighty
outcrop, 184 m high, on which stands
the little pilgrimage chapel of Notre-
Dame-du-Roc (1703). On the rock there
was once a Celtic oppidum which later
became Petra Castellana. In the 14th c.
the settlement was moved into the valley
and surrounded by a wall. To the rear of
the parish church at the eastern end of
the Old Town (not particularly
important) a path leads to the rear of the
limestone block and past the Stations of
the Cross up to the top, from where
there is a good view of Castellane and of
the river as it flows into the gorge.

Châteauneuf-du-Pape   E 4–5

Département: Vaucluse
Altitude: 117 m
Population: 2100

The famous wine town of Châteauneuf-
du-Pape lies between Orange and
Avignon in a gently undulating
landscape near the left bank of the
Rhône away from the main road.

Viticulture

Châteauneuf-du-Pape is the centre of an
area exclusively devoted to the growing
of vines, as the pebbly soil is unsuitable
for any other form of agriculture. From
some 3200 ha of vineyards 9.1 million
litres of wine are produced, 98 per cent
of which is red wine, considered to rank
with the wines of Bordeaux and
Burgundy as one of the best in France.
According to the *appellation controlée* the
wine must contain 12.5 per cent of
alcohol, the highest in France (it actually
contains 13–14 per cent). The wine is
made from 13 varieties of grape, so that
its character depends on the
establishment in which it is produced.

Châteauneuf-du-Pape is a strong, full-
bodied wine which takes at least four or
five years to reach maturity. A lighter
wine has been successfully produced
which can be drunk when it is younger,
but this is not the traditional
Châteauneuf-du-Pape.

The impetus for the standardisation
of the quality of wine and the
corresponding grading originated in
Châteauneuf (☛Practical Information,
Wine).

There are many opportunities to visit

the wine cellars and to taste the wines (*visite de cave, dégustation de vins*). The Caves du Père Anselme is aimed at tourists and has a Musée des Outils de Vignerons, with interesting exhibits on the history of viticulture. The cellars and bottling plant can also be visited. The wines on sale here, although not cheap, are not of the highest quality.
◎ *Daily 9am–noon, 2–6pm.*

Town
Châteauneuf-du-Pape lies on a gently sloping hill, clustered about the ruins of the château that the popes built as a summer residence at the time of their exile in Avignon and which gave the place its name. Only the high tower and remains of the walls survive, but there are rewarding views of Avignon, the Dentelles de Montmirail and Mont Ventoux.

★★Corniches de la Riviera

See Suggested Routes, 2b

Digne   E 13

Département: Alpes-de-Haute-Provence
Altitude: 608 m
Population: 17,000

Digne lies in the heart of Provence, approximately on a line joining Grenoble and Cannes, in the foothills of the Alps. It is a spa, the headquarters of lavender growing and the centre of the Hautes-Alpes nature reserve.

Town
The 15th c. Cathedral of St-Jérome has an elevated situation in the Old Town. In the Romanesque former cathedral of Notre-Dame-du-Bourg (12th–13th c.) are remains of wall paintings of the 14th–16th c. as well as a Merovingian altar.

Surroundings

Lac de Serre-Ponçon
There is a rewarding 60 km drive from Digne northwards (at first not on the direct road D900 but west of this on the D900A) through the Clue de Barles and the Clue de Verdaches, two romantic gorges; then over the Col de Maure

(1347 m) to the Lac de Serre Ponçon (☛Gap). After leaving le Vernet on the return journey take the D900 instead of the D900A and cross the Col du Labouret (1240 m).

Donzère-Mondragon   D 4

Région: Rhône-Alpes
Département: Drôme
Altitude: 64 m

The Rhône Dam was constructed to the north of Bollène on an arm of the Rhône between the two villages of Donzère and Mondragon (between Montélimar and Orange) and this gives it its name.

Rhône Dam
Between Donzère (in the north) and Mondragon (in the south) the 28 km-long Canal de Donzère avoids a narrow stretch of the Rhône, into which flow the rivers Conche and Ardèche (see entry). The Usine de Bollène, one of the river power stations, lies not far north of the village of the same name. As well as the buildings housing the turbines, it includes a lock for canal traffic. The construction was completed in 1952. On the downstream side a road crosses the canal and on the west side of this there is a car park. The interior of the power station is not open to the public.
    A short way downstream from Bollène there is a very good view of the canal from the suspension bridge carrying the D994 to Pont-St-Esprit (☛Ardèche).

Complexe Eurodif
About 2 km north of the dam lies the Complexe Eurodif, a diffusion plant for the enrichment of uranium, together with its associated installations. Its capacity is sufficient to produce some 25 per cent of the world demand for enriched uranium and it is therefore of great importance for the economic development of the Tricastin area. Eurodif is a joint project of Belgium, France, Italy and Spain.
    The four heavy-water reactors of the Tricastin nuclear power station, each with a capacity of 900 MW, produce over 20,000 million kilowatt-hours of electricity annually.

★Draguignan H 14

Département: Var
Altitude: 181 m
Population: 28,000

Draguignan lies about 27 km inland of Fréjus, north of the Massif des Maures and the Valley of the Argens river which borders these mountains.

History

In the 5th c. the area was converted by Hermentarius, the first bishop of Antibes. According to legend the bishop had won the confidence of the inhabitants by killing a dragon that had threatened the whole countryside and laid it to waste. The name of the town also recalls this episode; it appears to be derived from 'dragon' and the legendary monster figures in the arms of the town.

In the 17th c. when Anne of Austria was acting as regent for her under-aged son Louis XIV, the town was surrounded by a defensive wall. During the French Revolution Draguignan was the district capital and then the capital of the *département* of Var.

Townscape

The historic centre of Draguignan is clustered about the Tour de l'Horloge (clock tower) which stands on a rock from which there is a fine view. Normally the tower is closed but the key can be obtained at the Office de Tourisme. The broad streets south of the Old Town, which are unusual in a small town, were laid out by Baron Haussmann who was largely responsible for the infrastructure of Paris (he was prefect there from 1853 to 1870).

★Museum

Not far north-west of the clock tower, rue de la République, stands a former 17th c. Ursuline convent which was later the summer residence of the bishop of Fréjus. It now houses a museum which has a number of treasures (Rembrandt: *Child blowing soap-bubbles*; Franz Hals: *Kitchen Interior*, as well as paintings by van Loo, J Parrocel and Ziem, and a sculpture by Camille Claudel. Also notable are ceramics (Moustiers, Sèvres), furniture, French and Flemish 17th c. paintings, an illuminated manuscript of the *Roman de la Rose*, the most important work of courtly poetry in France (12th c.) and an illustrated Bible in Latin

with 2000 engravings, which dates from 1493 and which came from a workshop in Nuremberg.
ⓖ *Tue.–Sat. 10–11.30am, 3–6pm.*

Surroundings

Lorgues

The little town of Lorgues, 13 km south-west of Draguignan, is a centre for the production of olives and olive oil; it has a beautiful Old Town and a fine boulevard lined with plane trees. In the classical Collégiale St-Martin (parish church; 17th c.) can be seen a statue of the Virgin which is attributed to Pierre Puget.

Le Thoronet

See entry

★Entrecastaux

Entrecastaux, situated to the west of Draguignan (31 km via Salernes, or about 20 km from le Thoronet) has an impressive château; this dates essentially from the 17th c. and was the seat of the comte de Grignan, the stepson of Madame de Sévigné (☞Grignan). The

Draguignan: Tour d'Horloge

Entrevaux: town gate and citadel

château, which is open to the public, has been renovated and contains furniture and objets d'art. The spacious park was laid out by Le Nôtre who was also responsible for the park of Versailles. Entrecastaux itself, a typical medieval Provençal village, with narrow streets and house facades, is a protected monument. Worth seeing are the fortified Church of St-Sauveur, the 17th c. washing place and Nôtre-Dame-de- l'Aube, which dates from the 12th c.

★Entrevaux   F 16

Département: Alpes-de-Haute-Provence
Altitude: 515 m
Population: 700

Amid the picturesque scenery of the upper reaches of the Var river, 43 km north-east of Castellane and 70 km north-west of Nice, lies the town of Entrevaux on the left bank of the river. 135 m above the village towers a steep rocky crag crowned by a citadel. The finest view of the township and the citadel is to be had from the road to the Col de Felines/Col de Buis, which winds its way up the valley above the village.

History
Entrevaux was founded in the 11th c. Because of its position Louis XIV ordered Vauban to build new fortifications during the war between France and Savoy. In 1693 he linked the citadel with the village and had bastions and towers erected.

Entrevaux is the birthplace of Augustin Bonnetty (1798–1879) the founder of the Annales de la Philosophie Chrétienne.

Sights

Cathédrale
The cathedral (built 1610–27) is partly baroque, partly classical. The main altar has a fine retable depicting the Assumption of the Virgin Mary, which like the choir stalls dates from the 17th c. The *Descent from the Cross* (on the left) is ascribed to Jouvenet. On the left of the entrance stands the silver reliquary bust of St John the Baptist. Every year on the Saturday preceding June 24th this reliquary is taken to the Church of St-Jean-du-Desert, 12 km away. On the Sunday afternoon the solemn procession of the St-Jeannistes, wearing local uniforms, carries the bust back, running the last hundred metres through the town.

Motocycle museum
An old house on rue Serpente contains a small motorcycle museum. The oldest machine dates from 1901; all are in working order.

Steam trains
Entrevaux lies on the narrow-gauge railway Annot-Puget-Théniers, part of the line from Nice to Digne (☛Practical Information, Railways). On some Sundays from the beginning of May until the end of October a special train operates on this line; it is hauled by a steam locomotive of the Mallet type, built in 1923 by Henschel in Kassel, and is made up of old carriages. Information – indispensible, since there is only one return journey – can be obtained from:
CHEMINS DE FER DE LA PROVENCE
Gare du Sud, 33 avenue Malausséna, 06000 Nice
☎*0493882856.*

★Esterel (Massif de l'Esterel) H–J 16–17

Départements: Var, Alpes-Maritimes
Altitude: up to 618 m

The Esterel Mountains rise immediately behind the coast between St-Raphaël in the west and Cannes in the east. They are bordered in the north by the valley of the Argentière and in the west by the valley of the Reyran.

Topography

The Esterel Mountains are formed of volcanic rock, predominantly of porphyry, the characteristic red colour of which is a feature of the landscape. The conifers, cork oaks and coriaceous trees, which cover the entire massif, regularly fall victim to forest fires.

★Mont Vinaigre

The highest peak of the Esterel Mountains is Mont Vinaigre (618 m) near to its northern escarpment. It can be reached from Fréjus (see entry) on road N7, from which in 11 km a narrow forest road branches off. There is an extensive panorama from the summit.

★Pic de l'Ours

From the coastal village of Agay (☞St-Raphaël), situated on the Corniche de l'Esterel, a road leads inland and encircles (mostly as a single-track road) the Pic de l'Ours (496 m). This summit in the eastern part of the mountain range, from which there is an extensive view, is best reached from the nearby Col Nôtre-Dame, to which the mountain road climbs with numerous bends. From this stretch of road there are magnificent views of the indented rocky coast. It takes about 30 min. climbing to reach the summit of the Pic de l'Ours on which there is a radio and television transmitter. The panorama from here is breathtaking.

★Corniche de l'Esterel

The Corniche de l'Esterel (N98) is a charming road which winds its way along the rocky coast between St-Raphaël and Cannes. It runs through the resort of Boulouris, passes the impressive Cap du Drammont (lighthouse; offshore the little Île d'Or) and the village of Agay, which has a fine situation on a bay; on Pointe de la Baumette is a memorial to the aviator and writer

The coast of the Esterel Massif

Antoine de St-Exupéry. The road continues through Anthéor with the Pic du Cap-Roux (452 m; rewarding view) rising on the left, le Trayas, Miramar (with a marina), la Galère (in the holiday complex of Port-la-Galère are some remarkable grotto-like houses) and Théoule-sur-Mer. Cannes is then reached via la Napoule.

Étang de Berre   H–J 6–7

Département: Bouches du Rhône
Area: 15,000 ha

The Étang de Berre is a large lagoon to the north-west of Marseille. It is separated from the Mediterranean by the Chaîne de l'Estaque in the south, a ridge up to 279 m high; to the west extends the Plaine de la Crau.

Topography
The Étang de Berre is a popular recreation area for the people of Marseille district; nevertheless on the southern and eastern shores there is a great deal of industry as well as the large airport of Marseille Marignane and its associated satellite towns. The northern shore, however, with its quiet little communities and gentle landscape is reminiscent of the atmosphere of the lakes in northern Italy.
(☛Suggested Routes, 1c)

Martigues
See entry

Salon
See entry

★Fontaine-de-Vaucluse   F 6

Département: Vaucluse
Altitude: 80 m
Population: 600

The little village of Fontaine-de-Vaucluse, well known for its spring (the source of the Sorgue river) and for the Italian poet and humanist Petrarca, lies in the west of Provence about 30 km east of Avignon.
   The village, although often thronged with tourists, is charmingly situated at the end of the valley. The surrounding hills (*vallis clausa*) has given the place its name. Fontaine-de-Vaucluse can be reached on a byroad; there are extensive parking places near the village centre.

History
Fontaine-de-Vaucluse was made famous by the Italian poet and humanist Francesco Petrarca (Petrarch; 1304–74). He was born in Arezzo in Italy but took up residence in the papal town of Avignon and later withdrew to his country seat in the Vaucluse where he devoted himself entirely to his literary pursuits.

Sights

★Village
In the centre of the village lies the pretty place de la Colonne, shaded by plane trees; the column commemorating Petrarch was erected in 1804 to mark the 500th year of his birth. Around the square are restaurants and bars, some with terraces by or above the river.
   On the right bank of the Sorgue, in the house in which Petrarch is reputed to have lived, there is a little museum devoted to the poet and his works.
ⓖ *Apr. 15th–Oct. 15th Wed.–Mon. 9.30am–noon, 2–6.30pm; at other periods Sat., Sun. only.*

Church of St-Véran
Leaving the car park and before reaching place de la Colonne there can be seen on the right the Romanesque Church of St-Véran, dating from the first half of the 12th c.; in the crypt is the grave of St Véran who was Bishop of Cavaillon in the 6th c.

Musée d'Histoire
The interesting Musée d'Histoire was opened in 1990 in a former paper factory on the road to the source of the Sorgue. It is dedicated to the 'dark years' of the German occupation and the Resistance in the Vaucluse. Themes include the trauma of defeat, everyday life and its difficulties and the collaboration of the Pétain government with the Nazis.
ⓖ *Sep. 1st–Oct. 15th, Apr. 15th–Jun. 30th Wed.–Mon. 10am–noon, 2–6pm; Jul.–Aug. 10am–8pm; Oct. 16th–Dec. 31st Sat., Sun. 10am–noon, 1–5pm; Mar. 1st–Apr. 14th Sat., Sun. 10am–noon, 2–6pm.*

Fontaine de Vaucluse
The Fontaine de Vaucluse is a resurgent spring at the foot of a vertical rock wall

200 m high. Water seeping through the limestone of the Plateau de Vaucluse emerges here, and according to the amount of precipitation the level of the water and the force of the spring vary considerably. It is most impressive in the spring, when the snow is melting.

It is reached by a 800 m roadway which is generally only passable on foot because of the numerous stalls selling souvenirs of all kinds; there are no parking facilities. On the right at the edge of the village and by the river is a cave museum, Le Monde Souterrain.

Ⓖ Daily 10am–noon, 2–6.30pm; guided tours every 30 minutes which provide information about the nearby spring.

Further along the path is a paper mill with a great waterwheel, which has now been set up as a workshop open to the public in which paper is made according to 15th c. methods.

On the mountain spur on the far side of the river, which appears turquoise green on account of the water plants, are the ruins of the château built by the bishops of Cavaillon. The roadway continues upwards into the narrowing valley beside the river which is fringed with ancient plane trees and which rushes down in foaming cascades (hidden beneath the rocks when the water level is low). Set into the rock on the left above a small spring can be seen a tablet, placed here in 1963 by the Dante Society in memory of Petrarch and his beloved Laura.

Valley of Fontaine-de-Vaucluse

Surroundings

Branching of the Sorgue

Shortly before reaching the township of l'Isle-de-la-Sorgue the river divides into two arms. One winds its way northwards to Velleron, a typical Provençal village; the other flows through l'Isle to Thor, where the Romanesque Church of Nôtre-Dame-du-Lac (12th c.) towers above the water like a shipwreck.

L'Isle-sur-la-Sorgue

After the tourist attractions of Fontaine-de-Vaucluse the atmosphere of the former little industrial town of l'Isle-sur-la-Sorgue (17 km from Fontaine and 23 km from Avignon) comes as a welcome relief. By the Sorgue, which divides here into several canals and reminds the visitor of Venice, 70 watermills used to provide power for paper making, cereal production, oil pressing, woollen and silk mills and a tannery. A few watermills still exist and have been restored, including those on avenue des Quatre-Otages (on the edge of the park), in place E-Char and place V-Hugo.

The church dates from the 17th c. and has a richly decorated interior; during the Revolution the art treasures which had been confiscated from five abbeys were assembled here and formed one of the finest baroque collections in Provence. Other buildings worth seeing are the public corn store of 1779 (now the Office de Tourisme), the Hôtel Donadeï de Campredon, an L-shape palace of 1773–5 (rue du Dr-Tallet; exhibitions of important artists) and the Hospital (place des Fr-Bruns) with its wrought-iron gate of 1762 and the wood-panelled Apothecary, which houses a collection of Moustiers vessels and a gigantic bronze mortar.

★Fréjus   J 16

Département: Var
Altitude: 21 m
Population: 42,000

The town of Fréjus is situated in the
western section of the French Riviera
between the Massif des Maures and the
Massif de l'Esterel. Not far to the south-
west the Argens river flows into the
Mediterranean.

History
Whether the site of the Forum Julii,
founded by Caesar, was already settled in
pre-Roman times has not been
conclusively proved. Under Emperor
Augustus the place became a port and
was linked to the sea by a canal 1200 m
long and 30 m wide. In the 4th c. Fréjus
became the see of a bishop, and in the
10th c. it suffered from attacks by
Saracens. From the 12th c. onwards the
development was hindered by epidemics
of plague. The harbour had to be finally
abandoned in the 18th c. because of
silting. In August 1944 Allied forces
landed here.

The breaching of the Malpasset Dam
in 1959 was a catastrophe. The mighty
rush of water down the valley caused 421
deaths and buried the town under mud.

Fréjus: the cathedral cloister

Cathédrale

The cathedral, built in the 11th and
12th c., is almost completely surrounded
by other buildings; only the doorway
leading into the narthex (lobby) is
visible from the outside. Above rises the
tower with its spire, rectangular in the
lower part but octagonal above.
The narthex of the cathedral is entered
through the south doorway with its
impressive Renaissance doors (1530),
which, however, are usually protected by
wooden shutters and are shown only on
guided tours. Some of the carvings are
ornamental, others represent scenes from
the lives of the Virgin Mary, St Peter and
St Paul; in the borders can be seen
symbols of the Saracen wars.
◉ *Apr.–Sep. Wed.–Mon. 9am–7pm;
Oct.–Mar. Wed.–Mon. 9.30am–noon,
2–5.30pm; guided tours.*

★Baptistery
To the left of the narthex is the
Baptistery, a pre-Romanesque octagonal
building of the 4th or 5th c. The
arcades are borne on eight pillars; six of
these came from antique buildings
(three pairs of differing marble). In the
centre stands the font. There were
originally two doors to the chapel; the
person to be baptised came in through
the lower door and left by the higher
one.

Interior
Inside the cathedral can be seen, left of
the entrance, two marble tombs
(17th c.), a wooden Crucifix (16th c.)
and a beautiful 16–part altarpiece (15th
c.) by Jacques Durandi (d ca 1470; Nice
school); in the chapel to the left of the
high altar are two other bishops' tombs
(14th and 15th c.).

★Cloister
Steps from the narthex give access to
the two-storey cloister. It is composed
of delicate pillars and in the coffered
ceiling can be seen a cycle of scenes
from the Apocalypse, dating from the
14th and 15th c., not all of which have
been preserved. In the middle of the
cloister is a well, 16 m deep.

Musée Archéologique
On the north side of the cloister is a
double staircase, the steps of which were
once used as seats for the nearby Roman
amphitheatre. The upper storey of the
cloister was originally also enclosed on
all four sides, but a great deal was
destroyed in the French Revolution; only
one side of the gallery now remains. In
the adjoining room can be found the
Musée Archéologique with a Roman
mosaic floor and other finds of Greek
and Roman times.

Other Sights

Arènes
The Roman amphitheatre on rue Henri-
Vadon dates from 1st–2nd c. AD. It
measures 114 × 82 m and once
accommodated up to 10,000 spectators.
To a great extent it is unrestored and also
largely free of modern buildings. On the
north side the oval leans against the
slope, while on the south side an
elaborate vaulted construction supports
the steps from below.
*Apr.–Sep. Wed.–Mon. 9.30–11.45am
2–6.15pm; Oct.–Mar. Wed.–Mon.
9–11.45am, 2–4.15pm.*

Aqueduct
In the north-east of the town, on the N7,
there are remains of the Roman
aqueduct which brought water from the
Esterel Mountains.

Roman theatre
Not far west of the aqueduct are the
remains of a Roman theatre laid out in a
semicircle.

Pagoda
Outside Fréjus to the north, on the road
leading to the Esterel Mountains, can be
seen a pagoda, an unconventional sight
with its vivid coloration.

Fondation Daniel Templon
This private museum in the Capitou
industrial zone houses a collection of
major works by sculptors from the
region. Access is by the D37 to the
junction with the A8 in the direction of
Cannes; at the roundabout immediately
before the tollbooth turn into the
industrial zone, then along the A8.
Tue.–Sun. 1.30–5.30pm.

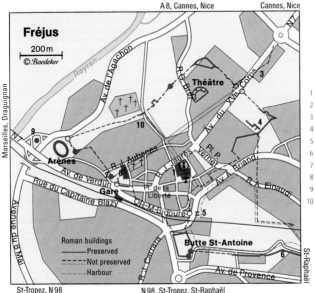

1 Cathedral/Cloister
2 Hôtel de Ville
3 Aqueduct
4 Platform (Praetorium)
5 Porte d'Oree
6 Lanterne d'Auguste
7 Porte des Gaules
8 St-François-de-Paule
9 Columns
10 Porte d'Agachon

Surroundings

Barrage de Malpasset

Access: follow road D37 which leads to the A8 motorway, but just before the junction turn right and follow the valley of the Reyran upstream. The road, which is much used by heavy lorries and in its final part not made up, goes under the motorway and ends not far below the Barrage de Malpasset, the dam which burst in 1959. About 90 min. should be allowed to wander around the remains of the dam; there is an explanatory diagram near the path.

The gigantic blocks of reinforced concrete, which were torn away by the flood wave and which today lie strewn about everywhere, give some idea of the enormous force of the water as it rushed towards the sea from the reservoir.

Le Muy

The lively community of le Muy, 11 km west of Fréjus at the confluence of the Nartuby and Argens rivers, is situated in an area of intensive agriculture. The 15th c. church and the round Tour Charles-Quint (tower of Charles V) are notable.

Anglo-American parachute troops landed here on August 15th 1944.

About 2.5 km south-west on the slope of the Montagne de Roquebrune (up to 372 m; fine views and peculiar rock formations) stands the Chapel of Nôtre-Dame-de-la-Roquette to which there are pilgrimages on March 25th, the second Monday after Easter and September 8th.

★Ganagobie (Abbaye de Ganagobie)   E–F 11

Département: Alpes-de-Haute-Provence
Altitude: 660 m

On a plateau which was already settled in prehistoric times, situated 350 m above the valley of the Durance, stands Ganagobie Abbey (12th c.), an example of Provençal Romanesque architecture. It is celebrated for its contemporary mosaics, which are some of the rarest surviving works of art of this size and importance. The view from the plateau is equally fine. Ganagobie is reached from Manosque by taking N96 and D30 (27 km) and from Digne along N85, D4 and N96 (35 km).

★★View

Going east from the church along allée des Moines, which is bordered by holm oaks, you reach a rocky ledge from which – as if from a balcony – the view extends over the valley of the Durance and the Plateau of Valensole as far as the area of the pre-Alps around Digne; on clear days the Alps themselves (Pelvoux, Monte Viso) can even be seen.

From the western edge (in the opposite direction from the church), past prehistoric standing stones, there is a prospect over the Forcalquier Depression to the Montagne de Lubéron.

Abbey

History

After the foundation of a monastery by the bishop of Sisteron, Jean III, and the assimilation of this monastery into the already powerful Cluny in 935, it is presumed – although there is no documentation – that the present buildings were erected in the 12th c. In good times there were more than a dozen monks in the community; the prior later acquired the title of baron and had a seat in the state council. Decline set in about 1400 and at times the office of prior was held by laymen and even by Protestants. At the Revolution the abbey was secularised and sold. In 1891 it came into the possession of Benedictines who began the rebuilding; meanwhile restoration (including the mosaic) was concluded.

Church

The exterior is simple, with wall arcades on the long sides as the only articulation. The doorway is both unusual and remarkable: in its archivolts and even in the door frames round-toothed decoration was inserted at a later date. The somewhat archaic representation and iconography of the tympanum is remarkable for the period, including as it does temporal power, Christ in the Mandorla, the four evangelists among the 12 apostles. The interior nave consists of three square bays articulated by arches and buttresses. Adjoining the twin bays of the transepts is the choir with a main apse and side apses. The northern one is externally circular and probably belongs to an earlier building. The gallery in the west wall is reminiscent of Cluny and its

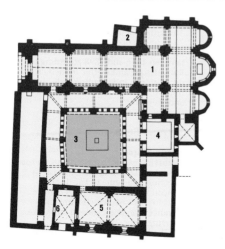

Ganagobie

1 Church
2 Tower
3 Cloister
4 Chapter house
5 Refectory
6 Kitchen

10 m
33 ft

liturgy, in which the singing of the choir is antiphonal. The sculptural decoration is modest, since it was accompanied by frescos (traces of which remain) and the mosaics in the eastern bay of the transept and in the apses (see below).

Cloister

The cloister, largely reconstructed with preserved medieval material, probably dates from the late 13th c. It was later joined to the church and chapter house. Its barrel vault is higher on the outside than on the inside, in order to minimise the weight on the arches. The eight arches of the garden sides are divided by double and quadruple pillars and separated by an intermediate pillar; the leaf decoration is similar to that in Notre-Dame, Vaison (see entry) which is under Burgundian influence. Each four arches are held together by a large relieving arch.

★★Mosaics

The mosaics in the choir and transepts were made between 1135 and 1170 and with their area of almost 70 sq m form the largest Romanesque floor mosaic in France. Dating is made possible by an inscription which names both the client, a certain Prior Bertrand, and the artist Petrus Trudbert. The themes and representation point to the influence of antiquity (especially in the ornamentation) and to the time of the crusades; incorporated with this is the overlying theme of good and evil which are given their traditional sides – good on the right, evil on the left. In addition to magical symbols (signs of the zodiac) fables are the principal subjects. In the left apse a galloping rider pursues a monster; there are centaurs, unicorns and elephants. Of particular note in the right transept is the fight between St George and the dragon and the stag as the symbol for Christ.

★Gap   B 12

Département: Hautes-Alpes
Altitude: 733 m
Population: 35,000

The busy *département* town of Gap is an important traffic junction on the Route Napoléon; it lies on the Luye river in the north of Provence and in about the same latitude as Montélimar. Gap has a charming situation, with a backdrop of the Alps to the north of the town. Its pleasant climate has led to its becoming a popular health resort and it is a base for winter sports.

History

The place was already populated when the Romans penetrated into this region. Almost every trace of the Roman settlement of Vapincum disappeared during the succeeding centuries, especially as the place lay on the crossing of important north-south and east-west routes and was always much sought after and consequently fought over. In 558 the Lombards sacked the town; in 1650 plague killed two-thirds of the population; and in 1692 Savoy troops burned down almost all the houses. In March 1815 Napoléon arrived on his way back from Elba and passed through Gap on his march to Paris.

Sights

Musée Départmental
On avenue du Maréchal Foch, a little to the east of the town centre, is the Musée Départmental, which houses Gallo-Roman antiquities, ceramics from Moustiers, furnishings from the Queyras and exhibits illustrating the history of the town and its surroundings. Its principal attraction is the mausoleum of François de Bonne, duke of Lesdiguières, constructed from black marble from Campsaur with an alabaster statue by Jacob Richier (1585–1640).

Cathédrale
The cathedral in the town centre has a 77 m tower; occupying the site of several previous buildings, it was constructed between 1866 and 1898 according to Romanesque and Gothic models. The decoration is in Byzantine style and is noteworthy for the use of local black, red and grey stone.

Surroundings

★Serre-Ponçon
By driving east for about 20 km on road N94 or on D900B in a south-easterly direction you come to Lac de Serre-Ponçon with its 120 m high barrage, built in 1955–61, which dams the Durance river and creates a large lake covering some 2700 ha.

The best excursion is a circular drive: from Gap take the above road as far as Chorges then turn right on to the D3 which winds its way south, with beautiful viewpoints, to the dam; the best general view of the dam is from the *belvédère* a little way north of the road. The D3 continues to the junction of the

Gap, with the Massif des Ecrins in the background

D900B. Take this road, cross the Durance and then, at varying distances from the water, follow the southern bank of the reservoir. In about 20 km turn west on the the D954. A little way from the road can be seen the Demoiselles.

Demoiselles Coiffées
Demoiselles Coiffées (ladies with head-dresses) is a group of earth pyramids. Still following the bank of the lake we reach the N94 near Savines-le-Lac and once again cross the lake and return to Gap via Chorges.

★La Garde-Adhémar   C 4

Région: Rhône-Alpes
Département: Drôme
Altitude: 185 m
Population: 1100

In the 13th c. la Garde came into the possession of the Adhémar family who also had a fortress at Grignan (see entry) in the 11th c. Since the 13th c. la Garde has borne their family name. Situated on the edge of the heights of the Tricastin above the Rhône valley (about 20 km south of Montélimar and 17 km west of Grignan) its beautiful position is best appreciated if it is approached from Grignan through the Val-des-Nymphes (see below).

Sights

Townscape
Outside the town on the north there is a car park from which the modest little town can be explored. Parts of the medieval town wall have been preserved on the north-east, including two gates. From the main door of the Church of St-Michel, one of the important monuments of the district, there is a fine view of the Rhône valley and the outlying hills of the Vivarais, with the Dent de Rez (719 m) among them.

★St-Michel
A chapel dedicated to St Michael is mentioned as early as 1105 but the present church was certainly not built until 40 years later (at the same time as the church in Bourg-St-Andéol on the other side of the Rhône, and the cathedral in St-Paul-Trois-Châteaux). The

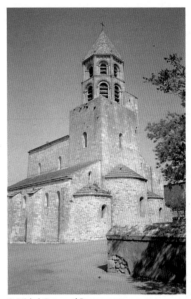

St-Michel, Provençal Romanesque

church was restored in 1849–50 at the instigation of Prosper Mérimée.

With its simple architectural forms St-Michel, although situated in the extreme south of the Dauphiné, is typical of Provençal Romanesque – a lack of figure decoration, little articulation and precisely shaped masonry. Its three aisles form a square; on the east side are three apses but no transept. The nave has a barrel vault and the side aisles a quarter-barrel which supports the weight of the vault. Only the south wall and the apses have sizeable windows, so that practically the only light entering the building comes through the door. The west apse is an extremely rare feature in French Romanesque. In contrast to the rest of the church the tower consists of a massive square base with delicate octagon above (the arches of the arcades have ovoid decoration and rest on pilasters with capitals modelled on those of antiquity). The west front, too, has bands of relief work, but these were probably added in the 19th c.

Chapelle du Val-des-Nymphes
Two km east, on the D572A are the ruins of the 12th c. Chapel of the Val-des-

Nymphes set in a well-watered green valley. In Gallo-Roman days this spot was probably a pagan shrine, as the name implies. The roof and arches of the Romanesque chapel are lacking. The west front is remarkable: the arch of the doorway has keystones from a Roman building and the tympanum has three niches, separated by fluted pilasters with imitation classical capitals. The arches which support the corner pilasters are later additions. Of interest is the articulation of the choir apse by wall arcades on two levels.

★Gordes F 7

Département: Vaucluse
Altitude: 373 m
Population: 1600

Gordes, some 40 km east of Avignon, is world famous for its extremely picturesque situation on the steep slope down from the Plateau de Vaucluse to the valley of the Coulon. In the 1950s Gordes was neglected, but today it is one of the most visited places in Provence. This *village perché* is dominated by its 16th c. château. The best view of Gordes is to be had from the the road leading up from Cavaillon.

Sights

Château
The château, flanked by corner towers, was not erected until 1540 yet it still has the air of a medieval fortress. Its age is indicated by the doorway and windows, as well as by the richly decorated fireplace (one of the largest Renaissance fireplaces in France) in the Great Hall.

The château was temporarily made available to the Hungarian-French artist Victor Vasarély for his Didactic Museum (Musée didactique) in appreciation of his having met the costs of restoration. From 1996, the **Musée Pol Mara** has been based here, which is dedicated to the work of the contemporary Flemish painter and honorary citizen of Gordes, Pol Mara; in a chronological sequence, examples of his surrealist and abstract works are shown here.

★Village des Bories
The Village des Bories lies 2 km south of

The picturesque town of Gordes

Gordes. From the main road a narrow carriageway branches off to the west, it is enclosed in places by walls made of boulders and in spite of stretches of one-way operation cannot be used by large motor or towed caravans.

Ⓖ *Daily 9am–sunset.*

Bories are built of flat stones without mortar (drystone work) and are generally without windows. The slope of the roof consists of a kind of false vaulting whereby each layer of stone overhangs the one immediately below on the inside, until the slopes meet in the middle. These constructions, which are quite common in Provence, used to serve generally as herdsmen's huts but, as in the case here, rural farms and whole settlements could consist of *bories*. Examples of this curiously archaic construction had their precursors in the Neolithic and were built in Provence until the beginning of the 20th c.; they could be put up by an experienced craftsman with no other tool than a hammer.

The settlement of *bories* near Gordes was thoroughly restored in the 1960s. It is probably the largest and most complete of its kind still remaining. The village is surrounded by a wall, scarcely as high as a man, enclosing the five groups of huts. Beside houses and stables there are a wine press and a bread oven; in a few of the *bories* farming implements of several periods are exhibited. In a two-storey 17th c. house there are diagrams about this method of construction and its corresponding forms in other countries.

The view to the south over the hills covered with *maquis* or *garrigue* (evergreen shrubs) is charming.

Musée du Vitrail

By the Moulin des Bouillons (5 km south on D148) can be found the Musée du Vitrail in which glass painting and the art of religious stained glass in Europe is presented.

Surroundings

★Roussillon

The little town of Roussillon lies 10 km east of Gordes in the well-known ochre area between the Plateau de Vaucluse and the Montaine du Lubéron. The whole town reflects the intensive colour of ochre which was mined here, and

which brought prosperity to the citizens as a raw material much in demand for the manufacture of paint, until the competition from synthetic pigments.

At the entrance to the town on the left is a car park which is often full (there are other parks on the road from Apt in the west on rue des Bourgades and in the north on the road leading to D2). From the main car park there is a signposted tour of Roussillon.

The town is entered through a charming clock tower. Further uphill cross the narrow steps of rue de l'Arcade and the very pretty place de la Mairie and go past the church to the Castrum, an observation platform with an orientation table. To the north can be seen the Plateau de Vaucluse and further on the broad shape of Mont Ventoux. All around among the woods are ochre rocks, the colours of which vary from violet to light yellowish brown.

Chaussée des Géants

Impressive ochre formations, the Chaussée des Géants (roadway of the giants) can be seen from the entrance to the town, to the south of the car park mentioned above. It takes some 30 min. to reach them; the path is waymarked and provided with information boards. Also impressive is the Val des Fées (view from rue des Bourgades to the south). Those with a special interest in ochre rocks are recommended to visit the Colorado of Rustrel (☛Lubéron).

Sénanque

See entry

Fontaine-de-Vaucluse

See entry

La Grande-Motte

Région: Languedoc-Roussillon
Département: Hérault
Altitude: sea level
Population: 4000

The modern holiday centre of la Grande-Motte lies on the Golfe du Lion, 10 km west of Aigues-Mortes and 20 km south-east of Montpellier. It is actually not part of Provence but of the adjoining région of Languedoc-Roussillon.

Roussillon: famous for its ochre rocks

Townscape

La Grande-Motte came into being in 1974 as the first of the modern holiday centres that sprang up around the lagoon and dune country west of the Camargue. These centres include Port-Barcarès, Port-Leucate, Valras-Plage and Port-Camargue (see below). Designed by Jean Balladur it has developed into a huge holiday town, with a sophisticated infrastructure of accommodation and entertainment and sporting facilities.

The place is grouped around the marina, on both sides of which stretches a beach of fine sand. The typical silhouette is formed by pyramid apartment blocks. On the east side of the harbour is a fine aquarium with more than 30 tanks. There is also a casino in la Grande-Motte. To the north and east of the main road through the town are holiday homes, various sports centres and a holiday village.

In the nearby lagoons, Etang du Ponant and Etang de Mauguio, fairly large groups of flamingoes can be observed. Here there are also opportunities for water sports and fishing.

Surroundings

Le Grau-du-Roi

Le Grau-du-Roi (3 km south-east), a more conventional place than la Grande-Motte, is in the *département* of Gard. It has developed around a fishing village which, however, has already been almost swallowed up by the usual concrete skyscrapers. To the north-west on the horizon can be seen the skyline of la Grande-Motte.

The lagoons, lying to the south-east, which extend into the countryside of the Camargue are used mainly for obtaining sea salt.

Port-Camargue

South of le Grau-du-Roi lies Port-Camargue, the newest and most easterly of the holiday towns on the coast of Languedoc-Roussillon. Port-Camargue has excellent boating facilities and broad sandy beaches. The complex of holiday homes and apartment blocks, generally only one or two storeys high, are built out into the lagoon so that boats can often be tied up right outside the door. Two broad roads run round the edge of this attractive place and finish on either side of the harbour keeping traffic away from the residential area.

Camargue
See entry

★Grasse   H 17

Département: Alpes-Maritimes
Altitude: 333 m
Population: 43,000

Grasse, at heart still an ancient little town and Sous-Préfecture of the *département* of Alpes-Maritimes, lies about 18 km north of Cannes. It has a sheltered situation on the slope of the Roquevignon some distance from the coast on the Route Napoléon. Even before the Côte d'Azur, Grasse was known as a winter health resort, on account of its mild climate. The town is famous as the centre of the perfume industry.

History
The area of Grasse is rich in finds from prehistory, especially the late Neolithic. It is believed that the place existed in Merovingian times (5th/6th c. AD). In the 12th c. Grasse gained its independence but in the 13th c. came under the control of the dukes of Provence. It was the seat of a bishop from 1244 until 1790. The perfume industry, which has made Grasse world renowned, was introduced in the 16th c. by Catherine de' Medici. The rococo painter Jean-Honoré Fragonard (1732–1806) was born in Grasse. Pauline Borghese, the sister of Napoléon Bonaparte, lived in Grasse (garden above the town, 2 boulevard Jeu-de-Ballon; from here the view extends from Nice to Cannes).

★Perfume industry
Grasse is the most important centre of the perfume industry, not just in France but in the whole of Europe. The material from which the perfume is extracted is provided by the large flower plantations and lavender fields of the surrounding area. In and around Grasse about 30 large firms process throughout the year several million kilograms of blossoms (orange, rose, jasmine, thyme, rosemary, mignonette, violet). For the manufacture of perfume from natural raw materials three main methods are used: the first is the old-fashioned

distillation process by means of steam; the second is an extraction process in which the perfumes together with fatty deposits are extracted by using alcohol; the third is a method of solution whereby the scents are extracted by chemical means. In order to obtain 1 kg of essential oil 1000 kg of orange-blossom, for example, are necessary. To obtain oil of lavender the plants are picked (either by machine or by hand), allowed to dry for a week and then treated with steam in vats. After the mixture is cooled the particles of lavender oils, which have a lighter relative density, float to the top of the brew and can be removed. About 40 kg of lavender plants are necessary to obtain 1 litre of oil of lavender. Most of the perfume factories in Grasse (e.g. Fragonard, Molinard, Galimard) have set up sales rooms and operate guided tours.

Musée de la Parfumerie
The Perfumery Museum (8 place du Cours) was opened in 1989 and has many exhibits – from antiquity to the present – illustrating the history and production of

La Grande-Motte

The Museum in the Parfumerie Fragonard

perfumes. Adjoining is a research centre and on the roof a garden of scented plants has been laid out.
Jun.–Sep. 10am–7pm; Oct., Dec.–May Wed.–Sun. 10am–noon, 2–5pm.

Sights

Because of the narrow thoroughfares in the Old Town, Grasse can only be visited on foot.

The tour begins at the Office du Tourisme (Tourist Office) in place de la Foux; not far east of here lies the Centre International de Grasse, a modern congress and conference centre. From the southern end of the square a double set of steps enclosing a fountain leads down into the Old Town.

Place aux Aires
The first place to be reached is the elongated place aux Aires where the lively market is held every morning and which also has a fountain; on the north side of the square stands the elegant Hôtel Isnard which was built by the wealthy Gerber Isnard (1781).

Place du Cours
From place aux Aires follow rue Amiral-de-Grasse southwards to place du Cours, from where there is a pleasant view over the parts of the town lower down the valley. In a curve of the street stands the pretty red facade of the Perfumery Museum (see above) and to the south the Parfumerie Fragonard, on the ground floor of which is a museum about the history of the perfumery industry since ancient times, and a collection of perfumes of Grasse. The basement contains part of the production process and can be visited.

To the south-west of place du Cours is the main boulevard of the town, the beautiful cours Honoré-Cresp. Here are the Municipal Casino and several perfumeries.

Musée Fragonard
A little to the south at 23 boulevard Fragonard is the Villa Musée Fragonard (a 17th c. town house). It was here that J-H Fragonard withdrew in 1791 after he had lost his aristocratic customers through the French Revolution. On the staircase can be seen grisaille pictures by Alexandre-Evariste, Fragonard's son, good copies of paintings by J-H Fragonard that were done for the countess du Barry, the mistress of Louis XV (the originals are privately owned and in the US), and other members of the family.
Jun.–Sep. 10am–1pm, 2–7pm; Oct., Dec.–May Wed.–Sun. 10am–noon, 2–5pm; closed pub. hols.

Musée d'Art et d'Histoire de Provence
To the east opposite the observation terrace on rue Mirabeau stands the former Hôtel de Clapiers-Cabris, a stately palace of 1771. It now houses the Musée d'Art et d'Histoire de Provence (Museum of Provençal Art and History; opening hours as for the Musée Fragonard) with historic furniture, ceramics and a collection devoted to the history of the town.

Notre-Dame-du-Puy
To the north-east behind the museum and right in the centre of the Old Town stands the Cathedral of Notre-Dame, originally 12th–13th c. and extended in the 17th and 18th c. The architecture shows influence by Lombardy and Liguria. Inside the basilican church are three paintings by P P Rubens (1601) –

Christ Crowned with Thorns, *The Crucifixion* and *St Helena*; a remarkable representation of the *Washing of Feet* by J-H Fragonard, one of the rare religious paintings by this master of rococo; and the Altar of St Honorat, which has been attributed to Bréa.

To the north, opposite the church, stands the Ancien Evêché, the former bishop's palace, built in the 13th c. and later considerably altered; it is now the Town Hall (Hôtel de Ville). From place du 24-Août, which adjoins the church, there is a fine view over the valley.

Surroundings

Cabris

Cabris is a picturesque village, once popular with artists, above the Grasse basin (8 km west). Of interest are the ruins of the 12th c. fortress, a church (1606–50) and the Chapel of Ste-Marguerite with an altarpiece of about 1500. At the western edge of the village stands the 16th c. Chapel of St-Jean-Baptiste.

★Gourdon

About 14 km north-east the little village of Gourdon is situated on a ridge. The château, built in the 13th and 17th c. on Saracen foundations, houses a museum

(Oriental and French weapons, pictures of the Cologne school of about 1550, primitive painting). The park-like terraces laid out by Le Nôtre partly belong to a botanical research station. From here there is a fine view of Cap d'Antibes and Cap Roux.

★Gorges du Loup

The gorge which the Loup river has cut deep into the rock is reached from Grasse via le Bar-sur-Loup and the D2210. The road (D6) through the gorge runs below rock walls up to 400 m high, past the Cascade de Courmes (altogether 70 m high) and near the 25 m high Saut du Loup. Near a winding stretch of the D3 which returns to Grasse there is an observation point (signed 'Surplomb des Gorges du Loup'), from which there is an almost vertical view down into the gorge and up to the 1248 m high Pic des Courmettes.

★Grignan   C 5

Région: Rhône-Alpes
Département: Drôme
Altitude: 197 m
Population: 1100

Townscape
The township of Grignan lies in hilly

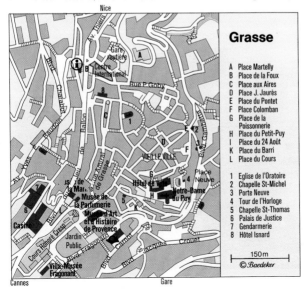

Grasse

A Place Martelly
B Place de la Foux
C Place aux Aires
D Place J. Jaurès
E Place du Pontet
F Place Colomban
G Place de la Poissonnerie
H Place du Petit-Puy
I Place du 24 Août
K Place du Barri
L Place du Cours

1 Eglise de l'Oratoire
2 Chapelle St-Michel
3 Porte Neuve
4 Tour de l'Horloge
5 Chapelle St-Thomas
6 Palais de Justice
7 Gendarmerie
8 Hôtel Isnard

150m
© Baedeker

terrain east of the Rhône valley about 30 km south-east of Montélimar. The little town nestles below the château and around the church, forming a charming picture. The Upper Town must be explored on foot; there are car parks in the lower town.

History

Grignan, which was a barony in the Middle Ages in the possession of the Provençal aristocratic family of Adhémar-Castellane, was made famous by the Marquise de Sévigné (1626–96). The letters which she wrote to her daughter, the wife of the last count of Grignan, and to other contemporaries were published in 1726 and became celebrated for their vividness and for the details they give of contemporary life. The marquise died in the château at Grignan.

Sights

Place Sévigné

On the northern edge of the Old Town lies place Sévigné with a fountain commemorating the marquise. The little square is dominated by the 12th c. belfry (a defensive civic tower). Continuing past this tower, the road leads to the Upper Town and the château; below on the right can be seen a classical pump room.

★Château

The château that dominates the whole town was originally a modest building of the late Middle Ages. About the middle of the 16th c. it was completely rebuilt by Louis Adhémar, a diplomat and officer, after the collegiate church had already been erected. At the time of the French Revolution a considerable part of the château had to be pulled down by order of the authorities. The fixtures which survived and the remains of the château were purchased at the end of the century by a descendant of the Adhémars. The present aspect is largely the result of a thorough but not particularly successful restoration at the beginning of the 20th c.

The complex is entered by a gateway flanked by towers. To the south extends a large courtyard adjoining a terrace, with the Church of St-Sauveur which was built about 1660. From here there is

Grignan with its château

an excellent view of Mont Ventoux in the south-east, of the Rhône plain and of the mountains of Vivarais in the north-west.

The principal attractions of the interior of the château include the apartments of the Marquise de Sévigné and several rooms with period furniture (Louis XIII, Louis XV) as well as Aubusson tapestries; an audio-visual presentation accompanies the visitor. ⊙ *Apr.–Oct. daily 9.30–11.30am, 2.30–5.30pm, Jul., Aug. to 6pm; Nov.–Mar. Thu.–Mon. 9.30–11.30am, 2.30–5.30pm, Tue.–Wed. 2.30–5.30pm; closed January.*

St-Sauveur

Below the château stands the Church of St-Sauveur, built 1535–9 on the order of the above-mentioned Louis Adhémar by Jehan Delanche for the canonry founded in 1484. In 1568 the Protestant Portal was destroyed. An inscription over the door commemorates its restoration in 1654. The left-hand wall of the nave abuts the hillside. A gallery in the church allows direct entrance (17 m above the ground) to the château; during the French Revolution it was walled up. With its ribbed vaults and traceried windows the building reveals elements of late Gothic (flamboyant). To the left of the gilded high altar, with its altarpiece showing the *Transfiguration*, can be seen the tomb of the Marquise de Sévigné beneath a marble slab. The panelling dates from the late 17th century.

Surroundings

Valréas

The lively little town of Valréas, 9 km south-east of Grignan, was until the French Revolution papal property and the area around it is still called Enclave des Papes. Historical relationships still prevail – the Enclave is a northern pocket of Vaucluse, isolated from the rest of the *département* by the *département* of Drôme which encloses it. Agriculture, commerce and packaging are important factors in the economy.

The Old Town is surrounded by spacious boulevards with plane trees which follow the line of the former town walls. Although of modest size the fine Hôtel de Ville (15th–18th c.),once the town house of the Marquise de Simiane, is impressive. The château's keep dates

from the 12th c. The 12th c. Church of Notre-Dame-de-Nazareth has a notable south door.

La Garde-Adémar

See entry

★Hyères   L 12

Département: Var
Altitude: 40 m
Population: 42,000

Hyères, an important agricultural centre (wine, flowers, early vegetables) and the oldest winter health resort of the French Riviera, lies only 20 km east of Toulon at the foot of the 204 m high Castéou, 4 km from the sea.

History

Near the town lay the Greek foundation of Olbia. The Romans fortified the settlement and the fortifications were subsequently extended, first by the lords of Fos and afterwards by Charles of Anjou. During the Wars of Religion (16th c.) the town suffered considerably; after a siege lasting a year the duc de Guise had the walls pulled down. At the beginning of the 17th c. the keep was destroyed (the remains have been preserved). Hyères was discovered in the 19th c. as a health resort.

Sights

Old Town

The heart of the Old Town is place Massillon, where the busy daily market is held and where the 12th c. Tour St-Blaise stands, the remains of a residence of the Knights Templar.

On rue Rabaton can be found the birthplace of the great preacher Jean Baptiste Massillon (1663–1742), court minister to Louis XIV and the bishop of Clermont. Continue along rue Ste-Cathérine to place St-Paul (orientation table; extensive view), with the church of the same name, originally built in the 12th c. and restored in the 16th when the side chapels were added. On the right of the steps leading to the main door stands a charming little Renaissance house with little corner turrets, beneath this extends rue St-Paul.

A few metres to the west stands the Porte des Princes, part of a former monastery. To the north of the square on rue Paradis are some pretty 13th c. houses (No. 24 on the left; No. 6).

South-east of place Massillon, on the edge of the historic centre, stands the 13th c. Porte de la Rade, the former main gate of the town which gives access to place Clemenceau. To the north lies place de la République with a monument to Massillon, and the 13th c. Church of St-Louis, (Romanesque–early Gothic) which stood outside the town walls. East of the apse of the church, on cours Strasbourg, is the theatre and behind it the attractive Jardin A-Denis.

The busy avenue du Général-de-Gaul leads west from place Clemenceau and forms the boundary of the New Town to the south.

New Town

The impressive avenue Gambetta leads south from place du Portalet into the New Town. To the east lies place Lefèbvre and here can be found the interesting Musée Municipal with archaeological, local and natural history collections.

Ⓒ *Mon., Tue., Thu., Fri. 10am–noon, 3–6pm; Sat., Sun. only during special exhibitions 3–6pm.*

★Jardins Olbius-Riquier

To the south of the inner town can be found the Jardins Olbius-Riquier, a fine garden of 6.5 ha with a great many exotic plants and birds.

Notre-Dame-de-Consolation

The suburb of Costebelle lies 3 km south of the town centre on a 98 m hill. The top of the hill was a place of pilgrimage as early as the 11th c. There is a fine view from the Chapel of Notre-Dame-de-Consolation, the tower of which is surmounted by a statue of the Madonna. A pilgrimage to this spot takes place on August 15th and 16th. From the chapel the 306 m high Mont des Oiseaux (view) can be climbed in about 1 hour.

St-Pierre d'Almanarre

Still further south are the ruins of the Monastery of St-Pierre d'Almanarre (Arabic *al-manar*, lighthouse).

Hyères-Plage

By the sea south of Toulon-Hyères Airport lies the resort of Hyères-Plage with a racecourse and the harbour of Port St-Pierre-de-la-Mer (marina).

L'Ayguade-Plage, le Ceinturon-Plage

North-east of the airport and on the far side of the mouth of the Capeau river are the seaside settlements of l'Ayguade-Plage and le Ceinturon-Plage which have beaches of fine sand. This was one of the places from which crusaders set sail.

Surroundings

Presqu'île de Giens

Near Toulon-Hyères Airport the Presqu'île de Giens juts out into the Mediterranean. To the east of this narrow tongue of land stretches the wide bay of Rade d'Hyères and to the west extends the Etang des Pesquiers, closed off on the west by a dike along which runs the Route du Sel (Salt Road); here are the Salins Neufs (salt pans; 500 ha). These two spits of land link the coast to the Giens peninsula, 6.5 km long and up to 1.5 km wide, which only became joined to the mainland in Roman times.

On the eastern spit, which is covered with pines, are long sandy beaches with opportunities for surfing, and the settlement of la Capte. The central point of the peninsula is Giens with its château ruins (52 m above sea level; good view). In the west near the village of la Madrague rises the highest point of the peninsula (118 m; signal station).

Some 2 km east of Giens the road from Hyères ends at the ruins of the former Fort de la Tour-Fondue, built in the time of Richelieu. Immediately adjoining is the mooring of motor boats for Porquerolles (see below). To the south of the Giens peninsula lies the Île du Grand-Ribaud, a rocky island with a lighthouse.

★Îles d'Hyères (Îles d'Or)

The Îles d'Hyères – Porquerolles, Port-Cros and the Île du Levant (as well as other islands) – continue the Giens peninsula to the east. Geologically they form part of the Massif des Maures (see entry) and are also called – probably on account of their glistening mica-bearing rocks – the Îles d'Or (golden islands). The islands are for the most part wooded, with steep fissured slopes; they have fine natural harbours and are popular not least because of their beaches, which are ideal for bathing. In the time of King

François I the islands were used as a base by pirates.

There are ferry services from Toulon, Hyères-Plage and la Tour-Fondue to Porquerolles; from Port-de-Miramar, le Lavandou and Cavalaire.

The **Île de Porquerolles**, almost 8 km long and about 2 km wide, is the largest of the archipelago. It has vineyards extending over some 200 ha and beautiful beaches with clear water which are especially popular with visitors. The beaches on the north coast are predominantly flat; the entire southern and eastern part falls steeply into the sea.

The principal place is Porquerolles on the main bay of the north coast. From here there is a rewarding walk (about 45 min.) through beautiful Mediterranean vegetation south to Phare de l'Ouseau, the southernmost tip of the island (96 m above sea level; lighthouse).

Going north-east from Porquerolles through the woods along the Plage Notre-Dame the Cap des Mèdes is reached in just over an hour. About half-way a path branches off on the right which leads past the Fort de la Repentance to the Sémaphore (signal station; 142 m; view).

East of the Île de Porquerolles lies the **Île de Port-Cros** (about 4 km long, 2 km wide). Since 1963 it and the surrounding offshore area has been a Parc National (nature reserve); only a few people live on this island.

The luxuriant Mediterranean fauna and flora (primeval forests, nesting sites of rare birds, fishing grounds) and the former Fort du Moulin (17th c.) at the entrance to the harbour of Port-Cros are of considerable interest. West of the harbour lies the little Île de Baguad (up to 59 m high). From Port-Cros a particularly rewarding walk (1½ hours) leads from the harbour south-east into the Vallon de la Solitude (valley of loneliness) and to the imposing Falaises du Sud (almost 200 m high cliffs). Also worth while is a 3-hour walk eastwards to the charming Pointe de Port-Man. The highest points are Mont Vinaigre (196 m) and la Vigie (207 m). The island is at its best during blossom time from March to May.

Still further east lies the geologically interesting lonely rock island, the **Île du**

Levant (8 km long and up to 1.5 km wide). It was formerly the possession of the Abbots of Lérins. It has become well known through the naturist colony of Héliopolis set up in 1932. Large parts of the island are military territory.

La, Le, Les

See main name

Le Lavandou   L 14

Département: Var
Altitude: 0–483 m
Population: 4700

Le Lavandou lies at the foot of the Massif des Maures, about half-way between Toulon and St-Tropez (40 km east of Toulon), on a broad bay facing south-east.

Townscape

This pretty former fishing village, now popular as a holiday resort, may owe its name to the lavender which extensively grows in the surrounding area. Holiday homes and numerous high-rise buildings are prominent features of the town. From the harbour, in the eastern part of which are mooring facilities for yachts, ferries leave for the Îles de Hyères (☛Hyères).

West of the harbour stretches the Rade de Bormes, a bay with fine sand, and along it runs boulevard de Lattre-de-Tassigny; from the boulevard there is a comprehensive view of the sea and the islands of Port-Cros and Levant (two of the Hyères Islands). In the south the bay is enclosed by the wooded slopes of Cap Bénat. Far to the east Cap Lardier rises from the sea.

Road N559 running east from le Lavandou, gives access to sandy beaches, interspersed with rocky stretches.

Cap Bénat

South of le Lavandou the wooded Cap Bénat extends out into the sea. The road leading to it comes first to the resort of la Favière (yacht harbour, beach) before reaching the settlement of holiday homes at Cap Bénat. On the highest point, les Fourches (205 m), stands a château and, on the extremity of the cape, a lighthouse.

In the Colorado de Rustrel

Lubéron (Montagne du Lubéron) G 6–9

Département: Vaucluse
Altitude: up to 1125 m

The Montagne du Lubéron rises in the interior of the region to the east of Cavaillon. On the south the mountain range is bordered by the Durance river, the plain of which is intensively cultivated (vineyards, cereals, orchards) and in addition there are some green areas; in the north the valley of the Coulon divides it from the Plateau de Vaucluse. The Montagne du Lubéron is a mountainous area of chalk which reaches a height of 1125 m in the Mourre Nègre. Usually a distinction is made between the Petit Lubéron in the west and the Grand Lubéron in the east, which are separated by the gorge of the Combe de Lourmarin.

History
A dark chapter was the massacre in 1545, which the baron of Oppède perpetrated in 24 villages (including Cadenet, Lourmarin, Ménerbes and Mérindol). Because his beloved, the baroness of Tour d'Aigues, would not marry him he had over 2000 inhabitants of her villages killed in every conceivable manner; he sold 800 men to be galley slaves and plundered and burned the houses. These people had the misfortune to be Waldenses (Christian followers of Peter Waldo), who had been threatened since the Parliament of Aix; the persecution lasted from 1524 until the baron obtained approval from King Francis I for his act of revenge.

Parc Naturel Régional du Lubéron
A large part of this mountainous area is taken up by the Parc Naturel Régional du Lubéron (nature park), established in 1977, which has an area of about 120,000 ha and which extends into the neighbouring *département* of Alpes-de-Haute-Provence.

Bories
In several places in Lubéron can be seen the characteristic *bories*, huts built of boulders without mortar (☞Gordes).

Rustrel
A good 10 km north-east of Apt (see

Surroundings

Bormes-les-Mimosas
The township of Bormes-les-Mimosas, 2 km north-west, is picturesquely situated on the flank of a hill. The best view is from the terrace near the château ruins. In place de la Liberté stands the handsome 16th c. Chapel of St-François-de-Paule (floodlit in summer), flanked by two cypress trees. A statue commemorates the beneficent deeds of St Francis of Paula during the plague of 1481. In the cemetery can be seen a memorial to the landscape painter Jean-Charles Cazin (1841–1901); some of his work is displayed in the Hôtel de Ville (Musée Arts et Histoire, rue Carnot). Also of interest is the Tour de l'Horloge, an 18th c. clock tower, and the Church of St-Trophime (also 18th c.; fine altar-piece). Below the church extends old Bormes, a typical Provençal town with steep streets (known as *rompi-cuou*, breakneck). With la Favière, Bormes-les-Mimosas has a good yacht harbour.

Collobrières
See Massif des Maures

below) is the village of Rustrel. Like Roussillon (☞Gordes) it is known for its deposits of ochre. Here the little Dôa river has cut a gorge, called the Colorado de Rustrel. This picturesque gorge can be reached by two roads going south from Rustrel. Footpaths lead to the ochre rocks.

Drive through the Lubéron range

Apt
The best starting point for a drive through the Lubéron range is Apt, situated in the basin of the same name, the Bassin d'Apt on the little Calavon river. Of interest is the former Cathedral of Ste-Anne, originally Romanesque but considerably altered in the 14th and 17th c. In the baroque Chapel of Ste-Anne is the reliquary of the patroness of the church. The treasury contains reliquaries from Limoges and illuminated manuscripts. The Archaeological Museum has, in addition to Gallo-Roman antiquities, a considerable collection of ceramics.

From Apt road D943 runs south to the Lubéron. It passes through a varied and scenically beautiful landscape with vineyards and orchards; ahead rises the mountain range of the Lubéron with the village of Bonnieux and, on the right, the village and château ruin of Lacoste. The château is associated with the notorious Marquis de Sade to whom it belonged; he withdrew here after the Arcueil affair in 1771.

★Bonnieux
100 m separate the highest and lowest parts of this little town on the north slope of the Lubéron. The upper church (12th and 15th c.) is reached by a flight of steps from place de la Liberté; it is surrounded by mighty cedars (in the 1860s cedars from the Atlas Mountains were planted in the Lubéron). From here the view extends across the Bassin d'Apt to Gordes and Roussillon and across the Plateau de Vaucluse to Mont Ventoux which dominates the landscape. In the Office du Tourisme (rue de la République) is the small Musée de la Boulangerie (bakery museum). The lower church contains four panels by a 15th c. German master (St Veronica; the martyrdom of Jesus).

Combe de Lourmarin
Road D934 leads to the dense, relatively low forest of holm oaks, sweet chestnuts and gorse in the Gorge of the Aigue Brun, below impressive, partly overhanging rock walls.

★Mourre Nègre
Just short of Lourmarin a narrow forest track branches off to the left, climbs up to the crest of the Grand Lubéron and in about another 15 km reaches the Mourre Nègre, the highest point of the range. The last short stretch must be made on foot; from the top there is a magnificent panorama.

Lourmarin
At the southern end of the Combe lies Lourmarin, overlooked by its 15th–16th c. château; from the tower there is a good view of the Lubéron, the plain of the Durance and the Montagne Ste-Victoire (30 min. guided tours morning and afternoon). The writer and Nobel prizewinner Albert Camus (1913–60) who settled here is buried in the churchyard.

In the Combe de Loumarin

The Drummer of Arcole in Cadenet

Marcoule   E 4

Région: Languedoc-Roussillon
Département: Gard
Altitude: 50 m

The nuclear research centre of Marcoule lies in the west opposite Orange on the right bank of the Rhône.

Usine Nucléaire
The extensive complex of this nuclear research centre, where 2200 people are employed, is situated by the river, the water of which is used for cooling the reactors. The principal task of the centre is, however, not the production of electrical energy but nuclear research and the obtaining of radioactive substances for medicine, science and industry, of tritium for military purposes and of nuclear fuel (plutonium) for power stations. For this purpose the reactor Phénix, the first fast breeder in the world, was started up in 1973. In Marcoule the fuels from French and Spanish gas-graphite reactors are also reprocessed.

Belvédère de Marcoule
The best view of the complex is from the *belvédère* (observation point) reached along a private road (🅖 *8am–7pm*). A large panoramic display gives a general view of the complex; an exhibition explains the layout and working of nuclear power stations and uranium enrichment, and the French atomic industry.

★★Marseille   J–K 8

Département: Bouches-du-Rhône
Altitude: 0–160 m
Population: 880,000 (conurbation 1,104,000)

Marseille, the oldest and second largest city, after Paris, and the most important port of France, is situated on the Mediterranean east of the Rhône delta. Marseille is the chief place in the *département* of Bouches-du-Rhône, a university town and the see of an archbishop.

Marseille has a charming situation on a broad bay which is enclosed on the north by the Chaîne de l'Estaque towards the Étang de Berre (see entry) and rises on bare limestone hills. It is

Cucuron
There is a worthwhile excursion from Lourmarin to Cucuron, about 10 km distant. The Romanesque and Gothic church is in poor condition; it has a pulpit with coloured marble intarsis work and an 18th c. altarpiece of the Resurrection by Puget. The Regional Museum in the Hôtel des Bouliers has exhibits illustrating prehistory as well as Gallo-Roman finds. Mourre Nègre (see above) can also be climbed from Cucuron.

Cadenet
The plain of the Durance and the Abbey of Silvacane (see entry) are reached via Cadenet, which is dominated by the ruins of an 11th c. fortress.

In Cadenet stands the statue of the Drummer of Arcole. According to legend this 19-year-old boy, who was a soldier in Napoléon's army, swam the river during the battle and beat his drum so loudly that the Austrians, thinking they were surrounded, surrendered. In the 14th c. church a Roman sarcophagus serves as the font.

dominated by the Church of Notre-Dame-de-la-Garde, the landmark of the city and the port. Although the oldest city in France there are few remains of ancient or medieval buildings.

Economy

The economy of the town is primarily determined by the importance of the port which predominantly trades with North Africa and south and east Asia. A third of French maritime trade is handled by the independent Port Autonome de Marseille. The annual turnover of goods amounts to about 100 million tonnes (almost 90 per cent imports), of which over 90 per cent is handled by the new installations of Fos-sur-Mer and Lavéra which extend to the west (mineral oil, oil products and ores). With some 1.2 million passengers annually Marseille is the third passenger port of France; a great proportion of this traffic is attributable to the busy ferries across the harbour basins.

Raw materials and heavy industry characterise the area of Marseille/Étang-de-Berre/Fos; four refineries produce 30 per cent of national capacity, steel production amounts annually to 3 million tonnes. The traditional industries of Marseille – shipping, the production of cooking oil and the manufacture of foodstuffs and soap – have suffered from recession, and both steel and petrochemical production have declined, with the result that Marseille has the highest unemployment in France. The position has been intensified by the significance of Marseille as an entrepôt between Europe and North Africa, that is as the principal arrival place for immigrants from Arabic and African countries. Over 100,000 Arabs live in Marseille; the Belsunce quarter north of the Canebière is also known as the 'Beirut of Marseille'; few European faces frequent this part of the city.

Marignane, Marseille's airport, with almost 5 million passengers a year is third largest in France, after Paris and Nice, a symbol of the local economy.

History

The town was founded in the 7th c. BC under the name of Massalia by Greeks from the town of Phocaea in Asia Minor. Until well into the time of the Roman Empire it was a centre of Greek culture.

The town experienced its first flowering in the middle of the 6th c. BC after Phocaea had been destroyed by the Persians, and the population was soon increased by streams of refugees. Massalia expanded to the north-east towards the present Butte des Moulins. Trade flourished, especially with the Ligurians who, it is generally believed, had their principal settlement in the nearby Oppidum d'Entremont (☛Aix-en-Provence).

The intervention of the Romans after the Second Punic War in favour of the Greeks culminated in the destruction of the Saluvian tribe in 124, whereupon Aquae Sextiae Saluviorum (Aix), the first Roman town on Gallic soil was founded. The quarrel between Caesar and Pompey led to a fateful clash with the Romans, when the people of Massalia sided with Pompey. Caesar conquered the town, added to it the extensive territory of the province of Arles and promoted the development of the Forum Julii (Fréjus).

Already in the 1st c. AD an extension of the now Roman town of Massalia was carried out by draining the extensive marshes to the east. The wall built in the Imperial Age enclosed the settlement until well into the 11th c.; at that time the town was composed of an Upper Town (temple, forum and other public buildings) and a Lower Town (port, dock installations).

After the fall of the Roman Empire the town came under the domination of the Visigoths, then of the Franks and finally passed to the kingdom of Arles. After its destruction by Saracens it was rebuilt in the 10th c. and was subject to the vicomtes de Marseille; in 1218 it became free until 1250 when Charles of Anjou conquered Marseille which was united to France in 1481.

The importance of the harbour increased enormously at the time of the crusades. In the Middle Ages defences were constructed as opportunity offered, for example the Tour St-Jean on the north side of the harbour entrance, erected by the Knights of the Order of St John, a bastion near the present-day pilgrimage church of Notre-Dame-de-la-Garde by François I and extensions to the Château d'If. Under Mazarin the forts of St-Jean and St-Nicolas were reinforced at the harbour entrance.

During the French Revolution, which saw violent clashes between the Jacobins and the merchants, the most unruly elements withdrew to Paris where they

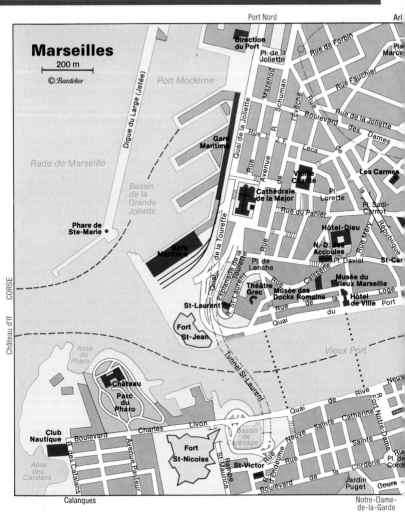

Marseilles

200 m

© Baedeker

Port Nord

Arl

Pla
Marce

Direction
du Port

Pl. de la
Joliette

Rue de Forbin

Rue Faucher

Port Moderne

Mazenod

Schuman

Rue

Boulevard

L'Évêché

Rue de la Joliette

des

Dames

Digue du Large (Jetée)

Quai de la Joliette

Avenue

de

Leca

Gare
Maritime

Rue

Rade de Marseille

Bassin
de la
Grande
Joliette

Vieille
Charité

Cathédrale
de la Major

Les Carmes

Pl.
Lorette

Pl. Sadi-
Carnot

Rue du Panier

République

Phare de
Ste-Marie

Gare
Maritime

Quai de la Tourette

Esplanade de la Tourette

Hôtel-Dieu

N.-D. des
Accoules

Pl. Daviel

St-Car

Rue

Cassérie

Musée du
Vieux Marseille

Chateau d'If   CORSE

Pl. de
Lenche

Théâtre
Grec

St-Laurent

Rue

Musée des
Docks Romains

Rue

de

Hôtel
de Ville

Loge

Port

Fort
St-Jean

Quai

du

Vieux Port

Tunnel St-Laurent

Anse
du
Pharo

Neuv

de

Rive

Fort Notre-Dame

Château

Parc
du
Pharo

Charles

Livon

Quai

Sainte

Catherine

Club
Nautique

Boulevard

Avenue Pasteur

R. des Catalans

Bassin
de
Carénage

Sainte

Rue Neuve

Fort
St-Nicolas

St-Victor

Rue

Rande St-Maurice

R. d'Endoume

Rue

de

la

Corderie

Pl. de
Cord

Anse
des
Catalans

Boulevard

Jardin
Puget

Cours

Calanques

Notre-Dame-
de-la-Garde

made popular the *Marseillaise* which had been composed by the army officer Rouget de Lisle, in Strasbourg.

In the 19th c., under Napoléon III, there were large extensions to the town, as in Paris where Baron Haussmann had laid out broad boulevards through the city. Notable among the improvements were rue de la République between the Old and New Harbours, numerous examples of prestigious architecture, including the triumphal arch in place d'Aix and the Palais Longchamps, all of which reflect the economic prosperity at the time of the Industrial Revolution.

The increase of French influence in North Africa from 1830 onwards and the opening of the Suez Canal gave an impetus to building (new housing, port installations) which has continued to the

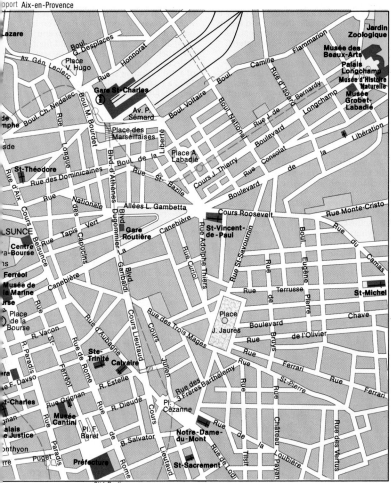

Aéroport Aix-en-Provence

St-Lazare

Jardin Zoologique

Musée des Beaux-Arts

Av. Gén Leclerc

Boul G Desplaces

Honnorat

Place V. Hugo

Camille

Flammarion

Palais Longchamp

Musée d'Histoire Naturelle

Rue

Gare St-Charles

Boul. Ch Nédelec

Boul. M. Bourdet

Av. P. Sémard

Boul Voltaire

Boul National

Rue d'Isoard

Bernardy

Longchamp

Musée Grobet-Labadié

Rue

Longue

Place des Marseillaises

Rue de la Liberté

Place A Labadié

Rue J. de

Consolat

Libération

de

St-Théodore

Blvd d'Athénes

Boul de la

Rue St-Bazile

Cours J. Thierry

Rue

Boulevard

la

Rue des Dominicaines

Rue d'Aix

Rue

des

Nationale

Allées L. Gambetta

Cours Roosevelt

Boulevard

Rue Monte-Cristo

Cours Belsunce

Rue Tapis Vert

Rue des Capucins

Blvd Dugommier

Canebière

St-Vincent-de-Paul

Rue Adolphe Thiers

Rue St-Savournin

Boul Eugène

Rue du Camas

LSUNCE

Gare Routière

Blvd Garibaldi

Centre a-Bourse

Ferréol

Rue Curiol

Musée de la Marine

Canebière

Rue

Terrusse

Pierre

St-Michel

Place de la Bourse

R. Vacon

R. St-

Rue d'Aubagne

Cours Lieutaud

Rue des Trois Mages

Place J. Jaurès

Boulevard

Rue Broys

de l'Olivier

Chave

era

Rue de Rome

Ferréol

Ste-Trinité

Calvaire

Cours Julien

Rue

Rue

Ferrari

St-Pierre

Rue

St-Charles

Rue Grignan

R. Estelle

R. Dieudé

Rue des 3 Frères Barthélemy

Rue

Rue

Ferrari

gnan

alais e Justice

Musée Cantini

Pl. F. Baret

Cours

Pl. Cézanne

Rue

de

Château

Rue des Vertus

onthyon

rre

Puget

Paradis

B. Salvator

Préfecture

Lieutaud

Rome

Notre-Dame-du-Mont

St-Sacrement

Rue de Lodi

Thist

la

Payan

Loubière

Cité Radieuse Cassis

Métro

present day (the slums of Marseille were known as *bidonvilles* – tin-can towns).

Part of the Old Harbour was filled in during the 1920s. During the second world war Marseille was the target of air raids, and on February 1st 1943 it was occupied by German soldiers and much of the historic centre was destroyed. The rebuilding followed plans by August Perret (1874–1954). In 1947–54 Le Corbusier created the modern housing complex Unité d'Habitation (Cité Radieuse).

Around the Canebière

La Canebière

The principal artery of the busy inner city is the Canebière (Provençal Canebiero), a broad highway which begins at the harbour. This street, about 1 km long, is lined with shops and offices. The name is derived from *cannabis* (hemp) and means rope-walk. Former hemp fields near the Old Harbour provided the raw material for the rope makers.

The former boulevard – it was once compared to the Champs-Élysées – now forms a social and cultural boundary, separating the poor Belsunce quarter in the north from the more affluent southern part of the city. Various redevelopment programmes are attempting to ameliorate the situation.

Bourse

Coming from the harbour, on the left of the Canebière stands the Bourse (Stock Exchange), an impressive building of 1852–60, with the Musée de la Marine (marine museum; collection of pictures and other artistic exhibits of the Marseille Chamber of Trade; many drawings and plans of 17th c. ships).

Musée d'Histoire de Marseille

The redesigned Centre de la Bourse (Stock Exchange Centre; department stores) gives access to the excavation site where remains of the Greek fortifications

of the port of Massalia (3rd–2nd c. BC) were uncovered, and which has been laid out as a park (Jardin des Vestiges) and open-air museum. On the ground floor of the Stock Exchange Centre can be seen a collection of the finds, including the hull of a 3rd c. Roman ship. In the summer of 1993 a relatively well-preserved Greek ship, about 2500 years old, was found by a workman in the Old Town.
◎ *Mon.–Sat. noon–7pm.*

★ Musée Cantini

South of the Canebière, at 19 rue de Grignan, which is reached by way of rue Paradis, is the Musée Cantini. As well as porcelain the museum has an important collection of 20th c. art (there are also temporary exhibitions).
◎ *Daily 10am–5pm; Sat., Sun. in summer noon–7pm.*

Not far to the east of the Stock Exchange the Canebière crosses the broad cours St-Louis (on the right) which leads into rue de Rome and on the left cours de Belsunce which is continued by rue d'Aix. This crossing is the intersection of the main roads leading east–west and north–south and is also the south-western corner of the Arab quarter which extends north as far as the Porte d'Aix and the Gare St-Charles.

About 250 m further on is the intersection with boulevard Dugommier (to the left) and boulevard Garibaldi (to the right). At the end of the Canebière stands the neo-Gothic Church of St-Vincent-de-Paul.

Around boulevard Longchamp

★ Palais Longchamp

At the eastern end of boulevard Longchamp, which runs parallel to boulevard de la Libération, the continuation of the Canebière, stands the Palais Longchamp with stately museum buildings on either side of a pillared hall (fountains). It was built by Espérandieu in 1862–69 at the end of the canal from the Durance to Marseille. On the left is the Musée des Beaux Arts with 16th and 17th c. paintings (Perugino, Rubens), works by Provençal masters (Puget, Serre, Mignard), modern sculptures and works by the caricaturist Honoré Daumier, born in 1808 in Marseille. (Opening hours as for the Musée Cantini.) On the right is the Musée d'Histoire Naturelle (Natural History Museum).

Fish market in the Old Harbour

Musée Grobet-Labadié

Boulevard Longchamp terminates in a circular open space, where stands the Musée Grobet-Labadié, a mansion with beautiful furniture, given to the town by Madame Grobet. On display are musical instruments, medieval sculpture and tapestries, 18th c. furniture and ceramics (opening hours as for the Musée Cantini).

Around the Old Harbour

★Vieux Port

In the west of the town, where the Canebière begins, lies the picturesque Vieux Port (**Old Harbour**; 25 ha, 4–7 m deep), which is now used only by fishing boats and sports craft. From here boats leave for the Château d'If and Calanques, near Cassis (☛Surroundings). The lively waterfront, especially quai des Belges on the east side (fish market every morning), is a focal point for tourists. At the harbour entrance two forts stand sentinel: on the left the Fort St-Jean and on the right the Fort St-Nicolas (17th c.; viewpoint).

Basilique St-Victor

To the east of Fort St-Nicolas is the fortress-like Basilica St-Victor, which once belonged to an abbey founded in the 5th c. In its present form, with its turreted towers, it is of 11th to 14th c.; the foundations go back to Early Christian and Carolingian times. In the crypt can be seen the original catacomb chapel and the Grotto of St Victor, and in the basilica a 13th c. Black Madonna. 🄖 *Daily 8am–noon, 2–6pm.*

Parc du Pharo

On a hill to the south of the harbour entrance, below which runs a road tunnel, the Tunnel St-Laurent, lies the Parc du Pharo, with the former great château of the Empress Eugénie (the wife of Napoléon III) and a naval memorial. In summer open-air plays are performed outside the château. From the park there is an extensive view of the port and the town.

★Notre-Dame-de-la-Garde

The 154 m limestone hill in the south of Marseille was used in ancient times at least as an observation point or guard post. In the 15th c. it was the official relay station for the royal intelligence

Notre-Dame-de-la-Garde

network (smoke and light signals). Today the Basilica of Notre-Dame-de-la-Garde on its summit is the landmark of the city, visible from afar. It was built on the site of a medieval pilgrimage chapel in 1853–64 by Espérandieu in neo-Byzantine style of light and dark stone. A gilded Madonna crowns the 46 m high belfry.

The whole of the interior of the church is clad in white and dark marble. In the crypt can be seen many votive tablets and model aircraft given by aviators.
🄖 *Summer 7am–7.30pm; winter 7.30am–5.30pm. Access by bus 60.*

★★View

From the terrace encircling the church there is a marvellous panorama including the offshore islands of Pomègues and Ratonneau and the Château d'If (☛Surroundings). At the north-west bastion is an orientation table.

Old Town

The Old Town with its steep crooked streets lies to the north of the Old Port.

The Old Harbour with Notre-Dame-de-la-Garde

On the north side of the harbour basin is quai du Port, with the Hôtel de Ville (Town Hall) built in the late 17th c. on a Genoese model.

Museums

The Musée du Vieux Marseille (history of the town, Provençal furniture and costumes, utensils of the 17th–19th c.) is housed in the Maison Diamantée to the north of the Old Harbour. The house is named from the diamond-shaped stone blocks of which it is built; it is a good example of bourgeois architecture of the end of the 16th c. Further west in place de Vivaux is the Musée des Docks Romains which is equally worth a visit. It is the only museum in Provence erected right above the excavations; on view is one of the few remaining Roman trading places. Opening hours of both museums as for the Musée Cantini.

St-Laurent

Near Fort St-Jean (see above) stands the Romanesque Church of St-Laurent, which was severely damaged in the second world war. The side chapels date

from the 15th and 16th c., the octagonal tower from the 18th c.

Cathédrale de la Major

On a terrace in the north-west of the Old Town, above the new port installations, stands the mighty Cathedral of the Major, with two domed towers and a 16 m high dome over the crossing. It was built between 1852 and 1893 in a mixture of Romanesque and Byzantine styles of alternate courses of white and green limestone. Choir and nave are part of an original 11th century building. A faience relief by Lucca della Robbia from the 11th century has also been preserved. With a length of 141 m it is the most spacious ecclesiastical building of the 19th c. The interior is richly decorated with marble and mosaic; in the crypt can be seen the tombs of the bishops of Marseille.

St-Lazare

The Cathédrale de la Major completely overshadows the former cathedral of St-Lazare (Cathédrale Ancienne Major, dating from the 4th to 12th c.) beside it.

In the Chapel of St-Severin there is reliquary altar, another (of St-Lazare) is in the left-hand aisle. The chapel to the left of the remarkable apse has an Interment by Robbia, and a Romanesque reliquary shrine dating back to 1122.

★Vieille Charité

Not far north-east of St-Lazare is the Vieille Charité, a hospice for the poor, built between 1671 and 1745 to plans by Jean and Pierre Puget (the latter is little known as an architect). This masterpiece of French hospital architecture of the end of the 17th c., with its chapel designed by Pierre Puget, is now a scientific and cultural centre.

The **Musée d'Archéologie Méditerranée** is housed here. It has a notable Egyptian department and pottery, bronzes and glass dating from Etruscan, Greek and Roman times. Also on display are drawings and paintings by a number of masters (Fragonard, Ingres, Boucher) and a collection of regional archaeology. Opening hours are as for the Musée Cantini.

Other sights

South of here is the Cour des Accoules, with a 19th c. Calvary chapel, overlooked by the Clocher des Accoules (bell tower), the remains of one of the oldest churches in Marseille. In the immediate vicinity in place Daviel stands the Hôtel-Dieu, which is reputed to have been founded towards the end of the 12th c. The plans for the construction of the new building were largely the work of the architects Portal and Mansart. In the front courtyard was a monument to the designer Honoré Daumier of Marseille, with a bronze by A Bourdelle. Also in place Daviel is the fine Palais de Justice (old lawcourts; 1743–7).

Northern Marseille

Port Moderne

Downhill from the cathedral, about 1 km from the Old Harbour, the Port Moderne (New Harbour; over 200 ha; 25 km of quays) was laid out from 1844. Most passenger ships (including ferries for Corsica) dock in the Bassin de la Grande Joliette, which is 20 ha in extent. On quai de la Joliette, opposite the end of boulevard des Dames, lies the Gare Maritime (Marine Railway Station) immediately above the harbour basin.

From the Jetée (mole; 5 km long, access only at weekends), there is a good view of the New Harbour. Going east from the port along boulevard des Dames we come to place Jules-Guesde, where stands the **Arc de Triomphe** (triumphal arch), erected in 1825–32 to commemorate the capture of Fort Trocadéro at Cadiz.

Southern Marseille

Avenue du Prado

The broad avenue du Prado (called the Prado for short), expansively laid out and shaded by plane trees, is the southern continuation of rue de Rome and leads to the Rond-Point du Prado. On the left are the Parc Amable Chanot and the exhibition grounds with the Palais des Congrès.

★Parc Borély

From the Rond-Point avenue du Prado continues south-west to the shore. On the left is the Parc Borély where the film of the tales of Marcel Pagnol (director

Unité d'Habitation by Le Corbusier

Yves Robert, premiere 1991) was shot, and the mansion which was built for a rich merchant called Borély in 1767–78.

Unité d'Habitation (Cité Radieuse)

About 1.3 km south of the Rond-Point, on the right side of boulevard Michelet, extends the Unité d'Habitation, also called the Cité Radieuse, a residential complex designed by Le Corbusier (built 1947–52) and intended to 'show the way ahead'. The huge rectangular construction, 165 m long and 56 m high, comprises on eight double storeys 337 flats of 23 different types. There are communal rooms, shops, a kindergarten, a bar, a theatre, and on some floors *rues intérieures* complete the internal facilities. The 'House', which is supported by seventeen pairs of concrete stilts – these also contain the supply services – represents a whole town for some 1600 inhabitants. The basic idea behind this construction was to provide accommodation for many people in the smallest possible area and to leave room for green open spaces. Le Corbusier has nevertheless sought to realise harmonious proportions and forms. Today this experiment is criticised for not permitting the spontaneity and individuality of modern city life.

Surroundings

★Château d'If

About 2 km south-west of Marseille, the fortified rock island in the Bay of Marseille with its Château d'If is famous on account of the novel *The Count of Monte Christo* (1844–5) by Alexandre Dumas the Elder. The fortress, built in 1524, was once used as a prison. There is a fine view from the top of the cliff.

Ratonneau, Pomègues, le Planier

West of the Château d'If lie the two fairly large islands of Ratonneau and Pomègues, linked by a causeway which encloses the Port de Frioul (yacht harbour; quarantine station). Further out to sea can be seen the little island of le Planier.

Europort Sud

See Martigues

Rove-Tunnel

From the Anse de l'Estaque in the north of the bay the Rove Canal used to run in a tunnel under the Chaîne de l'Estaque to the Étang de Berre. At 22 m wide and 15.4 m high it was the tunnel with the largest cross-section and ships with a draught of up to 4.5 m could use the 7 km canal. In 1963 it collapsed and has since been closed. From the N568 a path

View from Cape Canaille towards the Calanques

The Old Harbour and wharves in la Ciotat

under the railway line leads to the tunnel entrance.

Château Gombert
On the northern edge of the city, at the end of place des Héros, with its rows of plane trees, stands the Château Gombert. Here is the Musée des Arts et Traditions Populaires du Terroir Marseillais, a collection of Provençal art in the house of a pupil of Mistral.

Grottes Loubière
About 1.5 km north-west in the Massif de l'Etoile are the Loubière Grottos, a cave system with impressive karst features.

Allauch
The health resort of Allauch is situated amid magnificent hill scenery on the outskirts of Marseille, about 10 km north-east. In the Church of St-Sébastien can be seen a fine painting of the Ascension by Monticelli. To the south lies the attractive square allée des Grands-Vents, with four 16th c. windmills, one of which has been restored and now houses the Tourist Office. In place Pierre-Bellot is the Musée du Vieil Allauch (local history).

Above the village to the east stands the 12th c. Chapel of Notre-Dame-du-Château, from where there is a rewarding view.

Cassis
The little port of Cassis, 22 km south-east of Marseille, lies on a semicircular bay, framed by mountains. It was once the haunt of painters, including Vlaminck, Dufy and Matisse; nowadays it is an important recreation centre for the people of nearby Marseille. The white wine of Cassis is renowned (*appellation d'origine contrôlée*).

Of interest are the historic centre with remains of 12th and 14th c. fortifications, a château (1381) and the beautiful Fontaine des Quatre Nations.

In September 1991 a cave with important prehistoric paintings was discovered. The entrance is underwater.

★★Calanques
Between Marseille and Cassis lie the magnificent Calanques, narrow fiord-like coves between vertical rock walls. They are partly used as natural yacht harbours and are popular with rock climbers. The large Calanques, Port-Miou, En-Vau and Port-Pin, are particularly impressive; they are accessible from the land and can be reached by boat from Cassis (trips according to demand).

Warning During the holiday season cars are often broken into and thefts committed; visitors are, therefore, strongly urged to leave no valuables behind in their vehicles.

La Ciotat

The port and industrial town of la Ciotat, 30 km south-east of Marseille, can be reached via Cassis (see above). Given sufficient time, the visitor should not use the inland route D559 from Cassis but the somewhat narrow and winding ★★Corniche des Crêtes which runs just below the Falaises, the tallest cliffs in France, high above the sea to Cap Canaille (362 m). In the afternoon especially there is a splendid view of the coast from the Calanques to Cap Croisette. The whole stretch, barely 15 km long, leads via the Grande Tête to la Ciotat.

La Ciotat, a pretty fishing village with a once-important shipyard (now closed; dry dock for ships up to 300,000 tonnes) lies on the western side of the bay of the same name, dominated by the bold crags of the Cap de l'Aigle (Cape of the Eagle), 155 m high. Offshore is the little Île Verte (Green Island) with a fortress. In the attractive Old Town are many 17th and 18th c. houses, and near the Town Hall (1864) a turreted keep. Notable paintings are to be seen in the parish church at the Old Port. A visit to the Musée d'Histoire Locale (local history) is recommended.

Following the new harbour northwards we reach the district of la Ciotat-Plage, with hotels and a beach.

Martigues   J 6

Département: Bouches-du-Rhône
Altitude: sea-level
Population: 42,000

The picturesque town of Martigues lies on the western edge of the Étang de Berre, about 30 km north-west of Marseille.

Sights

Venice of Provence

The character of the surroundings of Martigues has been strongly influenced by the construction of the motorway and industrial plants. Nevertheless the town, which because of its situation on the Canal de Caronte is sometimes called the Venice of Provence, has retained to a considerable extent its atmosphere of bygone days. The Canal St-Sébastien and the picturesque corner – Miroir aux Oiseaux (Mirror of the Birds) – of the Île, the central part of the town, are given a particularly attractive appearance by fishing boats with their nets hanging up to dry. The canal is overlooked by the square tower of the 17th c. Church of Ste-Madeleine-de-L'Île with its wrought-iron bell cage.

Chapelle de l'Annonciade

In Jonquières, in the southern part of the town, near the Church of St-Genest (17th c.), is the Chapel of the Annonciade with 17th c. sculpture and paintings.

Musée du Vieux Martigues

In Ferrières, in the north of the town, can be found the Musée du Vieux Martigues with local history collections, and the Ziem Museum (Félix Ziem 1821–1911, landscape painter).

Surroundings

Europort Sud

With the petroleum harbour of Lavéra there begins the largest port and industrial complex in area of southern Europe. It comprises refineries, steelworks, production of man-made materials and oil storage installations. In this coastal zone, known as Europort Sud, more than 80 million tonnes of oil are handled every year. The 782 km long pipeline to Karlsruhe starts from here.

Cap Couronne

9 km south of Martigues and pleasantly situated on a hill above the Anse du Verdon lies the resort of la Couronne. 2 km south rises Cap Couronne, from which there is a good view of the sandy bays to the east.

Sausset-les-Pins

On a little bay, protected by the southern escarpment of the Chaîne de l'Estaque (which was one of the subjects of Paul Cézanne) lies the fishing port and resort of Sausset-les-Pins, 6 km east of la Couronne. It is popular as a recreation area for the people of Marseille.

Carry-le-Rouet

The fishing port and resort of Carry-le-Rouet, another 4 km east on the southern foot of the Chaîne de l'Estaque, is a popular resort and yacht mooring.

The sector of le Rouet-Plage at the end of the charming Vallon de l'Aigle is especially attractive. Just to the east lies the beautiful Calanque des Anthénors (yachting and bathing) and the little bay of Méjean.

Châteauneuf-les-Martigues

The largely agricultural community of Châteauneuf-les-Martigues, some 10 km east of Martigues, lies at the foot of the northern flank of the Chaîne de l'Estaque. The beach, the Plage du Jaï, is situated on the spit of land which encloses the Etang de Balmon.

Marignane

The township of Marignane, 16 km east of Martigues and 18 km west of Marseille, is considerably affected by traffic using the nearby airport, within which are situated the installations of Aérospatiale (air and space industry, Airbus).

Maures (Massif des Maures)   K 13–15

Département: Var
Altitude: up to 780 m

The Massif des Maures, on the coast between Hyères in the west and Fréjus in the east, is a hilly area some 60 km long and 30 km wide; it is composed of granite, gneiss and slate (reddish or dark grey in colour, with metallically glistening mica) and represents the remains of a land mass that once covered the whole of the western Mediterranean. The deeply fissured afforested uplands are still relatively isolated. The name has nothing to do with the Moors who in these parts were always called Sarrasins, but is derived from the Provençal *maure* or *moure*, meaning dark, uncanny.

★Corniche des Maures

The Corniche des Maures for the greatest part of the way is road D559 along the coast and, with its many bays and cliffs between le Lavandou and St-Tropez (see entries), has exceptionally fine scenery. It passes a considerable number of resorts; just beyond Cavalaire it skirts Cap Nègre (120 m) and, via Canadel-sur-Mer and Rayol, reaches the resort and port of Cavalaire-sur-Mer (château ruin) situated on a sheltered bay. To the north-west rises the 528 m high summit of les

Pradels. The Corniche continues around the peninsula of Cap Camarat near St-Tropez and ends near St-Tropez Bay.

Collobrières

Reached by road D41 going north from Bormes-les-Mimosas (see le Lavandou) for about 22 km, Collobrières lies in a hollow in the heart of the Massif des Maures. It is well known for its *marrons glacés* and Provençal joinery. Fossils and minerals have been found in the vicinity.

La Garde-Freinet

Also inland lies la Garde-Freinet, reached from Port-Grimaud along roads D14 and D558 (16 km). Situated on a pass with fine views, the village was a major Saracen stronghold, but had already been a Roman military post. Of interest are the ruins of the former Saracen fortress of Freinet on a hill to the north-east (about 30 min. walk), from where there is an extensive panorama.

Grimaud

See Port-Grimaud

★★Menton   G 21

Département: Alpes-Maritimes
Altitude: sea-level
Population: 25,500

Menton (Italian Mentone), at the eastern end of the Côte d'Azur on the Italian border, lies on the Golfe de la Paix which is divided by a rocky promontory into the Baie de Garavan on the east and the Baie de l'Ouest on the west. The situation and climate of Menton makes possible the cultivation of citrus fruits.

Lower Town

Casino

The focus of the town is the Casino (1932) on the west bay, and from here promenade du Soleil leads north to the harbour.

★Jardin Biovès

On its landward side in the valley of the Carei river (now diverted underground) is the fine Jardin Biovès with its exotic trees. In the park (avenue Boyer) stands the Palais d'Europe, a building of the belle époque housing the Congress and Cultural Centre and the Tourist Office.

★Musée Jean Cocteau
In the 17th c. harbour bastion at the beginning of the mole can be found the Musée Jean Cocteau, with pictures, drawings and stage designs.
From the end of both the moles of the Vieux Port there are fine views of the Old Town. From the Casino avenue Félix-Faure, the principal shopping street of the town, runs north-east parallel to the promenade.

★Hôtel de Ville
In the next parallel main street, rue de la République, stands the Italianate Hôtel de Ville (Town Hall). Of particular interest is the Salle des Mariages which was decorated by Cocteau (guided visits).

★★Musée Municipal, Musée des Beaux-Arts
The Musée Municipal, on rue Henri-Greville north of the Town Hall, has a comprehensive collection of local and prehistoric exhibits (including the negroid skull discovered in 1884 in the caves of Baoussé-Roussé, Italian Balzi-Rossi).

The collection of paintings is housed in the Palais Carnolès to the south-west, on avenue de la Madone.

Old Town

Harbour
The Old Town is reached by way of rue St-Michel, the continuation of avenue Félix-Faure. On the east side are the Harbour and the Plage des Sablettes, the principal beach which has been artificially improved.

Other sights
Further north along montée des Logettes and the narrow rue Longue, the former main street of the Old Town, the atmosphere of which is thoroughly Italian (a tunnel now runs under this area), you pass the remains of fortifications. On the left an imposing flight of steps (rampes St-Michel) leads up to an observation terrace. Here on the left side of place de la Conception stands the parish church of St-Michel (17th c.; altarpiece by Manchello 1569) and higher up is the Church of the Conception (1685). Both churches are in the Italian Jesuit style. On the old château hill, reached via rue du Vieux-Château or montée du Souvenir, lies the Old Cemetery (altitude 46 m; fine view) which was laid out in the 19th c. and has become the last

resting place for rich foreigners of various faiths.

Outer districts

★Jardin Botanique
From the cemetery boulevard de Garavan runs above the east bay to the Jardin Botanique on the right. This exotic garden on the site of the former Villa Val Rameh, contains many tropical and subtropical plants which flourish in the warm climate of Menton. From the terrace there is a view of the town and the sea. Above boulevard de Garavan lies the Jardin des Colombières, a park adorned with Mediterranean flora and ancient statues. The road now reaches the Pont St-Louis on the French-Italian frontier. From here it is possible to drive back to the town centre along quai Laurenti which follows the east bay.

Monastère de l'Annonciade
The Monastère de l'Annonciade (Capuchin monastery) lies outside the town to the north, high above the road to Sospel, with a marvellous panorama. Continuing under the motorway, there is a good view on the right of the typical Provençal village of Castellar.

Castillin Neuf
By following the road up the valley of the Caraï we reach Castillin Neuf, a village which was exemplarily rebuilt after the second world war.

Surroundings

Ste-Agnès
A narrow winding mountain road leads north-west to Ste-Agnès (11 km), a *village perché* in a most attractive situation with picturesque stepped streets. The hamlet is the starting point for fine walks in the mountains, including the ascent of the Pic de Baudon (1264 m; 2–3 hours), a climb which in places is very arduous but which rewards the climber with good views.

Villa Hanbury
There is a worthwhile excursion to the Villa Hanbury, near Mortola Inferiore 4 km inside Italy. The 18 ha park, originally laid out by an English merchant's family named Hanbury, contains 8 ha of typical Mediterranean vegetation with Aleppo

The Italianate harbour and Old Town of Menton

pines, and 10 ha of gardens in which, since 1898, 7500 different species have been planted (today it is estimated that there are still about 2000).

🕒 *Oct.–May Thu.–Tue. 10am–4pm; Jun.–Sep. 9am–6pm.*

Roquebrune
See Roquebrune-Cap-Martin

Col de Turini
See Suggested Routes 3b

Mercantour – Gorges des Alpes-Maritimes   C–F 15–21

Départements: Alpes-Maritimes, Alpes-de-Haute-Provence
Altitude: up to 3143 m

The Massif du Mercantour is situated in the extreme south of the Alpine chain, about 50 km north of Nice as the crow flies. The Franco-Italian border runs over its principal crest. A considerable part of this mountainous region forms the Parc National du Mercantour, 200,000 ha, founded in 1979, which is continued on the Italian side by the Parco Nazionale

della Argentera. Information:
PARC NATIONAL DU MERCANTOUR
23 rue d'Italie, BP 316, 06006 Nice.

Vallée des Merveilles
The attraction of the Mercantour has in some places caused problems, especially on Mont Bego in the Vallée des Merveilles. More than 100,000 figurative symbols, which Bronze Age people carved in the rocks here (1800–1500 BC) are under severe threat. The messages to the gods repeat over and over again a few motifs: the celestial bull which brings thunder and lightning; the three-edged dagger, typical of the Bronze Age; the scythe and geometric figures. Visitors contribute their own messages or help themselves to souvenirs and so certain areas have been closed and educational trails laid out. In Tende there is a museum devoted to the history of the herdsmen and the Vallée des Merveilles from the Bronze Age to the present day.

Access
The best route to the National Park from the Mediterranean coast is the N202 west of Nice which leads inland up the valley of the Var. From the north the stretch

from Gap via Barcelonnette to Auron
crosses the highest pass in the Alps, the
Col de la Bonette (2802 m).

Gorges des Alpes-Maritimes

The following description of the route
through the gorges to the south of the
Mercantour National Park is given from
south to north.

★Gorges de la Vésubie

About 23 km north of Nice airport the
D2565 branches off near Plan-du-Var
into the Gorges de la Vésubie, the
impressive ravines of the river of the
same name. Follow the road through
the narrow lower part of the valley for
10 km to the village of St-Jean-la-Rivière.
From here a narrow winding road on the
left comes, via the village of Utelle, to
the pilgrimage church of Notre-Dame-
des Miracles (Madone d'Utelle) which
was founded in the 9th c. From the
church, which is at a height of 1174 m,
the view extends over the mountains to
the Mediterranean.

★Défilé du Chaudan

After the diversion near Plan-du-Var
mentioned above, the main road
continues along the river which, not far
to the north, rushes through the Défilé
du Chaudan, a picturesque gorge framed
by vertical cliffs. At the far end of the
gorge the Route Nationale crosses the
river by the Pont de la Mescla. The
sloping limestone strata at the narrow
part of the gorge near where the D2205
turns off on the right, just short of the
bridge, make a very impressive sight.
Follow the D2205 into the valley of the
Tinée.

★Gorges de la Mescla

The Tinée river, which is now followed,
flows through the Gorges de la Mescla
just before its confluence with the Var.
The gorges are a highlight of this
magnificent stretch. The valley is quite
wide as far as Bancairon, then the road
again hugs the rock face. You pass the
villages of Clans and Marie, which are
built high up on outcrops and are worth
making a detour to see (very narrow
winding streets).

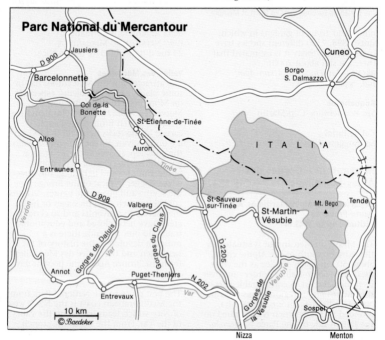

St-Jean-la-Rivière in the Vésubie valley

Beyond Bolinette the scenery changes. The white and grey limestone with its huge and often dramatically folded strata gradually is replaced by dark porphyry, a uniform brittle volcanic rock, which can also be seen in the Gorges Supérieures du Cians. The harmony of rocks and luxuriant vegetation is very beautiful.

About 21 km after leaving the Route Nationale, the D2565 turns right over the 1500 m high Col St-Martin into the beautiful upland valley of the Boréon, the starting point of many mountain footpaths. The D2205 continues to follow the main valley to the high mountain region which is popular both in summer and in winter for walking, mountaineering and skiing.

Beyond St-Sauveur (belfry of 1333, altarpiece of 1483) the D30 branches off and winds along amid a gentle alpine landscape, with terraced meadows and deciduous and coniferous forests, through the following small mountain resorts: the village of Roure (16th c. Church of St-Laurent with 13th c. belfry) perched boldly on the mountainside; Roubion (alt. 1200 m; on the left of the D38 before reaching the village are the

16th c. Chapel of St-Sébastien; wall paintings); and Beuil with a 15th c. belfry, a 17th c. church with interesting paintings and the 16th c. Chapel of the White Penitents with trompe-l'oeil paintings on the facade. Finally the road leads west to the winter sports village of Valberg, but by turning south we enter the Gorges du Cians.

★★Gorges du Cians

By following the N202 from the Pont de la Mescla (see above) for about 19 km you reach a junction on the right, the D28, which leads to the Gorges du Cians. The cleft which the Cians river has cut into the rock is up to 80 m deep, but in places only a few metres wide. The road runs alongside the river at the bottom of the gorge. The road first traverses the Gorges Inférieures, the 5 km long stretch dominated by 450 m high chalk pinnacles, to the Moulin de Rigaud. Then the road winds upwards into the more rugged and deeper Gorges Supérieures, 7 km long, which are entirely cut into the dark red porphyry.

★Gorges du Daluis

Still fully 20 km further up the valley of

the Var, beyond the village of Entrevaux (see entry), the D902 diverges from the N202 and climbs towards the top of the pass – the Col de Toutes Aures (1124 m) – 18 km to the west. The D902 follows the upper course of the Var and reveals another rewarding landscape. The Gorges du Daluis form an impressive 6 km long ravine, with the road reaching up to 200 m above the Var. Curious red porphyry walls, in places flecked with green, line the road which is led through them in tunnels or around them. Beyond Guillaumes this route continues to Valberg.

Lac de Castillon

By driving over the Col de Toutes Aures and past the attractive reservoir of Castillon, we reach Castellane (see entry) and continue into the magnificent gorges of the Verdon (see entry).

★★Monaco G 20

Principality of Monaco
Area: 1.95 sq km
Altitude: sea level to 65 m
Number of citizens: 4500
Number of inhabitants: 28,000

Flag   Coat of arms

The town of Monaco at the eastern end of the Côte d'Azur, close to the Italian border, is a principality. It was founded in 1297 by the Genoese noble family of Grimaldi and until 1861 also took in Menton and Roquebrune. To this day it is still ruled by princes belonging to the Grimaldi dynasty (since 1949 Prince Rainier III). Monaco is important today as a tax haven.

Monaco, formally the Principality of Monaco, has an area of 1.95 sq km, making it the second smallest European state after the Vatican City. The population, which is predominantly Catholic, consists of indigenous Monégasques (around 17 per cent , with their own local dialect,

Monegasco, which is a mixture of

Provençal and Ligurian), French (about 50 per cent), Italians (about 20 per cent) and the remainder made up of other nationalities. Residence on the rock of Monaco itself is reserved for the local Monégasques.

Two famous motor-racing events are closely associated with the principality: the Monaco Grand Prix (the weekend following Ascension Day), the only Formula One race in the world to be held on public roads, and the Monte-Carlo rally, the route of which in fact lies almost completely on French soil.

History

Prehistoric finds in the area occupied by the town of Monaco indicate that there were settlements here before the Stone Age. Around 900 BC Phoenicians dedicated a rock to the Baal of Tyre (the Melkart cult). After its development as a trading centre by the Greeks it became a port under the Romans and was given the name Herculis Monoeci Portus. Its subsequent history was influenced by the effects of population migrations and Saracen rule. From the 8th c. AD Monaco found itself under Genoese authority. The fief of Monaco was provided with a fortress in 1215, remains of which survive, and since 1297 has been ruled by the Genoese noble family of Grimaldi, which in 1612 was granted the title of prince. After a period under Spanish protection Monaco came under the control of the French line of Goyon de Matignon-Grimaldi and in 1793 was united with France. In 1814 it was returned to Prince Honoré IV and between 1815 and 1860 came under the protection of the kingdom of Sardinia, only to be transferred back to France in 1860. Prince Charles III protested at this and in return for ceding Mentone (Menton) and Roccabruna (Roquebrune) to France, the principality was given its independence. In 1866 the town of Monte-Carlo was founded. In 1911 Albert I drew up a constitution for the principality and in 1918 relations with France were put on a new footing. In 1949 Rainier III succeeded Louis II, who had reigned since 1922, and in 1956 he married the American film actress Grace Kelly (Princess Gracia Patricia; d 1982).

Government

The 1962 constitution defines the state as a constitutional hereditary monarchy. The reins of government are formally invested with the prince and are delegated by him to the minister of state. Apart from budgetary questions, the head of state has an absolute right of veto within the government.

The government is made up of a minister of state (Ministre d'État) and three government councils (Conseils de Gouvernement) for home affairs, finance and economics, and public works and social services. In addition there is also a council of state and a trade council.

Representation of the people consists of the National Council (Conseil National), elected for five years, with 18 members, and a Community Council (Conseil Communal) elected for four years. The actual parliament is the Conseil National, which meets twice a year.

In internal as well as external affairs, the government has close links with France, both in terms of customs and monetary union (dating from 1865 and 1925 respectively) as well as in taxation laws.

Stamps

The principality is part of France for the purposes of customs administration, but since 1885 it has issued its own stamps, which are used for letters sent from Monaco. The Office des Emissions de Timbre-Poste (2 avenue St-Michel) has set up a collectors' service, which can supply stamps (also by subscription). ◙ *Mon.–Fri. 8.30am–4.30pm.*

Economy

Gambling has made Monaco rich and famous. Today the receipts from the casino, the Café de Paris and the gambling room of the Hotel Loews represent a mere 4 per cent of the budget; nevertheless, apart from high taxes on consumer spending, which make up 55 per cent of its income, the state levies no other taxes, either on income, capital growth or wealth. The largest items of expenditure are culture and science.

Besides the Monaco of gambling and casinos, there is also an industrial and commercial Monaco which is of great importance. More than 2700 firms employ over 21,000 people, of whom half live in France. In the narrower industrial sector the number of firms has risen from 162 in 1949 to close on 400 at the present time. These industries include electrical and electronic goods,

Monaco: panorama from the Tête de Chien

publishing, chemical and pharmaceutical products, perfume and synthetic materials. Monaco also plays an important role as a financial centre. In less than 15 years three urban areas have been created by building out into the sea and the land area of the town has thereby expanded by 20 per cent with the addition of nearly another 2 sq km.

The principality sees its role today very much in the service sector. The primary money earner is tourism; in 1989 there were almost 250,000 overnight stays (28 per cent from Italy, 22 per cent from France, 12 per cent from the US, 9 per cent from the UK, 4.5 per cent from Germany). The tourist organisation whose presence is felt throughout Monaco is the Société des Bains de Mer (SCB), founded in 1856, whose brief was to bring money into the tiny and impoverished principality. The most important hotels and restaurants belong to it, as do the casino, the opera house, the golf club and other sports facilities. The largest hotel is the 636-room Loews Monte-Carlo, which also has a casino, nightclub, cabaret and swimming pool; its Grand Salon can welcome up to 1500 guests. In general Monaco has completely adapted itself to its role as a conference, convention, exhibition and festival centre. Besides the Centre de Congrès-Auditorium Monte-Carlo (in the Spélugues complex) whose amphitheatre will hold 1100 guests, there is the Centre des Rencontres Internationales and the Monte-Carlo Sporting Club with its famous Salle des Étoiles. In 1994 the Centre Culturel et des Expositions, which surpasses all the others in terms of size and facilities, opened.

Organised events

The cycle of organised events, of whatever kind, never halts in Monaco, from traditional festivals such as that of Ste Dévote (January 27th, when a boat is set on fire), car rallies, television festivals and flower parades, to the International Circus Festival in December (☞Events). The Monte-Carlo Opera and Philharmonic Orchestra are also renowned, with outstanding conductors and orchestras from all over the world

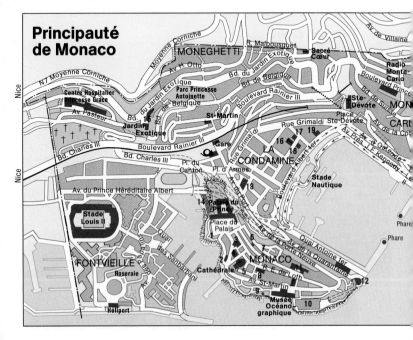

giving guest performances here. In Monaco Diaghilev founded his world-famous Ballet Russe in 1909.

Monaco-Ville

With its narrow streets Monaco-Ville, the oldest district and seat of the bishop, dominates a broad picturesque peninsula jutting out into the sea. Here remains of fortifications can be found.

★Place du Palais

In the western part of Monaco lies place du Palais with its bronze cannons dating from the time of Louis XIV; from here there is a beautiful view of Monte-Carlo. Dominating the square is the Palais du Prince, built in the 13th c. as a Genoese fortress. The changing of the guard takes place daily at 11.55am. Apart from providing this display, the Prince's Guard is also responsible for the security of the prince and his family and also appears at major events.

In the Palais there are splendid apartments, including the throne room

in Empire style, the York bedroom (18th c.) and beautiful 17th c. frescos (Genoese work). Tours take place when the prince and his family are absent (in which case the prince's flag on the Tour Ste-Marie is not raised) .

In the Palace Museum (officially Musée Napoléonien et des Archives Monegasques) can be seen many mementoes of Napoléon I, a stamp collection and a rock sample from the moon.

During the summer months concerts take place in the palace courtyard.
🄶 *Palais and Museum Jun.–Sep. daily 9.30am–6.30pm; Oct. 10am–5pm; Museum also Dec.–May Tue.–Sun. 10.30am–12.30pm, 2–5pm.*

Cathédrale

Rue du Tribunal leads from the palace to the cathedral, built between 1875 and 1884 in a Romanesque-Byzantine style. A chapel to St Nicolas, dating from 1252, was pulled down to make way for the building of the cathedral. Inside can be seen an altarpiece by Louis Bréa (ca 1500), other works of the Nice school, as

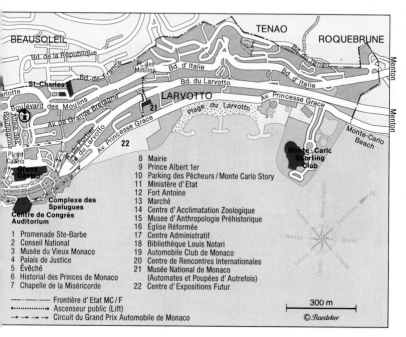

8 Mairie
9 Prince Albert 1er
10 Parking des Pêcheurs / Monte Carlo Story
11 Ministère d' Etat
12 Fort Antoine
13 Marché
14 Centre d' Acclimatation Zoologique
15 Musee d' Anthropologie Préhistorique
16 Église Réformée
17 Centre Administratif
18 Bibliothèque Louis Notari
19 Automobile Club de Monaco
20 Centre de Rencontres Internationales
21 Musée National de Monaco
    (Automates et Poupées d' Autrefois)
22 Centre d' Expositions Futur

1 Promenade Ste-Barbe
2 Conseil National
3 Musée du Vieux Monaco
4 Palais de Justice
5 Évêché
6 Historial des Princes de Monaco
7 Chapelle de la Miséricorde

———·——— Frontière d' Etat MC / F
▪▪▪▪▪▪▪▪▪▪▪ Ascenseur public (Lift)
→ · → · → · Circuit du Grand Prix Automobile de Monaco

300 m

© *Baedeker*

well as tombs of the princes (burial place of the princes of Monaco) and bishops. The grave of Princess Grace also lies here.

Opposite stands the Palais de Justice (lawcourts) and nearby the Historial des Princes (historical collection), as well as the notable Chapel of the Miséricorde of 1639; the first provost of the penitential monks resident here was Prince Honoré II. Inside there is a wooden statue of Christ, by François-Joseph Bosio, official sculptor of Napoléon, born in 1769 in Monaco (d 1845 in Paris).

★Musée Océanographique

The Jardins de St-Martin extend along the coast round the peninsula with a steep cliff on the seaward side, near which stands a statue commemorating Prince Albert I, a celebrated marine researcher. At the end of the gardens is the Musée Océanographique (marine museum); the facade facing the sea is 87 m high. The museum, which was opened in 1910 and took 11 years to build, houses valuable scientific collections (objects from Prince Albert's journeys of exploration, finds, submarines and diving equipment of Jacques-Yves Cousteau, pictures of marine plants and animals), also an important aquarium, laboratory and library and exhibits of model ships and educational film shows, especially about Jacques-Yves Cousteau. From the roof terrace (restaurant) it is possible to enjoy a superb view of the Italian Riviera as far as the Esterel Massif (also visible from Fort Antoine on the east of the peninsula).

🕐 *Jul., Aug. daily 9am–9pm; Apr.–Jun., Sep. 9am–7pm; Oct., Mar. 9.30am–7pm; Nov.–Feb. 9am–6pm.*

Centre d'Acclimatation Zoologique

On the western slope of the cliff is the Centre d'Acclimatation Zoologique (a centre for animal acclimatisation, a kind of zoo with tropical and African fauna), established in 1954.

Old Town

Fontvieille

A 222,000 sq m area was created and protected from the sea by a dam 30 m deep in order to form the district of Fontvieille. To the west, beneath the rock

The Palais de Prince in Monaco-Ville

Grand Prix de Monaco: the Ancien Gare curve

on which the Old Town rises, is the new Port de Fontvieille. Behind the harbour the Stade Louis II was opened in 1985, a sports stadium with 20,000 seats. There are guided tours.

🕐 *Tours daily 3pm, 4.30pm.*

Harbour
To the north, at the foot of the cliff, lies the busy, almost square, harbour which was constructed between 1901 and 1926. Large numbers of yachts, including from time to time the prince's private vessel, are moored here. On the western side of the harbour, near boulevard Albert-I, is the modern Stade Nautique Rainier III, a stadium for water sports.

Centre de Rencontres
Near the northern mole of the harbour on avenue d'Ostende is the Centre de Rencontres Internationales, an international meeting place.

La Condamine
Boulevard Albert-I is the main street of the district of la Condamine. In this quarter of the town there are numerous businesses, shops and public buildings (railway station, library, market). In the ravine-like valley on the northern edge of the town, below a road bridge stands the little Church of Ste-Dévote, dedicated to the patron saint of the town. The church has a fine 18th c. marble altar.

Moneghetti
Seemingly endless steps and roads with hairpin bends climb up the eastern slope of the Tête de Chien to the Moyenne Corniche (actually on French territory, N7; ☛Suggested Routes). These roads give access to the district of Moneghetti in the west of the principality, which is built on terraces with fine villas and gardens.

★★Jardin Exotique
The Jardin Exotique (Exotic Garden) is one of the most impressive of its kind. Because of the favourable climate, with little variation in conditions on the constantly warm and damp steep slope, a great variety of the most delicate, and in some cases unique, tropical plants thrive in the garden. In the grottoes, beautiful fossils can be seen. In the park there is also the interesting Musée d'Anthropologie Préhistorique

The Grand Casino, the landmark of the principality

(Museum of Prehistory and Anthropology), which not only exhibits bones discovered in the area but also a collection of coins and ornamental objects from the pre-Roman and Roman periods in particular. To the north of the museum lies the Parc Princesse Antoinette.
◎ *May–Sep. daily 9am–7pm; Oct–Apr. 9am–6pm.*

Monte-Carlo

The district of Monte-Carlo occupies a rocky promontory to the north of the port of Monaco. Its most elevated part is crossed by streets with shops and offices, including boulevard Princesse-Charlotte (in the west, the headquarters of Radio/Télévision Monte-Carlo), boulevard des Moulins (pavilion of the Office de Tourisme at its south-western end; a short distance to the north is the Church of St-Charles of 1883), and avenue de la Costa with its many luxury shops.

Casino

To the north of the harbour stands the magnificent Grand Casino, which was built by the architect of the Paris Opéra, Charles Garnier, between 1877 and 1879. It houses the legendary gaming rooms, opened in 1861, of the Société Anonyme des Bains de Mer et du Cercle des Etrangers (SBM). The company's full name makes reference to the fact that, to begin with, it was only allowed to open the doors of its casinos to non-Monégasques.

From the marble-covered atrium, surrounded by Ionic columns of onyx, you reach the Salle Garnier, the red and gold opera theatre, and the various gaming rooms. There is a room with games machines, the American room with American roulette and blackjack and the European salons with roulette, trente-et-quarante and baccarat. The doormen insist on appropriate dress.

★Les Spélugues

Below the casino extends the large-scale complex of the Congress Centre (called les Spélugues), which was opened in 1978. Boulevard Louis-II runs under the massive building which has been constructed on a hexagonal theme and includes the 636-room Hotel Loews, 100 apartments and a casino. On the roof level, of which there is an excellent view from the terrace in front of the casino, there is a striking mosaic of coloured tiles, which was designed in 1979 by Victor Vasarély and is called *Hexagrace-Le Ciel, la Mer, la Terre*. The Fondation Vasarély in Aix-en-Provence (see entry) was responsible for its execution.

Larvotto
In the south-west of the district of Larvotto stands the Centre Culturel et des Expositions. On avenue Princesse-Grace can be found the Musée National des Automates et Poupées d'Autrefois (museum of mechanical toys and dolls), housed in a belle-époque villa. On view are several hundred dolls, more than 80 automatons and over 2000 miniature objects, the purpose of which is to depict life in the 18th and 19th c. In the garden there are sculptures by Zadkine, Maillol, Rodin and Bourdeille.

Surroundings

Cap d'Ail
At the foot of the Tête de Chien amid sparse pine woods lies the holiday resort of Cap-d'Ail (2 km south-east of Monaco). Of interest are the ruins of the Tour d'Abeglio and the open-air theatre, designed by Jean Cocteau and decorated with mosaics. Several rocky promontories jut out into the sea near Cap-d'Ail.

La Turbie
The picturesque township of la Turbie is situated on the saddle between a ridge of the Tête de Chien and the Mont de la Bataille, 8 km to the north-west of Monaco. In the baroque Church of St-Michel-Archange (late 18th c.) there is a most remarkable communion rail made of agate and onyx, two paintings by Jean-Baptiste van Loo, a pietà of the Bréa school and a fine high altar of coloured marble, which was used during the French Revolution in Nice. Both town gates are relics of the fortifications begun in the 13th c.

La Turbie is dominated by a feature

visible from afar, the ★**Trophée des Alpes**, also called the Trophée d'Auguste. This monument was erected to the Emperor Augustus by the Roman senate in 6 BC as a memorial to the suppression of the Alpine tribes (14–13 BC). In the 14th c. it was converted into a fortress and in 1705 blown up (with little success) by Louis XIV during the War of the Spanish Succession. The monument was restored in about 1930, with American funds. The grounds around the monument have been laid out as a park; the steep south and south-eastern sides offer a marvellous view of the coast.

★Peillon
Peillon, situated at an altitude of 376 m in the hinterland of Monaco (5 km as the crow flies), is probably one of the finest examples of a Provençal *nid d'aigle*. In the Chapel of Notre-Dame-de-la Madone-des-Douleurs (or Chapel of the White Monks) there are frescos by Canavesi (15th–16th c.). In August the Fêtes du Vieux Village take place.

The Trophée des Alpes in la Turbie

Peille – a typical *village perché*

Peille
Another beautiful *village perché* (perched on a rock) is Peille, situated 630 m high above the Peillon river. The Romanesque church dating from the 12th c. boasts a rose martyry (16th c.) as well as beautiful naïve paintings. Over the village tower the ruins of a 13th c. fortress.

★Montélimar   B4

Région: Rhône-Alpes
Département: Drôme
Altitude: 81 m
Population: 30,000

Montélimar lies not far east of the Rhône, which is dammed in this section, some 150 km south of Lyon. The Roubion river flows past the town centre.

Montélimar, which derives its name from its château (Mont Adhémar), is known for its nougat industry, which uses locally grown almonds and honey.

The confectionery comes in many varieties, hard or soft, white or coloured, regular or in various flavours or 'perfumes': vanilla, honey, lavender, and so on. Shops selling it are found on allées Champs-de-Mars and boulevard A-Briand (ring road, car parking).

Château
To the east of the Old Town rises the château, built by the powerful Adhémar family (☛Grignan) in the 12th c. From 1340 to 1383 the château, together with the town, came into the possession of the popes, who were responsible for enlarging it. In the 16th c. it formed the north-east corner of the fortified town. From 1791 the château was used as a prison (until 1926) – a role which it had fulfilled on and off since the 15th c. Still preserved are the massive square Tour de Narbonne, the donjon (keep), logis (tower with living quarters) and the Chapel of St-Pierre, probably the oldest building in the complex, which displays the early southern French Romanesque style (11th c.) and has 14th c. frescos in its main apse.

From its terraces and tower the château offers a vantage point; in the north the cooling towers of the atomic power station at Cruas on the Rhône can be seen.

Montmajour – Fontvieille   G4

Département: Bouches-du-Rhône
Altitude: 15 m

★Abbaye de Montmajour

History
The former Benedictine abbey of Montmajour (Mont-Major), perched on a rocky hill 5 km north-east of Arles, rather like a fortress, was founded in the 10th c. and throughout the Middle Ages was an important place of pilgrimage. This pilgrimage could lead to the 'Pardon of Montmajour' and provided the monastery with a plentiful source of income. Other monasteries were founded by the monks from this abbey. The plain surrounding the hill was originally marsh and alluvial land and was not drained until the abbey was founded.

The château of the Adhémar family in Montélimar

At the start of the 18th c. the baroque buildings were begun, as the original 12th c. buildings had largely fallen into disrepair; however in 1785–6 the abbot, Cardinal Rohan, was implicated in the famous 'necklace' affair and the monastery was closed. In 1791, together with most church property, it was confiscated and sold.
🖸 *Apr.–Sept. daily 9am–6.30pm; Oct.–Mar. 9–11.30am, 2–4.30pm; closed pub. hols.*

Crypt

The first part of the monastery to visit is the huge Romanesque crypt, dating from the 12th c., which supports the church above, and which is partly built into the rock. The central space is surrounded by a vaulted corridor with apses in a semicircle.

Church

From the crypt the church above can be reached; this is a short, austere building with only two bays in the nave, a semicircular main apse and two side apses; at the end of the left transept is the square Chapelle Notre-Dame-la-Blanche. In the 18th c. plans were made to extend the nave westwards, but the scheme was never realised.

Cloister

The cloister adjoins the church on the south-west. It was probably built at the same time as the church, though only the east range shows the original Romanesque outline. The arches are divided by double pillars; rich ornamentation (comparable to that at St-Trophime at Arles; see entry) can be seen on the corbels which support the ribbed vaults. The cloister, in the middle of which stands a well on a plinth, is overlooked by the battlemented defensive keep, 26 m high, which was built in 1369 and boasts a superb view from its roof.

Baroque ruins

To the west of the Romanesque buildings are the ruins of extensions to it, which date from the baroque period

Montmajour Abbey: the cloister and keep

Moulin de Daudet

and are not open to the public. This enormous construction – a length of 135 m was planned, while a further 90 m were added during the building – was undertaken in 1703 by the architect Pierre Mignard. In 1726 a fire destroyed those parts which had been completed. Restoration of the damaged parts and further building under Jean-Baptiste Franque came to a halt in 1736.

Ste-Croix
On the right of the road about 200 m east of the monastery stands the little Chapel of Ste-Croix, dating from the 12th c. It was once the cemetery chapel of the monastery as is indicated by the tombs, which were hewn into the rock.

Fontvieille

★Moulin de Daudet
To the north-east of Montmajour (5 km), near Fontvieille, stands one of the most popular attractions of Provence for the French – the windmill made famous by the writer Alphonse Daudet in his book

Lettres de mon Moulin. Daudet did not live in the mill, however, and the *Lettres* were not written here but in Paris. Nevertheless it is a fact that Daudet derived the inspiration for a great part of his literary output in this region. Inside the windmill there is a tiny museum with mementos to the poet. There is a good view down the valley to the Rhône, with two old watchtowers in the distance.

Ⓖ *Museum daily 9am–noon, 2–7pm; Sun. only in Jan.*

Aqueducs Romains
On either side of the D33 road, about 3 km south of Fontvieille, the visitor will find the remains of two **Roman aqueducts**, which once provided water for Arles. The ruins have not been restored but are easily accessible.

★Montpellier	off map

Région: Languedoc-Roussillon
Département: Hérault
Altitude: 50 m
Population: 210,000

Montpellier, university city, diocesan city and capital of the *région* of Languedoc-Roussillon and of the *département* of Hérault, is situated some distance west of the Camargue on the Lez river, about 10 km from the coast of the Golfe du Lion. With its three universities, national élite schools (Grandes Écoles), agricultural college (the Agropolis agrarian research centre), libraries, conservatoire, it is an economic and cultural centre for the region.

Although Montpellier is not actually in Provence, it is an attraction for visitors touring the western part of the region and is therefore included in this book.

History

The town was established after the second destruction of the nearby settlement of Maguelone by Charles Martel (737). In the 13th c. it belonged to the kings of Aragon, then until 1349 to the kings of Mallorca as vassals of the French. As early as 1289 Montpellier had a university, where Francesco Petrarca studied from 1316 to 1319, and François Rabelais from 1530 to 1532 and from 1537 to 1538. At the end of the 16th c. the city was a headquarters of the Huguenots. In 1622 it was conquered by Louis XIII.

Sights

Place de la Comédie

Place de la Comédie with its Fontaine des Trois Grâces, a fountain dating from 1776, is the heart of the city. On the south-western side of the square stands the theatre (opera house). From here the great boulevards radiate around the area of the Old Town (the greater part a pedestrian precinct), which extends to the north-west on a hilltop. In the Old Town the 50 or so patrician and merchants' mansions from the 17th and 18th c. testify to the former wealth of the city.

★Promenade du Peyrou

From place de la Comédie the visitor can take rue de la Loge (pedestrian area) and rue Foch, impressive with its splendid 19th c. buildings, to reach promenade du Peyrou, an elevated park on two levels, dating from the 17th and 18th c., which offers a beautiful view as far as the Cévennes and the sea. At the intersection of the promenades stands an equestrian statue of Louis XIV, dating from 1828, while at the western end of the terraces is a water tower. The water is led through a canal 14 m wide which was constructed between 1753 and 1766 and which terminates in an imposing aqueduct 800 m long and up to 21.5 m high. On both sides of the water tower steps lead down to boulevard des Arceaux where the market is held.

Arc de Triomphe

Forming the gateway to the Old Town, the Arc de Triomphe (1691), a 15 m high triumphal arch in honour of Louis XIV, stands at the east end of promenade du Peyrou, on the northern side of which is the stately Palais de Justice (lawcourts).

Jardin des Plantes

Flanking boulevard Henri-IV, just to the north of the Arc de Triomphe, lies the Jardin des Plantes; laid out in 1593, it was the first botanical garden in France and has many exotic plants.

Musée Atger

The Musée Atger (boulevard Henri-IV) has drawings by French and Italian masters from the baroque period on display. The impressive building was originally a bishop's palace belonging to the Abbey of St-Bênoit (14th and 16th c.); since the French Revolution it has been the seat of the Faculté de Médecine, founded in 1221.

To the north of the museum stands the Tour des Pins, a relic of the medieval city fortifications.

Cathédrale St-Pierre

To the east of the Faculté de Médecine (rue de l'École-de-Médecine) stands the Gothic Cathedral of St-Pierre, founded in 1364 after the Wars of Religion and restored in 1867. The severe double-towered facade has a vaulted portico.

Hôtel des Trésoriers de la Bourse

The Maison d'Heidelberg, Centre Culturel Franco-Allemand (Franco-German cultural centre), is housed in the Hôtel des Trésoriers de la Bourse (rue du Bras-de-Fer).

★Musée Fabre

At the eastern edge of the Old Town, diametrically opposite promenade du Peyrou, lies its simpler counterpart, esplanade Charles-de-Gaulle. On the west side (rue Montpellieret) stands the Musée Fabre, which includes a picture gallery with works by Italian and Dutch painters, as well as older and more modern French masters and fine 18th c. sculptures.

Corum

At the northern end of ésplanade Charles-de-Gaulle Corum, the opera house and conference building by Claude Vasconi, was opened in 1990 (Opéra Berlioz, 2000 seats). From its roof terrace there is a beautiful view across the Old Town to the sea. To the east of the ésplanade stands the former citadel, built in 1624, which is today used for educational purposes (Lycée Joffre).

Antigone

To the east of the Polygone department store, between boulevard d'Antigone and allées du Nouveau-Monde, Ricardo Bofill has constructed the Antigone district, which stretches as far as the Lez river, and which is a shining example of postmodern architecture.

★★Mont Ventoux D–E 7–8

Département: Vaucluse
Altitude: 1909 m

Mont Ventoux is situated in the north-west of Provence in the latitude of Orange to the east of the Rhône, from which it is separated by the valley of the Ouvèze.

Mont Ventoux (Provençal *mont ventour*, windy mountain), which takes its name from the frequent and violent storms in the area, is a long limestone ridge, geologically a continuation of the Pyrénées. It towers in impressive isolation over the surrounding countryside, its summit completely devoid of vegetation, evidence of the drastic deforestation which the mountain has undergone. Above 1500 m there are extensive ski slopes.

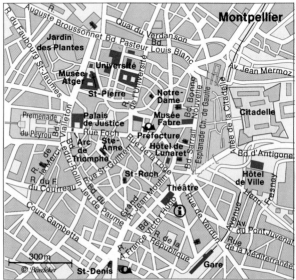

History

According to tradition, on April 26th 1336, the poet Francesco Petrarca climbed Mont Ventoux. This first ascent of a mountain for its own sake – albeit from religious and spiritual motives – reflects the increasing feeling for nature of a new age.

From 1902 until the 1970s the present road (D974) on the southern slopes of Mont Ventoux was a motor-racing course of international repute.

Drive over Mont Ventoux

North side

A typical starting point for a drive over the mountain is Vaison-la-Romaine (see entry) to the north-west of the Ventoux Massif. Follow the D938 as far as Malaucène, then turn left on to the D974. This stretch, which traverses exceptionally beautiful scenery with magnificent views on both sides, climbs fairly steeply through coniferous forests. Some 16 km beyond Malaucène, at an altitude of about 1400 m, there is a junction where a narrow road leads to the viewpoint of le Contrat. Beyond the junction the D974 is closed in winter, and even in early summer this road, which in any case is not particularly wide, may be further restricted by snow on the northern flank of Mont Ventoux. For the last 6 km the road winds upwards, the vegetation becoming increasingly scanty, until at 1829 m the highest point of the road is reached at the Col des Tempêtes (literally pass of storms), where there is an orientation table. From here there is a magnificent view over the valley of the Toulourenc and the mountains rising beyond it. At this point the pass is fully exposed to the frequent storms which roar violently over the crest.

Summit

On the summit of Mont Ventoux an observatory and a television transmitter have been erected, with a radar station a little lower down. Near the observatory can be found an observation platform facing south, from where the view extends to the Montagne du Lubéron (☞Lubéron).

Sunrise on Mont Ventoux

South side

The road downhill on the southern side is less steep, has fewer bends and is also wider than the road on the northern flank. It descends to the valley amid gravel slopes completely bare of vegetation. After 6 km there is a junction; the turning on the right, which formed part of the former racing circuit, goes to Bédoin and on to Carpentras. To the left the D164 goes via Sault to Apt. From Sault, though, the trip through the Gorges de la Nesque (☞Carpentras) is definitely not to be missed.

★Nice   G 19

Département: Alpes-Maritimes
Altitude: sea level to 20 m
Population: 400,000

Nice, capital of the *département* of Alpes-Maritimes, diocesan city and since 1966 a university town, lies on the Baie des Anges (bay of angels), surrounded by the foothills of the maritime Alps, in the eastern part of the Côte d'Azur, about 30 km from the Italian border. Its sheltered location and mild climate made Nice one of the classic winter resorts of the Côte d'Azur and up to the present day it has remained one of the most popular places for holidays.

History

Evidence of prehistoric settlement has been found in the caves of the château hill and in those of Mont Boron further to the east. Phocaeans from Marseille in 4 BC founded the strongpoint Nikaia Polis (town of Victory) on the château hill, in what is now the Old Town. Later the Romans settled on the Hill of Cimiez on the far side of the Paillon river further inland in order to protect the Via Julia.

Incursions by Saxons and Saracens wreaked havoc in the town, the former in the 6th c. and the latter in the 9th c. In the Middle Ages Nice formed part of the lands of the Count of Provence and from 1388 – after it had failed to recognise Louis of Anjou as heir to Provence – belonged to the dukedom of Savoy. In 1543 Nice, a Savoyard-Hapsburg city, was besieged by French and Turkish ships. In 1720 Savoy gained possession of Sardinia and it was at this period that the harbour and fortress were built (providing the only access to the sea for Piedmont). In 1792 Nice became

part of France, in 1814 it was incorporated into the Kingdom of Sardinia, but in 1860 as a result of a referendum it was returned to France.

Nice is the birthplace of the Italian freedom fighter Giuseppe Garibaldi (1807–82). The painters Dufy and Matisse are buried here, and Paganini died in a house on rue de la Préfecture.

Max Gallo, writer and first government spokesman of former President Mitterand, comes from Nice.

Economy

Its mild climate (average winter temperature 9°C) enabled Nice to become a popular winter health resort in the late 19th c. and one of the earliest centres of tourism – the initial British 'invasion' was triggered off in 1776 by the travel diaries of the Scottish doctor, Tobias Smollett. Until the 1920s Nice was merely a winter resort for rich elderly English gentry and Russian aristocrats, who whiled away their time at the gambling tables. After the first world war, in the wake of visits by American soldiers, artists and writers, the Riviera became well known as an area for holidays, and when in 1926 over 8000 American visitors spent July here it could be said that modern tourism as we know it today had arrived. Yet for many years after that the income from the winter months far exceeded that of the summer season; this situation did not change until 1936, when French workers began to receive holiday pay for the first time.

Today **tourism** to a large extent lives on the myth of the past: the wedding-cake style architecture of the luxury hotels is now juxtaposed with concrete apartment blocks; the magnificent promenade round the bay is now a six-lane motorway; corruption, property speculation, organised crime and casino violence are not unknown. Since 1928, under the rule of mayors Jean and Jacques Médecin, father and son, a 'Mediterranean Chicago' has evolved over the years (Jacques Médecin fled to Uruguay in September 1990) – 'La Côte, c'est fini', was the cry. However, with the impact of conference tourism and the establishment of high-tech industry (especially in Sophia-Antipolis, a European Silicon Valley) new fields of

Nice: Hôtel Negresco

activity are being opened up for investment. It should be noted that the Nice-Côte d'Azur airport, which was opened in 1962, is the second most important in France, even ahead of Marseille.

Carnival

The famous carnival, which has occurred in Nice since the 14th c., begins 12 days before Ash Wednesday. During this period various performances and festivities succeed one another on a 2 km stretch of the town. The focus is near place Masséna of the Jardin Albert-Ier. Processions of floats, cavalcades, masked balls, floral processions, showers of confetti and dancing in the streets are just a few of the highlights. The main Battle of Flowers is on the day after Ash Wednesday. The conclusion of the carnival is marked by a grand firework display on Shrove Tuesday which lights up the whole of the Baie des Anges. At Micarême (mid-Lent) a second celebration takes place.

Colline du Château

The first part of the city to be settled was the Colline du Château (château hill, 92 m high), which can be reached by lift from the shore promenade (quai des États-Unis) at the end of the Baie des Anges. The area at the top has been laid out as a park and offers an impressive panorama (orientation table). The citadel that once stood here was destroyed in 1706. Worth seeing are the remains of two churches built one above the other in the 11th and 15th c., which have now been excavated. Just to the east of the remains there is a good view of the harbour below.

Tour Bellanda

From the Colline du Château steps lead down to the promenade, passing the Tour Bellanda, a massive round tower built in 1880 on the site of the Bastion St Lambert, and in which Hector Berlioz composed his opera *King Lear*. The tower houses the Musée Naval (maritime museum).

Vieille Ville

The lively and picturesque Old Town, with its maze of tiny alleyways and streets, in which one could be forgiven

Nizza/Nice

250 m

© Baedeker

for imagining oneself transported to Italy, is popularly known as Babazouk. It opens out at the western end of the Colline du Château and in the north-west is bounded by spacious boulevards and parks, which extend over the Paillon (Jardin Albert-Ier, place Masséna, promenade du Paillon). In the south it is

bordered by the Ponchettes, in which fishmongers and grocers supplement the wares on display at the market on the adjoining cours Saleya.

Galerie de Malacologie

Near the eastern end of cours Saleya (No. 3), a short distance to the west of

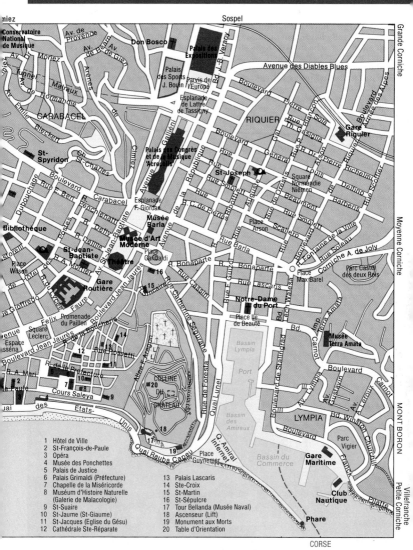

niez · Sospel · Grande Corniche · Moyenne Corniche · MONT BORON · Villefranche Petite Corniche · CORSE

1   Hôtel de Ville
2   St-François-de-Paule
3   Opéra
4   Musée des Ponchettes
5   Palais de Justice
6   Palais Grimaldi (Préfecture)
7   Chapelle de la Miséricorde
8   Muséum d'Histoire Naturelle
    (Galerie de Malacologie)
9   St-Suaire
10 St-Jaume (St-Giaume)
11 St-Jacques (Eglise du Gésu)
12 Cathédrale Ste-Réparate
13 Palais Lascaris
14 Ste-Croix
15 St-Martin
16 St-Sépulcre
17 Tour Bellanda (Musée Naval)
18 Ascenseur (Lift)
19 Monument aux Morts
20 Table d'Orientation

the steps descending from the château hill, can be found a department of the Musée d'Histoire Naturelle (Musée Barla, see below) with an aquarium and an interesting collection of shells.

Ⓒ Dec.–Oct. Tue.–Sat. 10.30am–1pm, 2–6pm.

Cours Saleya

An Italian atmosphere – Nice did not become French until 1860 – pervades cours Saleya, a long plain square without any obvious sights (even if in 1796 Napoléon, then chief commander of the Italian army, resided in the house on the south-western corner). Known for its flower market (Tue.–Sun. mornings), its attraction really lies in the richness of Nice's daily life. The market offers all the things which go to make up the cuisine of the Côte d'Azur, from Nice olives, sheep's cheese and home-gathered mushrooms to fish. Here fashionable young people and peasant women converge and it is possible to hear the *lenga nissarda*, a mixture of French and the Italian dialect of the Riviera, which is once again being taught in the schools. A flea market also takes place on the cours.

The flat roof of the Ponchettes (the double row of houses between cours Saleya and quai des États-Unis), which is several hundred metres long, is unfortunately not accessible.

The trilogy *The Bay of Angels*, in which Max Gallo describes the story of an Italian immigrant family in Nice, was written in the yellow baroque house on the east side of the cours. On the north side stands the baroque Chapel of the Miséricorde of 1736; inside there is an altar with the *Vierge de la Miséricorde* (Virgin of Mercy) by Jean Maralhet, dating from the early

15th c., and a picture of the Madonna ascribed to Bréa. This, the most beautiful church in Nice, is closed because of damage to the fabric of the building; a visit would only be possible at the discretion of the Palais Lascaris.

Palais Grimaldi

Adjoining the chapel to the north is the former Palais Grimaldi, built in 1611–13 and restored in 1907. Today it is the seat of the Préfecture (government administration). Nearby stands the Palais de Justice (law courts), completed in 1892.

★St-Jacques

On rue Droite, to the north-east of the Préfecture, stands the former Jesuit Church of St-Jacques (also known as the Église du Gésu, after the Il Gesó church in Rome), which dates from the early 17th c. and has a rich interior and colourful stucco decorations.

Cathédrale Ste-Réparate

The Cathedral of Ste-Réparate on place

Cours Saleya, the heart of Nice

Rossetti is the episcopal church and was built in the 17th c. It contains elaborate plasterwork, fine choir stalls and wooden panelling in the sacristy.

★Palais Lascaris

Further north on rue Droite, the Palais Lascaris is well worth a visit. This sumptuous baroque building dating from the mid-17th c. was the palace of the Lascaris-Vintimille family, counts of Castellar. On the ground floor are the fine entrance hall and a 18th c. apothecary's premises. In the rooms on view there are furnishings from the 17th and 18th c., Flemish tapestries, rich stucco work and ceiling paintings of the Italian school. Regular temporary exhibitions show the cultural tradition of the region.

ⓒ *Dec.–Oct. Tue.–Sun. 9.30am–noon, 2.30–6pm.*

Quai des États-Unis

Quai des États-Unis, the eastern part of the boulevard flanking the Baie des Anges, was called quai du Midi until 1917. Its change of name was a gesture of thanks to the US on the occasion of that country's entry into the first world war.

★Galerie des Ponchettes

On quai des États-Unis, a few steps from the western end of cours Saleya, the Galerie des Ponchettes (Musée Dufy) is housed in the former arsenal of the Sardinian navy. The gallery displays an outstanding collection of the works of Raoul Dufy (1877–1953), a gift from his widow to the city of Nice.

ⓒ *Tue.–Sat. 10.30am–noon, 2–6pm, Sun. 2–6pm.*

Musée Mossa

Also on quai des États-Unis (No. 59) is the Musée Alexis et Gustav-Adolf Mossa. Alexis Mossa (1844–1926), who conceived the idea of the Nice carnival procession, painted remarkable watercolour landscapes. His son Gustav-Adolf (1883–1971) continued this theme; his early work is however marked by surrealism.

Additional sights

To the west of this point is the opera-house, and beyond it the Church of St François-de-Paule (1736, Italian baroque) with a *Communion of St Benedict*, ascribed to van Loo. In the courtyard of the Hôtel de Ville (City Hall, a little further to the west) there is a representation of Orestes in front of the statue of Athene.

Ville Moderne

The buildings in the Ville Moderne include those situated on top of the covered-in Paillon river.

★Jardin Albert-Ier

The Jardin Albert-Ier is the park-like area between avenue des Phocéens and avenue de Verdun; here is situated the Théâtre de Verdure (open-air theatre). The gardens extend north as far as the busy place Masséna, where the Fontaine du Soleil, a fine fountain, and the Casino Municipal (1883) are situated. To the north extends the busy avenue Jean-Médecin, one of the principal shopping streets in the city, on which further north stands the neo-Gothic Church of Notre-Dame.

★Promenade des Anglais

To the west of avenue de Verdun, quai des États-Unis leads into promenade des Anglais and continues along the shingle beach of the Baie des Anges. This highway, which was laid down between 1822 and 1824 on the initiative and with the financial contribution of English visitors, and which has subsequently been widened on several occasions, is lined with numerous opulent buildings, among them the Palais de la Méditerranée (theatre and gambling casino), the Palais Masséna and the famous Hôtel Negresco, which is under a conservation order. The old Casino Ruhl, however, was replaced in 1970 by a commonplace modern building. For the future it is intended that promenade des Anglais should become a pedestrian area with gardens. Road traffic will be diverted into two tunnels, one on top of the other, each with three carriageways, which will run under the sea just off the coast. The shingle beach is to be replaced with sand.

★Musée d'Art et d'Histoire

The Musée d'Art et d'Histoire is housed in the Palais Masséna (65 rue de France). It contains artefacts of the Roman era, works of the Nice school

Private beaches, promenade des Anglais

of painting (Bréa, Durandi), Italian and Provençal porcelain, a collection devoted to regional history and culture and including the Nice watercolourists of the 19th c. A large collection of arts and crafts and the Félix Joubert collection of weapons can also be seen.
◉ *May–Sep. Tue.–Sun. 10am–noon, 3–6pm; Oct., Dec.–Apr. 10am–noon, 2–5pm.*

Les Baumettes

★Musée des Beaux-Arts
In the university district of les Baumettes, which adjoins to the west, is situated the Musée des Beaux-Arts Jules Chéret (33 avenue des Baumettes). This important art collection includes works by Chéret (d 1932 in Nice), as well as Italian and French paintings from the 17th–19th c. and modern classics.
◉ *May 2nd–Sept. 30th Tue.–Sun. 10am–noon, 3–6pm; Oct.–Apr. 10am–noon, 2–5pm, closed first 2 weeks of Nov.*

Musée d'Art Naïf
Even further to the west, on avenue Val-Marie, is the Musée International d'Art Naïf (Museum of Primitive Art), which originated in a bequest by the art critic Anatole Jakovsky and provides an excellent overview of primitive art throughout the world. Adjoining it there is a research and information centre.
◉ *May–Sep. Wed.–Mon. 10am–noon, 2–6pm; Oct.–Apr. 10am–noon, 2–5pm.*

St-Barthélemy

Prieuré du Vieux-Logis
From the eastern side of the university quarter the dead-straight boulevard Gambetta and its continuation boulevard de Cessole lead north to the district of St Barthélemy. In a 16th c. building, the Prieuré du Vieux-Logis, on avenue St-Barthélemy (No. 59), objects from the 14th to 16th c. have been assembled in order to show what the interior rooms of houses would have looked like at the end of the Middle Ages: study, dining room, a complete kitchen; French artisans' work and paintings of the French and Flemish schools are also to be seen.
◉ *Wed., Thu., Sat., 1st Sun. in the month 3–5pm.*

Cimiez

★Roman settlement
On a plateau in front of Mont Gros in the district of Cimiez can be seen the considerable remains of the Roman settlement of Cemenelum. The amphitheatre (over 5000 seats) and the baths, the largest complex in Gaul, are well preserved. The site of an Early Christian church has also been excavated.

Musée d'Archéologie
The Archaeological Museum is located within the area of the ancient settlement. Exhibited are finds from the excavations – coins, jewellery, Greek, Etruscan and Roman pottery.
◉ *May 2nd–Sept. 30th Tue.–Sun. 10am–noon, 2–6pm; Oct., Dec.–Apr. 10am–noon, 2–5pm; closed Sun. mornings.*

★Musée Matisse

The Musée Matisse occupies a 17th c. Genoese villa on the ancient site. Its contents (paintings, graphic designs, almost all his sculptures, pottery) derive from a gift by the family to the city of Nice. Notable are the sketches for the decorations of the chapel in Vence (see entry).

Monastère Notre-Dame-de-Cimiez

To the east, above the Roman ruins, stands the Monastery of Notre-Dame-de-Cimiez, a Benedictine foundation that was taken over by Franciscans in the 16th c. and extended in the 17th. Its present Gothic appearance is due to the restoration in 1850. The museum shows the life of the Franciscans in Nice from the 13th to the 18th c. and the Franciscan order in general. Inside the church there are fine altarpieces of the Nice school, including a Crucifix by Bréa dating from 1475. In the square outside (fine view) stands a marble cross dating from 1477.
ⓖ Mon.–Sat. 10am–noon, 3–6pm.

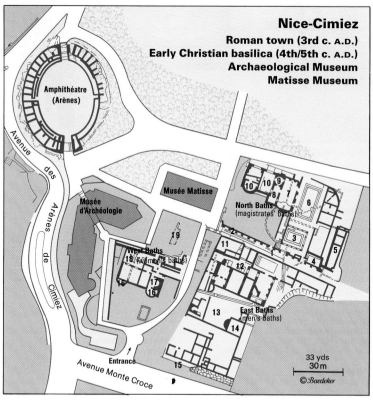

Nice-Cimiez
Roman town (3rd c. A.D.)
Early Christian basilica (4th/5th c. A.D.)
Archaeological Museum
Matisse Museum

Amphithéâtre (Arènes)

Avenue des Arènes de Cimiez

Musée Matisse

Musée d'Archéologie

North Baths (magistrates' baths)

West Baths (women's baths)

East Baths (men's baths)

Entrance
Avenue Monte Croce

33 yds
30 m
© Baedeker

1 Decumanus I	6 Courtyard (entrance)	11 4th c. AD building	16 Baths (3rd c. AD)
2 Early boundary wall (1st c. AD)	7 Frigidarium	12 Praefurnium (stove)	17 Choir of Early Christian basilica (5th c.)
3 Swimming bath	8 Tepidarium	13 Great courtyard	18 Baptisterium
4 Latrine	9 Sweat bath	14 School	19 Cardo
5 Reservoir	10 Caldarium	15 Decumanus II	

Musée d'Art Moderne, with a mobile by Calder

Carabacel

★Musée Marc-Chagall

Avenue de Flirey and the connecting boulevard de Cimiez lead south from the amphitheatre and baths. At the crossing with avenue du Docteur-Ménard stands the Musée National Message Biblique Marc Chagall, the most important exhibition of Chagall's works (paintings, etchings, lithographs, sculptures, stained glass, mosaics, wall tapestries on Biblical themes). Works by other artists are also displayed in the temporary exhibitions.
Wed.–Mon. Jul.–Sep. 10am–7pm; Oct.–Jun. 10am–12.30pm, 2–5.30pm.

Acropolis

Continuing along boulevard de Cimiez and then taking boulevard Carabacel to the south-west, the visitor will once again arrive at the area where the Paillon river has been covered in. Here stands the Acropolis, which is the name given to the Palais des Congrès et de la Musique (centre for conventions and other events); the Office du Tourisme is also located here.

Musée Barla

To the south of the Acropolis on boulevard Risso stands the Musée Barla, a branch of the Muséum d'Histoire Naturelle. Its collections deal with fungi, biological evolution, palaeontology, geology and mineralogy. There is also information about endangered species.
Mid–Sep. to mid–Aug. Wed.–Mon. 9am–noon, 2–6pm.

★Musée d'Art Moderne et d'Art Contemporain

Opposite the theatre, with which it was conceived to form an architectural unity, is the museum for modern and contemporary art, which was opened in 1990. The architects were Yves Bayard and Henri Vidal. Its four towers, faced in Carrara marble, show fine arts from the 1960s and 1970s: new realists and pop art, American abstracts, minimalists, the flux movement. In particular, are works on display by Yves Klein, the main representative of the Nouveaux Réalistes, who was born in Nice in 1928. A whole room is devoted to his work, and on the roof terrace, which has an exceptionally beautiful view across Nice, two *immatériels* stand, which were created for the museum in 1990.

ⓖ *Wed.–Sun. 11am–6pm, Fri. 10pm; closed pub. hols.*

Place Garibaldi

A short distance to the south-east is place Garibaldi, with its statue of the Italian freedom fighter who was born in Nice. Rue Cassini leads to the south-east from the square down to the harbour.

Harbour area

At the foot of Mont Boron (178 m), which bounds the Baie des Anges to the east, lies the harbour area with Port Lympia and the Avant-Port (outer harbour). Three- and four-storey plain residential buildings in the Italian style characterise the scene. Adjoining on the north is the district of Riquier, developed in a chessboard plan after 1780.

Surroundings

Observatory

In the north-east of Nice, on the edge of Mont Gros (375 m) and accessible by the Grande Corniche D2564, stand the white buildings, visible from a long distance, of the Observatory built by Charles Garnier. The dome, which at 24 m in diameter is the largest in Europe, was constructed by Gustave Eiffel in 1885.

ⓖ *Observatory visits Sat. 3pm, 3.30pm.*

Villefranche

On the far side of Mont Boron, 6 km to the east, lies Villefranche, a beautiful natural harbour developed in the early 14th c. by Charles II of Anjou. The town is surrounded by olive-clad hills and has such a mild climate that even bananas ripen here. In the south of the picturesque Old Town stands the Citadel (1580; fortifications on the seashore). In the Church of St-Michel, built in the Italian baroque style, is a figure of Christ carved in elm and another of St Rochus (16th c.).

The remarkable rue Obscure runs beneath huge shaded arches. By the harbour stands the fishermen's Chapel of St-Pierre (often closed) – the interior was decorated by Jean Cocteau – and the Palais de la Marine. Cocteau often stayed at both Villefranche and St-Jean-Cap-Ferrat and a scene from his film *Le Testament d'Orphée* is set in rue Obscure.

Cap Ferrat

See Beaulieu

Phénix

In the south-west, opposite the airport, is the newly built Arénas shopping centre. Between it and promenade des Anglais there is a large park with various attractions, an artificial lake and aviaries. Of particular interest is a glass greenhouse (110 m long, 25 m high) with tropical plants divided into seven climatic zones.

Parc des Miniatures

Halfway between the city centre and the airport, on boulevard Impératrice-Eugénie, lies the Parc des Miniatures. In a parkland setting it displays – on a scale 1:25 – episodes and monuments from the history of Nice from prehistoric times to the present day.

★★Nîmes   F–G 2

Région: Languedoc-Roussillon
Département: Gard
Altitude: 39 m
Population: 145,000

Nîmes, which has the greatest wealth of ancient buildings in France, is strictly speaking not part of Provence, but is described here as one of the principal attractions in this region.

The town is attractively situated in the foothills of the Cévennes, to the north-west of the Rhône delta between Avignon and Montpellier. It is the capital of the *département* of Gard, a diocesan town and the birthplace of the writer Alphonse Daudet (1840–97). Nîmes has an important textile industry (in particular, silk; the name denim used for jeans material comes from the words *de Nîmes*) as well as a thriving wine and spirits industry.

History

Ancient Nemausus was the capital of the Volcae Arecomici, who had built their town around a spring, the spirit of which was worshipped under the name

Nemausus. In 121 BC Nemausus submitted to the Romans and soon became one of the most important towns in Gaul, situated on the main route between Italy and Spain. The ancient buildings and extensive town walls bear witness to its eminence.

In the early Middle Ages until 1185 Nîmes had its own viscount and then passed to the counts of Toulouse. In the 16th c., since three-quarters of its inhabitants were Calvinist, the town suffered greatly during the Wars of Religion, and again in 1704 at the time of the uprising in the Cévennes. From the mid-18th c. the inexpensive *Indiennes* material was produced on a large scale in the town, initially by hand, and then machine printed, and this was to ensure Nîmes' prosperity. Today the town has had to yield importance to Montpellier as an economic and administrative centre.

★Modern architecture

In recent years extensive renovation work has been carried out, in particular in the Old Town. In addition, modern architecture has made its appearance in Nîmes. Raysse designed the Fontaine au Crocodile (the coat of arms of Nîmes shows a crocodile tied to a palm tree) on place du Marché, while Starck designed the Abribus (bus stop), including the seats and lighting, on avenue Carnot. On the esplanade a shopping centre by Valle has been opened, Norman Foster has designed a museum for contemporary art, while the roofing of the amphitheatre was produced by Michelin and Geipel. Those buildings planned, or already under construction, by such architects as Hendricks, Gregotti, Kurokawa, Balladur and Nouvel will turn Nîmes into a favoured destination for lovers of architecture.

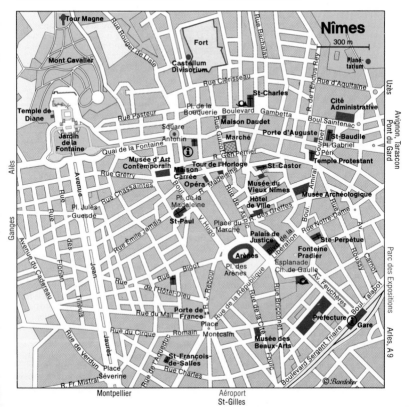

Été de Nîmes

In July/August the theatre, music and dance festival Été de Nîmes takes place, with performances in the Arènes and in the Jardins de la Fontaine. The emphasis is on jazz, rock and folk music. Information: ☎ 0466672802.

Sights

★★Arènes

The chief monument in Nîmes is the amphitheatre, which is located in the town centre. It dates from the 1st c. AD and is 133 × 101 m in area and up to 21 m high. With a seating capacity of 21,000 it is not one of the largest, but it is one of the best preserved of all the 70 known Roman amphitheatres, especially in the upper storey. The 62 arches of the exterior face are embellished in the lower part with pilasters and in the upper part with Doric half-columns. Brackets for the wooden masts of the awning can be seen on the top. The richly decorated main entrance faces north-west. The crowds thronging the theatre were able to leave by 124 exits in a few minutes.

In the 5th c. the Visigoths turned the arena into a fortress. In the Middle Ages it served as a château, then as dwellings for about 2000 people, who had their own chapel.

Since 1989 the amphitheatre has been covered with a 4800 sq m plastic roof, supported on 30 metal pillars, which are fixed in the non-Roman part of the fabric. In this way cultural events can be held here even in winter, while in summer the roof is removed.
⊚ May–Oct. daily 9am–6.30pm; Nov.–Apr. 9am–noon, 2–5pm.

Esplanade de Gaulle

To the east of the amphitheatre extends the esplanade Charles-de-Gaulle, a spacious square busy with traffic. Here stands the Fontaine Pradier, a marble fountain of 1848 representing a personification of Nîmes.

★★Maison Carrée

The Maison Carrée is situated on place de la Comédie and is reached from the amphitheatre by going north-west down boulevard Victor-Hugo. Standing on a podium, it is a splendidly maintained Roman temple which was erected at the time of Augustus between 20 and 12 BC.

The Arènes in Nîmes

Maison Carrée

In the Middle Ages the building was used on occasions as a convent. In the 18th c. it was thoroughly restored, then during the French Revolution sold to the *département* as national property. An art museum was established here in 1824.

Tall Corinthian columns bear the entablature with a frieze finely decorated with acanthus (front section missing). Fifteen steps lead up to the pronaos (antechamber) and the cella on the same level, which today serves as an exhibition room.

On the west side of the Maison Carrée, where the former theatre stood, is the Musée d'Art Contemporain, the architect of which is Norman Foster.

★Jardins de la Fontaine

West of the Maison Carrée, at the end of avenue J-Jaurès and on the edge of the city centre, lie the beautiful Jardins de la Fontaine (Gardens of the Source). They were laid out in the 18th c. in the area of the former fortified ramparts and include the ruins of an ancient sanctuary of a sacred spring. The gardens extend over several levels with waterways joining them. Groups of life-size baroque statues give atmosphere to the gardens.

Temple de Diane

On the western edge of the park under trees stands the so-called temple of Diana (it was in fact not a temple), a partly ruined, but harmoniously proportioned square building, which presumably formed part of the Roman baths and has been dated to the early 2nd c. on account of its decorations. The three aisles formerly had barrel vaults. As the building was used as a church since the Middle Ages, it was subsequently damaged during the Wars of Religion and its ruins later used as building stone.

Tour Magne

Above the Jardins de la Fontaine rises the 114 m high Mont Cavalier, with subtropical plants and shady footpaths. On its summit stands the Tour Magne, a 30 m high Roman monument, dating from the year 15 BC. The tower is the largest feature of the wall which surrounded the town in the Roman period. From the top an extensive view of the city and surroundings may be enjoyed.

Castellum Divisorium

To the west, beyond the fort, on rue de la Lampèze, the remains of an ancient water tower (Castellum Divisorium, Château d'Eau Romain) were discovered in 1884. Its purpose was to distribute the water supply for the town, which flowed over the Pont du Gard (see entry). The remains consist of a collecting basin, 6 m in diameter, from which ten supply channels (lead pipes 40 cm in diameter) led off to the individual areas of the town.

Cathédrale Notre-Dame et St-Castor

The Cathedral of Notre-Dame et St-Castor stands on place aux Herbes in the centre of the Old Town, almost due east of the Maison Carrée and reached from the latter along rue de l'Horloge with its 14th c. clock tower. Originally built in the late 11th c. and consecrated in 1096 by Pope Urban II, the cathedral has been renewed several times, in particular in the 19th c. in the Romanesque-Byzantine style. On the gable of the west front is an interesting Romanesque frieze, with scenes illustrating the story of the Creation, which is stylistically

related to St Gilles and may date from
the late 12th c.

★ Musée du Vieux Nîmes

Opposite the cathedral to the south
stands the former Bishop's Palace, in
which is housed the Musée du Vieux
Nîmes with its collection of regional
history and also the adjoining Musée
Taurin (Bullfighting Museum). Of
interest in the museum, which
developed from the private
ethnological collection of Henri
Beaucquier, are examples of local
textiles no longer manufactured in the
town, as well as furniture from
Provence and Languedoc, arts and
crafts.

★ Musée Archéologique

On boulevard Amiral-Courbet which
borders the Old Town in the east is
the Musée Archéologique (officially
Musée Lapidaire/Musée d'Histoire
Naturelle). Its exhibits include Gallo-
Roman finds and inscriptions,
sculptures up to the Middle Ages and
an exceptional collection of coins. In
the former chapel can be seen a
beautiful mosaic.

Porte d'Arles (Porte d'Auguste)

Near the northern end of boulevard
Amiral-Courbet stands the Porte d'Arles,
also known as the Porte d'Auguste, after
Augustus, who was instrumental in
having the town surrounded by walls.
This town gate, which was the starting
point of the road to Rome, dates from
15 BC and in the 14th c. was
incorporated into the walls of a fortress.
It was not uncovered again until 1752
when the fortress had suffered damage.
Today a bronze statue of Augustus (a
modern copy) stands near the gate. The
position of the side wings of the gate,
which were destroyed during the French
Revolution, are marked on the
pavement.

Musée des Beaux-Arts

The Musée des Beaux-Arts is on rue de
la Cité-Foulc which leads south from
the amphitheatre. Its collection of
paintings mainly includes works by old
masters of the 16th to 18th c.,
especially of France, Germany and the
Netherlands, but also of Italy and
Spain. On the ground floor there is a
remarkable ancient mosaic.
ⓖ *Daily 9am–12.30pm, 2–6pm.*

Surroundings

Perrier

At Codognan, about 20 km south-west of
Nîmes, is the bottling plant of the Perrier
mineral water firm (with its own glass
factory).
ⓖ *Guided tours Mon.–Fri. 9am, 10am,
1.30pm, 2.30pm, 3.30pm, also 5pm
Jun.–Sep.; closed pub. hols.*

Pont du Gard

See entry

Beaucaire

See Tarascon

St Gilles

See entry

★Orange   E 4

Département: Vaucluse
Altitude: 46 m
Population: 27,500

Orange lies in the lower Rhône valley,
where fertile alluvial lands are used for
intensive fruit and vegetable cultivation.
The town is famous above all for its
Roman buildings.

The Rhône flows past, about 6 km
distant from the town, at the point
where the Aigues river flows into it. The
motorway coming from the north
divides near the town into two
branches, one in the direction of
Marseille and the other in the direction
of Nîmes.

History

It was in front of the walls of Orange, or
as it was known in ancient times,
Arausio, that the first encounter took
place in 105 BC between the Roman
army and the Cimbri and Teutons – an
encounter in which 100,000 Romans lost
their lives. Three years later Marius
carried out the counter-attack at Aix. In
the period of the ensuing *pax romana*,
Orange had four times as many
inhabitants as it has today. Later it
became the capital of the tiny
princedom of Orange and in 1531 came
under the control of the Dutch house of
Nassau. For this reason the queen of the
Netherlands even to this today carries
the title of princess of Orange-Nassau. In
1713 Orange was ceded to France under
the Treaty of Utrecht.

Sights

★★Théâtre Romain

The Roman theatre, in the south of the city centre, is the best preserved and one of the finest of Provence's antiquities. It was set up at the beginning of the Imperial era (1st c. AD), but was probably renewed in the next century. With its back wall, composed of massive stone blocks, towering over every other building to a height of 38 m and a width of 103 m, with some of the rich decoration still intact, and its tiers of stepped seats, supported against the hillside, providing seating for 9000 people, it gives a good idea of a Roman theatrical auditorium. The theatre retains a statue of Emperor Augustus; it is 3.55 m in size.

ⓘ *Apr.–Sep. daily 9am–6.30pm; Oct.–Mar. 9am–noon, 1.30–5pm; closed pub. hols.*

Festival performances

During the summer months festival performances take place in the Roman theatre, the Chorégies d'Orange (concerts, operas), generally with above-average attendance. The exceptional acoustics of the building contribute greatly to their success. The overall impression of the auditorium and stage is only marginally affected by the technical installations. Information and tickets from: CHORÉGIES D'ORANGE BP 205, 84107 Orange Cedex ☎ *0490342424, 0490341552.*

Temple

Adjoining the theatre on the west are the ruins of a great Roman temple which was situated at the end of a 400 m long stadium. Directly opposite is the interesting Musée Municipal (Town Museum), which contains antique fragments and illustrates the architecture and techniques of the Roman theatre.

ⓘ *Apr.–Sep. Mon.–Sat. 9am–6.30pm, Sun. 9am–noon, 2–6.30pm; Oct.–Mar. 9am–noon, 1.30–5.30pm; closed pub. hols.*

Colline St-Eutrope

Above the theatre to the south a beautiful park has been laid out on Colline St-Eutrope; from its northern side there is a wonderful view of the theatre and town towards Mont Ventoux.

Old Town

The Old Town lies to the north of the Roman theatre. On place Clemenceau stands the Hôtel de Ville (Town Hall), dating from 1671, and nearby the Cathedral of Notre-Dame (1083–1126) which was severely damaged during the Wars of Religion.

★Arc de Triomphe

The arterial road (N7, avenue de l'Arc-de-Triomphe), which leaves Orange in a northerly direction leads to the Arc de Triomphe, situated outside the town and sited on a circular space framed by plane

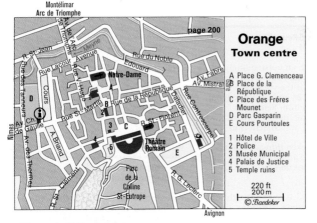

Orange
Town centre

A Place G. Clemenceau
B Place de la République
C Place des Frères Mounet
D Parc Gasparin
E Cours Pourtoules

1 Hôtel de Ville
2 Police
3 Musée Municipal
4 Palais de Justice
5 Temple ruins

220 ft
200 m
© Baedeker

◄ Orange: the Théâtre Romain

trees. It was erected after Caesar's victory in 49 BC. In spite of severe weathering it is the finest of its kind in France. Three arches with coffered vaulting form the gateways. Once there were a bronze Quadriga (four-horse chariot) and four statues on the top, while there is a representation of a Gallic battle on the frieze.

Surroundings

Sérignan

At Sérignan-du-Comtat, 8 km to the north of Orange (on the N7 and the D976; then right at the entrance to the village), the biologist and ethologist J-H Fabre retired to his Harmas estate, where he lived and researched for 36 years in almost total seclusion. The house has been turned into a museum and the study and a room with drawings and watercolours can be visited.

ⓒ *Wed.–Mon. 9–11.30am, 2–6pm, Oct.–Mar. 4pm; closed pub. hols.*

The statue of Fabre on the market square in Sérignan shows him with his most important instrument, his magnifying glass.

Châteauneuf-du-Pape
See entry

Marcoule
See entry

★★Pont du Gard   F 3

Région: Languedoc-Roussillon
Département: Gard

The Pont du Gard, an outstandingly well-preserved Roman aqueduct, spans the Gard river near the village of Remoulins about 25 km west of Avignon. In summer access from Remoulins is only possible along the left bank of the Gard (when a one-way system is in operation).
Cars are often broken into and thefts committed in and around the large car parks near the Pont du Gard.

Aqueduct
The Pont du Gard is a 49 m high and 275 m long aqueduct, spanning the deep valley of the Gard or Gardon. Probably built about 19 BC by Agrippa,

the son-in-law and co-regent of Emperor Augustus, the three-storey construction is one of the greatest and best-preserved Roman monuments. With the exception of the topmost arcade, the arches are of varying widths (getting narrower from the middle outwards) and the whole structure is asymmetrical, because of the differing gradients of the two banks. In this way any kind of monotony is avoided. In a channel in the topmost arcade ran the pipeline (some 50 km long) taking water to Nîmes. A height difference of only 17 m was possible between the water source and the distribution pipes. It is estimated that 20 million litres of water flowed across the aqueduct each day. The road on the first storey was added in 1743.

The plan to build a theme park around the aqueduct has been halted, thanks to campaigns in the press and from public pressure groups. Hotels, restaurants, reconstructions of Roman buildings and car parks were planned at great expense. Instead plans have been restricted to creating the necessary minimum infrastructure for the two million visitors who come each year (a cultural-historical trail, car parks at wide intervals), in order to counteract uncontrolled parking and a proliferation of souvenir stalls and snack stands.

Garrigue
Vast areas of land around the Pont du Gard are covered with *garrigue*. *Garrigue*, also *garigue*, in Provençal *garoulia*, is mainly found on rocky chalk soil. This thorny scrub does not grow much over 50 cm high and consists of box, thistles, oak, gorse and aromatic herbs such as thyme, lavender, sage and rosemary; hyacinths, irises, tulips and orchids also grow alongside.

Port-Grimaud   K 15

Département: Var
Altitude: sea level

Port-Grimaud is situated at the south-western corner of the bay of St-Tropez at the foot of the Massif des Maures; behind it stretches a plain which the

Garde and Giscle rivers have filled up with their deposits.

Townscape

The very attractive modern holiday resort of Port-Grimaud is reminiscent of a Venetian fishing and lagoon settlement, with its maze of channels. When the resort was translated from the drawing board to reality in 1966, great importance was laid on creating a townscape typical of the region.

The resort is free of traffic: there are car parks outside the town for holidaymakers and visitors. As well as motor boats plying regular routes, there are four-seater electric boats for self-drive hire on the canals.

By the canals, on which there are many fine sailing ships and cabin cruisers, there are boutiques, shops and restaurants; the market is held in the main square. Many of the apartment houses have their own moorings outside the front doors. Facing the sea stands the ecumenical Church of St-François-d'Assisi, designed in a Romanesque style; a coin-operated turnstile gives access to the tower from which there is an exceptional panorama of the little town, the lagoons and the mountainous hinterland.

Surroundings

Cogolin

Cogolin, situated on the south-western edge of the coastal plain of Port-Grimaud, is a centre of artisan and industrial wood and textile production. The main products are bamboo and cane furniture, carpets and pipes made out of *bruyère* (heather roots). In the village there is a pretty 16th c. church and a clock tower – the remains of an earlier fortification.

To the south of Port-Grimaud lies the yachting harbour of les Marines de Cogolin.

★Grimaud

Grimaud is situated inland on the site of a settlement which was used by the Ligurians; it is a *village perché*, high above the plain of Cogolin and with a particularly picturesque townscape. Of interest are the ruins of the fortress (11th c.; view) and the Church of St-Michel, also dating from the 11th c. Also well preserved is the Maison des Templiers (House of the Templars) with its Gothic arcades. 2 km east on the road from Port-Grimaud stands the charming Chapel of Notre-Dame-de-la-Queste.

Pont du Gard, a marvel of Roman architecture

La Garde-Freinet
See Massif des Maures

St-Tropez
See entry

★Roquebrune-Cap-Martin G 20–21

Département: Alpes-Maritimes
Altitude: sea level to 300 m
Population: 12,500

The municipality of Roquebrune-Cap-Martin is situated close to the Italian border, due west of Menton (see entry).

The inland community of Roquebrune is built like an eyrie on a greyish-brown conglomerate hill. Most of the narrow little streets are vaulted and are full of atmosphere; going uphill through these streets you reach the château, which dominates the whole town. It dates from the 10th c. and from its fortified tower there is a fine view.

★Vista Palace
To the west above Roquebrune on the

A steep street in Roquebrune

Grande Corniche stands the luxury hotel the Vista Palace (owned by the Grundig group), which has a breathtaking situation right on the mountainside and from which there is a marvellous view.

Cap Martin
Cap Martin, stretching like a tongue into the sea, offers beautiful walks; along the west shore runs promenade Le Corbusier (the architect drowned here in 1965), which has splendid views. At the foot of the Sémaphore (signal station) can be seen the ruins of the Church of St-Martin, built by the monks of Lérin in the 11th c. Among olive groves and pine woods there are many villas.

★★St-Gilles G 2

Région: Languedoc-Roussillon
Département: Gard
Altitude: 7 m
Population: 11,000

St-Gilles lies not far beyond the western border of Provence on the northern edge of the Camargue, 16 km from Arles. The town is primarily known for its 12th c. church, one of the most important Romanesque buildings in southern France.

St-Gilles is a starting point for trips into the Camargue (see entry).

★★St-Gilles
In the heart of the Old Town stands the church, built in the 12th c. and restored on a smaller scale in the 17th c. The west front is exceptionally fine (the light at its best in the late afternoon) with its three doorways and wealth of decorative figures, which include the first detailed representation of the Passion in Western sculpture. The damage inflicted on the church during the French Revolution makes the importance of its architecture all the more significant.

The entrance to the crypt is on the right of the facade. The interior of the basilican church, which has no transepts, is characterised by Gothic styles from the 17th c. rebuilding.

★Vis de St-Gilles
To the left of the facade a narrow lane leads to the ruins of the former Choir, which was destroyed in the 17th c. Here is the Vis de St-Gilles (Screw of St

St-Gilles church

Gilles), a now free-standing staircase dating from the 12th c; the complicated shape of the spiral staircase is witness to the stonemason's art. There are also remains of the apse (the bases of pillars).

Maison Romane

From the open space in front of the church (place de la République) a narrow lane leads to the charming little place de l'Olme. Here stands the Maison Romane (Romanesque House) which has capitals decorated with figures on its first and second storeys. Inside there is a museum with an Early Christian sarcophagus, fragments of sculpture and a natural history collection. From the hall on the second floor there is a fine view across the roofs of St-Gilles. Next door is the Office du Tourisme.

★★St-Maximin-la-Ste-Baume   J 11

Département: Var
Altitude: 303 m
Population: 8000

St-Maximin-la-Ste-Baume lies at the northern foot of the Massif de la Ste-Baume in the basin of a dried-up lake, about 50 km north-east of Marseille and 40 km east of Aix-en-Provence on the A8 autoroute.

The little basin was already settled at the time of the Roman occupation. The town became famous, not only for its church, but also as the place where, it is said, the bones of St Mary Magdalene were discovered.

History

Mary Magdalene is supposed to have landed by boat at Stes-Maries-de-la-Mer, accompanied by her sister Martha, her brother Lazarus, Maximin, Sidonius, her servant Sara and others, after their expulsion from Palestine. While Maximin and Sidonius went into the country as missionaries, Mary Magdalene, at God's behest, spent thirty years without earthly nourishment as a penitent in a grotto (Ste-Baume, see below). She was buried, it is said, in a mausoleum, which has been preserved as the crypt of the church. Just as Mary Magdalene represents a synthesis of many Biblical figures (the sinner, Mary of Bethany, Maria of Magdala), so the legend and its sequels are equally strange. In Vézelay in Burgundy St Magdalene was worshipped as long ago as the 11th c. It was maintained that her bones had been brought there at the end of the 9th c., from St-Maximin. Political quarrels – territorial conflicts, conflicts between pope and king – caused Charles II of Anjou in 1279 to search for the 'real' relics at St-Maximin and he was 'successful'; four handsome sarcophagi were discovered in the crypt. In the controversy over the authenticity of the relics Pope Bonifatius VIII decided in favour of Charles of Anjou; at a stroke Vézelay forfeited its pre-eminence.

★★Ste-Madeleine

History
The new church and the Dominican convent were begun in 1295 and intended for pilgrims who passed by. The choir and the first bay on the eastern side were finished in 1316, another five nave bays were not completed until 1404. In the last building period between 1508 and 1532 the western parts were added, while the facade and central doorway remained unfinished or temporary. A planned bell tower to the right of the doorway was not built. The staircase tower at the southern end was not completed until later and serves as a bell tower.

The French Revolution drove out the Dominicans; however Lucien Bonaparte, president of the local Jacobin club, set up a reinforcement camp here and thereby saved the building. Even the preservation of the huge organ can be attributed to Lucien; when the pipes were due to be melted down, he is supposed to have demanded that the *Marseillaise* should be played on the organ (although there is no mention of this in his memoirs).

Exterior
The tranquil little town is dominated by the massive structure of this, the largest and most important Gothic church in Provence. The building, 79 m in external length, is completely unified in its conception despite the many years which it took to construct. Immediately

Ste-Madeleine, the finest Gothic church in Provence

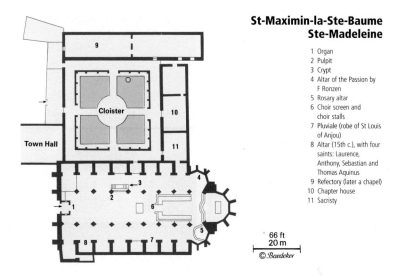

St-Maximin-la-Ste-Baume
Ste-Madeleine

1 Organ
2 Pulpit
3 Crypt
4 Altar of the Passion by
   F Ronzen
5 Rosary altar
6 Choir screen and
   choir stalls
7 Pluviale (robe of St Louis
   of Anjou)
8 Altar (15th c.), with four
   saints: Laurence,
   Anthony, Sebastian and
   Thomas Aquinus
9 Refectory (later a chapel)
10 Chapter house
11 Sacristy

66 ft
20 m
© Baedeker

striking are its flat silhouette, which is barely interrupted by any vertical lines, the enormous buttresses which flank the nave and the choir, and the complete absence of usual Gothic decorations. The austere simplicity might be explained by the building regulations of the Dominicans, but also by the country's inherent Romanesque tradition.

Interior

Just as simple, but at the same time giving an enormous impression of space, is the interior of the church. Even here there are unusual features: there is no transept, nor does the choir have an ambulatory. Instead the bays of the nave aisles are continued into chapels.

The interior is divided into three levels and is well lit. The bosses of the ribbed vaults are decorated with the coats of arms of the founders.

Fittings

In contrast to the restrained architecture the baroque fittings are very opulent: the splendid main altar (end of 17th c.), choir stalls and screens made of walnut (1692), and the organ

(by Isnard, 1773; one of the finest French organs of the 18th c.). In the left apse there is a special item of interest, the Passion Altar of 1520 by the Fleming François (Antoine) Ronzen, who had earlier worked in Italy (Rome, Venice); the 22 panels depicting the Passion of Christ are also of interest because of their precise details of places and buildings (Venice, Rome; oldest known picture of the Papal Palace in Avignon).

Pluviale

The chasuble (pluviale) of St Louis of Anjou (1274–97, son of King Charles II of Naples, bishop of Toulouse) shows in silk embroidery on a gold background 30 scenes from the life of Christ and the Virgin Mary. It is stored in a display cabinet (generally kept covered) in the third side chapel on the right.

Crypt

The crypt of the church is reached by a staircase (16th c.) from the north aisle (light switch on the wall). This low room with a barrel vault (4.24 × 4.48 m; formerly covered with marble), dating from ca 400, contains the

Ste-Madeleine: the organ of 1773

The crypt

sarcophagi, from the same period, of Mary Magdalene (made of fine-grained marble from the Sea of Marmara), St Maximin, Sidonius and Marcel and St Susanne. Their reliefs show scenes from the Old and New Testaments and are some of the oldest Christian monuments in France. The reliquary bust of gilded bronze (1860) contains a skull, supposedly that of Mary Magdalene.

Convent

The building of the convent was begun at the same time as the basilica in 1296. The cloister dates from the 15th c. The chapter house and sacristy (ribbed vaults), which connect the cloister to the church, today house the Collège d'Échanges Contemporains (a cultural centre; venue for concerts). Prior to this, between 1859 and 1966 the Dominicans were resident here. The cloister hostel dating from the 17th c. is today the Town Hall.

🅖 *Apr.–Oct. daily 10–11.45am, 2–4.45pm; Nov.–Mar. Mon.–Fri. 10–11.45am, 2–4.45pm.*

Surroundings

Nans-les-Pins

The wine village of Nans-les-Pins, 12 km to the south, lies in the northern foothills of the Massif de la Ste-Baume and is dominated by the ruins of a medieval fortress.

★Massif de la Ste-Baume

Beyond Nans-les-Pins road D80 leads up into the mountains. Some 8 km along this road, where it is joined by the D95 (a second route from the Hostellerie de la Ste-Baume, 1 km further), a footpath begins, which leads to the Ste-Baume (Holy Grotto), an opening in the calcareous rock face which has been converted into a chapel (return journey 1 hour). St Mary Magdalene is supposed to have lived there and has long been a place of pilgrimage. On July 22nd the saint's festival is celebrated with a midnight mass in the grotto.

The name Ste-Baume is derived from the Provençal word for grotto, *baoumo*. The forest retains a primeval character, unusual for the region, a result of the sacred location. The shady environment with a damp, cool microclimate enables deciduous trees, such as limes, beeches and maples, and a dense undergrowth to flourish.

★★St-Pilon
From the Carrefour de l'Oratoire a path (part of the GR9, red and white markers) brings walkers in 30 min. to the summit of St-Pilon (994 m), with a splendid view in clear weather (orientation panel) inland to Mont Aurélien and the Montagne Ste-Victoire as far as Mont Ventoux, and southwards to the sea.

Tourves
Tourves, at a road junction in an area of intensive agriculture (5 km south-east of St-Maximin), has the impressive remains of the uncompleted Château de Valbelle (18th c.). Nearby there are grottoes with prehistoric paintings.

St-Raphaël   J 16

Département: Var
Altitude: sea level
Population: 24,000

The port of St-Raphaël, halfway between St-Tropez and Cannes, has a charming situation on the north side of the gulf of Fréjus at the foot of the Esterel range.

Townscape
In the historic centre stands the 12th c. Church of the Templiers (a Templar church), with a tower which was built as protection against pirates. Adjoining the church on the north side is the Musée d'Archéologie Sous-Marine (Museum of Underwater Archaeology) with a notable collection of amphorae which were mostly rescued from ancient wrecks. Parallel to the shore runs promenade René-Coty, which is beautifully laid out and extremely popular in high season. From here and also from the pleasant avenue de Gaulle there is a good view of the strange rock

The monument and triumphal arch of Glanum, near St-Rémy-de-Provence

formations, the Lion de Terre (lion of the land) and Lion de Mer (lion of the sea) on the edge of the gulf.

Surroundings

Agay
The charming winding road along the red rocky coast leads (9 km eastwards) to the delightful resort of Agay on the bay of the same name, which is enclosed by Cap Dramont and the Pointe de la Baumette. At the latter there is a lighthouse and a memorial to the French airman and author Antoine de St-Exupéry.

Agay is a good starting point for trips to the Esterel range (see entry).

★St-Rémy-de-Provence G 4–5

Département: Bouches-du-Rhône
Altitude: 60 m
Population: 8,500

St-Rémy-de-Provence is situated about 20 km south of Avignon to the east of the Rhône in the northern foothills of the Alpilles. The town became famous because of Glanum, an important Greco-Roman town, and later as the place where Vincent van Gogh lived.

Van Gogh
Between May 1889 and May 1890 the painter Vincent van Gogh lived – not entirely willingly – in St-Rémy. In 1888 he had settled in Arles, where the scenery and the light of Provence influenced his new style of painting with bright vibrant colours. Gauguin, who was very close to him, visited him there in the December. A row between the two of them sparked off a crisis in van Gogh. He cut off his ear and was taken to the asylum of St-Paul-de-Mausole in St-Rémy, which is today the Van Gogh Dr Berron clinic. After Arles St-Rémy was the most important place for van Gogh as a creative stimulus and the source for many of his pictures.

Nostradamus
In the same way that the light and colours of Provence cast a spell over van

The Glanum excavations at the foot of the Alpilles

Glanum

near St-Remy-de-Provence

Burial ground of the Graeco-Roman town (2nd c. B.C.–3rd c. A.D.)

1 Basin of fountain

GREEK PERISTYLE HOUSES
2 Maison des Antes
(House of the Antes)
3 Maison de Cybèle
(Shrine of Cybèle)
4 Maison d'Atys
(House of Atys)

ROMAN BATHS
5 Heating chamber
6 Caldarium (hot water)
7 Tepidarium (tepid water)
8 Frigidarium (cold water)
9 Palaestra (courtyard)
10 Natatio (swimming pool; cold running water)

OTHER EXCAVATIONS
11 Maison de Capricorne
(House of the ibex; mosaics)
12 Building with apse
13 Basilica
14 House of Sulla (mosaics)
15 Covered water-channel
16 Forum
17 Wall with apse
18 Monument or altar
19 Roman theatre
20/21 Roman temple
(perhaps dedicated to Caius and Lucius, grandsons of Augustus)
22 Well
23 Buleuterion (council chamber ?)
24 Hall with Doric columns
25 Fortified gate
26 Nympheum (presumably above the sacred well of Glanum)
27 Altars (dedicated to Hercules)
28 Celtic shrine

55 yds
50m
© *Baedeker*

Gogh, so Nostradamus, born in St-Rémy in 1503, represents all that is mysterious in what we associate with Provence.

Frédéric Mistral
Maillane, 7 km to the north-east of St-Rémy, is the birthplace of the 'Homer of Provence', Frédéric Mistral. His house, in which he lived from 1876, has been turned into a small museum.

★Glanum ancient site

South of the little town, on the road into the Alpilles, lie the remains of the Graeco-Roman settlement of Glanum Livii (2nd c. BC and 1st–3rd c. AD), destroyed in the year 480 by the Visigoths.

Les Antiques
To the right of the road, in an open space

surrounded by plane trees is the impressive group of monuments known as les Antiques; here stand a monumental triumphal arch, a souvenir of the foundation of the town, and an 18 m monument in memory of Julius Caesar's two adopted sons; both date from the 1st c. BC. The lower part of the square base of the latter is decorated with reliefs of battle scenes; above the base rises a temple-like structure. The reliefs on the frieze of the archway of the triumphal arch and the coffered internal vaulting are notable but the reliefs on the outside of the walls (trophies, prisoners) are severely damaged.

Excavations

The extensive excavation site can be entered via the new exhibition room with its informative illustrations and models of life in ancient times.
Apr.–Sep. daily 9am–7pm; Oct.–Mar. 9am–noon, 2–5pm.

St-Paul-de-Mausole

Close to the excavation site and on the east side of the road is the former Monastery of St-Paul-de-Mausole with its Romanesque church and beautiful little cloister dating from the 12th c. It remains as it was a hundred years ago (indeed since 1807), when van Gogh lived here, a psychiatric hospital.

★St-Tropez   K 15

Département: Var
Altitude: sea level
Population: 6300

The little port and well-known resort of St-Tropez lies on the southern shore of the gulf of the same name at the foot of the eastern part of the Massif des Maures. There is a large car park to the west of the town at the Nouveau Port.

History

The settlement was known to the Greeks as Athenopolis; it was named Heraclea Cacabaris by the Romans. The present name is said to go back to St Tropez whose remains were discovered here. In the time of the Saracens the little coastal village was hard pressed but was able to recover and in the 15th c. became a republic.

St-Tropez was later a meeting place for artists: Liszt and Maupassant stayed here; Paul Signac bought a house here (la Hune) and as a result a whole string of painters moved to St-Tropez, so that at the beginning of the 20th c. the village became rather like an artist's centre (Matisse, Bonnard, Utrillo). From 1924 to 1938 the writer Colette lived in her villa la Treille-Muscate in St-Tropez.

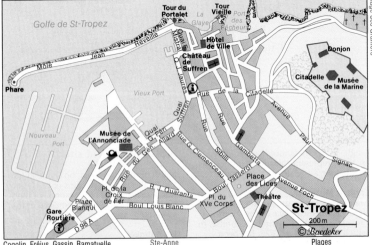

Cogolin, Fréjus, Gassin, Ramatuelle   Ste-Anne   Plages

St-Tropez, once a fishing village

After the second world war St-Tropez developed into an extremely popular resort, particularly with society, film stars and the newly rich. In 1955 Roger Vadim made the film *Et Dieu créa la Femme* (And God created Woman) with Brigitte Bardot in the principal role, while in the 1960s Gunter Sachs made *The Girls of St-Tropez*. However, it must be said that the gloss which the wealthy brought with them has paled somewhat in the face of mass tourism, even if St-Tropez is still a magnet for the rich and beautiful.

Sights

Citadel
High over the town towers the Citadel, built between 1590 and 1607. In the gateway is a large modern relief by Paul Landowski, depicting a ship's cannon being made ready for action. Within the fort is the Musée de la Marine et de l'Histoire Locale (Museum of Shipping and Local History), in which there is a good reproduction of a Greek galley. From the battlements there are good

views of the gulf of St-Tropez and the Massif des Maures.

🔘 *Jun. 16th–Sep. 14th Wed.–Mon. 10am–6pm; Sep. 15th–Jun. 15th 10am–5pm; closed Nov. 15th–Dec. 15th.*

Old Town
The Old Town of St-Tropez is situated to the west below the Citadel and is bordered on the other side by the harbour basin. Part of it has been laid out as a pedestrian zone where shops, boutiques and restaurants abound.

Rue de la Citadelle leads down into the centre; on the right on rue du Portail-Neuf stands the 18th c. church, in Italian baroque style, in which can be seen a bust of St Tropez and beautiful wood carvings (at Christmas time there is a fine Provençal crib).

North-west of the church near the harbour and the Hôtel de Ville (Town Hall) stands the former Palais des Bailli Pierre-André de Suffren (1729–88), bailiff of the Order of Malta and one of the most important admirals of the French fleet ('Scourge of the English'; his statue stands on the east side of the harbour).

From here it is not far on the right to the Mole Jean-Réveille, enclosing the harbour on the north, from where there is a good view of the town's seafront. Luxury yachts in the harbour provide a splendid spectacle, especially when the La Nioulargue regatta is being held at the end of September and beginning of October.

★Musée de l'Annonciade

At the southern corner of the harbour basin (quai de l'Epi) stands the former Chapel of Notre-Dame-de-l'Annonciade (the church of the White Penitents of 1510). It now houses the Musée de l'Annonciade, which contains the very remarkable collection of the Lyon industrialist Georges Grammont, pointillist and fauvist paintings, the creators of which have worked in St-Tropez – artists such as Signac, Derain, van Dongen, Rouault, Braque, Bonnard, Matisse and Maillol.

Ⓞ *Jun.–Sep. Wed.–Mon. 10am–noon, 3–7pm; Oct, Dec.–May 10am–noon, 2–6pm.*

Surroundings

Ramatuelle

On the hilly and for the most part wooded peninsula 12 km to the south of St-Tropez, lies the picturesque hill village of Ramatuelle, which has many superb views, besides its fortified houses with imposing gates, surrounded by vineyards and pine woods. In the tiny cemetery is the grave of the actor Gérard Philipe (1922–59).

To the north-west towers the 326 m high Moulins de Paillas, named after the former mill situated on its southern slope. A narrow road leads to the top, from which there is a fine view across the whole peninsula of Cap Camarat, westwards to the Massif des Maures, south-westwards to the bay of Cavalaire and northwards to the bay of St-Tropez. 5 km beneath Ramatuelle Cap Camarat extends into the sea; from its lighthouse there are more views over to the beaches of the bay of Anse de Pampelonne (to the north) and Plage de l'Escalet (to the south).

View from Cap Camarat over the beaches of St-Tropez

La Croix-Valmer
Coming from St-Tropez and passing
Ramatuelle the D93 road enters a scenic
but winding stretch over the Col de
Collebasse to the resort of la Croix-
Valmer which lies on the bay of
Cavalaire.

Ste-Maxime
On the far side of the bay to the north of
St-Tropez (14 km) lies the port of Ste-
Maxime, a popular holiday resort. In the
church to the west of the harbour is a
striking marble altar (18th c.) from the
Carthusian monastery of la Verna (in
Italy). To the north-east of the little town
there is the Sémaphore (signal station,
127 m) with fine views.
　　The **Musée du Phonographe et de la
Musique Mécanique** (on the road to Muy,
10 km) has a collection of over 300
musical instruments and phonographs.
Ⓖ *Easter–Oct. 10am–noon, 2–6pm.*

Cogolin
See Port-Grimaud

Grimaud
See Port-Grimaud

Stes-Maries-de-la-Mer　　　　J 2

Département: Bouches-du-Rhône
Altitude: sea level
Population: 2000

Stes-Maries-de-la-Mer is situated in the
extreme west of Provence, in the flat
country of lagoons and salt steppes of
the Camargue (see entry).

History
The place owes its name to the legend
whereby the three Marys – Mary (sister
of the Virgin Mary), Mary Salome
(mother of the Apostles James and John)
and Mary Magdalene (the penitent) – in
AD 45, with their black servant, Sara,
having been set adrift in a boat without
equipment or supplies, landed here and
converted Provence to Christianity
(☞St-Maximin-la-Ste-Baume).

Townscape
In recent years the town has been
extensively remodelled into a holiday
centre. In general the conversion has
been successful, the erection of tall
buildings having been avoided.
　　Stes-Maries is one of the most visited
places in Provence, especially at the time
of the pilgrimages in May and October.

Sights

★Église
The fortress-like church in the heavily
commercialised town centre (pedestrian
zone) dates from the 10th, 12th and
15th c.; inside is a well for use in case of
siege. In a chapel above the apse are the

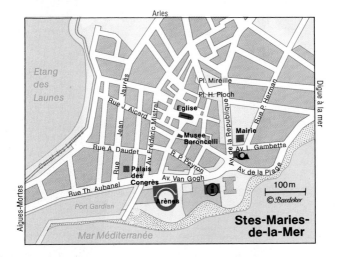

Stes-Maries-
de-la-Mer

reliquaries of the first two Marys, in the crypt those of their black servant Sara. Pilgrims come from far and wide to worship Sara (pilgrimages on May 24th, 25th and at the weekend after October 22nd). From the roof of the church (admission fee) there is a fine view.

Musée Baroncelli

The Musée Baroncelli is in the former town hall, a few metres south of the church (rue Victor-Hugo). It has collections dealing with local history and folklore from the Gallo-Roman period up to the beginning of the 20th c.; there are also illustrations of the animal and plant life of the Camargue plus archaeological finds from the vicinity. ⊚ *Apr.–Sep. daily 9am–noon, 2–7pm; Oct.–Mar. Wed.–Mon. 9am–noon, 2–5pm.*

Arènes

On the southern edge of the town between place du Marquis-de-Baroncelli and the beach, stands the arena, which is used for bullfights and similar events which take place during high season.

Musée Tsigane

The open-air Musée Tsigane (Pioch-Badet, on the D570, 10 km to the north of Stes-Maries) is devoted to Romany traditions. Painted caravans and other historical objects are on display; in one exhibition photos and maps are used to document over 1000 years of Romany history. Connected to the museum is an archive. There are video showings and guided tours. ⊚ *Daily.*

★Salon-de-Provence   H 6

Département: Bouches-du-Rhône
Altitude: 82 m
Population: 36,000

Salon-de-Provence is situated on the edge of the Plaine de la Crau, north of the Étang de Berre and north-west of Marseille.

History

Once on this site, on the hill of Valdemech, stood the Roman Castrum Salonense. The present-day town had its origins in the time of Charlemagne, after the salt marshes were drained. Salon was the native town of Adam de Craponne, who in 1554 built the canal named after him linking the

◀ Gipsy pilgrimage to the 'Black Sara'

lower Durance to the Crau and thereby starting the drainage and canal system between the Durance, the Rhône and the Étang de Berre. Nostradamus, who lived in Salon between 1547 and 1566 and here composed his *Centuries astrologiques*, is buried in the Church of St-Laurent.

Sights

★Château de l'Empéri

From its central position, the Château de l'Empéri dominates the town. Built by the archbishops of Arles between the 12th and 15th c., it is one of the best preserved and largest fortifications in Provence. The present site in essence goes back to Archbishop Jean des Baux (1233–58). The name Château de l'Empéri stems from the fact that Salon had fallen to the German emperors in 1032 with the rest of the kingdom of Provence and actually become part of the Empire. Of note is the beautiful Chapel of Ste-Cathérine (12th c.). ⊚ *Wed.–Mon. 10am–noon, 2.30–6.30pm.*

Musée de l'Empéri

The Musée de l'Empéri is housed in the château. It traces the history of French weaponry from the time of Louis XIV to the end of the first world war and includes uniform, equipment, firearms and swords.

St-Michel

East of the château on rue St-Michel stands the 12th–13th c. Church of St-Michel with its peculiar bell gable. The Romanesque doorway has an unusual tympanum, which is made up of sculptured blocks; in the middle at the top is the Archangel Michael, patron of the church, with two snakes (devil), and underneath a lamb with the cross, a symbol of the risen Christ. The other sections show stylised floral ornaments based on ancient models.

A short distance to the east the visitor passes through the Porte Bourg-Neuf, the remains of the town defences from the 13th c., which made way for the ring of boulevards around the town. To the right stands the fountain with the statue of Adam de Craponne and the attractive Town Hall (1655–8).

Maison de Nostradamus

The former house of the cosmologist Nostradamus (Michel de Nostre-Dame, 1503–66) – he spent the last 19 years of his life here – contains the note worthy Nostradamus Museum (2 rue

Salon-de-Provence: the tympanum of St-Michel

Nostradamus). It includes historical editions of his prophecies, mementos, and a reproduction of his study.
🕐 *Wed.–Mon. 2–6pm.*

Place Crousillat
The town gate Porte d'Horloge (mid-17th c.; bishop's arms over the gateway) leads to place Crousillat with its completely moss-covered fountain.

★St-Laurent
To the north of the town centre, on square St-Laurent, stands the Dominican Church of St-Laurent (14th–15th c.), which in its simplicity is an outstanding example of the Provençal Gothic style. Inside there is an alabaster statue of the Madonna (16th c.), a stone relief of the Descent from the Cross (15th/16th c.) and the tomb of Nostradamus which in its present form is a modern work.

Surroundings

La Barben
The little village of la Barben is charmingly situated in the Touloubre

valley 8 km east of Salon. About 1 km east of the village stands the Château de la Barben on a steep rocky height. It is surrounded by beautiful parkland with an animal compound and an aquarium.

Cornillon-Confoux
The picturesque village of Cornillon-Confoux, noted for its wine (*appellation d'origine contrôlée*), lies on a spur from which there is a fine view of the Étang de Berre. Of interest are the 17th c. château and the 12th c. church.

St-Chamas
The little fishing and yachting port of St-Chamas lies some 3 km south-west of Cornillon-Confoux on the Étang de Berre (see entry). The village is separated from the lagoon by a narrow mountain ridge, on top of which runs a canal. There is an aqueduct with a clock tower where the canal crosses a gap in the sea barrier. Well worth seeing are the prehistoric cave dwellings, the single-arched Pont Flavien (a bridge over the Touloubre, to the west of the village, with triumphal arches as gateways, dating from the 1st c. AD) and the 17th c. church with its baroque facade.

★Sénanque (Abbaye de Sénanque) F 7

Département: Vaucluse
Altitude: 480 m

The abbey of Sénanque, with those of Silvacane and le Thoronet (see entries), form a group of important Romanesque Cistercian monasteries in Provence – the 'three sisters of Provence', as they are called. Sénanque is situated on the southern edge of the Plateau de Vaucluse in the valley of the Senancole, to the north of Gordes (see entry). The name is derived from the Latin *sine aqua* (without water), as very little water flowed in the river.

On the approach from Gordes, 4 km on the D177, a narrow road with passing places which traverses dense *garrigue*, there is a good view of the monastery, deep down in the valley amid fields of lavender. The picture is at its most beguiling in July and the beginning of August, when the lavender is in flower.

The monastery, which is today the home of a Cistercian community, can be visited. Visitors may take part in the monks' services; the times are displayed at the entrance. In the monastery buildings exhibitions, cultural events, seminars and concerts (also church music, especially Gregorian chant) regularly take place.
🅖 *Mar.–Oct. Mon.–Sat. 10am–noon, 2–6pm, Sun. 2–6pm; Nov.–Feb. Mon.–Fri. 2–5pm, Sat., Sun. 2–6pm.*

History
Sénanque was founded in 1148 by the Cistercian monastery at Mazan (Ardèche). Building of the church was begun in 1160 and finished by the early 13th c. The monastery buildings were erected 1180–1220 (the buildings at Silvacane were begun in 1175, le Thoronet in 1160). The heyday of the abbey was during the 14th c., when the Cistercian Benedict XII was Pope in Avignon. Because of its growing wealth – Sénanque owned a vast amount of land between Mont Ventoux, Montagne de Lure and the Montagne de Lubéron – its strict discipline slackened, leading to its decline. In 1544 it was a victim of an uprising during the Wars of Religion, from which it never recovered. During the French Revolution the estate was confiscated and sold to a private owner who maintained the monastery. In 1854 a community of Cistercians returned but after setbacks during the anti-clerical Third Republic the last monks transferred to Lérin. Later Paul Berliet, the lorry and bus manufacturer, started up a cultural centre and in October 1988 a group of monks returned to Sénanque from Lérin.

Monastery buildings

Exterior
Sénanque's external appearance is defined by simple and harmonious proportions and its perfectly crafted stonework, which produce a monumental impression.

According to the rules of the Cistercian order, the rooms which were used for day-to-day living were to be by the river, whilst the church should occupy the most elevated position. At Sénanque this could only be achieved by having the church aligned north–south.

Except for the south wing, which was destroyed and then later rebuilt during the 18th c., and the refectory, Sénanque is largely preserved in its original state.

Dormitorium
The monastery buildings are entered from a wing connected to the north-west side of the abbey (19th c.; ticket office, books, souvenirs). The circular signed route leads first to the dormitorium (sleeping quarters) situated on the upper floor, an austere room, the Gothic pointed arches of which are a continuation of the vaulting which covers the transepts of the monastic church. The monks used to sleep here in their clothes on sacks of straw. An excellent set of displays provide information about building techniques (architecture, stonemasonry).

From the dormitorium there is direct access to the church; the monks assembled seven times a day for worship, including twice during the night. Thus there is one flight of stairs leading to the church, another leading down to the cloister.

Cloister
The cloister is barrel-vaulted; the arcades leading to the garden consist of

Abbaye de Sénanque

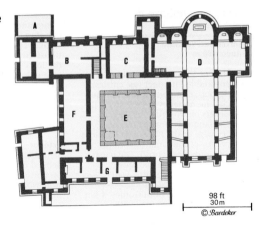

A	West wing (entrance)
B	Monks' hall ((scriptorium)
C	Chapter house
B & C	Dormitory above
D	Abbey church
E	Cloister
F	Refectory
G	Lay brothers' building

98 ft
30 m
© Baedeker

four bays per side, each bay containing three small round arches (hence twelve arches in all, a holy number). The rhythm of this sequence affords a sense of harmony; the cloister at le Thoronet, which is only slightly older, is far more archaic. The capitals of the arches show palm leaves, petals and water lilies; they are simple and beautifully crafted. Of the well which is situated in the south-west corner there remain only the pillars that supported the vault.

Chapter house
Below the dormitorium are the chapter house and the monks' hall. Together with the church, the chapter house was the centre of the abbey. Here matters pertaining to the day-to-day life of the monastery and the Cistercian order were discussed. The monks sat on the steps around the sides of the room. The ribbed vaulting (inserted at a later date) converges in two pillars with lavish capitals.

Monks' hall
On the same level as the cloister is the monks' hall, the only room in the monastery which could be heated. While in other monasteries belonging to the order the monks' hall was only used for purposes which required a warm environment (care of the sick, writing work), in Sénanque it also served as a general day room. It

possessed two chimneys; the one which has been preserved also passes through the dormitorium, where it gave off some heat. The roof is supported in the middle of the room by a thick column resting on a square base, here too with a richly worked capital.

Refectory
The refectory, which was destroyed in the 16th c. and rebuilt in the 19th, has regained its original appearance as a result of recent restoration. Today it is used by the monastic community as a chapel and during the week most of the services are conducted here. It is closed to visitors.

Church
The building of the basilican church was begun in 1160 with the north end (chancel transepts) and completed in the 13th c. with the nave. The alteration of the nave arcades to pointed arches and the irregularity of the side aisles probably came about as a result of later alterations. The height of the nave was also raised so that windows could be put in. Apart from these windows, the walls of the nave are bare up to the roof vaults. On the south facade there is no central doorway, merely two small doors leading through to the side aisles. The crossing is unusual in that it is vaulted by an octagonal cupola; most Cistercian churches only have a continuous ridge

The Abbaye de Sénanque, impressive in its simple architecture

or simple tower. The main monastery at Mazan and neighbouring Velay were models for the architecture.

Connected to the broad transept with its pointed barrel vault is the equally high choir and chancel ending in an apse with two side apses on each side. The altars, of which one dates from the Romanesque period and served as a model for the others, are original. In the right-hand transept there is a wheel window.

As a whole the bright airy building represents a realisation of the Cistercian concept of monastic living: seclusion, poverty and simplicity, prayer and hard physical labour – those qualities which Bernhard of Clairvaux prescribed when he renounced the worldly splendour of Cluny.

★Silvacane (Abbaye de Silvacane) G 8

Département: Vaucluse
Altitude: 230 m

The former Cistercian abbey of Silvacane

lies near the little village of la Roque-Anthéron on the left bank of the Durance, south of the Montagne du Lubéron (see entry), 25 km north-east of Salon and 26 km north-west of Aix-en-Provence.

Ⓖ *Apr.–Sep. daily 9am–7pm, Oct.–Mar. Wed.–Mon. 9am–noon, 2–5pm; closed pub. hols.*

History
The name of the abbey comes from the Latin *silva cannorum* (forest of reeds) and suggests that the area was formerly marshland. The monastery was founded in 1144 by Raymond des Baux and transferred to the Cistercians. Unlike other Cistercian monasteries, Silvacane does not lie far from civilisation, but is situated where important transport routes meet. Previously there had been a monastic community here which had cared for the spiritual well-being of travellers crossing the Durance. Work on the building was not begun until 1175 and the church was finished in 1230, during which period the Gothic style of architecture had already established

itself in the north of France. The cloister and monastic buildings followed around 1250–1300, while the refectory was not erected until the 15th c. during a short new burst of activity. In 1443 Silvacane came under the cathedral chapter of Aix-en-Provence and became the parish church of nearby la Roque-Anthéron, long after it had declined as a monastery. Like many other ecclesiastical properties it was sold during the French Revolution and was intended to have been torn down to provide building materials. However in 1846 the government acquired the estate and this resulted in an extensive restoration.

Monastery buildings

Church

Although Silvacane has a very simple design, the protracted period of its construction saw a certain watering-down in the strict building principles of the Cistercian Romanesque style (☞le Thoronet). The powerful buttresses on the facade, transept and choir convey a certain unity of structure. Over the doorway of the west facade is the coat of arms of the cathedral chapter of Aix; it was put up on the occasion of the transfer of Silvacane to the diocese in the 15th c.

Interior

The nave with its three bays and ogival barrel vault joins the transept; the choir chapels are also barrel-vaulted. The Gothic ribbed vault of the crossing was probably inserted at a later date. As a whole the interior of Silvacane is more solid than Sénanque or le Thoronet. The capitals are embellished with leaf decorations (partly archaic, partly revealing Gothic forms). A progression in both building techniques and in aesthetics can be detected in aisle vaults.

Cloister

As was usual in Cistercian monasteries, there was direct access from the church to the cloister and to the monastic buildings. A staircase leads down from the north aisle to the small cloister,

Abbaye de Silvacane

Abbaye de Silvacane

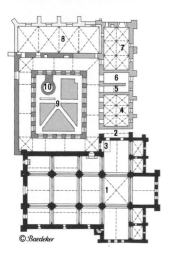

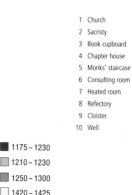

© Baedeker

1 Church
2 Sacristy
3 Book cupboard
4 Chapter house
5 Monks' staircase
6 Consulting room
7 Heated room
8 Refectory
9 Cloister
10 Well

■ 1175 – 1230
▨ 1210 – 1230
▨ 1250 – 1300
□ 1420 – 1425

1.6 m lower. It has barrel vaults. The simple Romanesque-looking round arcades which open to the garden were originally subdivided with a double pillar (which in some cases has been retained), which carries two pointed arches, and a round window between (oculus). In fact the cloister was erected in the late 13th c.

Conventual buildings
The conventual buildings are lower down. The chapter house vault is supported by two pillars. It is connected to the dormitorium on the upper floor by a staircase. The monks' hall was fitted with a fireplace and also served as a scriptorium. The refectory, which because of the natural slope was built at cellar level, dates from the 15th c. and has ribbed vaults; there is a rose window in the eastern bay.

The building for the lay brothers, which was a normal feature of Cistercian monasteries, has not been preserved.

★Sisteron   D 11

Département: Alpes-de-Haute-Provence
Altitude: 482 m
Population: 6500

Sisteron lies in the extreme north of the area covered in this guide on the Route Napoléon and to the north of the Montagne de la Lure; it is not far from the confluence of the Buëch with the Durance.

History
It is believed that the caves in the vicinity were lived in from very early times, but there is no actual proof of this. Augustus subdued the tribes of the Avantici and Vocones which were settled here and built Segustero at a narrow point of the Durance on the Roman Via Domitia. In the 5th c. Sisteron became the seat of a bishop and remained so until the French Revolution. In the 9th and 10th c. Saracens held the town; in 1348 half the population died of the plague. About the middle of the 14th c. a beginning was made on the defences, most of which can still be seen today. In 1481 Sisteron fell to the kingdom of France, but the Wars of Religion caused great devastation. On his journey from Elba to Paris Napoléon passed through the Defile of Sisteron without much difficulty. In August 1944 the town and citadel were bombed by American planes (over 300 casualties) in order to drive out German troops.

Sights

Townscape

Situated high above the place where the Durance breaks through its mountain ridge the Citadel of Sisteron crowns an unusually impressive landscape. In summer a little tourist railway (starting point at place de la République) runs up to the Citadel.

★Citadel

Above the town to the north on a high rocky hill, through which the N85 road runs in a tunnel, stands the Citadel, built in the 12th and extended in the 16th and 19th c. It is fortified on several levels and commands not only the river but also the entire north and south hinterlands. The greater part of the fortifications are the work of the architect Jean Erard (16th c.). From the highest turrets and the Guérite du Diable outwork there is an unusually impressive view to the north over the Alpine region and eastwards across to the other side of the river where the Rocher de la Baume rises, a steep rock face with almost vertical fault lines.

On the north side of the citadel an open-air theatre has been constructed.

Notre-Dame-des-Pommiers

In the centre of the lower town stands the former cathedral of Notre-Dame-des-Pommiers, built between 1160 and 1220. Like many churches in this area of the Alps it reveals the influence of Lombardy. Of special interest are the figure sculpture on the entrance, the capitals of the nave and the two baroque altars.

Town walls

To the south of the church on allée de Verdun can be seen three well-preserved semicircular towers that were once part of the town walls.

Old Town

In the Old Town of Sisteron are a number of fine 16th and 17th c. houses; a walk through the picturesque streets, which in places lead beneath flying buttresses, is marked by arrows.

◀ Sisteron: Rocher de la Baume

★Tarascon   G 3–4

Département: Bouches-du-Rhône
Altitude: 9 m
Population: 11,000

Tarascon is on the left bank of the lower course of the Rhône about halfway between Avignon and Arles.

Legend

Tarascon derives its name from the Tarasque, a fabulous man-eating creature of wild appearance said to have dwelled here and which only St Martha was successful in pacifying. It has become the heraldic animal of the town celebrated by a festival in June, the Fête de la Tarasque, when a terrifying effigy of the creature is led through the procession.

No less romantic is Tartarin de Tarascon, the hero of the novel by Alphonse Daudet. Short and somewhat stocky with a black beard and quite warlike in his behaviour, he is nevertheless more inclined to dream his adventures rather than carry them out; in the long run he values physical well-being more highly than war and deprivation, and with his lovable humanity he is, for many, the embodiment of the Provençal character.

Sights

Château du Roi-René

Immediately north of the road bridge (boulevard du Château), on the banks of the Rhône, stands the massive château. Its origins go back to the late 14th c. and it was named after René, duke of Anjou and former king of Naples (called 'le Bon Roi René'), who ordered the completion of the château in the mid-15th c. and who patronised artists and scientists.

Protected on one side by the river and on the other by a deep moat, the château resisted every siege and attack right up to the bombardment by Allied forces in 1944. From the battlements there is a fine view.

🄶 Daily 9am–4pm; guided tours on the hour; closed pub. hols.

Ste-Marthe

Diagonally opposite the château stands the Church of Ste-Marthe, originating

Tarascon: Château du Roi-René

in the 10th c., but now a predominantly Gothic building. The doorway to the south aisle is interesting, in spite of damage to the sculptures. Inside the church is a panel by Pierre Parrocel, a less well-known member of the family of painters; in the crypt can be seen the sarcophagus of St Martha, whose remains were found in Tarascon.

Hôtel de Ville

Not far from the château (rue des Halles) stands the Hôtel de Ville (Town Hall; 17th c.) In the Old Town there are a number of fine buildings.

Surroundings

Beaucaire

The little town of Beaucaire lies on the right bank of the Rhône opposite Tarascon and is in the *région* of Languedoc-Roussillon and the *département* of Gard. It was once famous in western Europe for its market (Foire de Beaucaire), which has existed since 1217 and which takes place from July 21st to 28th. Today it includes a historical procession, wine festival, concerts and bullfights. Noteworthy is the beautiful Hotel de Ville (Town Hall; 1679–83), built by J Hardouin-Mansart. Above the town are the ruins of a château of the 13th–14th c. from which there is a rewarding view.

Abbaye St-Roman

About 5 km to the north of Beaucaire, on the other side of the Rhône, is the Abbey (Troglodytique) of St-Roman, which is built into the rocks (5th c.). Access is by following the road parallel to the D986L; 15 min. walk from the car park.

Ⓒ *Jul.–Aug. Tue.–Sun. 10am–7pm; Apr.–June Wed.–Sun. 10am–6pm.*

From the top of the hill (go straight up the mountain from the turning off the D986L) there is a superb ★**view** across about 40 km of the Rhône valley from

Avignon to Arles (Fourques Power Station), the mountain chains of the Montagnette and the Alpilles, as well as Tarascon and Beaucaire.

★★Le Thoronet (Abbaye du Thoronet)   J13

Département: Var
Altitude: 142 m

The abbey of le Thoronet (26 km to the south-west of Draguignan on the D562) is the oldest and smallest of the three Cistercian monasteries in Provence (☛Sénanque, Silvacane) and has a secluded position in a wooded, hilly area to the south of the Argens.

Le Thoronet is the epitome of the Provençal Romanesque style and represents a model of Cistercian building principles, which derive from the strict rules of the order – absolute simplicity, clear lines and proportions, a complete absence of decoration. The severe exterior is tempered by the reddish hue of the stone from the Esterel Massif, the Provençal light and the beautiful setting.
ⓞ *Apr.–Sep. Mon., Wed.–Sat. 9am–7pm, Sun. 9am–noon, 2–7pm; Oct.–Mar. 9am–noon, 2–5pm.*

History

The convent and church were built, like Sénanque, by the monks of Mazan (Ardèche) between 1160 and 1190, after they had settled near there in 1136 at the instigation of Raymond Bérenger, count of Barcelona and Toulouse. Raymond ensured that the foundation should have a secure basis for its existence by transferring land to its ownership. One of the first abbots, Folco or Folquet (from 1201), had been a famous troubadour before he

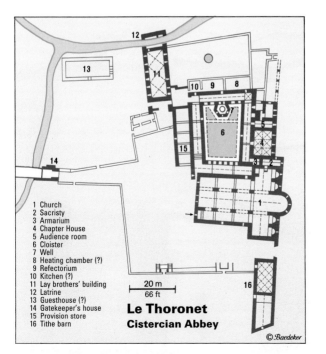

1 Church
2 Sacristy
3 Armarium
4 Chapter House
5 Audience room
6 Cloister
7 Well
8 Heating chamber (?)
9 Refectorium
10 Kitchen (?)
11 Lay brothers' building
12 Latrine
13 Guesthouse (?)
14 Gatekeeper's house
15 Provision store
16 Tithe barn

20 m
66 ft

Le Thoronet
Cistercian Abbey

© *Baedeker*

renounced worldly and amorous concerns and became a Cistercian monk in 1196. After a period of decline during the 14th c. the monastery was abandoned and in 1791 during the Revolution was confiscated by the state and sold off. It was bought back by the state in 1840 and preserved from dilapidation thanks to the efforts of the French writer Prosper Mérimée. The baroque additions in the 18th c. were removed during restoration work which took place after 1873.

Monastery buildings

Church

The stone belfry is unusual for a Cistercian church – normally only roof turrets were permitted. The masonry is impressive by virtue of the exactness with which the slabs of stone have been cut and laid; the slightly sloping roofs rest directly on the vaults. The facade does not have a central doorway – as there was no congregation – but merely two side doors (the left one was assigned to lay brothers).

Interior

The nave is built with four bays and pointed barrel vaults. The arms of the transept do not form a crossing with the nave, but are merely attached to it. Set in the eastern wall of the transept, to the left and right of the choir, there are two apses, while the choir leads to the eastern apse.

The transition to the Gothic style is heralded by the ogival barrel vault in the nave and transept and the half vault in the aisles, which divert the weight from the central vault on to the exterior walls.

The articulation of the interior is by the simple piers and a string course that marks the base of the vaulting. Light reaches the interior through a few small windows in the west, south and east walls and in the apses; the north side has no windows.

Cloister

The cloister is reached from the north aisle. The irregular shape of its plan (a

trapezium with unequal sides, the longest 37 m) and profile is caused by the land on which it is built. The building history is documented here in the various mouldings and vaults; the earlier south wing (ca 1160–70) has a barrel vault, while in the north-east and north-west corners are Gothic ribbed vaults. The round-arched arcades leading to the garden rest on rectangular piers and contain pairs of smaller round arches with simple capitals. Here it is possible to trace the tradition of Romanesque building techniques (cf. the Temple of Diana in Nîmes).

The terrace above the cloister, which is reached from the dormitorium, offers the best view across the site.

Well house

The well house on the north wing of the cloister is the only example in Provence to survive. The hexagonal building has a ribbed vault and round-arched windows with a separate entrance and exit. The fountain itself is modern.

Monks' buildings

Next to the northern transept on the same level is the wide sacristy and the tiny library (the Cistercians restricted themselves to only the most essential reading matter). Connected to it is the chapter house, the ribbed vault of which rests on two pillars. The sculptures on the capitals (leaves, palm branches, volutes) represent the only sculptural decoration in the whole complex; probably it was felt fitting to allow a certain degree of embellishment to what was, after the church, the most important room for monastic life.

The parlatorium (speaking room) is situated between the cloister and the monastery garden. Other buildings in the north of the site (warming room, refectory, kitchen and monks' hall) have not been preserved, although their plan is still discernible.

Following the Cistercian tradition, a staircase leads from the north transept directly into the dormitorium, the monks' sleeping room, which is situated above the chapter house.

Lay brothers

The lay brothers' building, which dates from the early 13th c., is connected to

View from the south transept towards the lay brothers' doorway

the north-west corner of the cloister. On the ground floor is the refectory with a ribbed vault; on the upper floor the dormitorium has an ogival barrel vault. The door in the north wall led to the latrine, now in ruins, which was directly above the stream.

Cellar
The store room built against the west range of the cloister dates from the end of the 12th c. It is a long room with an ogival barrel vault. Here there are alcoves for oil and wine, the remains of an oil press and an exhibition dealing with the restoration of the monastery and the building of the Cistercians.

Outbuildings
In the north-west corner of the site are the foundations of the guest house; in the south stands the former tithe barn.

★★Toulon L11

Département: Var
Altitude: sea level to 10 m
Population: 181,500

The port of Toulon lies about 70 km south-east of Marseille near the most southerly point of the French Riviera. The bay of Toulon forms an outstanding natural harbour; it consists of the inner Petite Rade (little harbour roads) and the outer Grande Rade (large roads) and is protected by the offshore promontory of St-Mandrier. Toulon is the most important military port in France.

History
The settlement, called Telonion by the Greeks, Telo Martius by the Romans, was important in ancient times primarily because of the purple dye obtained from the purple snails which lived in the sea. The conversion to a naval port did not occur until recent times. In 1487 Toulon passed into French hands under King Louis XI and became an important base by virtue of its strategic position (the largest natural harbour in the Mediterranean). The Tour Royale, which controlled the access to the Petite Rade, was built in 1514. The fortifications, which were installed towards the end of the 16th c. and strengthened by Vauban in 1660, withstood in 1707 the combined forces of Prince Eugene, Holland and

England. In 1793, during the French Revolution, the royalists delivered the town to the English Admiral Hood; it was reconquered by the revolutionary army after a six-week siege, during which the 23–year-old batallion commander Napoléon Bonaparte (later Napoléon I) gained particular distinction and was as a result promoted to brigadier-general. In the 19th c. it was from Toulon that the French troops left to go to war: to the Crimea, Italy, Mexico, Indo-China, Madagascar and Africa. Until 1939 the naval fleet constituted the main employer in the town. In the second world war Toulon was occupied by German troops in November 1942 and half destroyed by bombing; the French fleet went down on November 27th. When the Allied forces landed in August 1944 Toulon was one of the first towns to be liberated (see below Mont Faron). In 1974 Toulon became (after a lapse of 181 years) a prefecture again and capital of the *département* of Var.

Old Town

The Vieille Ville (Old Town), which was severely damaged during the second world war, lies by the Vieille Darse (Old Harbour), on the north-west of which stands the Préfecture Maritime; every day after sunset the Cérémonie des Couleurs takes place here. The fronts of the houses along quai Stalingrad, which leads south-east to the Rond-Point Bonaparte, were rebuilt after the second world war and are dominated by the tower of the new Town Hall. The caryatids by Pierre Puget (1620–94), originally in the Old Town Hall, which was also destroyed in the war, today adorn the entrance to the Municipal Information Centre. They have been copied over and over again all over Provence (for instance at cours Mirabeau in Aix-en-Provence), but here remain, unsurpassed in the vividness of their originality.

Just to the west from here the narrow, but very busy rue d'Alger runs north and leads into rue Hoche, at the end of which is place Puget with the Fontaine des Trois-Dauphins (1782, by Chastel), which, like many fountains in

Toulon and its harbours, seen from Mont-Faron

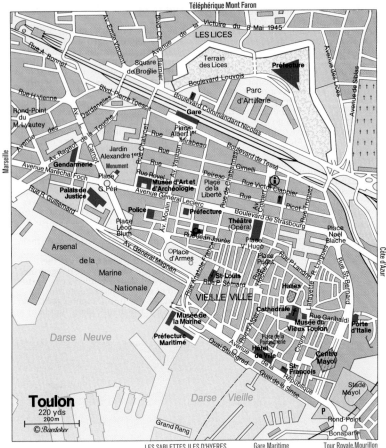

Toulon
220 yds
200m
© Baedeker

Provence, is overgrown and covered with deposits of lime.

Musée de la Marine
To the north of the Préfecture Maritime stands the Musée de la Marine (Naval Museum), which houses a collection of old models of ships, etchings and drawings and an exhibition about the development of artillery.
ⓖ *Wed.–Mon. 10am–noon, 1.30–6pm.*

Cathédrale Ste-Marie-Majeure
South-west of place Puget in the

centre of the Old Town stands the Early Gothic Cathedral of Ste-Marie-Majeure (13th c.; largely rebuilt in the 17th c.) with an 18th c. belfry. Nearby is the colourful Marché (market; vegetables, flowers) and (on cours Lafayette) the Musée du Vieux-Toulon with local history collections and sacred art.
ⓖ *Mon.–Sat. 2–6pm.*

Other sights
The Bibliothèque du Vieux-Toulon is also situated on cours Lafayette. At the east end of rue Garibaldi, which

branches off here, stands the impressive Porte d'Italie, a 16th c. bridge. Further on, to the south of the cathedral, place de la Poissonnerie, the fish market.

Leaving place Puget, the busy centre of the Old Town, by rue Muraire (also called Raimu) we come to the noteworthy Opera House (1862–4). North-west lies place de la Liberté with the Monument de la Fédération by Allard.

Further to the west, on boulevard Leclerc, is the **Musée d'Art et d'Archéologie** (Museum of Art and Archaeology; pictures from the 13th to 20th c., prehistoric and ancient artefacts; ◉ 1–7pm). In the same building is the Musée d'Histoire Naturelle (Natural History Museum; geological and fossil collections; ◉ 10am–noon, 2–6pm). Adjoining is the attractive Jardin Alexandre-Ier with magnolias, palms and cedars and to the south of this the large Palais de Justice (law courts).

Port

At the west end of quai Stalingrad along the Darse Neuve (New Harbour) begin the workshops, docks and stores of the Arsenal Maritime behind the fine Porte de l'Arsenal (1738).

Le Mourillon

Beyond the Rond-Point Bonaparte lies Mourillon, the south-east quarter. From the Tour Royale, an impressive fortification of the time of Louis XII at the southern end of the roadstead, there is an exceptional panoramic view. The contents of the Musée Naval Tour-Royale, which was once housed here, have been transferred to Paris. To the north-east stands Fort St-Louis (1707), which guards a small harbour.

★Corniche Mistral (Littoral F-Mistral)

Probably the finest street in Toulon is the Corniche Mistral, which leads along the Grande Rade de Vignettes of Mourillon past the Jardin d'Acclimatation (botanical garden) to the charming residential district of Cap Brun (103 m; fort, view). Below the coast road runs the Sentier des Douaniers (Customs Officers' Path), a winding footpath along the coast, which leads across the Batterie Basse du Cap Brun to the romantic bays of Méjean and Magaud.

★★Mont Faron

Corniche du Mont-Faron

The Corniche du Mont-Faron (Corniche Marius-Escartefigue), a road half way up Mont Faron, borders the districts of Ste-Anne (with the spacious Hôpital Maritime) and Super-Toulon. The last named has only been opened up recently and is characterised by fine villas situated on the slope. There are magnificent views early in the morning and shortly before sunset.

Summit

Mont Faron (542 m) dominates the city in the north; from Super-Toulon a cableway 1437 m long (boulevard Amiral-Vence, dep. every 10 mins; closed Mon.) goes up to the Mémorial du Faron and the Tour Beaumont (493 m). From here there is a very rewarding but narrow, steep and winding road (route du Faron; mostly one-way traffic and certainly not suitable for large motor homes or towed caravans), which starts in the

Toulon: Fontaine des Trois-Dauphins

west and climbs up past the Fort du St-Antoine to the **Musée Mémorial du Débarquement en Provence**. This martial building contains a collection explaining the landing of the Allied forces from August 15th 1944 (weapons; equipment; diorama; film presentation).
◎ *Tue.–Sun. 9.30–11.30am, 2.30–4.30pm; duration of visit 1 hour.*

From the roof of the fort (orientation table, telescope) there is a superb panorama of the city and of the mountains rising all round.

On the plateau on the summit, with its great variety of flowers, there is also a small **zoological garden**.
◎ *Daily 2pm–sunset.*

From the Mémorial the road leads eastwards past Fort Croix-Faron and Fort Faron and back down to Super-Toulon.

Surroundings

Cuers
Cuers, situated 22 km to the north in the country, is a well-known wine-producing and cork-processing centre. On the south-eastern edge of the Barre de Cuers (696 m) there are extensive areas of flower cultivation.

The centre of the village is picturesque with its fine parish church (organ of 1669), the medieval gateway and pretty little streets. Above the village stand the ruins of a château from which there are good views.

Ollioules
Ollioules, on the southern slope of the gorge of the same name (8 km to the west), is well known for its flower growing (auctions). There is a ruined château in the village.

★★Gorges d'Ollioules
Not far north of the village one reaches the Gorges d'Ollioules, which has been cut by the Reppe river with strange rock formations. Above the gorge on a sheer volcanic rock lies the village of Evenos, a *village perché* with the remains of a château, the keep of which, like the traditional houses, is built of blocks of basalt.

La Seyne-sur-Mer
La Seyne-sur-Mer, 4 km to the west of Toulon on the other side of the bay, is an industrial town with several parts; it has important shipyards, mussel beds and works for the processing of olive wood. Of interest are the 17th c. Church of Notre-Dame-du-Bon-Voyage, the former Fort Balaguier, also 17th c., and the Musée de la Seyne (local history). To the east lies the pleasant yacht and fishing harbour with a movable bridge.

Tamaris
Tamaris, which gets its name from the tamarisks which grow here, is a popular resort with a yachting harbour reached by following a beautiful coastal road around the promontory of Fort Balaguier. To the west above the resort stands Fort Napoléon, and behind it along the Rade du Lazaret is the district of les Sablettes which lies on a sandy spit between Cap Sicié and Cap Cépet. From here there is a particularly fine view of the roadsteads of Toulon and the sea.

Signes
The quiet vine- and fruit-growing village of Signes lies 30 km to the north of Toulon in a hollow on the edge of the headwaters of the Gapeau. It is reached either via Ollioules (west, N8, D402 and D2) or via Solliès-Pont (east, N97, D554 and D2). Here on place St-Jean stands a beautiful chapel (restored in 17th c.); inside can be seen pictures, votive tablets and penitents' garments. The square is embellished by an 18th c. fountain. In the Church of St-Pierre (16th c. belfry) the beautiful wooden altar (14th and 17th c.) is worthy of note.

Autodrome Paul-Ricard
On the western route to Signes, at the junction of the D402 with the N8, is the motor-racing track of Paul-Ricard, which until 1990 was the venue of the Grand Prix de France (Formula One). Since 1991 the race has been held at Magny-Cours, near Nevers in Burgundy.

Six-Fours-la-Plage
See Bandol

★Uzès   E 2

Région: Languedoc-Roussillon
Département: Gard
Altitude: 138 m
Population: 8000

The little town of Uzès lies beyond the
boundary of Provence, some 40 km west
of Avignon. It has a picturesque
situation above the wooded valley of
the Alzon. The town centre with its
narrow streets and alleys is surrounded
by a ring of boulevards shaded by plane
trees.

The best facilities for parking are on
the broad esplanade on the western edge
of the Old Town.

Sights

★Place aux Herbes

A short way east of the esplanade is
place aux Herbes, the beautiful main
square of the town, shaded by plane
trees and adorned by its fountain, which
is mainly overgrown. All round the
square are medieval houses with arcades.
On Saturdays the market takes place
here.

Hôtels

On rue de la République further north
stands the Hôtel de Joubert with a
pretty staircase and inner courtyard.
From here we turn east and on the far
side of the small place Dampmartin

(arcades with ribbed vaults) reaches
the equally interesting Hôtel
Dampmartin. To the north stands the
great complex of buildings of the
Château Ducal; entrance from place du
Duché.

Château Ducal

The former château of the dukes of Uzès
was built in various stages from the 11th
to the 17th c., but was again altered in
the 19th c. In the inner courtyard the
Renaissance facade (mid-16th c.)
between the keep and the chapel tower
deserves particular attention; it is divided
by pillars and decorated with relief
medallions. There is a good panorama
from the Tour Bermonde (11th c.;
balustrade 1839).
ⓘ *Apr.–Sep. daily 9.30am–noon,
2.30–6.30pm; Oct.–Mar. Tue.–Sun.
10am–noon, 2.30–5pm.*

Hôtel de Ville

Opposite the château gateway stands
the Hôtel de Ville (Town Hall) which
was erected in 1773 under Louis XVI.
The elegant facade facing the château
is original, while the north front,
where the main entrance is situated,
was renewed about 1900. The facades
of the courtyard are broken up by
pillars. The view of the ducal château
through the wrought-iron gate is
delightful.

Crypte

Opposite the north-east corner of the

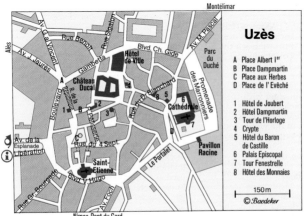

Montélimar

Uzès

A Place Albert Ier
B Place Dampmartin
C Place aux Herbes
D Place de l'Evêché

1 Hôtel de Joubert
2 Hôtel Dampmartin
3 Tour de l'Horloge
4 Crypte
5 Hôtel du Baron
   de Castille
6 Palais Episcopal
7 Tour Fenestrelle
8 Hôtel des Monnaies

150m

©Baedeker

Nîmes, Pont du Gard

Uzès: fountain on place aux Herbes

the Wars of Religion. The present facade was added in the 19th c.

The most interesting part of the medieval cathedral is the round **Tour Fenestrelle** (Window Tower), a 42 m high belfry erected in the 12th c. on a Lombardian model. Its six storeys, which narrow as they ascend, are divided up by wall arcaders, which from the third floor upwards contain round-headed openings. Because it served as a watchtower, the building escaped destruction by the Albigenses.

Hôtel du Baron-de-Castille

On the far side of the square opposite the bishop's palace stands the Hôtel du Baron-de-Castille, a classical building with an elegant pillared facade (18th c.).

St-Etienne

On the southern edge of the Old Town, on boulevard Victor-Hugo, is the Church of St-Etienne, a large baroque building (1765–78). The square tower standing alongside dates from the 13th c.

château is the entrance to the so-called 'crypt', an Early Christian cult chamber hacked out of the rock. On the walls in low relief are the figures of John the Baptist and an Orans (a figure praying with outstretched arms).

Palais Episcopal

From the château and the Town Hall going east past the Ancien Hôtel des Monnaies (former Mint) we reach the Ancien Palais Episcopal, the former Bishop's Palace (place de l'Evêché). Today the law courts and the library are situated here and in the second storey is a museum with exhibits of art, ethnology, prehistory and natural history, as well as mementoes of the writer André Gide, whose family originated from Uzès.
🅖 *Feb.–Dec. Tue.–Sun. 3–6pm.*

Cathédrale St-Théodorit

To the south by the bishop's palace stands the Cathedral of St-Théodorit dating from the 17th and 19th c.; the previous building was destroyed during

Surroundings

Musée du Bonbon

Not far to the south (D981), in Pont-des-Charrettes, the Musée du Bonbon presents the history and manufacturing process of the popular gummi bears.
🅖 *Jul.–Sep. daily; Oct.–Jun. closed Mon.*

Musée 1900

The small museum at Arpaillargues (4 km to the west, D982) displays an attractive collection of cars, motorbikes, carriages, agricultural tools and machines, as well as cameras and toys.

Haras d'Uzès

Founded in 1972, the Haras d'Uzès (about 4 km to the west, D407; signed) is one of 23 French national studs and has in excess of 70 horses of different breeds, including Arab and English. It is also used as a Gîte d'Étape by long-distance horse riders.
🅖 *Conducted tours. Jul.–Aug. Tue., Fri. 3pm.*

★Vaison-la-Romaine   D 6

Département: Vaucluse
Altitude: 200 m
Population: 6000

Vaison-la-Romaine lies to the north-west of Mont Ventoux, about 30 km north-east of Orange. To the south of the town extend the wine-producing regions of Séguret and Gigondas and the Dentelles de Montmirail.

History

In the 4th c. BC this was the chief place of the Celtic Vocones. Later the Romans founded Vasio Vocontiorum in the fertile region of the valley of the Ouvèze and over five peaceful centuries this developed into a flourishing community. As early as the 4th c. AD Vaison was the seat of a bishop and in 442 and 529 ecclesiastical councils were held here in the 12th c. Raymond, count of Toulouse, laid siege and conquered the town, robbed the bishop of his property and had a château built on the highest spot of the mountain which rises above the town.

In September 1992 the Ouvèze valley suffered a devastating flood during which the water engulfed 30 houses and a campsite was washed away; 18 people lost their lives at Vaison.

★Roman excavations

To the west and the east of place du 11-Novembre can be found the two separate Roman excavations. The eastern part corresponds to the Quartier de Puymin and the western to the Quartier de la Villasse.

⊚ Excavations and Notre-Dame: Apr., May 10am–12.30pm, 2–5.45pm; Jun.–Aug. 9am–12.30pm, 2–6.45pm. Guided tours 11am, 2.30pm. Museum: Apr., May 10am–1pm, 2.30–5.45pm; Jun.–Aug. 9.30am–1pm, 2.30–6.45pm. The combined entrance ticket to all the sights is valid for five days.

Quartier de Puymin

The gently sloping Quartier de Puymin

The Roman bridge over the Ouvèze river at Vaison-la-Romaine

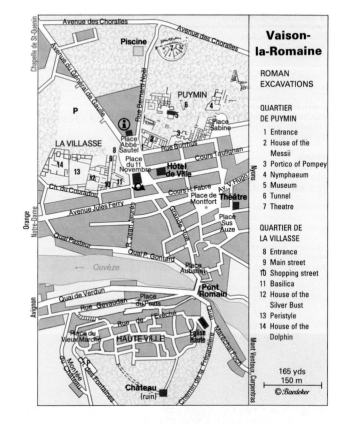

Vaison-la-Romaine

ROMAN
EXCAVATIONS

QUARTIER
DE PUYMIN

1 Entrance
2 House of the
   Messii
3 Portico of Pompey
4 Nymphaeum
5 Museum
6 Tunnel
7 Theatre

QUARTIER DE
LA VILLASSE

8 Entrance
9 Main street
10 Shopping street
11 Basilica
12 House of the
   Silver Bust
13 Peristyle
14 House of the
   Dolphin

165 yds
150 m

© Baedeker

is laid out like a park with oaks and cypresses. In the lower part foundations of walls have been uncovered including those of the House of the Messii, the Portico of Pompey (pillared hall) and the Nymphaeum. The statues set up on the excavation site are copies of the ancient originals which can be seen in the museum.

In addition to a large and very well arranged lapidarium (Roman tombstones, statues), the museum in the centre of this site includes a model of the theatre. Other specialised subjects concern the Roman dwellings and Gallo-Roman pottery. Of interest is a showcase containing urns for ashes, some of which are made of glass. Immediately by the entrance there is a map showing the Roman province of Gallia Narbonensis.

Theatre

Just above the museum a tunnel leads to the ancient theatre which is smaller than those at Arles and Orange. It has been restored and now serves its original purpose once more as an open-air theatre.

Quartier de la Villasse

Extending to the west on the far side of the square (information pavilion of the Office de Tourisme) and the park is the Quartier de la Villasse, the second large excavation site of Vaison-la-Romaine. It has not been so thoroughly restored as the Puymin site and provides a more natural impression. Of interest here are the great arch of the former basilica and the carefully paved Roman street which was provided with gutters. In some places mosaic floors survive.

Other sights

Notre-Dame
On the western edge of the Quartier de la Villasse stands the Church of Notre-Dame, the former cathedral. Its origins go back to Merovingian times, but the present building was erected between the 11th and 13th c.; its plan is smaller than that of its predecessor as shown by the foundations that have been uncovered near the church. Adjoining on the north of the church is the cloister dating from the 12th c. but which had to be extensively renovated in the 19th c. Of interest are the beautiful capitals of the arcades.

Upper Town
South of the Ouvèze river the Upper Town (Haute Ville) rises up the château hill. The river is crossed by a bridge originally built by the Romans and the path then passes through a medieval gate tower. In the romantic narrow streets of the Upper Town, which, protected by the château developed from the 14th c., artists and craftsmen have settled in recent times, producing pottery, olive-wood carving and other items. At the eastern edge of the Old Town stands the church and, from the open space in front of it, there is a good view of the valley below. The cubical ruin of the château (the interior is closed to the public) stands on the top of the Old Town and can be reached by a narrow footpath. From the rocky plateau which in the south and west falls sharply and is completely unprotected (caution!) there is a rewarding panorama.

Surroundings

Mont Ventoux
Vaison-la-Romaine is the northern starting point for the drive over Mont Ventoux (see entry).

Dentelles de Montmirail
The western foothills of Mont Ventoux

The cloister of Notre-Dame

between Malaucène and Gigondas are appropriately called Dentelles de Montmirail (*dentelles*, lace). The chalk rocks with their vertical strata give more of an impression of the Alps than Mont Ventoux does and in spite of their modest height (Pic St-Amand 734 m) they are a paradise for climbers; it is also a popular area for walkers.

Gigondas
In Gigondas, 15 km to the south-west of Vaison, the best vines in the area grow, equal to those of Châteauneuf-du-Pape, with their own *appellation d'origine contrôlée*. In the village square there are sales stands offering wine tastings.

★Vence   G 18

Département: Alpes-Maritimes
Altitude: 325 m
Population: 13,500

Vence is a superb *village perché* in the east of the Côte d'Azur slightly inland between Nice and Antibes.

Sights

Townscape

In the centre of the Old Town stands the former cathedral (St-Véran; 10th–15th c.). The interior has fine choir stalls and a Roman sarcophagus which serves as an altar. In the baptism chapel there is a mosaic by Marc Chagall which depicts the rescue of Moses from the Nile. The choir and the tower chapel retain Carolingian work. On the facade of the cathedral there are two Roman inscriptions with dedications to the emperors Heliogabalus and Gordianus.

East of the church, place Godeau, stands an ancient column; also of interest are the battlemented belfry and the charming Renaissance gate. In the west on the edge of the Old Town lies the attractive place du Peyra with the fountain of the same name. Also to the west, outside the town centre, on avenue Henri-Isnard, stands the 15th c. Chapel of the Pénitents-Blancs.

★Chapelle du Rosaire

On the northern edge of the town, to the right of the road D2210, can be found the inconspicuous Rosary Chapel, which belongs to a Dominican convent. It can be recognised by the linear representation of Mary, Jesus and St Dominic, by Henri Matisse over the doorway. The interior was also designed by Matisse (between 1947 and 1951) with bold graphics (black line drawings on white ceramic tiles) based on Biblical themes. These include the birth of Christ, St Dominic and the Passion of Christ (Way of the Cross). The simple room only receives colour through its glass window. The altar furniture and various chasubles were also designed by Matisse; they are kept in the Matisse Museum at Cimiez in Nice (see entry).

ⓖ *Tue., Thu. 10–11.30am, 2.30–5.30pm, or 4–5pm.*

Surroundings

St-Paul-de-Vence

The little town of St-Paul-de-Vence, which has managed to retain its medieval character, is attractively situated on a hill 3 km to the south. The well-preserved town wall dates from the 16th c.; there is also a civic defence tower. The early 13th c. church has a fine treasury with silver work, reliquaries, and a ciborium dating from 1439. On place de la Fontaine (with a fountain) stands the Musée Provençal. In the 1920s St-Paul was 'discovered' by painters such as Signac, Modigliani and Bonnard.

★★Fondation Maeght

On the Gardettes hill, 1 km to the north-west of St-Paul-de-Vence, lies the Fondation Maeght, a foundation established by the art dealers Aimé and Marguerite Maeght (husband and wife) and opened in 1960, an interesting concoction of nature, architecture (Josep Lluis Sert) and modern art. Alongside mosaics by Braque, Chagall and Tal-Coat, the ceramic sculptures of Miró are of special note, as well as the bronze figures of Giacometti and the stabile by Calder. The chapel was created by Braque and Ubac. In the museum there are works by artists such as Arp, Bonnard, Chagall, Giacometti, Kandinsky and Miró.

The Fondation Maeght also organises exhibitions, concerts and symposia.

Vence: place du Peyra

⊙ *Jul.–Sep. daily 10am–7pm, Oct.–Jun. 10am–12.30pm, 2.30–6pm. Visitors should allow at least two hours to tour the foundation.*

Tourette-sur-Loup

The charming fortified village of Tourette-sur-Loup, with its medieval towers, lies on a rocky plateau 5 km west of Vence above the valley of the Loup, surrounded by olive groves, pine woods and fields of violets. In the 14th c. church is a notable ancient altar and an altarpiece of the following of Bréa. Also of interest is the Musée d'Artisanat Local (Museum of Local Crafts).

★★Verdon (Grand Canyon du Verdon)   G 13–14

Département: Alpes-de-Haute-Provence

The Verdon, 175 km in length, is the most important tributary of the Durance. Between Castellane and the man-made Lac de Ste-Croix it flows through the Grand Canyon du Verdon, a 21 km series of magnificent wild gorges in the fossil-filled chalk of Haute-Provence. At their deepest the gorges descend to 700 m, the water of the river falling 153 m over its length.

Timetable

The round trip described below is about 120 km long. To have sufficient time to appreciate the scenery at least six hours should be allowed, and if possible a whole day.

Drive through the Grand Canyon du Verdon

Access

The best starting point for a circular tour of the Grand Canyon du Verdon is the little town of Castellane (see entry) on the Route Napoléon.

Take the road D952 in a south-westerly direction downstream through the Defile of Porte St-Jean and Clue de Chasteuil. At the fork (in about 12 km) bear left on the D955, cross the river (Pont de Soleils; signposted Rive Gauche) and continue south over attractive uplands. Some 6 km beyond the fork, near the picturesque village of Trigance with its dominating château on the

Fondation Maeght, centre for modern art

right, take road D90 as far as the D71 which is followed north-west.

Balcons de la Mescla

The Balcons de la Mescla (*mescla*, mixing, referring to the nearby confluence of the Artuby with the Verdon), provide the first highlight of the drive. Here there is a fine view into the gorge 250 m below. A little further on cross a boldly curved bridge over the Artuby, which joins the Verdon at this point.

Corniche Sublime

The road continues on a winding course, with breathtaking views high above the Verdon and through the Tunnels de Fayet (views between tunnels).

Falaises des Cavaliers

There is a viewing platform near the restaurant at the Falaises des Cavaliers, then the road continues along a magnificent 10 km stretch up to 400 m above the river in the ravine below.

Lac de Ste-Croix

After driving round the impressive cirque de Vaumale and crossing the 964 m high Col d'Illoire, the road winds its way down to the deep turquoise Lac de Ste-Croix (about 2500 ha), a lake formed by the damming of the Verdon. On the shore is a popular leisure centre (sailing, windsurfing, camping). Here the D19 joins the D957 which you follow to the right. At the point where the Verdon leaves the gorge and enters the reservoir cross the river by the bridge (fine view of the gorge on the right).

Some 7 km beyond the junction of the D19 with the D957 the D952 bears right just before Moustiers. This road borders the northern (right) bank of the Verdon. Passing the Belvédère de Galetas (viewpoint) and crossing the Col d'Ayen (1032 m) you reach Palud-sur-Verdon.

To drive along the winding Route des Crêtes first continue along the D952 and then turn right on to the D23; part of this road is one-way and can only be used in this direction.

★ Route des Crêtes

The 23 km long Route des Crêtes draws close to the edge of the Grand

◄ *The Gorges du Verdon from Point Sublime*

Canyon, and on its course passes several viewpoints – the Belvédère de Trescaire, the particularly impressive Belvédère de L'Escalès and the belvédères du Tilleul, des Glacières and de l'Imbut before leading back to la Palud.

★★ Point Sublime

The D952 heads for probably the finest viewpoint of the tour, Point Sublime. From the car park it is about ten min. walk to the viewing platform, from which the visitor can enjoy the classic view of the Gorge of the Verdon. The platform stands 180 m above the confluence of the Baou with the Verdon; there is a magnificent prospect of the resurgence of the river near the Couloir Samson.

Passing below the *village perché* of Rougon, with the romantic ruins of a château (rewarding detour) and through the defile of the Clue de Carejuan we reach, about 5 km beyond Point Sublime, a road junction near the Pont de Soleils and return to Castellane.

★★ Sentier Martel

The Sentier Martel footpath is named

after the great French speleologist Edouard Martel (1859–1938) who was the first in the 20th century to explore the entire length of the Gorge of the Verdon. The path runs along the bottom of the gorge and can be reached from the road at Point Sublime or at the Chalet de la Maline on the Route des Crêtes.

A walk along the entire length of this section is not particularly easy and will require from six hours to a whole day. Stout footwear, provisions, drinking water and suitable clothing (including a sweater and a waterproof) are essential; a pocket torch is desirable, as in places the path leads through tunnels.

Warning Its is dangerous to stay in the immediate vicinity of the river as, depending on the operation on the dam and the sluices, the water level can rise considerably in a very short time and a strong current can result. Therefore walkers should not linger in places where there is no escape path up the cliff.

Practical Information from A to Z

Practical Information

Air Travel

Airports

Aéroport International Nice-Côte-d'Azur
(5 km south-west of Nice centre)
☎ *0493213030, www.nice.aeroport.fr*

Aéroport International Marseille-Provence
(25 km north-west of Marseille at Marignane)
☎ *0442141414*

Airlines

International routes are flown by Air France, the national airline; inland traffic is handled by Air Inter. Both airlines are represented at all French airports. Abroad information for both companies is provided at the offices of Air France.

Air France
Head office:
1 square Max-Hymans, 75741 Paris Cèdex 15
☎ *0802802802*

UK:
177 Piccadilly, London W1V 0LX
☎ *(0845) 0845111*

US:
142 West 55th Street Fl 2, New York, NY 10019-5305
☎ *(212) 8304000*

Canada:
1510–2000 Rue Mansfield, Montreal H3A 3A3
☎ *(514) 8471106*

British Airways
Aéroport Nice-Côte-d'Azur:
☎ *0472682403*

UK:
156 Regent Street, London W1R 5TA
☎ *(0800) 050142*

Scheduled and charter flights
Numerous international airlines offer scheduled flights to the airports of Nice and Marseille. In addition, many smaller companies offer charter flights to cater for the demand for tourist, business and conference needs. Charter flights usually have restrictions, but flying to Provence may be cheaper than travelling by car, using the ferries or the Channel Tunnel.

Helicopter services

Héli Inter Riviera
The Héli Inter Riviera helicopters connect Nice airport, Terminal 1, with Monaco, Cannes and Sophia-Antiopolis near Antibes. Information and reservations:
Aérdodrome, Cannes
☎ *0493214646*

Héli Air Monaco
Héli Air Monaco connects Nice airport, Terminals 1 and 2, with Cannes, St-Tropez and Monaco; in addition there are various charter flights including long distance. There is a shuttle bus service from the heliport in Monaco to all parts of the town. Information:
HÉLI AIR MONACO
Héliport de Monaco, quartier de Fontvielle, MC 98000 Monaco
☎ *0493213459, email infodept@heliair-monaco.com*

Arriving

By air
The most important airports for the area covered in this guide are Marseille-Marignane and Nice, but there are good services to Nîmes and Montpellier, which are also served by local airlines as are Toulon/Hyères and St-Raphaël/Fréjus. There are direct flights from British airports to Marseille and Nice and numerous charter flights in connection with package holidays (☛Air Travel). From the US and Canada most visitors fly to Paris and connect from there.

By rail
The principal route from the north of France to Provence is via Lyon and Marseille to Toulon, Cannes and Nice. The journey time can be shortened by

◀ The Pont d'Arc over the Ardèche river

taking the TGV (Train à Grande Vitesse) from Paris.

By road
From the English Channel ports or tunnel to the Riviera is a distance of some 1125 km and, even if the motorway (Autoroute du soleil) is used, at least two days should be allowed for the journey. The motorway is subject to substantial tolls. The alternative *routes nationales* are good but liable to be crowded during the holiday season.

Visitors wishing to avoid the long journey by road from the Channel can use one of the motorail services to Avignon, Fréjus/St-Raphaël, Toulon and Nice.

Beaches

The stretches of sandy beaches with their shallow descent into the sea are especially suitable for families. The small bays along the La Côte Bleu, west of Marseille, have a rocky bottom and are good for exploring the underwater fauna and flora of the Mediterranean. With its hidden beaches it is considered an insider's secret.

There is a beach (la Roquille) with facilities for visitors with disabilities at Cap d'Agde on the western Mediterranean coast.

Naturism
Maison de la France have a brochure listing beaches where nude bathing is allowed (☛Information).

Warning As soon as visitors leave the beach they should cover even their swimming costumes and beachwear. Any violations of this rule are heavily fined.

Beach warning system
Since conditions of wind and current can change very quickly, most of the larger beaches have a warning system which should be strictly observed; coloured flags indicate the prevailing conditions.

Camping

Camping plays a more prominent role in France than in other European countries. Almost every place of tourist interest has one or often several campsites (*terrains de camping*), often run by the local council (*camping municipal*).

Classification
Sites are classified according to the comfort they offer from one to four stars. The cheap sites of the lowest category may not conform to expectations in terms of their sanitary facilities.

Reservation
During high season sites along the coast and on the main holiday routes are generally full (*complet*), so if you wish to stay at a seaside site you will need to book well in advance. It is to be recommended, though, to consider the more remote inland sites which are cheaper and more spacious.

Facilities
Several campsites offer child-care facilities and have children's playgrounds as well as swimming pools. Some also have shops, restaurants, bars and discos and a full programme of entertainment. Some offer facilities for visitors with disabilities and also hire tents, caravans, cabins or even bungalows.

Information
Space does not permit the inclusion of a detailed list of campsites. Information can be obtained from regional and local *offices de tourisme* and also from:
FÉDÉRATION FRANÇAISE DE CAMPING ET CARAVANING
78 rue de Rivoli, 75004 Paris
☎ 0142728408, fax 0142727021

Camping à la ferme
The French themselves are very fond of *camping à la ferme* (camping on a farm), for an informal holiday, usually for an extended period. Visitors from abroad who have a good knowledge of French may well find a farm holiday an enjoyable experience.

Camping au château
Of particular interest are campsites in the grounds of châteaux. Information can be obtained from:
CASTELS & CAMPING CARAVANING
PIBS-CP26, 56038 Vannes
☎ 0297425583, email
mail@les-castels.com

Camping outside sites
Outside the campsites, a stay on roads,

car parks or service stations is permitted for one night only, and generally forbidden in the countryside. Opportunities for overnight stops in caravan and camper van are becoming more and more restricted; you are advised to obtain information locally (☞Information).

Water supply
In high summer in Provence drinking water can be in short supply. Therefore economy in the use of water is necessary, and in many places attention is drawn to this by notices.

Car Rental

Booking
Visitors who wish to rent a car during their stay in Provence can make a booking before leaving home. During the high season (July, August) prior booking is recommended.

Local firms are often cheaper than international counterparts, but the latter will often permit the vehicle to be returned to a different place from where it was initially rented. Weekend or weekly rental are the norm, usually with unrestricted travel. Visitors are recommended to book their vehicle as a package together with air or rail travel. A passport and a driving licence (held for at least one year) must be produced. Usually, the driver must be at least 21 years old, older for certain vehicles. Personal liability insurance is included in the rental; other types of insurance can also be included.

Avis
Cannes:
69 la Croisette
☎ 0493941586
Gare de Cannes/Avis train + auto
☎ 0493392638

Marseille:
267 boulevard National
☎ 0491507011
Gare de St-Charles/Avis train + auto
☎ 0491647100
Aéroport de Marseille-Provence, Marignane
☎ 0442142167/42142163

Monaco:
☎ (377) 93301753

Nice:
2 rue des Phocéens, place Masséna
☎ 0493806352
Gare de Nice/Avis train + auto
☎ 0493879011
Aéroport Nice-Côte-d'Azur
☎ 0493213633

EuropCar
Cannes:
3 rue du Commandant-Vidal
☎ 0493397520
Palais des Festivals
☎ 0493397520
Aéroport Mandelieu
☎ 0493904060

Marseille:
121 avenue du Prado
☎ 0491175300
Aéroport Marseille-Provence, Marignane
☎ 0442782475

Monaco:
☎ (377) 93507495, 93052575

Nice:
6 avenue de Suède
☎ 0493 88 64 04
Aéroport Nice-Côte-d'Azur
☎ 0493213644 (Terminal 1),
0493214253 (Terminal 2)

Hertz
Cannes:
147 rue d'Antibes
☎ 0493990420
Aéroport de Mandelieu
☎ 0493904020

Marseille:
16 boulevard Charles-Nédelec
☎ 0491140424
27 boulevard Rabatau
☎ 0491792206
Aéroport Marseille-Provence, Marignane
☎ 0825091313

Monaco:
☎ (377) 93507960

Nice:
Pomenade des Anglais
☎ 0493871187
Aéroport Nice-Côte-d'Azur
☎ 0825342343 (Terminal 1)

Budget
Marseille:
40 boulevard des Plombières

☎ *0491644003, 42775930*
Aéroport Marseille-Provence, Marignane
☎ *0442142455*

Monaco:
54 route de la Moien-Corniche
☎ *(377) 93780545*

Nice:
Aéroport Nice-Côte-d'Azur
☎ *0493213650*

Conversions

To convert metric to imperial multiply
by the imperial factor; e.g. 100 km
equals 62 mi. (100 × **0.62**).

Linear measure

1 m	**3.28** ft
	1.09 yds
1 km (1000 m)	**0.62** mi.

Square measure

1 sq m	**1.2** sq yds
	10.76 sq ft
1 ha	**2.47** acres
1 sq km (100 ha)	**0.39** sq mi.

Capacity

1 litre (1000 ml)	**1.76** pints
	2.11 US pints
1 kg (1000 grams)	**2.21** pounds
1 tonne (1000 kg)	**0.98** ton

Temperature

°C	°F	°C	°F
–5	23	20	68
0	32	25	77
5	41	30	86
10	50	35	95
15	59	40	104

Currency

The unit of currency is the French franc
which is made up of 100 centimes. There
are banknotes for 20, 50 100 and 500
francs and coins for 10, 20, 50 centimes
and 1, 2, 5, 10 and 20 francs.
In Monaco the French franc is officially
used but Monaco also mints its own
coins, ranging in value between 10
centimes and 10 francs; however, these
are only accepted in Monaco and its
immediate surroundings.

Note
Travellers to France are advised to take
about 200 francs in small denominations
to pay for initial expenses (taxi,
telephone). In particular it is worthwhile
obtaining sufficient small coins to pay
for the tollbooths on the motorways
(*péage*).

Euro
On January 1st 1999 the euro became
the official currency of the France, and
the French franc became a
denomination of the euro. French franc
notes and coins continue to be legal
tender during a transitional period. Euro
bank notes and coins are likely to start
to be introduced by January 2002
(1 euro = 6.56 F).

Currency exchange
Foreign currency and traveller's cheques
can be exchanged at official bureaux de
change, banks and savings banks (*Caisses
d'Epargne Ecureuil*).

Rates of exchange
These fluctuate daily and often differ
according to whether francs/euros are
obtained before leaving home or actually
in France. Current rates of exchange can
be obtained from banks, tourist offices,
travel agents and are published in the
principal national newspapers.

Currency regulation
There are no restrictions on the import
of French or foreign currency. However,
cheques or monies. with a total value of
more than 50,000 francs must be
declared to French customs officials
on arrival in or departure from the
country.

Cheques
For the sake of security visitors are
advised to take traveller's cheques.
Because of a high occurrence of theft,
eurocheques are hardly ever accepted
now.

ATMs
Best value are the automated teller
machines where it is possible to
withdraw money using EC cards, as
well as credit cards, using a PIN
number.

Credit cards
Many hotels, shops and car-rental firms
accept credit cards (e.g. Eurocard, Visa,
Diners Club, American Express). Tolls on
motorways can be paid by using

Eurocard, Mastercard or Visa International.

If credit cards or cheques are lost or stolen the issuing office must be informed immediately.

Customs Regulations

Entry into France
Personal effects and sports equipment can be taken in without payment of duty. Video equipment must be declared on entry.

Allowances between EU countries
In theory there is now no limit to the amount of goods that can be taken from one EU country to another provided they have been purchased tax paid in an EU country, are for personal use and not intended for resale. However, customs authorities have issued guidelines to the maximum amounts considered reasonable. These are: 10 litres of spirits or strong liqueurs, 20 litres fortified wine (port, sherry), 90 litres of wine (of which not more than 60 litres may be sparkling wine), 110 litres of beer, 800 cigarettes or 400 cigarillos or 200 cigars or 1 kg tobacco).

During spot checks you will need to be able to prove that all items are destined for your personal consumption.

Entry from Non-EU countries
For those coming from a country outside the EU or who have arrrived from an EU country without having passed through custom control with all their baggage, the allowances for goods obtained anywhere outside the EU for persons over the age of 17 are: 1 litre spirits or 2 litres of fortified wine or 2 litres table wine, plus a further 2 litres table wine; 200 cigarettes or 100 cigarillos or 50 cigars or 250 grams tobacco.

Cycling

Provence is an ideal region for exploring by bicycle and traffic is mercifully light on most of the smaller roads. However a cycling tour can be quite strenuous; the hilly and often mountainous terrain, the intensive sunlight from early spring and (especially in the Rhône valley) the often strong or even stormy wind (☛Facts and Figures, Climate) should be

taken into account when planning. If possible the coastal roads of the entire Côte d'Azur, which are very busy practically throughout the year, should be avoided.

Information
The French Tourist Office with the help of other organisations promotes cycling holidays (brochure *Cycling in France*; suggested tours, booking facilities). In addition special cycle paths have been constructed. Details can be obtained from French cycling clubs:
BICYCLUB DE FRANCE
8 place de la Porte-Champerret 75017 Paris
☎ *0147665592, fax 0143803568*

FÉDÉRATION FRANÇAISE DE CYCLOTOURISME
8 rue Jean-Marie-Jégo 75010 Paris
☎ *0144168888, fax 0144168889,*
www.ffct.org

Organised cycling tours
Various holiday organisations offer cycling tours of differing types (duration, route, sporting standard) with accommodation ranging from tents to comfortable hotels (many of the latter as a gourmet tour). Access by plane or bus. Information from travel agents.

Cycle tours around Porquerolles:
Office du Tourisme in Hyères
(☛Information)

Cycle tours in the Montagne du Lubéron:
Comité Départemental du Tourisme in Avignon (☛Information)

Mountain biking in the Camargue:
BOUCHES-DU-RHÔNE, LOISIRS ACCUEIL
☎ *0490594939, fax 0490591675*

Gîtes d'Étape
Cyclists, for whom contact with the country and its people is more important than comfort, may find the Gîtes d'Étape interesting (☛Hotels).

Bicycle rental
Bicycles can be rented even in small towns. The French National Railways (SNCF) keep bicycles for rental at about 250 stations (train + bicycle). The relevant stations at described in this guide are: Antibes, Arles, Bandol, Cagnes-sur-Mer, Cannes, Gap, le Grau-de-Roi, Hyères, Juan-les-Pins,

Montpellier, Nîmes, St-Raphaël. Cycles can be returned to any station.

Electricity

France is committed to introducing the international norm (adopted in 1983) of 230 volts AC by the year 2003. In the meantime there is no difficulty with British equipment using 240 volts AC. An adaptor to accommodate British or American type plugs is necessary.

Embassies and Consulates

UK
Embassy:
35 rue du Faubourg-St-Honoré, 75008 Paris
☎ 0142669142

Consular section:
16 rue d'Anjou, 75008 Paris
☎ 0142669142

Consulate-General:
24 avenue du Prado, 13006 Marseille
☎ 0491157210

There is also a consulate at Nice.

US
Embassy:
2 avenue Gabriel, 75008 Paris
☎ 0142961202, 42618075

Consulate-General
12 boulevard Paul-Peytral, 13286 Marseille
☎ 0491549200

There is also a consulate at Nice

Canada
Embassy:
35 avenue Montaigne, 75008 Paris
☎ 0142259955

Consular section:
35 avenue Montaigne, 75008 Paris
☎ 0147230101

Consulate-General:
24 avenue du Prado, 13006 Marseille
☎ 0491371937, 0491371940

Emergencies

Contacting travellers in France
In cases of life or death of visitors in France or their families at home local radio stations will transmit emergency calls: Radio Monte-Carlo, Radio France (local stations Côte d'Azur, Vaucluse, Provence, Marseille).

Entertainment

Son et Lumière
In tourist centres *son et lumière* (sound and light) spectacles take place after sunset during the summer. Accompanied by lighting effects, historical or legendary episodes are presented to the audience as a kind of radio play.

Events

January
Avignon Cheval Passion (centred around the horse)
Cannes MIDEM – Marché international du Disque et de l'Edition Musicale (music fair, only for professional visitors)
Département Var truffle festivals
Monaco Rallaye Monte-Carlo; International Circus Festival

February
Nice (and other towns) Carnival
Mormes-les-Mimosas Mimosa festival
Cannes MILIA – Marché International du Livre Illustré et des Nouveaux Médias (international book and new media fair)
Côte Bleue (west of Marseille), Carry-le-Rouet La Fête de l'Oursin (every Sunday in February, all about the sea urchin)
Monaco International Circus Festival
Monaco International Television Festival
St-Raphaël Mimosa Festival

Mid-February to early March
Nice Carnival de Nice

End February to early March
Cannes Festival International de la Musique (international festival of classical music)
Cannes Festival International des Jeux (international games festival)
Menton La Fête du Citron (Shrove

Tuesday lemon festival, traditional celebration of the 'golden fruit')

March
Antibes, Juan-les-Pins New Orleans les Pins Jazz Festival
Hyères Coupe du Monde de Fun Board (Fun Board World Cup)
Maillane Festival to honour its famous citizen, Frédéric Mistral
Monaco Grand Prix de Magie de Monte-Carlo
Monaco Rose ball of the Monte-Carlo Sporting Club
Tourette-sur-Loup Fêtes des Violettes (festival of the violet)

From mid-March
Mornas Reconstitution Historique (everyday life in a French fortress in the 18th century)

End March–early April
Avignon, Menerbes, Isle sur la Sorgue, tower of Aigues Arts Baroque en Provence (every year the Vaucluse region revives baroque traditions)

April
Arles La Féria Pascale (Easter festival, first bullfight of the season)
Bandol Printemps des Potiers (at Easter large spring festival of the potteries)
Monaco International tennis championships of Monte-Carlo
Monaco Spring arts at Monte-Carlo (ballet, concerts)

End April–early May
Pays d'Apt Jazz festival

May
Cannes Festival International du Film (international film festival)
Caromb cherry festival
Grasse Expo-Roses (exhibition of roses)
Monaco Grand Prix de Formule 1 (car race)
Nice Fête Traditionelle de Maïs (traditional maize festival)
Stes-Maries-de-la-Mer Pilgrimage of Sinti and Romany families with a procession of St Sarah to the sea
St-Rémy-de-Provence Festival of driving livestock up to the alpine pastures
St-Tropez Bravade (cheerful military performance; the inhabitants of the town dress up in army and navy uniforms)

Vaucluse region Fête de la Vigne et du Vin (open day in all the wine cellars)

June
Boulbon La Bénédiction des Bouteilles (homage to the few vintners who settled in the mountains in order to grow vines)
Cagnes-sur-Mer Fête de la Brocante (antiques fair)
Coaraze Journée des Fêtes Médiévales (medieval festival)
Coursegoules Arts and crafts fair
Marseille Garlic market
Martigues La Fête des Pêcheurs de la St-Pierre (hundreds of boats congregate on the Grand Canal for the fishermen's festival)
Monaco Folk festival to celebrate the Fête de St Jean
Nice Festival de Musique Sacrée (festival of church music)
Roquebrune-Cap-Martin Foire à la Brocante et à l'Artisanat Local au Village (antiques and crafts fair)
Roquebrune-Cap-Martin Fête Traditionelle des Genêts (traditional gorse festival; procession of costumed children and other events)
Tarascon Festival of the Tarasque (parade with the heraldic animal of the town)
Valbonne Sophia (Antipolis) Fête du Sport 'Sportipolis' sports festival
Valréas Nuit de Petit St-Jean (giant historical spectacle)

June/July
Salon-de-Provence La Reconstitution Historique (celebration of Nostradamus and the Renaissance)

July
Aix-en-Provence International opera festival
Antibes (Juan-les-Pins) Musique au Cœur d'Antibes (music in the heart of Antibes)
Cabris Fête Provençale (Provençal festival)
Cagnes-sur-Mer Festival International de la Peinture (international festival of painting)
Istres Setting sail of fishermen
Juan-les-Pins Jazz à Juan (international jazz festival)
Le Thoronet Festival de la Musique Sacrée (festival of church music)
Martigues Venetian Nights
Monaco Concerts in the Palais du Prince
Monaco Festival International de Feux

d'Artifice (international fireworks festival in the harbour)

Mougins Les Arts dans la rue (art in the streets)

Nice Nice Jazz Festival

Nice Les Grandes Nuits du Folklore International (the great nights of international folklore)

Orange Performances in the Roman theatre

Ramatuelle Festival du Jazz

Roquebrune-Cap-Martin evening performances in the square in front of the château throughout the month (music, theatre, dance)

St-Cézaire-sur-Siagne Fête de l'Huile et de l'Olive (festival of the oil and the olive)

Toulon Music Festival

Valensole Lavender festival

Visan Fête du Vin et de la Moisson (colourful wine and harvest festival)

Early July–early August
Avignon Theatre festival

Early July to mid-August
Arles Rencontres Internationales de la Photographie (international days of photography)

Mid- to late July
Cannes Les Nuits Musicales du Suquet (romantic evening concerts)

Vallauris-Golfe-Juan Festival Jean Marais (theatre, dance, concerts)

End July to mid-August
Aubagne Santon market (market of crib figures)

Cagnes-sur-Mer Fête Médiévale (medieval festival)

Côte d'Azur In Romanesque churches inland: Musique en Pays de Fayence (chamber music concerts)

Grasse Jasmine Festival

Grimaud, Marseille Pilgrimage to St Mary

Menton Festival du Musique de Chambre (international festival of chamber music on the church square of St-Michel)

Monaco Concerts in the Palais du Prince

Monaco Festival International de Feux d'Artifice (international fireworks festival in the harbour)

Monaco Gala of the Monaco Red Cross

Seyne-les-Alpes Mule drivers demonstrate their skills

Sisteron Nuits de la Citadelle (concerts, ballet, theatre)

Valensole Exhibition of small crib figures

September
Biot Fête des Vendanges (grape harvest festival)

Cannes Carlton Intercontinental Cannes Golf Cup

Monaco Rally of vintage cars in Monte-Carlo

Monaco Monaco Yacht Show in the harbour

September–October
Apt, Cassis, Cogolin, Orange Vintners' festivals

Arles Premices du Riz (festival of rice germination)

Collobrières Festival of sweet chestnuts

October
Collobrières Fête de la Châtaigne (delicacies made from chestnuts)

Monaco SPORTEL – international meeting for the world of sports and television

November
Avignon Baptème des Côtes du Rhône Primeurs (the arrival of the young wine is celebrated)

Marseille Santon Nativity market (crib figures)

Monaco Monegasque National Festival (Nov. 19th)

Vaison-la-Romaine, Aups Wine and truffle markets

December
December is devoted to Nativity traditions; families produce mangers and traditional *santons*, colourful crib figures made from clay or dressed in the Provençal costumes. The climax is the Provençal Christmas midnight Mass, when a young lamb is often still slaughtered.

Bandol Fiete des Vins (celebration of the young wine on the first weekend in December)

Cannes Festival International de Danse (international dance festival)

Istres La Fête des Bergers (shepherds drive their herds into the town and a thanksgiving Mass in Provençal dialect is held)

Monaco Ballet

Monaco International regatta, laser class

Excursions

Guided tours
Many historic buildings and parts of churches (crypt, treasury) can only be visited with a guide. As the majority of tourists are French, commentary in English is infrequent. However, explanatory texts in English are sometimes available on loan. The guide expects a tip at the end of the visit.

Recorded commentary
In many places of interest a coin-operated audioguide is frequently encountered. This provides a commentary in French and sometimes in other languages as well.

Food and Drink

French cuisine is world famous, both for its quality and for its variety. Great importance is paid to a varied menu. Undue haste in serving and eating is unknown and at least one hour should be allowed for a meal. Even modest, unpretentious country inns often have a remarkable culinary standard – reflected in the way in which the table is set (clean tablecloths, polished cutlery, sparkling glasses, flowers) – in which regional dishes play an important role.

White bread, cut from crusty baguettes, is always provided, and fresh drinking water is freely available.

Gastronomy
Places providing food and drink are called variously restaurants, rotisseries, bistros (usually simple hostelries, but can also be places offering excellent service), and brasseries (originally the small bars of breweries, but now more generally restaurants). Snacks (sandwiches) are also served in cafés, tea rooms and bars. In the larger towns there are reasonable self-service restaurants and at railway stations and airports quick-service buffets.

Prices
At first glance prices may seem high, but when the quality and variety are taken into account this impression will generally be revised.

Prices on the menu are usually inclusive of service and taxes. For exceptionally good service a tip of about 5–10 per cent of the bill is the norm. It is customary to round-up the bill in any case.

Meals
The various meals are: *petit déjeuner*, a simple breakfast of coffee, bread, butter and jam and/or the popular croissants; *déjeuner* (lunch) is served approximately noon–2pm; and *dîner* or *souper*, served from 7–9pm. In most restaurants there are one or more *menus* (set meals), with starters, main courses and sweets, or a customer can choose from an à la carte menu.

Provençal cuisine

Provençal cuisine makes use of the wide range of local produce. Although not very varied, it is characterised by the freshness and quality of its ingredients which makes it a culinary experience for people from northern and central Europe. Among the most common ingredients, apart from lamb, fish and seafood, are aubergines, peppers, tomatoes, courgettes, onions and olives as well as olive oil, garlic (*ail*) and rosemary, thyme, sage, basil, mint and aniseed, a mixture called *herbes de Provence*. *Pèbre d'ai* is a mixture of savory and thyme. The favourite vegetable is chard, the fleshy leaves of which are eaten as a side dish, in gratins and omelettes, as dumplings and, combined with apple and pine kernels, even as a cake.

The classic collection of Provençal recipes is *Le Cuisinier Durand*, published 1830 and compiled by Charles Durand. Durand (Alès 1766–Nîmes 1854), the *carême* of Provençal cuisine, was chef to the bishops of Alès, Nîmes and Montpellier and his work made the cuisine of his home region famous throughout the region.

Soups
Among soups fish soup occupies a special place. One of the best known is bouillabaisse, originally a simple fishermen's dish which they prepared after returning to port, throwing the poorest fish of their catch into a large pot. Bouillabaisse is prepared from various fish, even mussels and crustaceans, with olive oil, garlic and herbs, especially saffron, together with

dried orange peel. The seafood and the soup may be served separately, the latter poured over slices of white bread (in Marseille there is a particular bread called *marette*). However there were and are so many different recipes that in 1980 the chefs of Marseille published a charter for the 'Real Bouillabaisse'.

Bourride is similar but contains green beans, carrots and potatoes in addition to fish, and is enriched with *aïoli* (garlic mayonnaise). *Aigo-Saou* is a soup prepared from white fish and potatoes.

Another soup which should be mentioned is *soupe au pistou*, consisting of beans and tomatoes and served with *pistou*, a herbal mixture of garlic, olive oil, bacon and basil.

Meat
A typical Provençal method of cooking meat is to cut it into small pieces and braise it with a great variety of additional ingredients; the whole dish is then called *daube*, which may consist of beef, lamb or poultry with tomatoes and olives. Lamb is the principal meat eaten and is sometimes cooked over a charcoal fire. Connoisseurs appreciate *pieds et paquets*, lamb's feet braised with tomatoes and olive oil and little packets of lamb entrails. *Saucisson d'Arles* (sausage from Arles) is a popular delicacy; the original recipe included pork and also donkey meat.

Fruit and vegetables
The valleys of the Rhône and the Durance are the largest vegetable and fruit growing areas of France, and it is not surprising that vegetables of all kinds feature largely in the menu. The traditional recipe for *Salade Niçoise* includes tomatoes, green peppers, black olives, small artichokes, anchovies and tuna fish, sliced hard-boiled eggs and a dash of olive oil. *Tomates à la Provençale* are tomatoes with olive oil, parsley and garlic, baked or grilled; aubergines and courgettes are similarly prepared. *Fleurs de courge farcies* (stuffed courgette flowers) are an exotic speciality. Ratatouille consists of onions, courgettes, aubergines, tomatoes, peppers, garlic and herbs, stewed in olive oil. Also popular are artichokes, fennel and chard, often grilled or fried.

In Tricastin, in the north of Provence, truffles are harvested; their marketing

centres are Valréas and Carpentras (☛Shopping).

Seafood
Fish and crustaceans (*poissons et crustacés*) play a major part in Provençal cuisine, even though fish has tended to become relatively expensive. In addition to the soups already mentioned, popular fish dishes are *brandade*, a mousse of cod (sometimes dried), olive oil, cream, garlic and lemon, as well as grilled barbel, sole, bream and other sea fish. The visitor should also try cuttlefish or squid (*calmar, seiche*) which are prepared in various ways, mussels (*moules, coquilles*), oysters (*huîtres*), crayfish (*langoustes*), shrimps (*crevettes*) or crabs (*tourteaux*). Sea urchins (*oursins*) are often sold along the roads; cut open and spooned out raw, they are a popular snack.

Pasta
Pasta is often served as a side dish, especially as an accompaniment to braised meat, such as *daube*. Noodles (*pâtes*), differing from Italian pasta in being usually made with eggs are designated as 'fresh' or 'speciality of the house'. As well as the different varieties of pizza and *pan bagnat* – a kind of bread filled with olives, tomatoes and anchovies and baked in oil – there is *pissaladière*, a popular savoury flan of onions, olives and anchovy fillets. In Nice, with its Italian past, but also elsewhere, the Italian influence is obvious and pasta such as ravioli, tortellini, cannelloni, lasagne and gnocchi is frequently served.

Cheese
The numerous varieties of Provençal cheese (*fromage*) are for the most part made from sheep's or goat's milk. They bear such names as *Annot, Banon* (prepared from sheep's milk in winter and from goat's milk in spring), *Bossons* (as well as the variety marinated in olive oil together with spices, *Bossons macérés*) *Brousses, Cachat, Claqueret* (a soft cheese served with diced onions), *Picodon, Poivre d'Ane* (with Provençal herbs) and *Sospel*.

Desserts
There is a great variety of fruit from the huge plantations along the Rhône and Durance and the coastal plains, where oranges and lemons also thrive. The figs of Solliès are renowned.

Cakes and pastries

Cakes and pastries are available in many kinds (see glossary below). A favourite is white nougat which consists of honey, sugar, egg white, almonds, pistachios and vanilla, occasionally also with dark chocolate and flavoured with liqueur and enriched with orange pieces; the most famous concoctions if made by the manufacturers Escobar in Montélimar (☛Shopping).

Drinks

The French national drink continues to be wine (see entry), but beer (*bière*), mostly from breweries in Alsace, is growing in popularity and so is *bière panaché*, beer with lemonade. There are many brands of mineral water, either carbonated (*gazeuse*) or still (*plat*). The springs and filling plants of the well-known Perrier water are situated to the west of the Rhône delta between Nîmes and Montpellier.

Spirits

The fiery distillate called *marc*, a by-product of winemaking, is excellent. From the region around Nice comes a popular grape brandy called *branda*. *Lérinade* is a liqueur formerly made by monks. The bitter-sweet liqueur from the abbey at Sénanque is supposed to have curative properties for digestive ailments. The aniseed liqueur pastis, which is second only to wine as a national drink, is generally drunk diluted with ice-cold water; it is also pleasant when mixed with mint or grenadine syrup.

Glossary of specialities

Aïoli Garlic mayonnaise (served with cooked vegetables, fish and eggs)

Beignets de fleurs d'acacia Acacia flower pancakes

Berlingots de Carpentras Peppermint sweets from Carpentras

Bouillabaisse Traditional fish soup from Marseille

Brandade Purée of dried cod and olive oil

Brousse Fresh sheep's cheese, eaten on its own or flavoured with orange-blossom water

Caladons de Nîmes Delicious pastries made from honey, almonds, flour, orange and vanilla (speciality from Nîmes)

Calissons d'Aix Confectionery made from almond paste with melon and honey (speciality from Aix-en-Provence)

Chichi fregi Crisp pastries made from sweet choux pastry (known in Marseille, for example)

Coussins de Lyon Desserts made from chocolate cream and almond paste flavoured with Curaçao liqueur and covered with a bright green icing

Estocaficada Dried smoked salt cod, cooked with vegetables (tomatoes, onions, peppers and new potatoes)

Fruits confits Candied fruits, for example in Apt, Grasse, St-Rémy-de-Provence

Gardiano Lamb stew with potatoes (a speciality from the Camargue)

Génépi des Alpes Herbal schnapps made from black rue

Palets d'Or A mixture of dark chocolate and crème fraiche (speciality from Lyon)

Panisses Deep-fried or baked little cakes made with a chick pea batter

Papalinos d'Avignon Little chocolate balls; the are covered in a pink icing that is flavoured with l'Origan du Ventoux, a herbal liqueur made from heathers (speciality from Avignon)

Pissaladière An onion tart with anchovies and olives

Polenta Semolina made from maize and flavoured with Parmesan cheese

Ratatouille A Provençal vegetable stew

Rouille Mayonnaise with paprika, served with fish

Soupe au pistou Vegetable soup, flavoured with basil

Tapenade Purée of olives, capers and anchovies

Tartarinades de Tarascon Chocolate balls filled with almonds and nuts, as well as raisins and other fruits that have been preserved in *eau de vie* (a speciality from Tarascon)

Tourte Bléa A flat cake of chard, raisins and pine kernels

Gastronomic tours

All about the **truffle** (including searching for truffles, truffle meals), information and reservation:
AGENCE BREMOND
Rue Jean-Aicard, 83300 Draguignan
☎ *0494680501, fax 0494470059.*

Thyme and basil in flower: information and reservation from Comité Départemental du Tourisme de Vaucluse in Avignon (☛Information).

The tourist route, **Route de l'Olivier**, leads between St-Rémy-de-Provence, Arles and Salon-de-Provence among olive plantations and groves past olive mills, olive producers and restaurants which cook exclusively with olive oil. Information (and reservation) as well information on culinary Provence:
BOUCHES-DU-RHÔNE, LOISIRS ACCUEIL
Domaine du Vergon, 13370 Mallemort
☎ *0490594939, fax 0490591675.*

The farm of **Bas Chalus** gives an insight into the production of milk and cheese. Information and bookings:
OFFICE DU TOURISME
8 place de Bourguet, 04300 Forcalquier
☎ *0492751002, fax 0492752676,*
www.forcalquier.com.

Vineyards: see Wine.

Health

Medical assistance
French medical services are excellent and the country is well supplied with doctors, many of whom speak English. British visitors will find it helpful to obtain a free booklet prepared by the Department of Health and available from post offices *Health Advice for Travellers* (containing form E111) which gives advice about health precautions and how to get urgent medical treatment when abroad.

Hotels

See also Camping, Youth Hostels.

Gîtes de France

Gîtes de France offer various types of

holiday in the country which give the visitor the opportunity to enjoy the beauty of the French countryside and the French way of life: Gîtes Rural (holiday flats and houses), Gîtes d'Étape (simple accommodation along footpaths and cycling routes), Chambre/Table d'Hôte (accommodation with families/private lets, including breakfast and/or meals to get to know regional specialities) Camping à la Ferme (camping in a farm).
  The Chambres d'Hôte, France's answer to British bed and breakfast accommodation, especially in country districts, are an excellent and comparatively inexpensive alternative to rooms in hotels of modest or average standard. In addition they often have a very pleasant atmosphere. Visitors should look out for the green traffic signs to houses which are generally situated away from main roads.

Meublés
Furnished rooms and apartments can be rented from private landlords in both small and large towns. They are officially classified in three categories – regular, comfortable and luxury – and are usually rented for at least a week. (Regular private rooms which are taken for only one night come into the category of Chambre d'Hôte.)

Information
Information is available from the local Office du Tourisme, the local Comité Départemental du Tourisme in Avignon, Digne, Draguignan, Gap, Marseille, Nîmes, Privas or Valence (☛Information) as well as from:
GÎTES DE FRANCE
56 rue St-Lazare, 75009 Paris
☎ *0149707575.*
  Current lists of private rooms and holiday homes can be obtained from any Comité Départemental du Tourisme or Office du Tourisme and also from Gîtes de France.

Hotels

Hotels in France are generally good and within their categories will satisfy every requirement. Apart from in the larger towns rooms are often furnished with the *grand lit*, the French double bed, and the charge for occupancy of such rooms by two people is the same or only slightly more than for single occupancy.

Full/half board
In many hotels, particularly those on the coast and in winter-sports areas, both full board (*pension complète*) and half board (*demi-pension*) are offered.

Classification
Most hotels are classified by the Ministère du Tourisme as Hôtels de Tourisme and are designated by one star (lowest category) to four stars (highest category) with the addition of the suffix L for luxury hotels.

Hotel lists
A list of the hotels in the Provence-Alpes-Côte-d'Azur region is available from the Maison de la France (☛Information) and from:
HÔTELS DE LA RÉGION
27 place Jules-Guesde, 13002 Marseille
☎ *0491575078*

Price categories
Prices vary considerably within each category and according to season. The following list gives the price per night for two persons in a room with bath; single rooms are rarely available. In most hotels approximately 30 per cent extra is charged for a third bed in a room.

Category	Double room	in this guide
L✱✱✱✱	From 1000F	★L
✱✱✱✱	700–1600F	A
✱✱✱	300–700F	B
✱✱	20–400F	C
✱	150–300F	D

Logis de France
A considerable number of hotels of various categories, especially in areas in which tourism is encouraged, have been modernised with help from the Fédération Nationale des Logis de France (83 avenue d'Italie, 75013 Paris). They are mostly small and medium-size family-run hotels, usually found outside the larger places in small towns and villages, with personal attention and comfort at reasonable prices. A guide is issued every year.

Relais
Many hotels, especially on the roadside outside built-up areas, are designated as *Relais* (the word actually means a posting house where horses were changed). They

are mostly good independently run places and include the Relais de Campagne et Château-Hôtels and Relais du Silence.

The inexpensive Relais Routiers are principally used by long-distance truck drivers and are, therefore, situated on main roads. They are generally simple but nevertheless good. A *Guide des Relais Routiers*, with over 3500 entries, is available.

Information
Current lists of the organisations mentioned can be obtained free from the Maison de la France and the Offices du Tourisme in the larger towns (☛Information), and sometimes in bookshops. In addition each Office du Tourisme publishes a local hotel list.

Reservations
Advance booking is recommended. Reservations can be made in two ways: either by a simple payment (*acompte*) or by a deposit (*arrhes*), which can be retained by the hotel in the event of cancellation by the visitor or in a case where the hotel has defaulted on the booking can be recovered two-fold by the visitor.

Forty Offices du Tourisme are associated with the Accueil de France organisation; in the area covered in this guide these are in Avignon, Cannes, Nice, Nîmes and Toulon. Here hotel rooms can be reserved seven days in advance in the town concerned and in other places where the organisation is represented. Any reservation fee will be reimbursed by the hotel.

Valuables
In France the proprietor of a hotel is responsible if a car is broken into while in a secured hotel car park. If a hotel room is burgled the proprietor's liability is limited to 100 times the cost of the room. Nevertheless, valuables should be deposited in the hotel safe.

Abbreviations
r	room
sr	single room
dr	double room
ap	apartments
ip	indoor pool
sp	swimming pool

Aigues-Mortes
ST-LOUIS
10 rue Amiral-Courbet, 30220 Aigues-Mortes

☎ *0466537268, fax 0466537592*
A; 22 r. A comfortable family-run hotel in the heart of the medieval town, with spacious rooms furnished in the Provençal style. When the weather allows, breakfast is served in the courtyard, in the shade of trees. The restaurant – with open fireplace – serves grilled specialities for dinner.

Aix-en-Provence
★ VILLA GALLICI
Avenue de la Violette, 13100 Aix-en-Provence
☎ *0442232923, fax 0442963045*
L; 15 r, 4 ap; sp. Part of the Relais chain, this attractive country mansion offers extraordinary comfort (including a beauty salon) in pleasant surroundings. Lunch is served in the summer house; dinner, served in the restaurant, consists of Provençal specialities and wines from the area around Aix, Bordeaux and Burgundy.

LE PIGONNET
5 avenue Pigonnet, 13090 Aix-en-Provence
☎ *0442590290, fax 0442594777*
A; 52 r; sp.

MERCURE PAUL CÉZANNE
40 avenue Victor-Hugo, 13100 Aix-en-Provence
☎ *0442263473, fax 0442272095,*
A, 55 r. A pleasant, upmarket tourist hotel, with remarkable furnishings, in part antique and valuable.

Antibes/Cap d'Antibes
★ HÔTEL DU CAP EDEN-ROC
Boulevard Kennedy, 06160 Antibes
☎ *0493613901, fax 0493671383*
L; 123 r; sp. Situated in the middle of a magnificent palm-fringed park on the coast, this hotel of the luxury class offers everything needed for dream holidays: pleasant atmosphere, a wide view across the sea and the coastline up to the Esterel mountains, fine sandy private beach, sea-water swimming pool, tennis courts and fitness rooms.

Antibes/Juan-les-Pins
★ JUANA
25 avenue Georges-Gallice, 06160 Antibes
☎ *0493610870, fax 0493617660*
L; 46 r; sp. An elegant house of the highest standard. The restaurant, La Terrasse, is well known by locals.

AMBASSADEUR CONCORDE
50–52 chemin des Sables, 06161 Juan-les-Pins Cédex
☎ *0492937410, fax 0493677985*
A; 254 r, 6 suites; ip, sp. Palm-fringed hotel, situated in the heart of Juan-les-Pins, 200 m from the fine sandy beaches of the Mediterranean. The hotel has a restaurant, a brasserie, a summer grill and a piano bar, as well as a fitness centre and balneotherapy.

Arles
LOU MARQUES JULES CÉSAR
9 boulevard des Lices, 13200 Arles
☎ *0490934320, fax 0490933347*
A; 52 r; sp. Based in a former monastery, the Jules César satisfies the highest requirements. The cloister is decked in flowers and is very atmospheric.

SAINT-TROPHIME
16 rue de la Calade, 13200 Arles
☎ *0490968838, fax 0490969219*
B; 22 r. 17th c. hotel in the heart of the Old Town, with attractive courtyard. All rooms have bath or shower and toilet; telephone and colour TV. In summer, breakfast is served in the courtyard.

Avignon
★ LA MIRANDE
1 place de l'Amirande
☎ *0490859393, fax 0490862685*
L; 20 r. Small, noble hotel, in the middle of the Old Town, close to the Papal Palace. In the past, the building was used as a residence for cardinals. Today it offers its guests all modern comforts and a good restaurant serving Provençal food.

CLOÎTRE ST-LOUIS
20 rue Portail-Boquier
☎ *0490275555, fax 0490822401*
A; 80 r; sp. A former monastery in the south of the Old Town, it has been transformed into a comfortable, modern hotel with an extension, The contemporary interior is noteworthy.

Avignon – le Pontet
AUBERGE DE CASSAGNE
450 allée de Cassagne, 84130 le Pontet-Avignon (junction A7, Avignon–Nord)
☎ *0490310418, fax 0490322509*
B, 35 r; sp. Comfortable hotel, situated 5 km outside the centre of Avignon, in the suburb of le Pontet. Rustic-elegant public rooms, comfortable private rooms (most with balcony), furnished in the

Provençal style; elegant restaurant with international and Provençal specialities and an extensive wine list.

Bandol
★ ILE ROUSSE
17 avenue Louis-Lumière, 83150 Bandol
☎ 0494293300, fax 0494294949
L; 55 r. Upmarket hotel.

Beaulieu-sur-Mer
★ LE MÉTROPOLE
15 boulevard du Maréchal-Leclerc, 06310 Beaulieu-sur-Mer
☎ 0493010008, fax 0493011851
L 48 r, 3 ap; sp. White villa built in the style of Italian palaces. The rooms and apartments are luxuriously furnished, some with balconies. Private beach. Restaurants serves local specialities according to the season and has French wines.

Les Baux-de-Provence
★ OUSTAU DE BAUMANIÈRE
chemin départemental 27, 13520 les Baux-de-provence
☎ 0490543307, fax 04905440 6
L; 12 r, 8 ap; sp. A member of the Relais chain, this 500-year-old country house has romantical luxuriously furnished rooms and suites with antique furniture, four-poster beds, beamed ceiling and open fireplace. The restaurant offers the finest specialities from Provence.

Cannes
★ MARTINEZ
73 boulevard de la Croisette, 06406 Cannes
☎ 0492987300, fax 0493396782
L; 423 r (incl. 16 suites); sp; tennis. Built in the 1920s and renovated to the original style, this palm-fringed hotel is world famous and regarded as *the* meeting place in Cannes. There is a heated open-air swimming pool, a private sandy beach, seven tennis courts and an activity programme for children, as well as a beauty salon. The restaurant, La Palme d'Or, has been furnished in the style of the 1930s and serves excellent food.

SOFITEL LE MÉDITERRANÉE
2 boulevard Jean-Hubert, 06400 Cannes
☎ 0492997300, fax 0492997329
A; 150 r; sp. Comfortable hotel, situated at the foot of the Suquet, the historic centre of Cannes, beside the harbour and only a few paces from the Palais des Festivals. Highly recommended for those with a sense of adventure and night owls.

CROISETTE BEACH
13 rue du Canada, 06400 Cannes
☎ 04992188800, fax 0493683538
B; 94 r; sp. Quiet tourist hotel, not far from the Croisette.

ABRIAL
24–26 boulevard Lorraine, 06400 Cannes
☎ 0493387882, fax 0492986741
C; 47 r. Tourist hotel in a central location, with small garden and terrace.

Eygalières en Provence
★ LE MAS DE LA BRUNE
13810 Eygalières
☎ 0490959077, fax 0490959921
L; 9 dr, 1 sr; sp. Charming and very exclusive, 16th-century former consular building, situated 30 min. by car from Arles, les Baux and Avignon; member of the association Guest in a Château. Comfortable, air-conditioned rooms, extensive park and heated swimming pool. Provençal food is served under the plane trees or in the vaulted cellars of the former olive press.

Eze-Village
★ LES TERRASSES D'EZE COUNTRY CLUB
1138 route de la Turbie, 06360 Èze-Village
☎ 0493415555, fax 0493415510
L; 81 r; sp; tennis. The hotel is built into the terraces of the mountain slope, affording a unique view of the Mediterranean and St-Jean-Cap-Ferrat. High degree of comfort and tastefully furnished rooms with balcony or terrace. Organised sports programme in July and August. Excellent restaurant with local and international specialities.

Fréjus
L'ARÉNA
139 rue du Général de Gaulle, 83600 Fréjus
☎ 0494170940, fax 0494520152
A; 19 r; sp. Charming small Logis de France hotel, situated in the historic centre, not far from beach and golf courses. Furnished in the Provençal style, with beautiful garden and gourmet restaurant.

Gap
CLARINE
Avenue d'Embrun, 05000 Gap
☎ 0492523737, fax 0492520646

B; 66 r; sp. Privately run hotel and restaurant.

Gordes
See Joucas

La Grande-Motte
MERCURE
Rue du Port, 34280 la Grande-Motte
☎ *0467569081, fax 0467569229*
A; 135 r; sp. The rooms in this hotel are decorated in contemporary style and have good views of the coastline.

Grasse
GRASSE COUNTRY CLUB
1 route des 3-Points, 06310 Grasse
☎ *0493605544, fax 0493605519*
A; 15 r; sp. Hotel situated in a park, with good views; opportunity to play golf.

Grignan
★MANOIR LA ROSERAIE
Route Valréas, 26230 Grignan
☎ *0475465815, fax 0475469155*
L; 15 r; sp; tennis; bicycle hire. 19th c. country house situated in 2 ha of magnificent park; comfortable, tastefully furnished rooms. The restaurant serves Provençal specialities.

Hyères
LES PRINTANIÈRES
20 impasse St-Joseph, 83400 Hyères
☎ *0494353737, fax 0494659476*
B; 48 r. Situated 4 km from the beach; spacious, air-conditioned rooms. Garden; Provençal cuisine. Sports and tourist activities on offer.

Joucas (near Gordes)
★LE MAS DES HERBES BLANCHES
Route de Murs, 84220 Joucas
☎ *0490057979, fax 0490057196*
L; 13 r, 6 ap; sp. Farmhouse in magnificent heathland, member of the Ralais chain; numerous terraces, rooms furnished with Provençal fabrics. The dining room has antique furniture and has an open fireplace. Regional dishes and wines from Provence. The inner courtyard has a well.

Juan-les-Pins
See Antibes – Juan-les-Pins

Le Lavandou
LES ROCHES
1 avenue des Trois-Dauphins, Aiguebelle
☎ *0494710507, fax 0494710840*
A; 35 r. A member of the Relais chain, situated in a grandiose rocky bay. The rooms are furnished with antique furniture and original paintings by Provençal artists. The restaurant is based on a steamship in the sea and offers, amongst other dishes, bouillabaisse; other specialities are grilled fish dishes and local cheeses, all served with exquisite wines.

Lourmarin
★LE MOULIN DE LOURMARIN
Rue du temple, 84160 Lourmarin
☎ *049060669, fax 0490683176*
L; 22 r; sp. Luxurious hotel with comfortable rooms in a former 18th c. mill house. The restaurant, housed in the oldest part of the mill, serves regional specialities.

Mandelieu-la-Napoule
★ROYAL HÔTEL CASINO
605 avenue du Général-de-Gaulle, 06210 Mandelieu-la-Napoule
☎ *0492977000, fax 0493495150*
L; 211 r; ip, sp; tennis. Beautifully situated beside the sea, next to the golf course of Mandelieu, this hotel offers an elegant holiday. The rooms are tastefully furnished and very comfortable, each one with balcony and view of the sea. The hotel has its own casino (blackjack, roulette, slot machines and bar), as well as a Turkish bath and fitness rooms. The restaurant, Le Féréol (sun terrace), offers seafood and other regional specialities; the Poker café has Turkish and Mexican dishes. Piano bar Le blue Wave.

Marseille
★LE PETIT NICE
Anse de Maldormé/160 corniche Kennedy, 13007 Marseille
☎ *0491592592, fax 0491592808*
L; 15 r; sp. A small, privately run hotel and restaurant in a magnificent location above the sea. The cuisine is renowned and serves mainly Provençal specialities.

SOFITEL MARSEILLE VIEUX-PORT
36 boulevard Charles-Livon, 1307 Marseille
☎ *0491155900, fax 0491155950*
A; 130 r (incl. 3 suites); sp. Close to the beach, an upmarket hotel with magnificent panoramic view of the old harbour. In the restaurant, Les Trois Forts, try the fresh fish dishes, or grilled dishes with *herbes de Provence*.

Climat de France Vieux Port
6 rue Beauvau, 13001 Marseille
☎ *0491330233, fax 0491332134*
B; 50 r. Situated only a few steps from the old harbour, this is an ideal base for exploring the town.

Marignane
Sofitel Marseille Aéroport
13728 Marignane
☎ *0442784278, fax 0442784270*
A; 180 r. (incl. 3 suites).

Menton
Ambassadeurs
3 rue Partouneaux, 06500 Menton
☎ *0493287575, fax 0493356232*
A; 50 r. Elegantly furnished hotel

Monaco (Principality of Monaco)
★De Paris
Place du Casino, MC 98000 Monaco
☎ *(377) 93163000, fax 93163849*
L; 141 r, 59 suites; sp. This grandiose hotel has rooms with sea view and air conditioning as well as a large terrace, and is directly linked with the Thermes Marins. Le Louis XV is a top restaurant and serves, among other dishes, local vegetables, black truffles as well as the wines of Bandol. There is an equally excellent grill restaurant on the 8th floor of the hotel (the roof can be opened) which offers a magnificent view over the principality; here grilled fish and meat dishes are served.

★Monte-Carlo Grand Hotel
12 avenue des Spélugues, Monte-Carlo, MC 98007 Monaco
☎ *(377) 93506500, fax 93300157*
L; 625 r; sp. The hotel rises directly above the sea, in characteristically jagged architectural style. All rooms have sea view, their own bath and air conditioning. The guest is spoiled by the cuisine in the hotel's six restaurants. There is a swimming pool on the roof terrace.

Beach Plaza (Le Meridien)
22 avenue Princesse-Grace, Monte-Carlo, MC 98000 Monaco
☎ *(377) 93309880, fax 93502314*
A; 313 r; sp. The magical Beach Plaza is in a unique location, directly on the beach. All rooms are elegantly furnished, everyone with bath and air conditioning. There are conference rooms for up to 300 delegates. The breakfast buffet is served on the splendid hotel terrace.

Mougins
★Le Mas Candile
Boulevard Clément-Rebuffel, 06250 Mougins
☎ *0493900085, fax 0492928556*
L; 23 r; 2 sp; tennis. Part of the Châteaux et Hôtels Indépendants chain, this upmarket hotel is situated about 15 min. outside Cannes. The terraces afford wonderful panoramas; the restaurant serves typically Provencal dishes.

Nice
★Negresco
37 promenade des Anglais, 06007 Nice Cédex
☎ *0493166400, fax 0493883568*
L; 140 r, 18 suites. The Negresco, part of the Leading Hotels of the World chain, is one of the most luxurious hotels in the world and a historical emblem of Nice, with its elegant rooms, furnished in the French style. Precious wall coverings, magnificent paintings and fantastic carpets give this hotel a special touch. The restaurant, Le Chantecler, is a Mecca for gourmets; La Rotonde is a brasserie, the Le Relais bar has evening entertainments and is one of the meeting places of society.

Beau Rivage
24 rue St-François-de-Paul, 06007 Nice
☎ *0492478282, fax 0492478283*
A; 118 r. A old, traditional house with added glamour. Anton Chechov resided here over a century ago (memorial plaque). Good private beach.

Novotel Nice Centre
8–10 Parvis de l'Europe, 06300 Nice
☎ *0493133093, fax 0493130904*
A; 173 r; sp. A well-run tourist hotel with all modern comforts. Charming swimming pool on the roof terrace with magnificent views.

Nîmes
Imperator Concorde
Quai de la Fontaine, 30900 Nîmes
☎ *0466219030, fax 0466677025*
A; 62 r. Atmospheric hotel in central location. Meals are served in the restaurant or the well-kept garden.

L'Orangerie
755 rue Tour de l'Evêque, 30000 Nîmes
☎ *0466845057, fax 0466294455*
A; 31 r; sp. Situated near the Old Town, shaded by plane trees in a small park, this pleasant hotel has modern rooms

(some with balcony or terrace) and soundproof windows. Regional and classic dishes are served in the restaurant; there is a small grill next to the pool.

Orange
ARÈNE
Place de Langes, 84100 Orange
☎ 0490114040, fax 0490114045
A; 30 r. Pretty, small, privately run hotel situated in the Old Town, not far from the Hôtel de Ville and cathedral, in the traffic-calmed place de Langes, under shady plane trees. Air-conditioned rooms with minibar; telephone and satellite TV; restaurant with Provençal cuisine.

La Palud-sur-Verdon
LES GORGES DU VERDON
Route de la Maline, 04120 la Palud-sur-Verdon
☎ 0492773826, fax 0492773500
A; 28 r; sp; tennis. Logis de France hotel situated in the picturesque Canyon du Verdon, on a small hill with beautiful views of the little village of la Palud. The restaurant serves Provençal specialities.

Port-Grimaud
★GIRAGLIA
Place du 14 Juin, 83360 Port-Grimaud
☎ 0494563133, fax 0494563377
L; 49 r; sp. Upmarket hotel with beautiful view of the bay.

Ramatuelle
LA FERME D'AUGUSTIN
Route du Tahiti, St-Tropez, 83350 Ramatuelle
☎ 0494559700, fax 0494974030
A; 35 r; sp. This romantic hotel is situated about 5 min. outside St-Tropez, 100 m from the Tahiti beach, within parkland. The rooms are furnished with antique furniture and offer great comfort; some have a view of the sea, a vineyard or the park and the swimming pool. Breakfast is served in the room, under a tree or on the terrace. The restaurant, only open to residents, serves regional specialities.

Roquebrune-Cap-Martin – Monte-Carlo
★VISTA PALACE
Route de la Grande Corniche, 06190 Roquebrune-Cap-Martin
☎ 0492104000, fax 0493351894
L; 42 r, 26 suites; sp on two levels; free shuttle bus to and from Monaco. Quiet

location 300 m above the sea, surrounded by Mediterranean-style gardens, the Vista Palace Hotel is one of the Leading Hotels of the World. Every room is elegantly furnished and has a marble bath, balcony or terrace with magnificent views of the French or Italian rivieras. Some suites have their own swimming pool or whirlpool. The fitness centre has saunas, sports room and gym as well as squash courts. The excellent restaurant, Le Vistaero, serves classic French cuisine with a Provençal touch; the restaurant Le Panorama has fantastic views, and is well suited for dinner, receptions and dance parties. The Icare is the place for cocktails, and Le Cap is popular for its evening entertainment.

Stes-Maries-de-la-Mer
LE MAS DE STE-HÉLÈNE
RN 570, ch. Bas des Launes, 13460 Stes-Maries-de-la-Mer
☎ 0490978329, fax 0490978928
A; 15 r. Situated in the centre of a nature reserve, on the Etang des Launes lake. Every room has its own terrace with view of the lake. Breakfast is taken in the room or in the neighbouring hotel, from a large buffet.

St-Jean-Cap-Ferrat
★ROYAL RIVIERA
3 avenue Jean-Monnet, 06230 St-Jean-Cap-Ferrat
☎ 0493763100, fax 0493012307
L; 72 r, 5 suites; sp. Built in 1904 and completely renovated, the hotel has magnificent French-style gardens, a heated swimming pool and private sandy beach. It is one of the Leading Hotels of the World and offers all comforts. The elegant restaurant Panorama serves excellent meals; La Perla offers grilled meals by the pool and a lunch buffet; the La Bedford cocktail bar is on the terrace.

St-Paul-de-Vence
★LE ST-PAUL
86 rue Grande, 06570 St-Paul-de-Vence
☎ 0493326525, fax 0493325294
L; 19 r. 16th c. mansion, part of the Relais chain, with beautifully furnished rooms and suites. Tables are attractively laid out in the dining room with vaulted and beamed ceiling, where delicious regional specialities and wines are served.

St-Raphaël
EXCELSIOR
193 boulevard Félix Martin, 83700 St-Raphaël
☎ 0494950242, fax 0494953382
A; 36 r. Beautiful views from the Logis de France hotel; meals are served outside if the weather permits.

St-Rémy-de-Provence
★VALLON DE VALRUGUES
Chemin de Canto-Cigalo, 13210 St-Rémy-de-Provence
☎ 0490920404, fax 0490924401
L; 49 r; sp. Elegantly furnished hotel, rooms in the Provençal style, situated in a 3 ha park. Meals are served in the elegant restaurant or on the terrace when the weather is good. Fitness room.

St-Cyr-sur-Mer
★LA FRÉGATE
Route de Bandol, RD 559, 83270 St-Cyr-sur-Mer
☎ 0494293939, fax 0494293940
L; 133 r. Attractive holiday complex at the foots of the vineyards of Bandol; Provençal style, rustic interior.

GRAND HÔTEL
83270 St-Cyr-sur-Mer
☎ 0494262301, fax 0494261022
A; 57 r; tennis. Idyllically situated in 3 ha of parkland, only 200 m from the fine sandy beach and yet in a central location, the hotel promises a pleasant stay and excellent food; snack bar next to the pool.

St-Tropez
★BYBLOS
Avenue Paul-Signac, 83900 St-Tropez
☎ 0494566800, fax 0494569801
L; 47 r, 55 suites; sp; fitness centre. The Byblos was built in the centre of St-Tropez in the style of a small Mediterranean village, with attractive patios and gardens. All the rooms are individually furnished in the Provençal style. The restaurant Les Aracades next to the pool offers Provençal specialities; another restaurant serves Italian food and is open late. In summer the disco Les Caves du Roy is a popular meeting place.

Ste-Maxime
★GOLF PLAZA HÔTEL & COUNTRY CLUB
83120 Ste-Maxime
☎ 0494566666, fax 0494566600
L; 106 r; ip, sp; tennis. Hotel next to the golf course, with good views of the bay of St-Tropez, offering sport and relaxation. The rooms are furnished in the Provençal style; every suite was individually decorated by a different artist. The gourmet restaurant serves local and international specialities; cosy English bar. Balneotherapy centre. Shuttle transfer to the private beach as well as to and from Nice airport.

Salon-de-Provence
★ABBAYE DE STE-CROIX
Route du Val-de-Cuech, 13300 Salon-de-Provence
☎ 0490562455, fax 0490563112
L; 19 r, 5 ap; sp. Part of the Relais chain, a beautifully restored 12th c. abbey, with comfortable rooms in the former monks' cells, some with country furniture. Vaults and cloisters remind of the original monastery. The restaurant (with panoramic terrace) serves Provençal specialities, and excellent cheeses and wine from the region.

Sisteron
LES CHÊNES
Route de Grenoble, RN 85, 04200 Sisteron Nord
☎ 0492611508, fax 0492611692
B; 21 r; sp. Logis de France hotel with viewing terrace and extensive gardens; play ground, tennis court, opportunities for swimming, paragliding and hang-gliding nearby.

Toulon
NEW HÔTEL LA TOUR BLANCHE
Boulevard de l'Amiral-Vence, 83000 Toulon
☎ 0494244157, fax 0494224225
A; 92 r; sp. Hotel situated in its own gardens, near the cable lift to the Mont Faron; excellent views of the bay of Toulon.

Uzès
HÔTEL D'ENTRAYGUES
Place Évêché, 30700 Uzès
☎ 0466223268, fax 0466225701
A; 19 r; sp. The hotel dates from the 15th c.; meals are taken in the restaurant Jardins de Castille or outside.

Vence
LE CHÂTEAU DU DOMAINE ST-MARTIN
Avenue des Templiers, 06140 Vence
☎ 0493580202, fax 0493240891
L; 15 r, 10 ap. The grand former residence of the Knights Templar is

situated in a 13 ha estate, surrounded by ancient olive trees. Today part of the Relais chain, the hotel has elegant rooms and a restaurant serving international and regional specialities and wines.

Verdon
See la Palud-sur-Verdon

Information

Maison de la France

The name Maison de la France combines various French tourist organisations. References to Maison de la France in this book have the same meaning as tourist office. Most local tourist offices are designated Office de Tourisme, some are also known as Syndicat d'Inititiave (SI). Other names: the reception office is called Bureau d'Acceuil, the tourist information point Point Information Tourisme. In smaller towns, the town hall (*mairie*) or the communal house (*commune*) also give information.

Internet
www.franceguide.com
www.provencetourism.com
www.crt-riviera.fr

Headquarters
MAISON DE LA FRANCE
8 avenue de l'Opéra, 75001 Paris
☎ *0142961023, fax 0142868052*

Information outside France
UK:
MAISON DE LA FRANCE
178 Piccadilly, London W1V 0AL
☎ *(09068) 244123, email info@mdlf.co.uk*

US (www.francetourism.com):
MAISON DE LA FRANCE
444 Madison Avenue, New York NY 10020
☎ *(212) 7571125, fax (212) 8387855*
676 North Michigan Avenue, Chicago IL 60611
☎ *fax (312) 3376339*
9454 Wilshire Boulevard, Suite 715, Beverly Hills CA 90212
☎ *fax (310) 2762835*

Canada:
1981 McGill College Avenue, Suite 490, Montreal, Quebec, H3A 2W9
☎ *fax (514) 8454868*

30 St Patrick Street, Suite 700, Toronto, Ontario, ONT M5T 3A3
☎ *fax (416) 9797587*

Information in France

Comité Régional du Tourisme
Provence-Alpes-Côte-d'Azur
Espace Colbert, 14 rue Ste-Barbe, 13231 Marseille
☎ *0491393800, fax 0491566661,*
www.provencetourism.com

Riviera-Côte-d'Azur
55 promenade des Anglais, 06000 Nice
☎ *0493377878, fax 0493860106,*
www.crtriviera.fr

Languedoc-Roussillon
20 rue de l'Aiguillerie, 34000 Montpellier
☎ *0467228100, fax 0467580610*

Comité Départemental du Tourisme
Alpes-de-Haute-Provence
19 rue du Dr-Honnorat, BP 170, 04005 Digne-les-Bains Cedex
☎ *0492315729, fax 0492322494*

Ardèche
8 cours du Palais, 07000 Privas
☎ *0475640466, fax 0475642393*

Bouches-du-Rhône
Le Montesquieu, 13 rue Roux de Brignoles, 13006 Marseille
☎ *0491138413, fax 0491330182*

Drôme
31 avenue du Président-Harriot, 26000 Valence
☎ *0475821926, fax 0475560165*

Gard
3 place des Arènes, BP 122, 30011 Nîmes
☎ *0466210251, fax 0466361314*

Hautes-Alpes
5ter rue Capitaine-de-Bresson, BP 46, 05002 Gap
☎ *0492536200, fax 0492533160*

Var
1 boulevard Foch, 83003 Draguignan
☎ *0494505550, fax 0494505551*
1 boulevard de Strasbourg, 83000 Toulon
☎ *0494185960, fax 0494185961*

Vaucluse
Place Campana, 2 rue St-Étienne, BP 147,
84008 Avignon
☎ *0490864342, fax 0490868608*

Local tourist offices

Aigues-Mortes
Porte de la Gardette, 30220 Aigues-
Mortes
☎ *0466537300*

Aix-en-Provence
2 place du Général-de-Gaulle, 13100
Aix-en-Provence
☎ *0442161161, fax 0442161162*

Antibes
11 place du Général-de-Gaulle, 06600
Antibes
☎ *0492905300, fax 0492905301*

Arles
35 place de la République, 13200 Arles
☎ *0490184120, fax 0490931717*

Avignon
41 cours Jean-Jaurès, 84000 Avignon
☎ *0490826511, fax 0490829503*

Bandol
Allées Alfred-Vivien, 83150
☎ *0494294135, fax 0494325039*

Les Baux-de-Provence
Hôtel de Manville, 13520 les Baux-de-
Provence
☎ *0490543439*

Beaulieu-sur-Mer
Place G-Clemenceau, 06310 Beaulieu-sur-
Mer
☎ *0493010221, fax 0493014404*

Cagnes-sur-Mer
6 boulevard Maréchal-Juin, 06801
Cagnes-sur-Mer
☎ *0493206164, fax 0493205263*

Cannes
SMEC, Palais des Festivals et des
Congrès, 1 boulevard la Croisette, BP
272, 06403 Cannes
☎ *0493392453, fax 0493394019*
Railway station (Gare SNCF)
☎ *0493991977*

Carpentras
170 avenue Jean-Jaurès, 84200
Carpentras

☎ *0490630078/90635788, fax
0490604102*

Castellane
Rue Nationale, 04120 Castellane
☎ *0492836114, fax 0492837689*

Châteauneuf-du-Pape
Place du Portail, 84230 Châteauneuf-du-
Pape
☎ *0490837108, fax 0490835034*

Digne
Rond-Point, 04000 Digne
☎ *0492314273, fax 0492322724*

Draguignan
9 boulevard Clemenceau, 83300
Draguignan
☎ *0494686330, fax 0494471076*

Fontaine-de-Vaucluse
Place de l'Église, 84800 Fontaine-de-
Vaucluse
☎ *0490203222, fax 0490202137*

Fréjus
325 rue Jean-Jaurès, 83601 Fréjus
☎ *0494171919, fax 0494510026*

Gap
12 rue Faure-du-Serre, 05000 Gap
☎ *0492525656, fax 0492525657*

Gordes
Place du Château, 84220 Gordes
☎ *0490720275*

La Grande-Motte
Place de la Mairie, 34280 la Grande-
Motte
☎ *0467290337, fax 0467290345*

Grasse
22 cours Honorée-Cresp, 06130 Grasse
☎ *049336666*

Grignan
Grande Rue, 26230 Grignan
☎ *0475465675*

Hyères
Rotonde Jean-Saluffe, BP 721, 83412
Hyères
☎ *0494651855, fax 0494358505*

Juin-les-Pins
1 boulevard Guillaumont, 06160 Juan-
les-Pins
☎ *0492905305, fax 0492905301*

Le Lavandou
Quai Gabriel-Péri, 83980 le Lavandou
☎ *0494710061, fax 0494647379*

Manosque
Place du Docteur-Joubert, 04100
Manosque
☎ *0492721600, fax 0492725898*

Marseille
4 la Canebière, 13001 Marseille
☎ *0491138900, fax 0491138920*

Martigues
Quai Paul-Doumer, 13500 Martigues
☎ *0442803072, fax 0442800097*

Menton
Palais de l'Europe, avenue Boyer, 06500
Menton
☎ *0492417676*

Montélimar
Allées Champ-de-Mars, 26200
Montélimar
☎ *0475010020, fax 0475523369*

Montpellier
78 avenue Pirée, 34000 Montpellier
☎ *(04)672206 16, fax 0467223810*

Nice
Railway station (Gare SNCF), avenue
Thiers
☎ *0493870707;*
2 rue Massenet
☎ *0493876060;*
Promenade des Anglais
☎ *0492144800;*
Nice airport
☎ *0493214411*

Nîmes
6 rue Auguste, 30000 Nîmes
☎ *0466672911, fax 0466218104*
Railway station (Gare SNCF)
☎ *0466841813*

Orange
Cours Aristide-Briand, 84100 Orange
☎ *0490347088, fax 0490349962*

Roquebrune-Cap-Martin
20 avenue P-Doumer, 06190
Roquebrune-Cap-Martin
☎ *0493356287, fax 0493285700*

St-Gilles
Place F-Mistral, 30800 St-Gilles
☎ *0466873375, fax 0466871628*

St-Raphaël
Rue W-Rousseau, 83700 St-Raphaël
☎ *0494195252, fax 0494838540*

St-Rémy-de-Provence
Place Jean-Jaurès, 13210 St-Rémy-de-
Provence
☎ *0490920522*

St-Tropez
Quai Jean-Jaurès, 83990 St-Tropez
☎ *0494974521, fax 0494978266*

Stes-Maries-de-la-Mer
Avenue Van-Gogh, 13460 Stes-Maries-de-
la-Mer
☎ *0490478255, fax 0490977115*

Salon-de-Provence
56 cours Gimon, 13300 Salon-de-
Provence
☎ *0490562760, fax 0490567709*

Sisteron
Avenue Paul-Arène, 04200 Sisteron
☎ *0492611203, 92613650, fax*
0492611957

Tarascon
59 rue des Halles, 13150 Tarascon
☎ *0490910352, fax 0490912296*

Toulon
8 avenue Colbert, 83000 Toulon
☎ *0494627387 and 0494625798*

Uzès
Avenue de la Libération, 30700 Uzès
☎ *0466226888, fax 0466229519*

Vaison-la-Romaine
Place du Chanoine-Sautel, 84110 Vaison-
la-Romaine
☎ *0490360211, fax 0490287604*

Vence
Place du Grand-Jardin, 06140 Vence
☎ *0493580638, fax 0493589181*

Villeneuve-lès-Avignon
1 place Charles-David, 30400 Villeneuve-
lès-Avignon
☎ *0490256155, fax 0490259155*

Principality of Monaco
DIRECTION DU TOURISME ET DES CONGRÈS DE
LA PRINCIPAUTÉ DE MONACO
2a boulevard des Moulins, MC 98030
Monaco
☎ *(377) 92166166, fax 92166000*

Media

Radio

British radio programmes can be received in the south of France on the short waveband (BBC World Service).

During the holiday season some French stations (including Radio Provence, from Marseille, Avignon, Digne, Gap and Toulon) transmit daily programmes in English for the benefit of visitors.

Television

French television uses a different system (SECAM) and British portable sets (PAL) cannot receive French programmes.

Motoring

Traffic regulations

As in other continental European countries vehicles in France travel on the right. Drivers and passengers must wear seat belts (including those fitted on rear seats).

Motorcyclists must wear a helmet. Children under 10 may not travel in front seats.

Priority roads

Priority roads are indicated before a junction with the sign *Passage protégé*. In general a vehicle approaching from the right has priority (*Priorité à droite* signs are often displayed); at a roundabout, however, vehicles actually negotiating the roundabout have priority. Roads without priority generally are signed *Vous n'avez pas la priorité* or *Cédez le passage*.

Horn

The horn can only be used to warn other drivers. Between sunset and sunrise flashing of the headlights must be used instead. In built-up areas the use of the horn is permitted only when danger is imminent. Priority on roads terminates at the entrance of a village or town (marked by settlement sign).

Headlights

In rain and snow dipped headlights must be used. Motorcyclists must use headlights at all times. When vision is less than 50 m speed restrictions to 50 kph or less apply. Foreign motorists are not compelled to convert headlights to the yellow beam normal in France. Spare bulbs for all lights must be carried.

Towing

Towing by private cars is forbidden.

Speed limits

Maximum speeds for vehicles:
- motorways 130 kph; when wet 110 kph
- main roads with two lanes in each direction 110 kph; when wet 100 kph
- national and country roads 90 kph; when wet 80 kph
- built-up areas 50 kph

Mopeds are normally restricted to 45 kph.

Drivers who have held their licence for less than two years may not exceed 80 kph on national roads and 110 kph on motorways.

Violation of traffic rules is punishable by high fines, hit-and-run driving by arrest. If you are able to pay on the spot, you will receive a discount; foreign drivers have to pay in cash.

Traffic signs

Ralentir or *Ralentissez* Slow down
Rappel Remember (previous traffic signs, usually speed restrictions)
Déviation Diversion
Passage interdit Passage forbidden

Drinking and driving

The alcohol limit is 0.05 per cent. Penalties for exceeding the limit are severe; a positive test can result in confiscation of the driving licence, and if an accident has occurred, even if no injury has been caused, a prison sentence of two months to two years and very high fines can be expected. If anyone is injured the penalty can be imprisonment and confiscation of the car.

Accidents

In the event of an accident the drivers concerned must each make a statement (*constat amiable d'accident automobile*) and sign it. Automobile clubs will provide the necessary forms. Where damage has occurred it is advisable to have the circumstances of the accident and details of damage confirmed by a *huissier* (a kind of lawyer's clerk). He is paid by the person or persons who summon him according to the time taken. The police need only be called if there are personal injuries or if a driver has driven off after an accident; the police are not concerned with accident damage. In the case of severe damage the offices of an expert should be obtained so that assessment can be simplified and expedited.

Fuel

Lead-free petrol (*essence sans plomb*; 95 octane) is available everywhere. Also available are lead-free super (98 octane), replacement lead fuel and diesel (*gazole*). Petrol stations on the motorways are open all day, but others, especially in smaller villages or in the countryside, may be closed at night and on Sundays. Most credit cards are accepted, and some petrol stations have an automatic card-operated service. Some automatic pumps accept only 10F coins.

Breakdown assistance

There are emergency telephones on all motorways and on some national roads in the case of breakdown or other motoring emergency.

Motorists from the UK should obtain European breakdown cover from their motoring organisation before travelling or contact:
AUTOMOBILE ASSOCIATION
☎ *(0870) 6000371, www.theAA.com.*

Roads

The French road network is very extensive and even minor roads are generally in good condition.

Since the network is so dense and the population density generally quite low, traffic is not particularly heavy; delays occur principally at holiday times and particularly at the beginning and end of the school holidays (beginning of July/end of September) on the major trunk routes.

Motorways
Apart from short stretches bypassing large towns such as Lyon or Marseille motorways are subject to tolls (*péage*; Eurocard, Mastercard and Visa International can be used). Toll booths at frontiers accept foreign currency. Normally, a ticket is given on entry onto a fee-paying motorway section; the same

ticket is then handed over to the cashier on leaving this stretch of motorway and paid for. In some areas coins can be thrown into a funnel to open the barriers – it is therefore advisable to travel with sufficient amounts of coins.

As far as the area covered in this guide is concerned the motorways (especially the A7 Autoroute du Soleil and the A8 Autoroute Provençale) function only as access routes; the toll stations and the entry and exit junctions are situated considerable distances apart which makes it advisable for visitors to use the national roads instead for exploring the area.

Motorway tolls
For information contact:
ASSOCIATION DES SOCIÉTÉS FRANÇAISES D'AUTOROUTES
Départment Information
3 rue Edmond-Valentin, 75007 Paris
☎ *0147059001, email asfa@autoroutes.fr, www.autoroutes.fr.*

National roads
Long-distance traffic still makes great use of the excellent national roads (*routes nationales*), which correspond approximately to A roads in the UK. They are designated by red and white kilometre posts which bear the road number (e.g. N555) and frequently have three lanes, the centre lane being used for overtaking. Provincial roads (*routes départementales*) are marked by yellow and white kilometre posts (e.g. D666); important stretches are of similar quality to the national roads.

Maps
Visitors who are travelling away from the major holiday routes should take a detailed map in addition to the general map provided with this guide. Below is a selection:

1:200,000 (1 cm = 2 km)
Michelin detailed maps of France; for the area covered in this guide sheets 80, 81, 83 and 84

1:100,000 (1 cm = 1 km)
IGN maps 60, 61, 66, 67 and 68

Parking

At the popular tourists sights there is generally sufficient parking available (mostly paying; many with attendant). Larger villages and towns are generally well provided with public car parks. It is usually easiest to park in one of these; the fees are relatively low.

Blue zone
In town centres there is the well-known *zone bleue* (signed) where a parking disc must be used; the maximum parking time is usually limited to one hour (except on Sundays and public holidays). Parking discs can be obtained from the police and from automobile clubs.

Parking regulations
In towns drivers can only wait or park facing the direction of the traffic. In one-way streets both sides can be used unless otherwise indicated. Often parking is allowed free on one side of the street only, the sides alternating on a half-monthly basis. Outside the towns drivers should always park parallel to the road. Yellow lines along the edge of the road mean parking is forbidden.

Parking ticket machines
Towns with public parking areas usually have *horodateurs*, centrally situated machines where a parking permit can be obtained. The ticket is bought with coins (fee according to length of parking time) and must be prominently displayed behind the windscreen.

Caravan drivers
Many public car parks, particularly in central areas, do not allow caravans. In practice a horizontal bar is fixed at a height of 1.9 to 2 m to prevent high vehicles from entering.

Warning
At all the large parking areas at the important sights and in busy holiday centres cars are often broken into, therefore no valuables should be left in the vehicle.

Opening Hours

Banks
Not all banks have the same closing day; some are closed on Saturdays, others on Mondays. Hours of business also vary; as a general rule banks are open 9am–12am, 2pm– 4pm; in some larger towns also 9am–4.30pm without closing at lunchtime. They close at noon on the eve of a public holiday.

Museums
See entries for individual museums.

Most national museums are closed on Tuesdays; municipal museums on Mondays. Most museums are closed on public holidays. Entry is normally permitted up to half an hour before closing time.

The ticket **Carte Musées Côte d'Azur** gives free or reduced admission to 58 museums and cultural institutions in the Département Alpes-Maritimes. Tickets for 3 days (70F) or 7 days (140F) are available from tourist offices and the museums.

Post offices
See Post

Shops
There are no official early closing days in France and no regulations as to when a shop may be open. Retail shops are normally open 9.30am–6.30pm. Grocers and supermarkets frequently open very early, but most close 12.30pm–3/4pm and remain open in the evening until quite late.

Normally shops are closed on Sundays, but in areas frequeneted by tourists and during the high season many shops also open on Sundays and public holidays; bakers, butchers, wine dealers and florists are often open until noon or 1pm. Shops which open on Sundays generally close on Mondays and sometimes also on Wednesdays.

Department stores
Department stores and large shops are open Mon.–Sat. 9.30am–6.30pm.

Shopping centres
Even quite small places usually have a large and well-stocked supermarket, often situated on the edge of the built-up area.

These shopping centres (*centre commerciale, supermarché*) are generally open Mon.–Thu. 9am–8pm (Fri., Sat. to 10pm). Frequently establishments that stay open late are closed on Monday morning.

Bookshops, hairdressers, small shops
These shops are usually closed on Mondays.

Places of interest
Many places of interest (*châteaux*, excavation sites and some churches) are closed from noon until 2pm. However, there are exceptions during the main holiday season. Visitors should, of course, refrain from looking round a church while a service is in progress.

Post

Opening hours vary; in the larger towns they are open Mon.–Fri, 8am–7pm; in smaller places 9–11.30am, 2–5.30pm. On Saturdays offices are generally open 8am–12am.

Stamps
Stamps (*timbres-poste*) can be bought from tobacco kiosks (*tabac*), newspaper kiosks and stationers as well as in post offices.

Postage rates
Letters within France and to other EU countries (up to 20 grams) cost 3F; to the US and Canada (air mail up to 10 grams) 2.7F.

Post within Monaco needs to be stamped with Monacan stamps.

Currency exchange
Some post offices also have a bureau de change.

Public Holidays

Fixed holidays
January 1st: Jour de l'An, New Year's Day
May 1st: Fête du Travail, Labour Day
May 8th: Armistice (1945)
July 14th: National holiday (storming of the Bastille 1789)
August 15th: Assomption, Assumption of the Virgin Mary
November 1st: Toussaint, All Saints Day
November 11th: Armistice (1918)
December 25th: Noël, Christmas Day

Movable feasts
Lundi de Pâques (Easter Monday)
Ascension (Ascension Day)
Lundi de la Pentecôte (Whit Monday)

Monaco (additional holidays)
January 26th and 27th: Festivités de la Ste-Dévote (festival of the patron saint of the Principality of Monaco)
Fête Dieu: Corpus Christi

November 18th and 19th: Manifestations de la Fête Nationale Monégasque (National holiday)
December 8th: Immaculate Conception

Public Transport

Buses and coaches

France has an extensive network of bus routes operated by private firms. Timetables and details of routes can be obtained from local tourist offices (☞Information).

Rapides Côte d'Azur (RCA)
The Rapides Côte d'Azur bus company operates inclusive tours between Cannes and Menton and also inland (Grasse, Aspremont, Peille, Sospel) which are good value. Information from the bus station (Gare Routière) and rail station (SNCF) in Cannes and also from the bus stations in Grasse, Antibes and Nice.

Excursions
Many French and English coach companies offer inclusive tours to the French Mediterranean coast, often with excursions inland. Information from travel agents in the UK or in France.

Europabus
Europabus, a subsidiary of eight European railway companies, operates a number of one-day tours from Avignon; these include Roman Provence, The Wine Road, The Wild Camargue and The Heart of Provence. Information can be obtained from Avignon railway station.

Railways

The most important railway route to Provence is the line from Paris and the channel ports via Lyon to Avignon, Arles, Marseille, Toulon, Nice and Monaco into Italy. This route is served by express (*rapide*) trains, many of which have evocative names such as Paris–Côte d'Azur, Rhône–Azur, Phocéen, Rouget de Lisle and the historic Train Bleu.

TGV
Since 1981 the Train à Grande Vitesse (TGV) has run between Paris and Lyon, with a continuation to Avignon and Marseille, and to Montpellier and Nice;

this is one of the fastest trains in the world in a regular timetable, reaching speeds of up to 300 kph. In the area of the French Riviera rail services are good. In addition to the route mentioned above there are lines from Avignon via Salon, Fos-sur-Mer to Marseille and from Nice to Turin via Breil and Tende. A branch line goes from Marseille to Hyères. The mountainous hinterland of Haute-Provence is served by the line from Marseille to Aix-en-Provence, Sisteron and Gap, with a branch to Digne. The Pine-cone Train runs from Nice to Digne. This rail-bus is an excellent shuttle service for walking excursions in the area of the lower Var and a trip on the antiquated narrow-gauge line gives the passenger a special feeling of actually being in Provence. On the stretch between Puget-Theniers and Annot trains are hauled by steam locomotives on certain days (☞Sights from A to Z, Entrevaux).

Special fares

Joker tickets So-called Joker tickets can be bought by everyone, They are valid on TGV as well as all other trains. From Paris and some other towns, many destinations in France can be reached at a lower price. There are two types: Joker 30 gives a reduction of up to 60 per cent as long as the ticket has been bought 30–60 days before travelling; Joker 8 reduced the fare by up to 40 per cent if the ticket has been bought 8–30 days before departure.

Reductions for young people Carissimo gives 20–50 per cent reductions for young people 12–25 years old. There are two types (valid for one year): Carissimo *4 trajets* for four single journeys; Carissimo *8 trajets* for eight single journeys.

Euro Domino Jeunes is a system of vouchers for unrestricted travel for three, five or ten days which have to be used within one month (also valid in numerous other countries in Europe). InterRail (also valid in many other European countries) gives unrestricted travel for 14 days or one month.

Reductions for senior citizens The Carte Vermeil (also in two types) gives 20–50 per cent reduction for senior citizens: Carte Vermeil Quatre Temps for those who travel only occasionally; Carte Vermeil Plein Temps for those who travel regularly.

Reductions for couples and families The Carte Couple gives a 25 per cent reduction for couples and families. Families receive reductions of up to 75 per cent, depending on the number of under-age children.

Billet Séjour A 25 per cent reduction of the fare is obtained by covering at least 1000 km on a return journey.

Car rental

In association with various firms French Railways (SNCF) operate the service Train + Auto (car at the station). Within the area covered in the guide this sevice is available at Aix-en-Provence, les Arcs/Draguignan, Antibes, Arles, Avignon, Beaulieu-sur-Mer, Cagnes-sur-Mer, Cannes, Gap, Hyères, Marseille, Menton, Monaco, Montélimar, Montpellier, Nice, Nîmes, Orange, St-Raphaël, Toulon.

Excursions

Partly in association with local undertakings French Railways organise sightseeing and excursions by rail, boat and bus under the title Excursions, Services de Tourisme SNCF. Starting points include Aix-en-Provence, Arles, Aubenas, Avignon, Cannes, Cap d'Agde, Gap, la Grande-Motte, Grasse, Hyères, Marseille, Menton, Montpellier, Nice, Nîmes, St-Raphaël, St-Tropez, Toulon. Further information can be obtained at any local Office de Tourisme and at railway stations.

Information

Details of services and fares can be obtained from:

FRENCH RAILWAYS (SNCF)
179 Piccadilly, London W1V 0BA
☎ (08705) 848848, www.raileurope.co.uk
610 Fifth Avenue, New York NY 10020
☎ (212) 7571125
1500 Stanley Street, Montreal H3A 1R3
☎ (514) 2888255/6

Restaurants

Most hotels have a restaurant. In the list below these restaurants are only given in exceptional cases; otherwise they can be found under Hotels.

Aigues-Mortes
ARCADES
23 boulevard Gambetta
☎ 0466538113
Restaurant in a 16th c. building; meals also served outside.

Aix-en-Provence
★ **CLOS DE LA VIOLETTE**
10 rue de la Violette
☎ 0442233071
Very good restaurant; outside eating possible.

AU BOUCANIER
46 place Forum des Cardeurs
☎ 0442219389
Creole cuisine.

JAPONAIS YOJI
7 avenue Victor-Hugo
☎ 0442384876
Japanese speciality restaurant with large garden terrace.

LA SOFRA
11 rue St-Jean (opposite the Palais de Justice)
☎ 0442273132
Tunisian cuisine.

BRASSERIE LE CINTRA
14 place Jeanne-d'Arc
☎ 0442263524
Buffet with starters, regional cooking, cheeses and desserts; children's menu.

Antibes
AUBERGE PROVENÇALE
61 place Nationale
☎ 0493341324
Provençal cuisine; tables in the garden.

★ **PAVILLON EDEN ROC IN THE HÔTEL DU CAP**
Boulevard Kennedy, Cap d'Antibes
☎ 0493613901
Gourmet restaurant in a magnificent location on a rock with fantastic views of the coast and islands.

Arles
L'OLIVIER
1 bis rue Réattu
☎ 0490496488
Very good restaurant; meals also served outdoors.

ESTRAMBOR
Route Arles–Sambuc, le Sambuc
☎ 0490972010

Speciality: *pieds et paquets* (☞Food and Drink)

Avignon
CHRISTIAN ÉTIENNE
10 rue de Mons
☎ 0490861650
Excellent restaurant in a 13th–14th c. building near the Papal Palace.

SHIP RESTAURANT MIREIO
Information: Grands Bateaux de Provence, allée de l'Oulle
☎ 0490856225
Breakfast cruises to Port St-Louis, Arles, Châteauneuf-du-Papes; candlelight dinner to Avignon and Villeneuve-lès-Avignon.

Bandol
AUBERGE DU PORT
9 allées J-Moulin
☎ 0494294263
Restaurant with good view of the harbour; meals also served outdoors.

Les Baux-de-Provence
★ **OUSTEAU DE BAUMANIÈRE**
(☞Hotels)

LA CABRO D'OR (RELAIS)
Route d'Arles, 1 km to the south-west
☎ 0490543321
Beautifully situated house; seasonal specialities: asparagus, game, lamb, sole and wines from the region.

Bormes-les-Mimosas
JARDIN DE PERLEFLEURS
100 chemin de l'Orangerie
☎ 0494649923
Provençal cuisine; specialities: entrails in rosé, shrimp soup, rabbit.

Cagnes-sur-Mer
LES PEINTRES
71 Montée de la Bourgade, Haut-de-Cagnes
☎ 0493208308
Seasonal specialities and wines from Provence.

Cannes
★ **LA PALME D'OR**
Hôtel Martinez (☞entry), 73 boulevard de la Croisette
☎ 0492987414
Top gourmet restaurant. Specialities: foie gras, lamb.

★La Belle Otéro
7th floor Hôtel Carlton, 58 la Croisette
☎ 0493680033
Top gourmet restaurant. Rooms with
wooden panelling and oil paintings;
piano music at night; terrace. Fish and
seafood specialities.

La Poêle d'Or
23 rue des États-Unis
☎ 0493397765
Elegant restaurant. Specialities: lobster
with asparagus and morels, duck, soufflé.

La Palmeraie
45 boulevard de la Croisette
☎ 0493381545
Unique view of la Croisette from the
restaurant's garden and terrace.
Traditional cuisine and specialities,
such as seafood, lamb and delicious
desserts.

La Taverne Sicilienne
16 quai St-Pierre.
☎ 0493394679
In the old harbour. Italian specialities,
pizza from the wood-burning oven,
pasta, meat from the grill.

Le Festival
52 boulevard de la Croisette
☎ 0493380481
Traditional brasserie, terrace opposite the
sea. Specialities: seafood salad, grilled
salmon, grilled sardines, home-made
desserts, ice cream and sorbet.

Le Grand Bleu
50 boulevard de La Croisette
☎ 0492997093
Luxury brasserie, terrace with sea view.
Speciality: lobster salad.

Carpentras
Vert Galant
12 rue Clapies
☎ 0490671550
Provençal cuisine, lamb dishes.

La Colle-sur-Loup
Hostellerie de l'Abbaye
Avenue de la Libération
☎ 0493326677
Regional cuisine; meals also served
outside in the shaded courtyard.

Digne-les-Bains
L'Origan
6 rue Pied-de-Ville
☎ 0492316213

Regional cuisine, meals also served
outside.

Eze
★Château Eza
☎ 0493411224
Top restaurant with magnificent view of
the coast and the peninsula. Provençal
specialities and wines.

Fontaine-de-Vaucluse
Philip
☎ 0490204431
Restaurant with service outside, good
views of the rapids.

Fréjus
Le Vieux Four
57 rue Grisolle
☎ 0494515638
Meals in rustic surroundings.

Gap
La Roseraie
Rue de Villarobert (N85)
Regional cuisine; meals also served
outside, good views.

Le Golfe-Juan
Tétou
☎ 0493637116
Nounou
☎ 0493637173
Both restaurants on the beach are
famous for their delicious bouillabaisse
and also offer fantastic sea views. The
dry Côte de Provence wines are a tasty
accompaniment to the soup.

Gordes
Les Bories
Route Vénasque
☎ 0490720051
Restaurant in a very comfortable hotel;
service also outside, great views of the
Montagne du Lubéron.

Mas Tourteron
Route des Imberts, 4 km to the south-
west
☎ 0490720016
Elegant restaurant in a Provençal
residence.

Grasse
Restaurant Golf Grasse Country Club
Route de Digne
☎ 0493605544
Beautifully situated; service also outside,
park, golf course.

Hyères
LA FRÉGATE
Port Pothuau, Salins d'Hyères (6 km to the east of Hyères)
☎ 0494664029
Beautifully situated restaurant with great views, serving regional cooking; also outdoors.

Le Lavandou
ROCHES
Aiguebelle (4.5 km outside le Lavandou)
☎ 0494710507
Excellent situations, beautiful seaside terraces; specialities include seafood.

Lorgues
BRUNO
3 km to the south-east, on the route des Arcs
☎ 0494739219
Speciality: truffle dishes and regional wines.

Lourmarin
LA FÉNIÈRE
Rue du Grand-Pré
☎ 0490681179
Excellent cooking; specialities including lamb dishes.

Mandelieu-la-Napoule
★ L'OASIS
La Napoule area of town
☎ 0493499552
Widely renowned gourmet restaurant with extraordinary atmosphere. The cuisine includes Provençal specialities. A *confiserie* is attached which produces home-made sweets and pastries.

Marseille
MIRAMAR
12 quai du Port
☎ 0491911040
Very good cuisine, service also outside. Specialities: bouillabaisse, seafood and regional dishes.

LES ARCENAULX
25 cours d'Estienne-d'Orves
☎ 0491547706
Restaurant-bookshop-gallery; antique furnishings.

LA MAISON DES FONDUS
1 avenue de la Pointe-Rouge
☎ 0491726642
Fondue dishes.

AUBERGE IN
25 rue du Chevalier-Roze
☎ 0491905159
Vegetarian restaurant.

AUBERGE DU VIEUX MOULIN
12 rue de Province
☎ 0491493755
Regional, traditional cooking.

Martigues
HOSTELLERIE PASCAL
3 rue Lucien-Toulmond
☎ 0442421689
Specialities: fish dishes, mussels, bouillabaisse.

LE DOMUS
Avenue Carro
☎ 0442428048
Specilaities: pizza from the wood-burning oven; terrace restaurant, good views of the sea.

Menton
VIVIERS BRETON
6 place Cap
☎ 0493352424
Fish and seafood dishes; service also outside.

Monaco
Hotel-restaurants, see Hotels

CASTELROC
Place du Palais
☎ (377) 93303668
Monegasque specialities.

LA PORTE D'OR
9 rue Grimaldi
☎ (377) 93251415
Chinese cuisine.

PIEDRA DEL SOL
2 rue du Portier
☎ (377) 93506213
Mexican food, cafeteria, cocktail bar.

RESTAURANT DU PORT
Quai Albert-1er
☎ (377) 93507721
Italian cuisine, fish dishes; terrace by the sea.

CHARLES III
15 galerie Charles-II
☎ (377) 93505763
Terrace restaurant opposite the casino gardens; Italian and Provençal cuisine.

Montélimar
Francis
Route de Mareille, 2.5 km
☎ *0475011167*
French cuisine.

Montpellier
★ **Le Jardin des Sens**
11 avenue St-Lazare
☎ *0467796333, fax 0467721305*
Grand restaurant, part of the Relais chain, in contemporary style with elegant dining room; excellent cooking and lovingly assembled wine list. Specialities: veal and fish dishes.

L'Olivier
12 rue Aristide-Olivier
☎ *0467928628*
French specialities.

Mougins
★ **Moulin de Mougins**
Route de Valbonne, quartier Notre-Dame-de-Vie
☎ *0493757824*
Part of the Relais chain. In a former 16th c. oil mill the guest, seated under rustic beams or in the garden next to a brook, is spoiled with gourmet meals, for example lobster fricassé and rare wines.

Le Manoir de l'Étang
Quartier Bois Font Merle, route d'Antibes
☎ *0493909107*
Charming Provençal hotel-restaurant, situated in the countryside.

Moustiers-Ste-Marie
La Bastide de Moustiers
☎ *0492704747*
The restaurant is housed in a 17th c. building, in 4 ha of parkland. Vegetables with country bacon, rabbit terrine and hen pheasant are some of the specialities served here.

Nice
Le Grand Pavois – Chez Michel
11 rue Meyerbeer
☎ *0493887742*
Excellent fish dishes, bouillabaisse and lamb specialities with Provençal herbs as well as excellent wines.

Le Florian
22 rue A-Karr
☎ *0493888660*
Provençal and northern French cuisine.

Le Grand Bleu
24 cours Saleya
☎ *0493622951*
Once the market stalls have gone, the owner also serves his fish specialities outside.

Le William's
29 quai Lunel
☎ *0493564737*
Small, family-run restaurant in the harbour; nautical interior decoration.

Café de Turin
5 place Garibaldi
☎ *0493622952*
Traditional fish restaurant, dating to the late 19th c. Rustic pub atmosphere.

Nîmes
Alexandre
Garons, route d'Aéroport
☎ *0466700899*
A short way outside the centre, this excellent restaurant offers great comfort and a beautiful garden.

Orange
Le Parvis
3 cours Pourtoules
☎ *0490348200*
Meals also served on the terrace.

Peillon
Auberge de la Madone
Place Auguste-Arnulf
☎ *0493799117*
Restaurant in attractive location, with garden and flower-decorated terrace.

Port-Grimaud
Port Diffa
La Foux, 2 km south of Port-Grimaud on the N98
☎ *0494562907*
Moroccan cuisine; service outdoors.

Roquebrune
★ **Restaurant Le Vistaero**
Vista Palace Hotel, Grande Corniche
☎ *0492104000*
Restaurant in fantastic location, with excellent views of Monaco and the coast; also outdoor service.

St-Jean-Cap-Ferrat
Le Provençal
2 avenue D-Séméria
☎ *0493760397*
Elegant restaurant serving French cuisine.

St-Martin-du-Var
★ JEAN-FRANÇOIS ISSAUTIER
3 km along the N202
☎ 0493081065
Excellent Mediterranean food.

St-Raphäel
LE SIROCCO
35 quai Albert-1er
☎ 0494953999
Excellent cuisine; service also outside;
great views.

St-Rémy-de-Provence
LA MAISON JAUNE
15 rue Carnot
☎ 0490925614
Pleasant atmosphere; service also
outside.

St-Tropez
AUBERGE DES MAURES
Rue Docteur-Boutin, corner of 43 rue
Allard
☎ 0494970150
Stylish and romantic restaurant.

CHRISTOPHE LEROY
38 rue Clemenceau
☎ 0494974878
Culinary creations of the highest quality,
yet at affordable prices.

LE MAS DE CHASTELAS
Quartier Bertau, route de Gassin
☎ 0494560911
Excellent and highly recommended
cuisine; restaurant is outside the town,
in a converted farmhouse (reservation
for evening meal required).

BISTRO DES LICES
Place des Lices
☎ 0494972900
Restaurant with terrace, serving excellent
French food, in the most beautiful spot
in St-Tropez.

CAFÉ DES ARTS
Place des Lices
☎ 0494970225
Traditional meeting point of boule
players and much prasied for its
aperitifs.

Stes-Maries-de-la-Mer
L'HIPPOCAMPE
Rue Camille-Pelletan
☎ 0490978091
Good cuisine; service also outside.

LA MANADE
10 avenue Frédéric-Mistral
☎ 0490979806
Speciality: seafood.

Salon-de-Provence
SALLE À MANGER
6 rue Maréchal-Joffre
☎ 0490562801
Elegant restaurant in a town house;
service also outside.

CHÂTEAU DE RICHEBOIS RESTAURANT
Route d'Eyguières
☎ 0490565744
Restaurant in a magnificent park.

Tarascon
RESTAURANT-PIZZERIA LE PAS DE LA BERGÈRE
1 boulvard Gambetta
☎ 0490912047
Italian specialities; pizza to take away.

Toulon
AU SOURD
10 rue Molière
☎ 0494922852
Fish dishes; service also outside.

Uzès
JARDINS DE CASTILLE
Place Evêché
☎ 0466223268
Service also outside.

Vaison-la-Romaine
BATELEUR
1 place Aubanel
☎ 0490362804
Regional cuisine.

Venasque
AUBERGE LA FONTAINE
Place de la Fontaine
☎ 0490660296
Restaurant in a quiet location; also has a
bistro.

Vence
AUGERBE DES SEIGNEURS
Place Frêne
☎ 0493580424
Provençal dishes.

Villefranche-sur-Mer
LA TRINQUETE
Quartier Darse
☎ 0493017141
This restaurant, situated in the harbour,
is the meeting point for fishermen and
for the wealthy residents who have their

villas on the Cap Ferrat. Speciality of the house: deep-fried small, round, grey fish.

Villeneuve-lès-Avignon
AUBERTIN
1 rue de l'Hôpital
☎ *0490259484*
Excellent cuisine.

Shopping

A speciality of Provence is perfume (especially in Grasse) and herbal essences (lavender oil, scented bags). Also popular are the *herbes de Provence*, aromatic herbs which are on sale everywhere; nougat from Montélimar of various kinds, soft or hard, perfumed or plain; and callissons, a tangy marzipan confection, from Aix-en-Provence.

Other popular souvenirs are candied fruits and flowers, liqueurs and jams made according to traditional recipes and freshly pressed olive oils from the traditional olive mills (many can be visited).

Household articles and craft objects made from olive wood can be found in great variety; the same is true of pottery (especially from the world-famous potteries of Vallauris). Unusual souvenirs are *santons* – Provençal crib figures. It must be remembered that all these things are produced specially for tourists.

The typical pleasantly rural-looking cotton material of Provence, which is used for women's clothes, has small floral patterns printed on a plain coloured background.

Music lovers will also be attracted by records, cassettes and CDs of Provençal songs.

Other attractive souvenirs from a holiday in Provence are copperplate engravings of the countryside from le Castellet and carpets from Cogolin.

The well-known resorts of the Côte d'Azur all have similar luxury shops stocking items that are of good quality and also expensive; the range extends from haute couture through jewellery and perfumes to luxury cars. A large part is taken up by the antique trade; many exclusive shops are found north of the harbour in Nice. The markets, with all kinds of culinary products and second-hand bric-a-brac (*brocante*), and the narrow lanes of the old parts of these towns are particularly attractive. Tourists in self-catering accommodation will find an almost inexhaustable range of goods of a high quality and at reasonable prices in the numerous supermarkets on the edge of towns. Worth mentioning are stores of the chains Carrefour, Cora and Géant.

Selected shops

Aix-en-Provence
AIX'S PARADOX BOOKSTORE
15 rue du 4-septembre
☎ *0442264799*
International bookshop.

BOUTIQUE CHANEL
1 bis, rue Fabrot
☎ *0442274022*
Exclusive women's fashion.

BOUTIQUE LACOSTE
7 rue Ancienne-Madeleine
☎ *0442380936*
Clothes for women, men and children.

DESIDERATA
1 avenue Pasteur
☎ *0442234141*
Reproductions, sculptures, masks, crafts, jewellery, gifts.

PRO SHOP – TOUT POUR LE GOLF
Domaine Riquetti, 9 chemin Départemental, les Milles
☎ *0442242118*
Everything for the golfer.

Antibes
CERRUTI
1881 Mazza Boutique, 12 bis boulevard Wilson
☎ *0493342521*
Exclusive fashions for women and men.

LA CUIVRERIE S'ANTIBES
6 rue de la République
☎ *0493344162*
Copperware.

Antibes – Juan les Pins
EPICERIE PROVENÇALE
11 avenue Philippe-Rochat
☎ *0493338844*
Provençal delicacies.

Arles
SOUVENIRS DE PROVENCE
143 avenue Stalingrad
☎ *0490931800*
Souvenirs from Provence.

Biot
LA POTERIE PROVENÇALE
1689 route de la Mer
☎ 0493656330
Provençal pottery; clay vases for the garden

VERRERIE LUZORO
1520 route de la Mer
☎ 0493655218
Glass blowers.

Cannes
ALEXANDRA BOUTIQUE
Rond-Point Duboys-d'Angers
☎ 0493384129
Exclusive ladies' fashion from famous designers such as Christian Dior, Emanuel Ungaro, Rocco Barocco, Claude Montana and Findi.

ART ET CADEAUX 1000 IDÉES
3 rue 14-août
☎ 0493684953
Art and gifts.

ATELIER DE LA POUPÉE
2 rue Venizélos
☎ 0493682928
Porcelain dolls.

BRUNO
50 rue d'Antibes
☎ 0493392663
Sweet shop, speciality candied fruits, crystal glass and gifts.

BULGARI
Hotel Majestic, 14 la Croisette
☎ 0492991800
Jewellery.

CERRUTI
15 rue des Serbes
☎ 0493382520
Exclusive men's fashions.

CHANEL
5 la Croisette
☎ 0493385505
Haute couture for women.

CHAUSSURES CHARLES JOURDAN
47 rue d'Antibes
☎ 0493398842
Elegant shoes.

GALERIES STEMPERT
11 rue Jean-de-Riouffe
☎ 0493393477

Porcelain from Limoges, crystal ware, silver, gifts.

HERMÈS – PARIS
17 la Croisette
☎ 0493390890
Jewellery, leatherware, fashion (further shops in Monaco and Marseille).

PAVILLON CHRISTOFLE
9 rue d'Antibes
☎ 0493390172
Porcelain and silver.

LOUIS VUITTON
44 la Croisette
☎ 0493398787
Leather goods, suitcases.

VAN CLEEF ET ARPELS
61 la Croisette
☎ 0493941508
Jewellery.

Châteauneuf de Grasse
ETAINGS DE TONGE
610 route Valbonne-Plascassier
☎ 0493421183
Gifts.

Grasse
FRAGONARD
20 boulevard Fragonard
☎ 0493364465
Museum and exhibition laboratory on the history of scent; factory shop.

Mandelieu-la-Napoule
PÂTISSERIE DES RESTAURANTS L'OASIS
Rue Honoré-Carle-la-Napoule
☎ 0493499552
Extraordinarily good cakes and pastries.

Marseille
DRAGÉES NOUCHIG
45 rue Vacon, corner of rue Paradis
☎ 0491550606
Confectionary, chocolate, wine and spirits.

HERMÈS – PARIS
93 rue Paradis
☎ 0491532457
Beautiful things for the table, silver, porcelain, crystal; also perfumes of Hermès, Equipage, Aamzone, Calèche, Bel-Ami.

LES CHEMINS DE MER
9 rue Euthymènes

☎ *0491544449*
Books, gifts, games, posters; gallery.

Monaco
BULGARI
Avenue des Beaux-Arts
☎ *(377) 93508840*
Jewellery.

BOUTIQUE MARKYA
7–9 boulevard des Moulins
☎ *(377) 39301041*
Exclusive handbags, leather goods, shoes, belts; scarves by Paloma Picasso, Gucci and Burberry.

CAROLINE PARFUMS
19 rue Princesse-Caroline
☎ *(377) 93507966*
Perfumes.

CARTIER
Place du Casino
☎ *(377) 93308658*
Jewellery.

CHRISTIAN DIOR BOUTIQUE
Avenue des Beaux-Arts
☎ *(377) 93500204*
Exclusive women's fashions.

LANVIN MONTE-CARLO
Place du Casino
☎ *(377) 93300453*
Men's fashions.

TEMPLIER
3 avenue St-Michel, Jardins du Casino
☎ *(377) 93250043*
Jewellery, gems, antiques, paintings.

Montélimar
PÂTISSIER ESCOBAR
Place du Chapeau-Rouge
☎ *0475012553*
White nougat (☛Food and Drink).

Nice
LA VINOTHÈQUE
21 rue Lépante
☎ *0493624214*
Wines, spirits, champagne; gifts.

LIVRAFLORE
Cours Saleya
☎ *0493134977*
Fresh flowers directly from the flower market; flower deliveries.

NEWAY
23 bis avenue Auguste-Vérola

☎ *0493319595*
Sale and repair of surf boards, sports clothes.

SASHKA KEV
Pedestrianised zone, 15 rue Masseena
☎ *0493168036*
Watches from Cartier, Ebel, Swatch and others; gems.

Opio (Alpes-Maritimes)
MOULINS DE LA BRAQUE
2 route de Châteauneuf
☎ *0493772303*
Oil mill; olive oil of Provence and regional produce.

Markets

The markets of Provence – be they food, crafts, antiques, fish or flower markets – present a particularly colourful picture of the region. It is recommended to check the dates for markets with local tourist offices. Here follows a selection:

Antibes
Crafts market

Apt
Market (Sat.)
Farmers' market (Jun.–Oct. Tue. am; particularly wonderful cherries in June)
Antiques and bric-a-brac market (Jul.)
Pottery market (Jul.–Aug. Tue.)
St Lucas Market, Salon of Nativity scenes (Dec.)

Avignon
Bric-a-brac market, place Crillon (Sat. am; also Whit holiday and in Sep. in the allée de l'Oulle)
Flower market, place des Carmes (Sat. am)
Flea market, place des Carmes (Sun. am)
Fun fair, rempart St-Michel (Sat. am, Sun. am)
Les Halles (mornings except Mon.)

Beaumes-de-Venise
Pottery market, street festival of painters, day of the book (Jul.)

Bollène
Market (Mon.)
Fleamarket (every second Sat.)

Cadenet
Market (Mon.)
Farmers' market (Apr.–Oct. Sat.)

Cannes
Les Antiquaires à Cannes (antiques; mid-Jul.)

Carpentras
Truffle market (Nov.–Mar. Fri. am)
Fleamarket (Sun. am)
Wine market Côtes du Ventoux (Jul.–Aug.)
Bric-a-brac, trade and agricultural market (Nove.)

Cavaillon
Market (Mon.)

Châteauneuf-du-Pape
Market (Fri. am)
Fruit festivals (bric-a-brac and medieval crafts; Aug.)

Gordes
Market (Tue. am)

Grasse
Antiques market

Grillon
Market (Sat.)
Lamb and asparagus market (May)

Jonquières
Fleamarket (Sun. am)

Le Thor
Market (Wed., Sat.)
Trade and crafts market (Palm Sun.)
Bric-a-brac (in the high season every 2nd Sun. in the month)

L'Isle-sur-la-Sorgue
Market (Thu., Sun.)
Bric-a-brac (Sun.)
Antiques market (Easter)

Malaucène
Market (Wed.)
Bric-a-brac, fun fair, potters' market (Jun.)

Monaco
Market la Condamine, place d'Armes (incl. sale of plants)

Mormoiron
Asparagus, bric-a-brac and trade fair (May)

Nice
Market on the cours Saleya: the market has everything needed in the Provençal cuisine: olives, sheep's cheese, mushrooms, fish, flowers (Tue.–Sun.); bric-a-brac (Mon.)

Oppède
Large market (crafts and bric-a-brac; Sep.)

Orange
Market (Thu. am)
Large antiques fair (Apr.)

Puyméras
Provençal market (Sat. in summer from 4pm)

Richerenches
Market (Sat. am)
Flower market (May)
Truffle market (Nov.–Mar. Sat. am)

Sault
Market (Wed.)
Fair of St Jean (St John's Market; Jun.)

Vacqueyras
Crafts market and wine festival (Jul.)

Vaison-la-Romaine
Market (Tue. am)
Farmers' market (Thu. am, Sat. am)
Provençal market in the upper town (Jun.–Sep. Sun. am)
Whit market and children's procession (May)
Gourmanderie days: young wine, Bacchus procession (Nov.)

Valréas
Market (Wed., Sat.)
Truffle market (Nov.–Mar. Wed am)
Easter market (Apr.)
Great St Jean market (Jun.)
Bric-a-brac market (Jun.)

Velleron
Fun fair (Wed. am)
Farmers' market (in the high season daily; rest of the year Tue., Fri., Sat.)

Vence
Antiques market

Sport

Water sports

The region Provence-Alpes-Côtes-d'Azur with its 700 km of varied coastline (rocks, coves, sandy beaches), and its numerous rivers, lakes and mountain streams is a paradise for water-sports enthusiasts.

Sports boats
See entry

Wind-surfing
Among the internationally famous windsurfing areas are: Six Fours, Cap Nègre, Place de Carro. Funboarders congregate near Stes-Maries-de-la-Mer and Port-St-Louis-du-Rhône.

Diving
The rockier sections of the coast, for example along the Corniche de l'Esterel and the Corniche des Maures, have many attractive bays and good diving grounds. Unfortunately, the diversity and density of marine life have been considerably reduced in recent years due to overfishing, intensive underwater hunting and water pollution. The introduction of a protective zone for marine mammals in 1992 and an increase in other protective measures seem to bode well for a regeneration of the marine habitat. Information from:
FÉDÉRATION FRANÇAISE D'ÉTUDES ET DE SPORTS SOUS-MARINS
24 quai de Rive-Neuve, 13007 Marseille
☎ 0491547743
    The *Annuaire officiel* published by the above association contains a list of diving clubs and courses available.

The coastline of Monaco is an **underwater reserve**; diving is strictly controlled; fishing and hunting are forbidden.

Other water sports
White-water rafting along 100 km of navigable river is possible at Verdon and Ubaye. For beginners, canoeing is good at Issole, Guil and Drag, while more advanced rafting (in inflatables) and canyoning (rambles in gorges) are possible at the foot of the Meije and in the gorges of the Ardèche. Information from the Maison de la France (☛Information) and from:
(Canoeing, rafting, canyoning)
ATALANTE
36–37 quai Arloing, 69256 Lyon
☎ 0472532480, fax 0478646062
(Rafting and canoeing)
GIE MEIJE PROMOTION
Route Nationale 91, 05320 la Grave
☎ 0476799124, fax 0476799124

Other sports

Flying
In the French southern Alps all kinds of flying is possible. Well known centres for gliders are at Fayence/Tourette, Sisteron-Vaumeilh as well as Château-Arnoux in the valley of the Durance. There are also various places for paragliders and hang-gliders. Courses in all kinds of flying sport can also be taken.
    Information from the departmental tourist offices (☛Information). A paragliding flight across the Verdon can be booked, for example, with Verdon Accueil, Office de Tourisme in Castellane.

Hot-air balloons
Information about hot-air ballooning can be obtained, for example, from:
OFFICE DE TOURISME
8 place de Bourguet, 04300
Forcalquier
☎ 0492751002, fax 0492752676.

Golf
Golf clubs which are affiliated to the France Golf International organisation always welcome visiting golfers. The relevant golf courses are at Brignoles, Châteauneuf-de-Grasse, Digne-les-Bains, la Garde, la Martre, la Motte, Mallemort, Mandelieu-la-Napoule, Plan-de-Grasse, St-Cyr-sur-Mer, St-Raphaël, Nans-les-Pins, Mouries, les Baux, Morière-les-Avignons, Ste-Maxime (with good views over the bay of St-Tropez, the Massif d'Esterel and the Montagnes des Maures), Avignon/Vedène.
    Information is available from the Maison de la France (☛Information) as well as:
GOLF INTERNATIONAL
Paris
☎ 0143267739
FÉDÉRATION FRANÇAISE DE GOLF
69 avenue Victor-Hugo, 75116 Paris
☎ 0144176332, fax 0144176363.
    A guide to the golf courses in the *départements* Var and Alpes-Maritimes (and two golf passes) is available from:
COMITÉ DÉPARTEMENTAL DU TOURISME
Toulon (Var *département*)
☎ 0494185960, fax 0494185961.

Golfing holidays are on offer from:
COMITÉ DÉPARTEMENTAL DU TOURISME
Toulon (Var *département*)
☎ 0494185960, fax 0494185961.
BOUCHES-DU-RHÔNE, LOISIRS ACCUEIL

Domaine du Vergon, 13370 Mallemort
(Provence)
☎ *0490594939, fax 0490591675.*

Rock climbing

Rock climbing is possible, for example,
in the Dentelles de Montmirail, Alpilles,
Calanques, in the Chaînes de la Ste-
Baume, the Montagne de Ste-Victoire
and in the Massif d'Esterel.
Rock climbing courses are offered,
among others, by the Comité
Départemental du Tourisme in Avignon
(☛Information).

Cycling

See entry

Riding

Horse riding along the coast on
Camargue horses is popular, and the
Lubéron also has rides to distant
mountain villages, The bridlepaths of the
Queyras lead through high mountains
and require some expertise in the saddle.
   The Maison de la France
(☛Information) gives further
information. A seven-day inclusive
holiday 'Horse and Nature in the
Lubéron' is available from the Comité
Départemental du Tourisme in Toulon
(☛Information).

Walking

See entry

Winter sports

It is little known that the Provence does
not only offer sunshine and beaches, but
also has some excellent winter-sports
facilities. The Maritime Alps are only $1\frac{1}{2}$
hours away from Nice and offer the best
in the region: the combination of
exceptionally good snow conditions and
warm sunshine. Because of the great
heights (1400–2450 m) skiing and
toboganing are possible well into March.
There are about 1200 km of piste for all
degrees of expertise, including 250 km
for cross-country skiers, served by 115 ski
and chairlifts as well as cable cars.
Information about the skiing stations
'Alpes d'Azur' can be obtained from
www.french-ski.com.

Among the **leading resorts** are:
Isola 2000 (2450 m; 85 km from Nice)
Auron (1600–2450 m; 95 km from
   Nice)
Valberg/Beuil (1430–2100 m; 80 km from
   Nice)

Roubion (1410–1920 m; 75 km from
   Nice)
Gréolières-les-Neiges (1400–1800 m; 55
   km from Nice)
La Colmiane/Valdeblore (1400–1800 m;
   65 km from Nice)
L'audibergue (1400–1650 m; 55 km from
   Nice)

Spectator sports

Pétanque

The Provençal boule game, *pétanque*, is
very popular with players and spectators
alike. Its origins hark back to a disabled
boule player who changed the rules of
the *boule à la longue* in such a way that
the player needed to stand within a small
circle, with both feet touching (*pieds
tanqués*), when throwing the ball. The
length of the track is fixed at between 6
and 10 m. At first, a small ball, the
cochonet (literally, the little piglet) is
thrown, which the larger metal balls are
then trying to get as close as possible to.
The opponent's balls can be dislodged
(*rouler* and *pointer*). When balls end up
almost equidistant from the cochonet,
the players are at great pains to measure
the distances accurately, and the winner
will finally be declared with much ado.

Bullfighting

In the Camargue bullfighting is a
traditional sport and attracts hundreds of
spectators into the arenas. This is a
peaceful version of the game, without
any bloodshed. Information from the
tourist offices (☛Information).

Sports boats

There are 40 yachting and sailing clubs
along the Côte d'Azur. A trip along the
Calanques is spectacular: the rocky cliffs
reach up to 400 m above the sea, and in
the fjord-like inlets there are hidden bays
with small beaches. Detailed information
about boating holidays in France are
available from the Maison de la France
(☛Information).

Boat hire

Sailing boats can be rented in most
seaside resorts. Information about boat
hire with captain from:
BOUCHES-DU-RHÔNE, LOISIRS ACCUEIL
Domaine du Vergon, 13370 Mallemort
☎ *0490594939, fax 0490591675.*

Organised holidays on yachts
Holidays on boats on the French coast are available from:
SUNSAIL
☎ UK (023) 92222222, US (800) 3272276.

Boats with cabins
Holidays on boats with cabins are increasingly popular; the best time for such holidays in the south is from March to November. In most cases, not even a boating licence is needed. It is possible, for example, to leave from Aigues-Mortes on the Canal du Rhône. Information can be obtained from the Maison de la France.

Several companies also offer boating excursions from Arles into the Camargue. Information from the tourist office in Arles.

Telephone

Most telephone boxes accept only *télécartes* which can be obtained from post offices, tobacco kiosks (*tabac*), the offices of France Telecom, railway ticket offices, and other outlets (showing *Télécate en vente ici*). A card is valid for 50 or 120 units.

A local call from a coin-box costs 1F per unit.

International telephone codes
From the UK to France: 00 33
From the US/Canada to France: 011 33
From France to the UK: 00 44
From France to the US/Canada: 00 1
After dialling 00 wait for the dialling tone before continuing.

When dialling from France the zero prefixed to the local dialling code must be omitted.

Monaco
When dialling Monaco, use the international code (00 or 011) and then the area code 337.

Time

France observes Central European Time, one hour ahead of Greenwich Mean Time. Summer Time (two hours ahead of Greenwich Mean Time) is in force from the last Sunday in March until the last Sunday in October. France is therefore one hour ahead of the UK all year round.

Tipping

Tips (*pourboire*) are normally given in similar circumstances and in similar amounts to those in the United Kingdom. In restaurants a tip of 5–10 per cent is a recognition of good service (a service charge of 15 per cent is normally included in the bill – *service compris*). At the very least, one should round up the amount.

In addition a tip is usual in hotels, for porters (per piece of luggage) and chambermaids, in museums and châteaux for the guides, in cinemas and theatres for the usher(ette)s, as well as for taxi drivers, hairdressers and toilet attendants.

Travel Documents

Passport
Visitors from Britain and other EU countries only require a valid passport (a British Visitor's Passport is acceptable). Visitors from the US and Canada do not require a visa for a stay of up to three months in France.

Vehicle documents
National driving licences and car registration documents are accepted in France. Although nationals of EU countries do not need an international insurance certificate (green card) it is desirable to have one, since otherwise only third-party cover is provided.

All foreign cars must display an oval nationality plate.

Health insurance
See Health

Pets
Pets (dogs, cats) must have an international vaccination certificate and an official health certificate (not older than five months). Vaccination against rabies has to be at least 30 days old, but no older than one year. Animals younger than three months may not be taken.

Advice
In case papers are lost photocopies are very helpful (for example so that the Police can disseminate details and the consulate can issue provisional documents). These copies should be kept separately from the originals.

Visitors with Disabilities

In the brochure *Touristes quand même! promenades en France pour les voyageurs handicappés* the French association for the disabled (see below), gives details of 90 French towns which are suitable for disabled visitors. It also contains information concerning accommodation, transport and public institutions for visitors who are disabled or hearing or sight impaired. Contact:
COMITÉ NATIONAL FRANÇAIS DE LIAISON POUR LA RÉADAPTATION DES HANDICAPÉS (CNFLRH) 38 boulevard Raspail 75007 Paris
☎ 0140786900, fax 0145894057

Rail travel
The brochure *Guide pratique voyageur: supplément à l'intention des personnes à mobilité réduite*, published by French Railways SNCF (☛Public Transport) gives information concerning facilities and reduced fares for passengers with disabilities.

Walking

The hinterland is an interesting and a rewarding area for walkers, but the Provençal coast is also becoming more and more popular. A paradise for nature-lovers and mountain walkers is the Mercantour National Park. It is important to remember that even outside the narrow areas of the Alps there are stretches of an Alpine character and so equipment must always be in good order and weather and conditions taken into account when embarking on a walking holiday.

Long-distance footpaths

A few long-distance footpaths (*sentiers de grande randonnée* – GR for short, plus the number of the footpath) in the area of Provence are summarised below:

GR 9
GR 9, coming from Grenoble, reaches the area covered in this guide near Dieulefit. It runs first via Nyons through the baronies to Brantes, follows the northern slope of Mont Ventoux and descends to the gorges of the Nesque. Beyond Apt and Buoux it climbs the Montagne du Lubéron (Mourre Nègre),

crosses the Durance at Pont-de-Mirabeau and comes to Vauvenargues at the Montagne Ste-Victoire. After ascending the Croix de Provence it continues east along the crest, turns south and via Trets reaches the Massif de la Ste-Baume (St-Pilon). Still going east it leads via the Barre de Cuers and Rocbaron into the Massif des Maures; it then skirts la Garde-Freinet before reaching the sea near Port-Grimaud.

GR 4
GR 4 first leads through the area of the Gorges de l'Ardèche (with several alternative paths), crosses the Rhône at Pont-St-Esprit and reaches Mont Ventoux via Vaison-la-Romaine and Malaucène. It continues along the northern foot of the mountain to Brantes; part of the path coincides with the GR 9, then it leads via Sault, Simiane-la-Rotonde and the Canyon d'Oppedette to the eastern part of the Lubéron and to Manosque. Near Grenoux-les-Bains it reaches the Verdon, follows the Colostre as far as Moustiers and descends to the Gorges du Verdon, following the river as far as Castellane. In a great curve the path skirts Entrevaux on the upper Var, turns south-west into the area of the Alpes-Maritimes, crosses the Montagne du Cheiron to Gréolières and arrives at Grasse across the Plaine des Rochers.

GR 5
GR 5 leads from Nice over Mont Chauve near Aspremont to the gorges of the Vésubie. From here it climbs to Utelle, crosses Mont Tounairet and via St-Sauveur-sur-Tinée comes to the area of Mont Mounier. It then continues north into the Queyras National Park and to Briançon.

GR 98/90/51
This series of long-distance paths covers the immediate hinterland of the Mediterranean coast from Marseille to Menton.

Information
Apart from the Maison de la France and travel agents specialising in walking tours, information (also about night hikes and walking without luggage) can be obtained from:
FÉDÉRATION FRANÇAISE RANDONNÉE PÉDESTRE 9 avenue Georges V, 75008 Paris
☎ 0147237232, email
ffrp.paris@wanadoo.fr, www.ffrp.asso.fr

MAISON DE LA RANDONNÉE (information for young people)
2 rue Voltaire, 75011 Paris
☎ 0143711309
FÉDÉRATION DES PARCS NATURELS
4 rue Stockholm, 75008 Paris
☎ 0142949084, email
info@parcs-naturels-regioneaux.tm.fr
CLUB ALPIN FRANÇAIS
14 avenue Mirabeau, 06000 Nice
☎ 0493625999

Transhumance

By prior arrangement it is possible to accompany shepherds as they move with their flocks among the mountain pasture. The walk lasts between three and ten days. Information from:
OFFICE DU TOURISME
Place Bourguet, 04300 Forcalquier
☎ 0492751002, fax 0492752676, email
oti@forcalquier.com, www.forcalquier.com

Maps and guidebooks

The walkers' guide in the Topo series *Topo-Guide des sentiers de Grande Randonnée* (short form *Topo Guide*) includes maps to a scale of 1:50,000 and, with information about routes, accommodation, time planning, geography, nature and culture, is an excellent reference book for a successful walking tour. It can be obtained in bookshops in France or it can be ordered from:
EDITIONS CHIRON
40 rue de Seine, 75006 Paris
☎ 0143264756.

When to Go

Spring early summer and autumn (September–October) are the best times to visit Provence or the Côte d'Azur. During these seasons the weather is fine (or at least not liable to unexpected changes) and the French school holidays are avoided. A visit in winter can also be a pleasant experience.

Spring

Because of the relatively mild climate blossom appears early: mimosa blossom from the end of January; from early March the pink blossom of the almond trees can be seen in the gardens; from the end of April to June magnolias are in blossom and rhododendrons flower in May and June; the flowering broom is celebrated in Roquebrune-Cap-Martin in June (☞Events). This and the pleasant water temperature early in the year make spring an ideal time for a visit to the Côte d'Azur. It must be added, however, that during this season there is quite a lot of welcome rain (many fossils washed out of the rocks on the hillsides can be found). For places at a higher altitude late spring and early summer are more suitable for a visit.

Summer

A stay at the coast in July and August, during the main holiday season (the school holidays last from the end of June until mid-September), may be slightly impaired by overcrowding (traffic jams, fully booked hotels). Yet the happy beach life in the daytime, the open-air festivals in the evening, and especially the dreamy nights by the sea, walks along romantic harbours with their lit-up yachts and along the beach promenades, or a chat with the locals in the popular street cafés more than make up for the crowds and turn a summer holiday in Provence into an unforgttable experience.

In the very dry summer season, the heat of which is often interrupted by the cold currents of the mistral, the real character of Provence comes into its own, especially when the lavender is in flower all around the perfume town of Grasse. At this season the gorges of Haute-Provence, which at other times are accessible only with difficulty, can be explored, or the Calanques to the east of Marseille can be visited without undue risk.

To the west of Marseille, in the region of Carry-le-Rouet, mosquitoes can be unpleasant in the summer; you are advised to take insect repellant with you.

Autumn

Thanks to the warm temperatures, swimming in the sea is possible until well into the autumn – generally a time of rainfall.

Winter

The particularly mild winters were the starting point for the most recent wave of tourism. Well-known and well-equipped winter-sports resorts are found chiefly in the Alpine parts of Haute-Provence and in the Alpes-Maritimes.

Wine

Viniculture in Provence goes back to the Greek colonisation in the 7th and 6th c. BC – it has therefore the longest tradition in France. It is carried on essentially in two areas, the lower Rhône in a triangle between Montélimar, Avignon and Apt, and Provence in its narrower sense, that is the country between Aix, Marseille and Nice.

AOC wines

There are 10 AOC (*appelation d'origine contrôlée*) areas in the Provence-Alpes-Côtes-d'Azur region, offering the entire range of the wine palette from a full-bodied red wine to sparkly whites and velvety dessert wines.

The AOC seal is only given to wines that fulfill the strict quality rules and regulations of the wine makers' associations: clear definition of vineyards and produce, restriction of quantities and strict quality control. Wine is classified according to AOC regions.

Rhône wines

Côtes du Rhône

The grands crus (the best sorts of wine, such as Châteauneuf-du-Pape, which was appreciated already by the popes of Avignion) is produced from 13 varieties of grape – every estate has its own recipe – and the vines are grown on the gravelly plains of the Rhône in widely separated rows. Châteauneuf-du-Pape is a full-bodied dark-red wine (minimum alcohol content 12.5 per cent) that requires four to five years to reach maturity; recently attempts have been made to make the wine less heavy and thinner, so that it can be drunk after only two years. The wines of Gigondas and Vacqueyras are similarly full-bodied red wines with an international reputation. Here too are the Côtes du Rhône Villages which (in about 16 communes) produce mainly red wine on 3,600 ha of land.

From Rasteau, Beaumes-de-Venise and Lunel come very aromatic white wines (muscat), the residual sweetness of which is achieved by the addition of spirit.

Côtes du Ventoux

The south-east includes the 7,680 ha area of Côtes du Ventoux where red, white and rosé wines are made.

Côte du Lubéron

On an area of 2,730 ha red, white and rosé wines are made in the Côtes du Lubéron area.

Provence wines

Some 60 per cent of the wine produced in Provence is the fruity aromatic rosé; red wine accounts for 35 per cent and white for 5 per cent.

Côtes de Provence and Côteaux Varois

The Côtes de Provence, on a planted area of 14,700 ha, and the Côteaux Varois, on an area of 1,575 ha, produce fresh rosé wines. The rosé – the typical wine of Provence, recognisable in its shaped bottles – is still largely considered to be an uncomplicated table wine even in the south of France. This is very unfair; despite its freshness it is by no means light or bland. Acidity, bouquet and alcohol content are perfectly balanced and characterise a wine that like no other embodies the landscape. An old proverb says: 'a good rosé goes with the Provence like the rouille to the bouillabaisse'.

Côteaux d'Aix-en-Provence

The Côteaux d'Aix-en-Provence go back to Roman times and have enjoyed a good reputation ever since.

Vins des Baux

The red and rosé wines of Baux have only recently been awarded an AOC.

Palette

Palette is a small area (20 ha) in front of the town gates of Aix-en-Provence, which mainly produces red wines.

Cassis

The very dry, full-bodied wines of Cassis (160 ha) have been famous since the Middle Ages.

Bandol

The mainly red Bandol wines are also widely known beyond Provence (1,250 ha).

Languedoc-Roussillon

Sand wine

One needs to add the areas between Nîmes and Stes-Maries-de-la-Mer: a speciallity here is the Listel, a 'sand wine' (*vin des sables*) which is grown to the east of Aigues-Mortes.

Wine routes through Provence

Route du Mont Ventoux
This route leads around the Mont Ventoux through the vineyards (and lavender fields) to the cellars of Séguret and Beaumes-de-Venise.

Route des Côteaux d'Aix-en-Provence
A route which leads to country residences (*bastides*), which wealthy citizens had built for themselves in the 18th c., outside the town gates.

Route des Côtes de Provence
This route links les Arcs with the new Maison du Vin and with the vineyards of Bandol, and touches on the cellars of Vidauban, Brignoles and Pierrefeu.

Information
Visitors are welcome in the wine cellars. Further information is available from the Comité Départemental du Tourismne de Vaucluse in Avignon (☞Information). The Comité Départemental offers, for example, a holiday 'The Vineyards of Provence' (with accommodation in walkers' cabins, picnics and evening meals, guide, luggage transport and wine tastings).

Youth Hostels

The French youth-hostel organisation FUAJ operates some 200 youth hostels, which can be used by young people holding a card issued by their national youth-hostel association.

In July and August (school holidays) advance booking is necessary; generally in the main holiday period a stay in any one hostel is limited to three nights.

Towns with hostels
In the area covered by this guide there are hostels in Aix-en-Provence, Arles, Cassis, Fontaine-de-Vaucluse, Fréjus, Jausiers, la Foux-d'Allos, Manosque, Marseille, Menton, Montpellier, Nice, Nîmes, la Palud-sur-Verdon, Savines-le-Lac, Stes-Maries-de-la-Mer, Tarascon, le Trayas (near Théoule-sur-Mer) and Séguret (near Vaison-la-Romaine).

Information
Fédération Unie des Auberges de Jeunesse 27 rue Pajol, 75018 Paris
☎0146077060, fax 0144898710, email *centre-national@fuaj.org, www.fuaj.org*

UCRIF
Ideally suited, for example, for school holidays, language courses and sport activities are the centres for youth encounters (open all year round) run by the Union Centres de Rencontres Internationales de France, which offer accommodation and meals as well as the opportunity to explore the tourist and cultural sights of the region. Information from:
Union Centres de Rencontres Internationales de France (UCRIF)
27 rue de Turbigo, 75002 Paris
☎0140265764, fax 0140265820, *www.ucrif.asso.fr*

Holidays for young people
France could be described as the classic country for young-people's holidays; the school holidays are chiefly spent by the sea, in the countryside or in other towns.

The Maison de la France (☞Information) publishes a brochure containing all necessary details and information about travel (fare reductions), accommodation (from youth hostels and campsites to centres where young people from other countries can be met, and student houses), activity holidays (language courses, sport, cultural work, even jobs) and all technical matters.

Index

Source of Illustrations

Imprint

121 photographs, 41 maps and plans, 1 large fold-out map

German text: Peter M Nahm, Vera Beck, Dr Fritz Nohr
Additional text: Dr Bernhard Abend
Cartography: Christoph Gallus, Hohberg-Niederschopfheim; Gert Oberländer, München; Mairs Geographischer Verlag GmbH & Co, Ostfildern (large fold-out map)
General direction: Rainer Eisenschmid, Baedeker Ostfildern
Editorial work German edition: Baedeker-Redaktion (Peter M Nahm)

English translation: Julie Bullock, David Cocking, Alec Court, Crispin Warren, Sylvia Goulding
Editorial work English edition: g-and-w PUBLISHING
Design: The Company of Designers, Basingstoke, Hampshire, UK

4th English edition 2001

© Karl Baedeker GmbH, Ostfildern
Original German edition 2000

© Automobile Association Developments Limited 2001
English language edition worldwide

Published by AA Publishing (a trading name of Automobile Association Developments Limited, whose registered office is Norfolk House, Priestley Road, Basingstoke, Hampshire RG24 9NY; registered number 1878835).

Distributed in the United States and Canada by:
Fodor's Travel Publications, Inc.
201 East 50th Street
New York, NY 10022

A CIP catalogue record of this book is available from the British Library.

Licensed user: Mairs Geographischer Verlag GmbH & Co, Ostfildern

Typeset by Fakenham Photosetting Ltd, Fakenham, Norfolk, UK
Printed in Italy by G Canale & C SpA, Turin

ISBN 0 7495 2963 6

Only a selection of hotels and restaurants can be given; no reflection is implied therefore on establishments not included.
   In a time of rapid change it is difficult to ensure that all the information given is entirely accurate and up to date, and the possibility of error cannot be eliminated.
   Although the publishers can accept no responsibility for inaccuracies and omissions, they are constantly endeavouring to improve the quality of their guides and are therefore always grateful for criticisms, corrections and suggestions for improvement.